My Memo

Volume. IV

1830 to 1831

Alexandre Dumas

(Translator: E. M. Waller)

Alpha Editions

This edition published in 2024

ISBN : 9789357966672

Design and Setting By
Alpha Editions
www.alphaedis.com
Email - info@alphaedis.com

Contents

BOOK I

CHAPTER I

My *Christine* rehearsals had opened Mademoiselle Georges' house to me, as those of *Henri III.* had given me the entrée to that of Mademoiselle Mars.

The house that my good and excellent Georges occupied, No. 12 rue Madame, was, if I remember rightly, made up of very original inhabitants. First of all, in the attics lived Jules Janin, the second tenant. Then came Harel, the principal tenant, who lived on the second floor. And on the first and ground floors were Georges, her sister and her two nephews. One of these two nephews, who is now a tall, fine, clever-looking young fellow who bears the name of Harel, had for a long time figured regularly on his aunt's playbills, both in the provinces and in Paris, for she could not do without him, either at the theatre or about town.

My readers will recollect the phrase which never varied for five or six years running—

"Young Tom, aged ten, will take the part of," etc.

The other names would vary from that of Joas to that of Thomas Diafoirus; but the age never varied: young Tom was always ten.

We ought to be fair to young Tom; he hated acting and, every time he had to go on the stage, he would mutter between his teeth—

"Curse the theatre! If only it could be burnt down!"

"What is that you are saying, Tom?" Mademoiselle Georges would ask.

"Nothing, aunt," Tom would reply; "I am only repeating my part."

His brother Paul, who was called "le petit Popol," was by far the funniest looking object that was ever seen: he had a charming head, with fine dark eyes and long chestnut hair, but his body was too small to carry the head. This disproportion gave the child a very grotesque appearance: he was immensely clever, a gourmand like Grimod de la Reynière, and the very opposite of Tom in that he would have stuck to the stage all his life, if he could only have managed to get plenty to eat thereby.

At the time when I first became acquainted with him, he was only a little monkey of six or seven years of age, and already he had devised a way of establishing a credit account at the café at the corner of the rue de Vaugirard and the rue de Molière, by means of all sorts of ingenious excuses. One fine day it was found out that little Popol's account amounted to a hundred crowns! In three months he had run through three hundred francs' worth of all kinds of confectionery and drinks, which he had asked for in his mother's name, or in that of his aunt, and which he had eaten or drunk on staircases, in corridors or behind doorways. He it was who, in *Richard Darlington*, was placed in such a manner as to make him appear the height of an ordinary man, representing the Speaker of the House of Commons. In this capacity he had a bell at his right hand and a glass of eau sucrée at his left; he rang the bell with the gravity of M. Dupin, and drank the glass of eau sucrée with the dignity of M. Barrot. The little beggar never would learn his prayers, and this gave the Voltairian Harel immense delight; however, all at once (it was during an epidemic of cholera), they found out that little Popol said a prayer, morning and evening, which he had, no doubt, improvised to suit the occasion.

They were curious to know what this prayer was and, hiding themselves to listen, overheard the following:—

"O Lord God! take my Aunt Georges; take my Uncle Harel; take my brother Tom; take mamma Bébelle; take my friend Provost, but leave little Popol and the cook!"

But the prayer did not bring the poor little fellow the luck he fervently wished: cholera took him, and carried him off, with fifteen hundred others in the same day.

We have said who his brother Tom was; we have all seen how "mamma Bébelle" acted under the name of Georges the younger: now let us say a few words about Aunt Georges, the most beautiful woman of her day, and about Uncle Harel, the wittiest man of his time.

Well, Georges' aunt was a splendid-looking creature of about forty-one. We have already given a sketch of her portrait by the clever pen of Théophile Gautier. Her hands and arms and shoulders, her neck, teeth and eyes, were of indescribable charm and beauty; but, like the lovely fairy Melusina, there was a certain weariness visible in her movements which was increased by the wearing of far too long dresses—why, I know not, for her feet were as lovely as her hands.

Mademoiselle Georges' idleness, except in matters connected with the theatre, wherein she was always alert, was incredible, Tall and majestic, aware of her beauty, with two emperors and three or four kings for admirers, Georges loved to lie on a big couch, in velvet robes, furred pelisses and Indian cashmere shawls, during winter; in summer, in teagowns of batiste or muslin. Thus extended, in a pose that was always careless and graceful, Georges received the visits of strangers, sometimes with the majesty of a Roman matron, at others with the smile of a Grecian courtesan; whilst from between the folds of her dress, the openings of her shawls and the skirts of her teagowns, there would peep out the heads of two or three hares of the very best breed, looking like as many snakes' heads. Georges' love of cleanliness was proverbial: she would perform a preliminary toilet before she entered her bath, so as not to soil the water in which she stayed for an hour; here she received her familiar friends, fastening up her hair with golden pins, from time to time, when it came down; her splendid arms uplifted entirely free of the water, her throat and bosom seeming as though sculptured in Parian marble. And it was a singular thing that these actions, which in another woman would have been provocative and lascivious, were simple and natural in Georges, like those of a Greek of the time of Homer or Phidias; as beautiful as a statue, she looked simply like a statue surprised at its own nudity, and she would, I am sure, have been much surprised if a jealous lover had forbidden her to show herself thus in her bath, where, like a sea-nymph, she made the water heave with the motion of her shoulders and her white breasts.

Georges made everybody round her clean in his habits except Harel. But Harel was another matter altogether. Cleanliness meant an immense sacrifice to him, and this sacrifice he would only make under strong pressure and constraint. So Georges, who adored him, and could not do without his delightfully witty chatter at her ears incessantly, declared to all comers that it was only his mind she loved, and that, as to the rest of his personality, she left him free to do what he liked with it.

At that period Georges still possessed magnificent diamonds and, among them, two buttons which had been given her by Napoleon and which were each worth nearly twelve thousand francs. She had had them set as earrings and wore them in preference to all others. These buttons were so large that Georges very frequently, on returning home in the evening, after acting, took them off, complaining that they pulled her ears down. One evening, we returned with her and sat down to supper. When supper was over, we ate almonds; Georges ate a great number and, whilst eating, complained of the weight of these earrings, took them out of her ears and laid them on the tablecloth. Five minutes later, the servant came, brush in hand, to brush the crumbs off the table, swept earrings and almond shells together into a basket, and both earrings and shells were thrown clean out of the window into the street. Georges went to bed without remembering her earrings, and slept peacefully; philosophic though she was, she would certainly not have done this if she had known that her servant had thrown twenty-four thousand francs' worth of diamonds out of the window.

Next day, Georges the younger came into the room to wake her sister.

"Well," she said, "you may well boast of being lucky indeed! Look what I have just found."

"What is it?"

"One of your earrings."

"Where did you pick that up?"

"In the street."

"In the street?"

"Yes, my dear ... in the street, at the door.... You must have lost it when you came back from the theatre."

"No, I had them on at supper."

"Are you sure of it?"

"So sure that, because they tired me, I took them out and laid them by my side. What can I have done with them afterwards?... Where can I have put them?"

"Why, good gracious!" exclaimed Georges the younger. "I remember now: we were eating almonds and the servant swept the table with the brush."

"Ah! my poor earrings!" cried Georges, in her turn. "Go downstairs quickly and look, Bébelle!"

Bébelle was already at the bottom of the staircase and, five minutes later, she returned with the second earring, which she had found in the gutter.

"My darling," she said to her sister, "we are very lucky. Have a mass said, or some great misfortune will overtake us."

We have referred to Harel's dislike of cleanliness: it was universally well known, and he himself took a kind of pride in it; he was a man who delighted in contradictions and it amused him to enlarge upon this odd superiority. When he saw Georges lying on her couch surrounded by her well washed and combed dogs with their morocco leather collars round their necks, he sighed with ambition. For his ambition—and it was one he had often expressed but never realised—was to keep a pig! He considered Saint

Anthony was the happiest of saints and, like him, he was ready to retire into a desert if Providence would condescend to allow him the same companion. As Harel's birthday approached, Georges and I decided to crown his modest desires: we purchased for twenty-two livres *tournois* a pig three or four months old; we put a diamond crown upon its head, a bouquet of roses at its side, rings of precious stones round its feet and, conducting it in state like a bride, we entered the dining-room at what we believed to be the most suitable moment to favour Harel with this sweet surprise. At the cries the new arrival uttered, Harel at once abandoned his conversation with Lockroy and Janin, attractive though it was, and ran towards us. The pig held a complimentary letter in one of its feet which it presented to Harel. Harel leapt upon his pig— for he guessed instantly that the pig was for him—pressed it to his heart, rubbed his nose on its snout, made it sit next him in Popol's high chair, tied it in the chair with one of Georges' scarves and began to stuff it with all sorts of dainties. The pig was christened there and then, and received from Harel (who vowed to undertake the obligations of a godfather towards his godchild) the euphonious name of Piaff-Piaff. That very night, Harel retired to his second storey with Piaff-Piaff and, as nobody had thought of the animal's bed, Harel carried away with him one of Georges' velvet gowns and made a litter of it for the pig. This theft led next day to a tremendous altercation between Georges and Harel, in which we, who were called in to judge between the two, sentenced Harel to pay Georges two hundred francs' indemnity for the night's use. The dress was sent to a shop, and page-boys' costumes were made out of it. Harel's love for his pig became quite fanatical. One day he came up to me at a rehearsal and said—

"Do you know, my dear fellow, I am so fond of my pig that I sleep with him!"

"So I understand," I replied. "I have just met your pig, who told me exactly the same thing."

I believe this was the only quip to which Harel never found a retort.

In common with all over petted animals, Piaff-Piaff grew conscious of his power, abused it, and one day things ended by turning out very badly for him. Piaff-Piaff, well fed, well housed, constantly petted, sleeping with Harel, attained to the honourable weight of a hundred and fifty pounds; which— for we calculated it—was fifty pounds more than Janin weighed, thirty pounds more than Lockroy, ten pounds more than I, fifty-five pounds less than Eric Bernard; it was decreed in a council from which Harel was excluded, that when Piaff-Piaff reached the weight of two hundred pounds he should be made into black pudding and sausages. Unfortunately for himself, each day he committed some fresh depredation in the house, which led to a general threat to hasten the hour of his demise, and yet, in spite of all these ill deeds, Harel's worship of Piaff-Piaff was so well known that the strictest resolutions always ended by granting him pardon. But, one day, Piaff-Piaff was prowling round a kind of cage where a magnificent pheasant was kept that I had given to Tom; the pheasant had the imprudence to poke its neck through two bars to peck at a grain of corn, and Piaff-Piaff stretched out his snout and bit off the pheasant's head. Tom was only a few steps off, saw the deed accomplished, and set up loud shrieks. But the pheasant, when decapitated, was only fit to be roasted. Piaff-Piaff, in attacking everybody else, had had the sense to respect Tom's property; he had, as we have said, frequently benefited by the plea of extenuating circumstances, but this last clumsy outrage left him no sympathiser, however eloquent, who could save him from being killed. Georges emphatically declared that he deserved death and no one, not even Janin, dared contradict the sentence. Judgment declared, it was decided to take advantage of Harel's absence to put it into execution, and, whilst everybody was hot against the offender, the butcher was sent for and told to bring his knife. Five minutes later, Piaff-Piaff raised shrieks loud enough to rouse the whole neighbourhood. The street door was held fast to keep Harel out if he happened to come back at that moment; but we had forgotten that the garden possessed an exit to the Luxembourg and that Harel might come in that way. Suddenly, as Piaff-Piaff was uttering the doleful notes which signified that his death was drawing near at hand, the door opened and Harel appeared, crying out—

"What are you doing to my poor Piaff-Piaff? What is the matter with him?"

"Well," said Georges, "your horrid Piaff-Piaff had grown too unbearable."

"Ah! poor animal! poor beast!" cried Harel; "they are cutting his throat!" Then, after a moment's pause, he said in sorrowful tones, "At any rate, I hope you told the butcher to put plenty of onions in the black pudding—I adore onions!"

And that was Piaff-Piaff s funeral oration.

CHAPTER II

M. Briffaut, Censor and Academician—History of *Ninus II.*—M. de Lourdoueix—The idea of *Antony*—The piece received by the Français is stopped by the Censorship—The Duc de Chartres—Negotiations for his presence with that of his two brothers at the first representation of *Christine*—Louët—An autograph of the Prince Royal

It was into the midst of such society as this, differing greatly in its humour from that of the Comédie-Française, that the rehearsals of *Christine* carried me. Just as in the case of *Henri III.*, all our artist friends offered their services to me: Boulanger had designed one half the costumes and Saint-Ève the other, when suddenly we received the official intimation—"The piece is stopped."

First *Marion Delorme* was stopped, then *Christine!* Truly the Censorship was getting its hand in.

I went to the Ministry and found that my play was in the hands of M. Briffaut, author of *Ninus II.* The history of *Ninus II.* might surely make M. Briffaut indulgent to others. But forgive me, perhaps you do not know the history of *Ninus II.* I will tell it you.

M. Briffaut had, in 1809 or 1810, written a play under some title or other, the scene of which was laid in Spain. But it was stopped by the Censorship. A friend of M. Briffaut appealed to Napoleon against the decision of the Censors. Napoleon read the play and found it contained some lines in praise of Spaniards.

"The Censorship was right to forbid it," he said. "It does not at all suit me to have a people praised with whom I am at war!"

"But, sire, what is to become of the author?" the friend asked humbly and sympathetically. "He has composed but this one play and may never write another all his life long; he was counting upon this as an opening to many ambitions—sire, you will ruin his career!"

"Very well, then; if he puts his action, say, in Assyria, instead of in Spain, I will raise no objection; and, instead of calling his hero Pélage, he calls him Ninus I. or Ninus II, I will authorise it."

Now M. Briffaut was not going to be stopped by such conditions as these, so he called his play *Ninus II.*; then, wherever the word *Spaniards* came in, he altered it into *Assyrians*, and *Burgos* into *Babylon*: it made it awkward in altering the rhymes, but that was all;—and the play was authorised and played; it was, no doubt, on account of this herculean feat, that they made M. Briffaut a member of the Academy. He was, on the whole, a very good fellow, and not unduly proud of having done nothing—a superiority which renders many of my colleagues insolent.

We discussed at length, not the literary, but the political, defects of the unhappy *Christine*. It seemed she bristled with them; and the poor Censor, whose touch was very delicate, did not really know where to lay his hands on them. There was in particular this line which Christine recites in allusion to her crown—

"C'est un hochet royal trouvé dans mon berceau!"

which was looked upon as a crime. In that line, I was attacking the legitimacy, the divine right, the succession! I cannot tell you the number of things I was attacking in it! For the moment I fancy I must, without knowing it, have written my play in that fine Turkish tongue of which Molière gives us a specimen in *Le Bourgeois gentilhomme*, which is capable of expressing a great deal in very few words. Then there was the sending of the crown to Cromwell—a very dangerous suggestion for the Monarchy! It was in vain I protested that the incident was true to history; that Christine had really sent the crown to the Protector, who had had it melted down. To recall to humanity, which seemed to have forgotten the episode, that it had really taken place, was looked upon as a revolutionary and inflammatory act. Indeed, from M. Briffaut's manner of dealing with history in *Ninus II.*, it was obvious he did not trouble himself much about historical facts. But, in spite of my discussions with M. Briffaut, pleasant as they were rendered by his affability, no progress was made, and thus, as Harel was pressed for time, I was prevailed on to try and engage the good offices of M. de Lourdoueix, the head of the Censorial staff.

I had been advised to get an introduction to M. de Lourdoueix by a lady of high repute who was one of his friends; I do not know what her name was, but I was given to understand that this was the only channel by which he could be got at; like Raoul, however, in the *Huguenots*, I was full of confidence in the justness of my cause; so, without any introduction whatever, I made an expedition to the South Side, where M. de Lourdoueix was to be found. I do not know whether M. de Lourdoueix had composed a *Ninus III.* or *Ninus IV.*, whether he belonged to the Academy, or simply to the Caveau Club; but he was far from being as courteous in his manner as M. Briffaut. Our interview was a brief one; after five minutes' conversation, decidedly bitter on both sides, he said—

"After all, monsieur, it is no use your saying anything further; for as long as the Elder Branch is on the throne and I act as its Censor your work will be suspended."

"Very well, monsieur," I replied, bowing; "I shall wait!"

"Monsieur," M. de Lourdoueix ironically remarked, "that decision had been already arrived at."

"Then I repeat it," I said, and left him.

But it was a sufficiently serious threat: I had no longer the support of M. de Martignac, that man of resource. The Polignac Ministry had succeeded his, and I had no means of approaching the new President of the Council. So I waited; the only weapon left me was patience and, while I was waiting, one day when I was walking on the boulevard I suddenly stopped and said to myself—

"A man who, when discovered by his mistress's husband, kills her,—vowing that she had offered resistance to his addresses, and dying on the scaffold for the murder,—saves the wife's honour and expiates his crime."

The idea of *Antony* was found; and, as I believe I have said elsewhere, the character of the hero was suggested to me by that of Didier in *Marion Delorme*. Six weeks later, *Antony* was finished. I read the piece to the Français, but the reading did not receive a very warm welcome. I distributed my two leading parts between Mademoiselle Mars and M. Firmin; but it was quite evident they would rather I had chosen other interpreters for those characters. I sent the play to the Censor, and it was stopped like *Christine*. This made a brace of them. But, whether at the time there was a certain feeling of modesty which has since been lost sight of, or whether I had some friend at the background who was working for me—and I have always suspected the excellent and highly cultivated Madame du Cayla of having been that friend—whether, indeed, Harel really had the influence with the Government he made out, the play of *Christine* was returned to me without any very great alteration, early in March. They had even left in the famous line about the *hochet royal*, inflammatory though it was said to be, and the sending of the crown to the Protector, in spite of any possible catastrophe that might result from this historical reminiscence! So the interrupted rehearsals were taken up again.

However, in the midst of all my worries, I still went constantly to the Palais-Royal library, where I had made a new acquaintance. My fresh acquaintance was the Duc de Chartres. He was at that time a charming boy and has since become a charming prince; a bad enough scholar, whatever his masters may say;—and for fear lest, for the honour of the scholastic profession, they should give me the lie, I will just give, as illustration, an anecdote thereon. The Duc de Chartres was then, as I say, a winning lad of seventeen and, as I was twenty-seven, the difference of age between us not being as great as that between him and Casimir Delavigne, or between him and Vatout, it was to me he generally turned. Moreover, at this time my name was being talked about a great deal; all sorts of adventures were attributed to me, as a host of sayings have since been put down to my account. I had the passions of the African, they said, and they pointed to my frizzy hair and dark complexion, which neither could nor would deny its tropical origin. It all added to the curious interest felt towards me by a boy on the verge of manhood, who had sympathy towards Art as expressed by us, or, rather, as expressed by me, since at that date Hugo had not yet published anything in the dramatic line. *Hernani* was not to be performed until 25 February 1830, and the intimacy of which I am speaking began about the end of 1829. So the Duc de Chartres looked upon me as a man, if not of his own age, at least not so very much older, and whenever he could get away, he would come and have a chat with me. I should mention that the conversation was soon diverted and passed from Art to artists, from the play to actors, and that we were as much interested in discussing the relative merits of Mademoiselle Louise Despréaux, of Mademoiselle Alexandrine Noblet and of Mademoiselle Léontine Fay, as of *Henri III.* and *Christine*. But our meetings never lasted long, for, at the end of a few minutes, we heard the Duc d'Orléans chanting his mass, or some gentleman or other shouting out the name of the Duc de Chartres, and the young prince who, as a grown man, still trembled before the king, would run off through some hidden door, stammering—

"Oh, Monsieur Dumas, do not tell them you have seen me!"

Some time before the performance of *Christine*, he had expressed his anxiety to be present, with his two young brothers, at the production of my second drama; but he was afraid permission would not be granted him. Why did the poor lad come to me to help him? He came to beg me to tell the Duc d'Orléans of my wish that his children should be present at the performance of my play. I was quite prepared, on my side, to make this request; and, the first time I saw His Highness, I ventured to do so. The prince "*hummed* and *hawed*" a little, to express his mistrust with regard to the morality of a play which had ever come under the ban of the Censorship; but I reassured him as best I could; and, after a little pressure, I obtained leave for the young princes to be present at the performance. I took good care to go to the library on the Thursday following, for I felt certain I should see the Duc de Chartres there, and he came, but he was accompanied by M. de Boismilon; however, he managed to pass by me and to say in a whisper—

"We are going! Thank you."

But I have promised to give an anecdote illustrative of the idleness of the Duc de Chartres—a fault they did their utmost to hide from his father; the prizes young princes are usually loaded with serving to divert his suspicions.

I will keep my promise.

In 1835 I took a journey to Italy with Jadin. Our intention was to travel as real tourists, on foot, on horses or mules, in carriages, *corricolo* or *speronare* or by boat; in short, just as we could. We decided to leave France by way of the Gulf of Genoa; consequently, at Hyères, we hired a sort of driver who, for a hundred francs, was to take us to Nice, skirting the shores of the Gulf of Jouan, which would enable us to stop for half a day. Jadin intended to make a drawing of the shore where Napoleon had landed in 1815, meaning to have it engraved later. The vetturino had stipulated, as his share of our bargain, to be allowed to add four persons to our number, on condition that they offered no opposition to a first halt of five or six hours at Cannes, and a second halt at Grasse. Among the travellers accompanying us was a young man of twenty-four or twenty-five, who was clad in a blue dress coat, nankeen trousers, coloured stockings and laced shoes. In my *Impressions de voyage*, I gave him the name of Chaix; in my Memoirs, I must give him his real name, which was Louët. For a day and a half, he never addressed a word to us; but our conversation appeared to interest him enormously; he smiled at our jokes and listened attentively to our much rarer serious remarks. At table, his place was always laid by ours and, at our first sleeping-place, he arranged not to be separated from us by anything more than a partition. When we reached the Gulf of Jouan, he stopped and, whilst Jadin made his drawing, I flung myself into the water for a bathe. Just as I was undressing, Louët came up to me and, speaking to me for the first time, asked permission to bathe with me. I did not at first detect the punctilious politeness with which the request was put, and laughingly replied that he was perfectly free to do whatever he liked. He thanked me for the permission and took the most rational and least eventful of baths I ever saw, in three and a half feet of water; then, when the drawing and bathing were finished, we climbed into our carriage and slept at Nice that same night. Three of our companions had already left us, one at the heights of Draguignan and the two others at Grasse. Louët alone remained faithful to us as far as Nice, which surprised me the more as I had heard him tell the others who had accompanied him to the carriage, just as he was parting from them, that he was on his way to Paris.

Now Louët must have given a very wide meaning to the proverb, "Every road leads to Rome," if he could persuade himself so far as to think that the road from Toulon to Nice would take him to Paris. This strange conduct on the part of our travelling-companion roused Jadin's curiosity and mine, but it was at length explained by a request the vetturino made on Louët's behalf, who dared not put it to us himself. Louët had really started from Toulon to go to Paris, but he had been so charmed with our fascinating conversation on the journey that, instead of travelling only as far as Luc and there leaving for Draguignan and Castellane, he had told the vetturino that, as he had never seen Nice, he would go on to that place. When he reached Nice, he asked through the vetturino whether, as a great favour, we would allow him to continue the journey with us; hastening to tell us that his society should cost us nothing, for he would pay a third of whatever our expenses amounted to; the vetturino added, by way of parenthesis, that Louët, whom he knew, had just come into a legacy of about thirty thousand francs and was returning to Paris with it when he fell in with us: after which he did not see how he could find a better way of spending a portion of his money than in our society. The request was proffered with such graceful entreaty and Louët seemed such a good sort of young fellow that we did not even think of discussing the question, but intimated that we should be delighted to have his company; that, as he proposed, the expenses should be divided into thirds, and the very next day we would tell him our plan of travel, so that he might then see if our itinerary suited him. He replied that we need not trouble to give him such a programme, that he had no settled aim—it was us and not the journey he wanted—that, since we had honoured him with leave to accompany us, he would go to China with us, or wherever we wished. Certainly no one could have been more accommodating and, indeed, Louët went the entire Italian journey with us and proved himself throughout an excellent travelling-companion. I related this story in my *Impressions de voyage* with the light gaiety of narrative that is natural to me, and in 1838 I had a visit from Jadin.

"You will never guess who is coming to see you to-morrow...?" he began.

"I cannot."

"Louët."

"Nonsense!"

I had not seen Louët since my return from Italy three years before.

"Yes," Jadin went on, "and I am sent to announce the visit to you."

"What! is he by any chance coming to ask satisfaction from me for bringing him into my *Impressions de voyage*?"

"No, quite the reverse; he is delighted to figure in the book and is coming to ask a favour from you."

"Ah! he will be very welcome. What is it?"

"He wishes to tell you what it is himself."

"Good! I will expect him."

Louët came the next day, and was exactly the same excellent, simple fellow, except that he seemed to have advanced considerably in the art of dressing himself.

"Well, Louët, here you are! Why, my friend, you look like a millionaire."

"Yes, because I am better dressed than formerly; but, otherwise, it is exactly the reverse. I haven't a halfpenny."

"What? You haven't a halfpenny?"

"No. I risked my little fortune and lost it."

"Absolutely?"

"The whole of it."

"Ah! poor fellow!"

"So I have come to ask ..."

"What? Not for advice how to make a new fortune, surely?"

"No: for your influence."

"With the Government?" I asked, with growing astonishment.

"No."

"The king?" I asked, more surprised still.

"No."

"With the Duc d'Orléans?"

"Yes."

My countenance fell. I desired to keep the revered and loyal friendship I had vowed to the duke pure from all motives of interest, so that he might be sure of the genuine nature of my attachment; accordingly, every time I was asked to obtain some favour from the prince royal it caused me real pain.

"The Duc d'Orléans!" I repeated. "What in the world do you want me to ask the Duc d'Orléans on your behalf, my dear Louët?"

"Some small post...."

"A small post!" I repeated, shrugging my shoulders.

"He surely will not refuse you it," Louët added.

"On the contrary, my friend, he will refuse it me, because I shall be the first to tell him to refuse my request."

"Why?"

"Because you have no sort of claim upon the Duc d'Orléans—you do not even know him."

"Indeed I have some excuse, I do really know him," said Louët to me. "I was a college chum of his."

"At Henri IV.?"

"Yes."

"You are certain?"

"Why, of course."

"Would he remember you?"

"I was in the same class with him; besides, if he has forgotten me, I possess a little note in his own writing that will revive his memory."

"A note from him?"

"Look here: you shall see it for yourself"; and he showed me three lines on a scrap of foolscap in small handwriting containing these words:—

> "MY DEAR LOUËT,—Translate for me from Ασκρωνδη
> as far
> as ὅλος, and I shall be infinitely obliged to you.
>
> "DE CHARTRES"

I seized the paper eagerly.

"Oh!" I said, "that being the state of things, my dear Louët, you are saved, and I will answer for everything."

"You will undertake the matter for me, then?"

"With the greatest of pleasure."

"When shall you see the duke?"

"To-morrow morning."

"When shall I come back?"

"To-morrow at noon."

"I shall have my post?"

"I hope so."

"Upon my word, my dear sir, you will have done me an immense service."

"I will do it for you. Go and sleep soundly, without a care. And the day after to-morrow you will wake up with a salary of twelve hundred francs."

Louët went away with this pleasant prospect before him, and I wrote to the prince royal to ask him for an interview next morning. A quarter of an hour later, I received his assent. I was then lodging at No. 22 rue de Rivoli. My windows were exactly opposite those of the Duc d'Orléans and he often used to answer by a sign requests such as I had just addressed to him. Such demands on my part were seldom asked; I always waited until the prince sent for me, for I knew that the king, and particularly the queen, looked askance at my visits to their son. So, next day, when I presented myself to the prince, he said—

"Ah, here you are! Why the deuce are you in such a hurry to see me?"

"Ah, monseigneur, to ask a favour which I am sure you will grant me with great pleasure."

"For whom, or of what is it about?"

"I do not know, monseigneur, why you are so categorical with me; you know I am no purist."

"Never mind, it is a good thing to prove that, although prince royal, I have had a college education."

"Exactly, and it is of one of your college companions, monseigneur, I have come to speak."

"Is there a single one left, by any chance, without a berth?" he asked.

"Yes, monseigneur; I have discovered him."

"Oh! you! You are capable of discovering any mortal thing."

"Well, monseigneur, since I am the discoverer of the Mediterranean...!"

"Well, what more have you discovered now?"

"I have told you, one of your Royal Highness's college companions."

"What is his name?"

I drew the slip of paper from my pocket, ready for use at the first opportunity.

"Louët, monseigneur."

The duke uttered a cry.

"Oh! that dunce!" he said.

I looked at him with a smile and made a show of putting the paper back in my pocket.

"Then, monseigneur," I said, "that alters matters."

"How so?"

"I have nothing further to ask your Highness."

"Why?"

I shrugged my shoulders.

"Well, what is that slip of paper which you are putting back into your pocket and which you are dying to show me?"

"I am still very anxious to show it you, it is true, monseigneur."

"Very well, then, show it me!"

"I dare not."

"Give it me!"

I held out my hand towards the prince and with the greatest submission, I handed him the paper.

"Good!" he said; "it is sure to be some infernal machine."

"Read it, monseigneur."

The prince cast a glance at the scrap of paper and blushed red to his eyes.

He blushed very easily, and granting this to be a weakness in him, it was one he shared in common with the Duc de Nemours and the Duc d'Aumale.

"Ah! ah!" he said, when he had read it.

Then, looking at me—

"Well, what does that prove?" he said. "That I was a bigger dunce even than he."

"Monseigneur, you will, in that case, surely, do something to help your superior?"

"What do you want me to do?"

And at this he went quietly up to the fireplace, rolling the scrap of paper between his fingers.

"Well, monseigneur, I sincerely hope you will find him a post."

"Where?"

"Near your own person."

"In what capacity?"

"Why, if it were only as a future tutor to your children, he would translate for them from the Greek for *Ασκρωνδη* right on to λος."

"Not that," he said; "but I have an idea."

"Upon my word, it does not surprise me."

Whereat the prince began to laugh.

"Do you think he would learn German?"

"He would learn anything you wanted, monseigneur."

"Very well. I will make him a secretary attached to Madame la Duchesse d'Orléans; when he knows German, he will translate the letters she receives from Germany ... that is the only post I have to offer him."

"When will the salary begin?"

"From to-morrow; tell him to call at Asseline's house."

"I thank you, both on his behalf and on mine, monseigneur."

He came nearer and nearer to the fireplace, rolling all the time the little bit of paper between his fingers. Finally he stretched out his arm towards the fireplace, but, holding my hand between the paper and the flames, I said—

"Pardon, monseigneur."

"What do you want?"

"That bit of paper...."

"Why?"

"It is my brokerage."

"What will you do with it?"

"I will have it framed."

"Oh, I know you are quite capable of doing that. Let me burn it."

"Monseigneur, I will hide it in a pocket-book and only show it once a week."

"Do you promise?"

"On my word of honour!"

"In that case, you can take it, and as you are longing to leave me to go and tell the good news to your protégé, go along with you."

"Oh, monseigneur, you shall not have the trouble of telling me twice."

"Go, go."

He waved me off with his hand, and I left him.

Poor prince! I have many anecdotes to tell of him like this one; and I mean to tell them. It was because of his goodness of heart and the loyalty of his patriotism that he became popular. And, when he died, I wrote these prophetic words:—

"God has just taken away the only obstacle that exists between the Monarchy and a Republic."

That is why you died, monseigneur: you were an obstacle: the Republic was a necessity.

CHAPTER III

The first representation of *Hernani*—The old ace of spades—The old man has a quarrel—Parodies—Origin of the story of Cabrion and of Pipelet—Eugène Sue and Desmares—Soulié returns to me—He offers me fifty of his workmen in the capacity of applauders—First representation of *Christine*—A supper at my lodgings—Hugo and de Vigny correct the objectionable lines

Hernani had been returned to Hugo almost without being examined; and we had not given them time to re-read it, as Taylor wanted to stage the play before his departure for Egypt. We were asked to hear it read before the Committee when the actors were present, as the play had been accepted beforehand.

The reading of *Hernani* made a profound sensation; nevertheless, I preferred, and still continue to prefer, *Marion Delorme*.

We were in the theatre by two o'clock on the day of the performance. We knew well enough that the victory achieved by de Vigny was not far-reaching. It was not of Shakespeare or Goethe or Schiller that sensible people were doubtful, it was of ourselves. What we wanted was a theatre that should be national, original, French, and not Greek or English or German; and this it was our mission to create.

Henri III., whether good or bad, was, at least, an original piece of work, drawn from our own chronicles, wherein traces of the influence of other theatres could be discerned, but no slavish imitation. *Marion Delorme*, which could not be got back from the Censorship, and *Hernani*, which was soon to be played, were both pieces of the same type. But *Henri III.* was intrinsically a stronger piece of work, whereas *Hernani* and *Marion Delorme* were more remarkable for their style.

Unluckily, French comedians were rigid in certain of their traditionary habits: it was usually quite an impossibility to get them to pass from tragedy to comedy without their making some dreadful slip in expression or even intonation. We have recounted the anecdote of Michelet and the four lines with reference to the cupboard scene. We ought also to mention that, in Hugo's work, comedy and tragedy often intermingle without any intermediate stages, and that this renders the interpretation of his thought more difficult than if he had attempted to set up an ascending or descending scale to bridge over the gulf between familiarity and grandeur of situation.

The English language, when rhymed, scanned and divided into short or long syllables, has a great advantage over ours, of which advantage Shakespeare availed himself to the full: his plays were generally written in three styles—in prose, in blank verse and in rhymed verses. Now, the people, the lower classes, talk in prose; the middle classes in blank verse; and princes and kings in rhyme. Moreover, if the ideas of the plebeian become exalted as he speaks, Shakespeare puts at his disposition two ascending styles in which to express his thoughts; if baser thoughts spring to the lips of kings and princes, he allows himself the liberty of making use of the language of the common people, or even of the middle classes, rather than injure that particular expression of thought. But the public that listens to our work knows nothing at all of these matters and is quite indifferent to all these shades of distinction: they merely come to applaud or to hiss; they applaud or hiss, that is all.

The first performance of *Hernani* left a unique impression upon theatrical annals; the suspension of *Marion Delorme*, the talk there had been about *Hernani*, had excited public curiosity to the highest pitch, and they were right in looking forward to a stormy night. The people attacked before they had heard a word, and defended without understanding what they were defending. When Hernani learns from Ruy Gomez that he has entrusted his daughter to Charles V., he exclaims—

"... Vieillard stupide, il l'aime!"

M. Parseval de Grandmaison, who was a little deaf, mistook it for

"Vieil as de pique, il l'aime!"
("Old ace of spades, he loves her!")

and, in his unaffected indignation, he could not refrain from shouting out—

"Oh! but really that is going a little too far!"

"What is going too far, monsieur?" my friend Lassailly inquired, who was on his left and had heard M. Parseval de Grandmaison's remark, but had not caught what Firmin said.

"I say, monsieur," the Academician replied, "that it is going a little too far to call a respectable, worthy old man like Ruy Gomez de Silva, 'old ace of spades'!"

"What! It is too strong an expression?"

"Yes, say what you like, it is not good taste, especially coming from such a young man as Hernani."

"Monsieur," Lassailly replied, "he had a right to say so. Cards were invented—they were invented in the time of Charles VI.; Monsieur l'Académicien, if you are not aware of that fact, I acquaint you with it. Hurrah for the old ace of spades! Bravo, Firmin! Bravo, Hugo! Ah!"

You can understand how hopeless it was to attempt to reply to people who attacked and defended in this fashion.

Hernani met with great success, although it was more strongly contested than *Henri III*. It is simple enough to find the reason for this: beauties of form and style are least readily appreciated by the vulgar mind, and these were Hugo's particular charms. On the other hand, these beautiful touches, being purely artistic, made a great impression on us, and on me in particular.

Hernani received all the tributes customary to triumph: it was outrageously attacked, and defended with equal violence; it was parodied with a clever astuteness directed against the traditionary dramatic customs, under the title of *Arnali, ou la Contrainte par Cor* (Arnali, or Constraint by Acclamation), a French work translated from the Gothic. And with regard to parodies,—let us make note of a historical fact, the date of which might else be lost in the mists of time, if we did not jot it down here.

The story—for such it is—of Cabrion and of M. Pipelet goes back to the month of March 1829. This is what happened, and it caused so much uneasiness to the porters of Paris that they have remained a melancholy race ever since!

Henri III., foreordained to meet with a great success, or at any rate to make a sensation, had also to have its parody; to facilitate the execution of this important work, I had sent my manuscript in advance to de Leuven and Rousseau; then, at their request, I had worked with them at the piece to the best of my ability, and we called it *Le Roi Dagobert et sa Cour*. But the Censorship regarded this title as lacking in respect to the descendant of Dagobert. The descendant of Dagobert, that worthy company which bears, for arms, scissors sable upon a field argent, meant His Majesty Charles X. It confused descendant with successor, but gentlemen on committees of examination are known to be above the consideration of such a mere trifle as that. So we altered the title to that of *La Cour du roi Pétaud*, to which the Censorship raised no objection. Just as if nobody were descended from le roi Pétaud!

So the parody of *Henri III. et sa Cour* was played at the Vaudeville under this title. It parodied the play, scene for scene. Now, at the conclusion of the fourth act, the farewell scene between Saint-Mégrin and his servant was parodied by one between the hero of the parody (unfortunately I have forgotten his name) and his porter. In this extremely tender, touching and sentimental scene, the hero asks the porter for a lock of his hair to the tune of *Dormez donc; mes chères amours!* which was all the rage just then, and most appropriate to the situation. On the night of the performance everybody went away singing the refrain and the words of the song. Three or four days afterwards, a party of us were dining at Véfours, including de Leuven, Eugène

Sue, Desforges, Desmares, Rousseau, several others and myself. At the end of the dinner, which had been exceedingly lively, we sang the famous refrain in chorus:—

"Portier, je veux
De tes cheveux!"

Eugène Sue and Desmares decided to carry into effect this flight of our imagination and, as they entered the house, No. 8 rue de la Chaussée-d'Antin, where Eugène Sue knew the name of the concierge, they asked the good man if his name were not M. Pipelet. He answered in the affirmative. Then, in the name of a Polish princess who had seen him and fallen desperately in love with him, they asked, with many entreaties, for a lock of his hair, and, to get rid of them, the poor Pipelet ended by giving it them. He was a lost man, after he had committed such a weakness! That same evening three other requests were addressed to him on behalf of a Russian princess, a German baroness and an Italian marchioness; and, every time the request was put to him, an invisible choir sang under the great doorway—

"Portier, je veux
De tes cheveux!"

The joke was continued the next day; we sent everybody we knew to ask Master Pipelet for a lock of his hair, so that he eventually only answered the bell with horror, whilst to no purpose whatever did he remove from his door the traditional notice—

Address yourself to the Porter.

On the following Sunday, Eugène Sue and Desmares decided to give the poor devil a serenade on a grand scale: they entered the courtyard on horseback, with guitars in their hands, and began singing the persecuting air. But, as we said, it was Sunday, and, the householders being away in the country, the porter quite expected they would try to embitter his Sabbath as on other days, not allowing him the rest God had conceded to Himself. Having informed every servant throughout the house, he slipped behind the singers, shut the street door and made a pre-arranged signal, whereupon five or six servants ran to his assistance, and the troubadours were compelled to turn their musical instruments into weapons of defence: they came away with nothing but the necks of their guitars in their hands. Nobody ever knew the details of this fight, which must have been a terrible one; the combatants kept it to themselves; but it was known to have happened; and the porter of the rue de la Chaussée-d'Antin was voted a literary outlaw. From that moment the wretched man's life became a premature hell to him: even his night's rest was not respected; for every belated littérateur had to take an oath to return home by way of the rue de la Chaussée-d'Antin, were he living even at the Barrière du Maine. The persecution endured for over three months; at the end of that time a new face appeared to answer the accustomed demand: Pipelet's wife came weeping to the grating to say that her husband had fallen a victim to this persecution and had been carried off to a hospital with an attack of brain fever. The unlucky man was in a delirium and, in his raving, repeated incessantly, over and over again, the refrain that had cost him his reason and his health. This, then, is the real truth about the celebrated persecution of the Pipelets, which made a great sensation during the years 1829 to 1830.

Now let us return to *Christine*. When the play was returned from the Censorship it was rehearsed with a will. Romanticism, which had taken possession of the Théâtre-Français, had just spread to the other side of the Seine and had turned aside from the Academy—as in the case of a fortress which a great general scorns to attack at a time of invasion—and threatened to carry the Odéon by assault.

It was creating quite a revolution in the Latin quarter. Further, in order to give more effect to the next performance, Harel constantly suspended the play—a means of advertisement and a way of publishing hitherto quite unknown.

On the morning of the general rehearsal I received a line from Soulié; it was, with the exception of the slight correspondence previously mentioned and the sending of places for *Roméo et Juliette*, the only sign of his existence he had given me for a year. He asked me for a pass for this rehearsal. I sent him at once a pass for himself and any of his friends who might wish to accompany him. The rehearsal took place the same night. Now, in those days, general rehearsals were actual performances of the play as it would be presented finally. Friends were not yet sick of it, success had not made them indifferent or jealous, and there really seemed to be a general interest taken in the outcome of some of them. The cause we were upholding was that of every obscure aspirant who hoped to become famous some day; and they would share a good deal of the influence acquired by us, in order to make their path more sure and brilliant. Egotism made them devotees. So the general rehearsal of *Christine* was an enthusiastic success.

I left the orchestra after the fifth act, and went to pay my respects to Soulié. He was greatly moved and held out his arms to me. I embraced him with deep emotion; it had distressed me to be on cool terms with a man whom I loved and whose talent I admired more than others did, because, better than others, I appreciated that talent.

"Ah!" said he, "you were certainly well advised in writing your *Christine* alone. It is an admirable piece of work, but parts of it suffer as regards composition;

that will come. Some day you will be our leading dramatist, and we your humble servants."

"Come now, my dear friend," I said, "you must be mad to say such things!"

"Not so; I mean what I say, upon my honour. To tell you that it gives me immense pleasure would be going too far; you would not believe me, but nevertheless it is so."

I thanked him.

"Look here," he said, "let us talk seriously: I know there is a plot organised against your play and that they are going to make it hot for you to-morrow night."

"Oh, I felt certain of it."

"Have you fifty places left in the pit?"

"Yes."

"Then let me have them and I will bring all my workmen from the sawmill, and we will back you up against them, never fear!"

I gave him a packet of tickets without counting them, and, as they were waiting for me on the stage, I again embraced him and we parted.

I think this man possessed certain brotherly and trusting qualities which one looks for in vain in theatrical circles: he who had been hissed three or four months previously in the same theatre, and under similar circumstances, now asked his rival for fifty places, in order to back up a play the success of which would but intensify the failure of his own, and from a rival who, with lavish generosity, gave him at once, without the slightest hesitation or misgivings, a pile of tickets quite sufficient in number to ruin the best play in the world if they fell into the wrong hands. We were, probably, rather absurd figures, but we were unquestionably well-meaning.

As no delay had been considered necessary, the play was performed the next day.

Frédéric had told me the truth. There had been organised by someone—by whom I had not the slightest idea, perhaps spontaneously and without any other incentive than the hatred borne towards us—the roughest sort of opposition I ever witnessed. As usual, I was present in a box at my first night, so I lost none of the incidents of that terrible battle which raged for seven hours; during which the play was knocked down a dozen times and always rose up again, ending at two in the morning by forcing the panting, horrified and scared public to go down on its knees.

Oh! I repeat it with an enthusiasm that has not diminished after twenty-five years of fighting, and in spite of my fifty or more triumphant successes, the contest between the genius of man and the ill-will of the crowd, the vulgarity of the audience, the hatred of enemies, is a grand and splendid spectacle. There is an immense satisfaction in dramatic quarters in feeling the opposition forced down on its knees and slowly made to bite the dust in utter defeat. Oh! what pride would victory produce, if it were not that, amongst honest men, it is a cure for vanity!

It is quite impossible to give any idea of the effect that the arrest of Monaldeschi produced on the audience, after the monologue of Sentinelli at the window, which had been hooted at. The whole theatre burst into roars of applause, and when, in the fifth act, Monaldeschi, saved by the love of Christine, sends the poisoned ring to Paula, there were furious outcries against the cowardly assassin, which were turned into frantic cheers when they saw him drag himself, wounded and bleeding, to the feet of the queen, who, in spite of his supplications and prayers, gives utterance to this line, which Picard had pronounced *impossible*—

"Eh bien, j'en ai pitié, mon père.—Qu'on l'achève!"

At last the whole audience was won over and the success of the play was assured. The epilogue, which was calm, and cold, and grandiose, a kind of vast cavern with damp floors and I dank vaults, where I buried the bodies of my characters, detracted from its successful acceptation. Those guilty souls with blanched heads and dead affections, meeting one another again after thirty years' separation, the one without hatred and the other without love, gazing in wonder at each other and asking forgiveness for the crime they had perpetrated, presented a succession of scenes that were more philosophic and religious in spirit than dramatic in art. Confronted with my own work, I recognised my mistake; but, having erred, I must atone; so I cut out the epilogue, which was really the best piece in the whole work, as regards style, although far from being perfect. Let us hasten to say that the rest was not very striking; it was written in imitation of a language in which I had then only just begun to stammer, in faltering accents.

I had not lost sight of Soulié during the performance: he and his fifty men were there. Even if I had put a mask over my face, I should not have dared to do what he had done for the success of my play!

Oh! dear and loyal-hearted friend! Known to and appreciated by few, I, who did know and appreciate you during your lifetime, and defended you after your death, I still extol your virtues!

But to conclude my story: the whole of the audience left the theatre without a single soul being able to tell whether *Christine* was a success or a failure.

I had a supper-party afterwards, for any of my friends who liked to come. If we were not fully triumphant at the victory, we were, at all events, excited by the fight. There were about twenty-five of us to supper—Hugo, de Vigny, Paul Lacroix, Boulanger, Achille Comte, Planche (Planche, who had not yet been bitten by the dog of hatred, and who only later showed an inclination to madness), Cordelier-Delanoue, Théodore Villenave—and I know not who besides, of the noisy youthful crew full of life and activity that surrounded us at that time; all the volunteers belonging to that great war of invasion, which was not in reality as terrible as it pronounced itself to be, and, after all, only threatened to capture Vienna in order to obtain possession of the Rhine frontiers.

Now listen to what happened: the event I am going to relate was almost a duplicate of the episode in connection with Soulié; and I will answer for it as being unique in the annals of literature.

There were some hundred lines in my play which had to be altered, and which, to make use of an expressive vulgarism, had been *empoignés* (seized upon) at the first night's performance; they were to be held up to hostile criticism, for they would not fail to be dropped on afresh at the next performance; besides some dozen cuts which had to be made and dressed by skilful and by fatherly hands; this needed doing immediately, that very night, so that the manuscript could be sent back the next morning for the alterations to be made at noon, and the piece acted that same night. Now it was out of the question that I, who had twenty-five guests to entertain, could do it. But Hugo and de Vigny took the manuscript, and, telling me to set my mind at rest, they shut themselves up in a small room, and, whilst the rest of us were eating and drinking and singing, they worked. They toiled for four consecutive hours with the same conscientious energy they would have employed upon their own work; and when they came out at daybreak, finding us all gone to bed and asleep, they left the manuscript, ready for the performance, on the mantelpiece, and, without waking anybody, these two rivals went off arm in arm, like two brothers!

Do you remember that, dear Hugo? Do you recollect that, de Vigny?

We were roused from our lethargic condition next morning by the bookseller Barba, who came to offer me twelve thousand francs for the manuscript of *Christine*—that is to say, double the sum for which I had sold *Henri III*. It was, then, unquestionably a success!

CHAPTER IV

A passing cab—Madame Dorval in the *Incendiaire*—Two actresses—The Duc d'Orléans asks for the Cross of the Legion of Honour on my behalf—His recommendation has no effect—M. Empis—Madame Lafond's Salon—My costume as Arnaute—Madame Malibran—Brothers and sisters in Art

The day after, or rather the evening of the second day after my first representation, I was crossing the place de l'Odéon at one o'clock in the morning, passing from the lighted theatre into the darkness of the street, and from the noise of the applause of a crowded house to the silence of an empty square, from intoxication to reflection, from reality to dreams, when a woman's head appeared at the door of a cab calling me by name. I turned round, the cab pulled up and I opened the door.

"Are you M. Dumas?" the person inside inquired.

"Yes, madame."

"Very well, come inside and kiss me. Ah! you possess marvellous talent, and you don't draw women badly either!"

It made me laugh, and I kissed the fair speaker. She who spoke thus to me was Dorval—Dorval to whom I could have retorted in the same words—

"You have marvellous talent, and you take off women rather well."

The fact is that since we had seen Dorval act Malvina in the *Vampire* she had improved immensely. In the *Incendiaire*, especially, she had been perfectly magnificent. Those who read these lines now will not know what the play was: I can only recollect a priest's part, which Bocage played excellently well, and a confession scene in which Dorval was sublime. Picture to yourselves a young girl who has had a torch put into her hands; how, or by what means, I no longer remember, but no matter; besides, that was twenty-two or twenty-three years ago, and I have forgotten the drama and, I repeat, I can only recollect the actress. She acted the confession scene, referred to above, on her knees: it lasted a whole quarter of an hour, during which space of time one held one's breath or only breathed in weeping. One night Madame Dorval was more beautiful, more tender and more pathetic than ever: and I will tell you why. You will have seen pictures by Ruysdael and Hobbema, and will recall how rays of sunlight stray across their landscapes, lighting up a corner of the grey sky, and illuminating the misty atmosphere, where the great oxen graze in the tall grass. Well, then, listen to this. When the player is fatigued, having played the same part over from ten to fifty times, inspiration gradually dies down and genius slumbers and emotion gets deadened; the actor's sky grows grey and his atmosphere clouded, and he searches for rays of sunshine like those that illumine the canvases of Hobbema or Ruysdael. The sight of a friend among the spectators, a talented fellow-artist leaning over the dress-circle, is, to him, as a ray of sunlight; a thoughtful face with eyes shining in the dim light of a box. Then communication is established between the house and the stage; the electric current is perceived and, thanks to it, the player returns to the days of the earliest performances; all the slumbering chords awake, and suddenly weep, mourn and sob more quiveringly than ever; the public applauds and shouts bravo, and thinks that it is for it the player works these wonders. Poor deluded public! It is towards some kindred soul, unsuspected by you, that all this effort, those cries and tears are directed! You simply get the benefit of it as from dew or light or flame. But, after all, what matters it to you who pours the dew down, who spreads this light, who lights this flame, since in this dew and light and flame you refresh and light and warm yourself? So, one night, Dorval had surpassed herself—for whom? She had not the slightest idea. It was for a woman in the audience—a woman who for three hours had kept her spellbound beneath her eagle glance; for three hours Dorval saw none of the other people in the house, she wept and talked and lived and, in a word, acted for that one woman alone: when she applauded and cried "Bravo!" the actress had been paid for her labour, rewarded for her pains and compensated for her talent! She had said to herself, "I am satisfied since she is." Then the curtain had fallen and, breathless, crushed, almost dead from exhaustion, like a pythoness when removed from her tripod, Dorval went to her room; from victress she became victim, and fell half fainting upon her couch. Suddenly the door of her dressing-room opened, and the unknown woman appeared on the threshold. Dorval sprang up trembling and took her by both hands as though she were a friend. For a few minutes the two women looked at one another in silence, smiling, with tears in their eyes.

"Forgive me, madame," the unknown said, with incredible sweetness of voice; "but I could not return home without telling you of the joy, the emotion, the happiness I owe to you. Oh! it was wonderful, sublime, exquisite!"

Dorval looked at her and thanked her with her eyes, and an inclination of her head and a motion of the shoulders peculiarly her own, all the while interrogating her, inquiring with every muscle of her countenance—

"But who in the world are you, madame? Who are you?"

The unknown guessed her thoughts, and replied—only those who had heard that wonderful siren speak can conceive the sweetness of her tones—

"I am Madame Malibran."

Dorval uttered a cry and pointed to the only picture which adorned her room. It was a portrait of Madame Malibran as Desdemona. Henceforth Madame Dorval possessed one of the two things she had hitherto lacked before she could become a woman of the highest merit: a friend who would be true to her but, at the same time, discriminating; and such a friendship Madame Malibran offered her. Now that she had her portion of friendship, it rested with Providence to bestow upon her that of love.

After Madame Dorval had played the parts of Adèle d'Hervey and Marion Delorme, she played Kitty Bell; by that time she had developed into a most accomplished woman and a consummate actress. Dorval's exclamation when she stopped me near the Odéon, and the artistic freemasonry she frankly sealed with a fraternal kiss, made me very happy! For pride to be satisfied, praise must come from a higher source or, at the very least, from as high a one as that of the recipient. For the praise that comes from above is ambrosial, that from below is but incense.

One day, Michelet wrote to me (I had never either seen or spoken with him previously).

"Monsieur," he said, "I like and admire you; you are one of the forces of nature."

This letter gave me keener and more real pleasure than if I had received the news that the grand Cross of the Légion d'honneur had been bestowed upon me. Mention of the Légion d'honneur suggests a few words relative to the sensation caused by the successes of both *Henri III.* and *Christine.*

Christine had been played on 20 February, and on 9 March, very probably at the request of the Duc de Chartres, who had been present, at his own desire, at the first representation, the Duc d'Orléans wrote as follows to M. Sosthène de la Rochefoucauld:—

> "PALAIS-ROYAL, 9 *March* 1830
>
> "I hear, monsieur, that you intend to submit to the King the suggestion of granting the Cross of the Légion d'honneur to M. Alexandre Dumas, when the season comes round at which he usually grants promotions to that order.
>
> "M. Alexandre Dumas' success as a dramatist, indeed, seems to me to deserve such a mark of esteem, and I shall be the more pleased for him to get it, since he has been attached to my secretarial staff and in my forestry department for the past six years, during which time he has supported his family in a most praiseworthy way. I am told

he intends to travel in the north of Europe, and that he sets great store by the nomination taking place before his departure. I do not know whether 12 April would be a suitable occasion on which to submit the proposition to the King; but I wish to suggest the idea to you, as a token of the interest I take in M. Dumas.

"Allow me to take advantage of this opportunity to offer you the assurance of my sincere regard for you.—Yours affectionately, LOUIS-PHILIPPE D'ORLÉANS"

One day, when I was in the library, M. le Duc de Orléans came in with a letter in his hand. I had risen at his entrance and remained standing as he advanced towards me.

"Look here, Monsieur Dumas," he said, "this is what has been asked on your behalf. Read it."

Intensely astonished, I read the letter I have just transcribed above. I knew that M. Sosthène de la Rochefoucauld, who was very friendly towards me, had been urged by Beauchesne to send my name in to M. de la Bouillerie's office; but it was far enough from my thoughts that the Duc d'Orléans would ever consent to recommend me himself. I blushed excessively, stammered out a few words of thanks and asked him to whom I owed the good fortune of being recommended by him.

"To a friend," he replied, and that was all I could extract from him.

Unfortunately, the duke's recommendation was of no avail. I have since been informed that it was M. Empis, head clerk of the king's household, who frustrated the kind intention of the prince and of M. de la Rochefoucauld. M. Empis belonged to an entirely opposite school of literature from mine; he had written a very remarkable play called *La Mère et la Fille*, the leading part in which was created by Frédérick Lemaître, upon his first appearance at the Odéon, and the piece was extraordinarily successful. I said above "Unfortunately the duke's recommendation was of no avail." Let us explain the word *unfortunately*. Unfortunate it was, indeed; for at that time the Cross of the Légion d'honneur had not been bestowed broadcast, and it would have been a rich prize had I obtained it. I was young and full of hope and vigour and enthusiasm; I was just on the threshold of my career; and therefore the fact of my nomination would have given me very great delight. But it is among the misfortunes of those who have the power of giving such honours that they never know how to give them in time; this cross, that the Duc d'Orléans asked for me in 1830, King Louis-Philippe only gave me in 1836, at the Fêtes of Versailles; even then it was not he himself but the prince royal who gave it me, upon the occasion of his marriage, when the orders at his disposal were one grand'croix and two croix d'Officier and one croix de Chevalier. The grand'croix was for François Arago; the two "croix d'Officier" were for Augustin Thierry and Victor Hugo; the croix de Chevalier was for me.

Having reached this period of my life, I will tell all the stories connected with this order, and how M. de Salvandy, so that he might be forgiven for presenting the croix d'Officier to Hugo and the croix de Chevalier to me, felt obliged to give one at the same time to an excellent fellow, whose name was so totally unknown as to preserve, by its very obscurity, the celebrity of our own. The result was that I put my cross inside my pocket, instead of pinning it in my buttonhole.

And this reminds me of the story of the father of one of my literary confrères, a wealthy cotton merchant, who, having received the cross, because he had lent Charles X. two million francs, only wore the ribbon in the buttonhole of his fob. Thus I had, for the time being, to deprive myself of the red ribbon. I was angry at first with M. Empis for having defeated my pretty dream, but far more angry with him later for having written *Julie, ou la Réparation*!

However, we managed to find endless diversions during that happy winter of 1830, severe though it was. It is a remarkable fact that revolutions almost always surprise people in the midst of dances, and kings in the midst of fireworks. There were, too, any number of masked balls. There was a Salon held in Paris in those days by Madame Lafond, which was entirely comprised of artistic society. Madame Lafond was, at that date, a woman of between thirty-six and thirty-eight years of age, in the zenith of her beauty, which was that of a brunette, and she was admirably preserved: she had dark speaking eyes and black wavy hair, add to these charms a most bewitching smile, the most graceful hands imaginable, and an intellect that was remarkable both for its power and its kindliness, and you will still only have a very imperfect impression of the mistress of that Salon. Her husband was the musician Lafond, who was a talented violin player: he was small and fair, and supported his wife to perfection at her soirées, playing the same part Prince Albert plays at the Court of Queen Victoria. I believe he was killed by a carriage accident. He had two sons a great deal younger than I, who still wore little round jackets and turned-down collars, and were sent to bed at eight o'clock. They have grown up into two delightful young fellows, whom I have since met at various Embassies.

In those days, neither the costume of pierrots nor that of dock labourers had become the fashionable rage; Chicard and Gavarni were still hidden in the dark depths of the future; and the Opera ballet had not emerged from the traditional domino in which it would have been a difficult matter to thread those mad galops, to the sound of that terrible music, which won Musard the nickname of "the Napoleon of the Cancan." The real cancan, which was a capital national dance, the only one which possessed the elements of spontaneity and of the picturesque, was consigned to the outskirts of civilisation, with other contraband goods proscribed by custom.

Now, the choice of a suitable costume was a very serious business to an author of twenty-six, who had already begun to possess the reputation, whether erroneously or not, of being quite an Othello. I had made the acquaintance at Firmin's balls—I do not know why I have never yet spoken of those delightful réunions of his, where one was sure to find, without powder or paint, the youngest and prettiest faces in Paris—of a clever young fellow, a pupil of M. Ingres, and who has since become the celebrated antiquary Amaury Duval. He had just returned from Greece, where he had taken part in an artistic expedition that had been sent to the land of Pericles, after the battle of Navarino. He appeared at one of Firmin's balls in the disguise of a Pallikar. The Pallikar was all the rage then; Byron had introduced, it, and all our pretty women had collected funds for that mother of lovely women, the land of Greece. From this time I became great friends with Amaury and, later, I gave his name to one of my romances, in remembrance of our youthful friendship; or, rather, let us say, of the friendship of our youth. He proclaimed himself a fanatical partisan of my works, and he it was, it will be recollected, son and nephew of an Academician, who was said to have demanded the heads of the members of the Academy, after the first representation of *Henri III*. So I went and hunted him up, for it was most important at a fancy dress ball to make the most of one's natural advantages. I have said that I never was good-looking, but I was tall and well built, although rather slight; my face was thin, and I had large brown eyes, with a dark complexion; in a word, if it was impossible to create beauty, it was easy enough to form character. So we decided that the dress of an Albanian would suit me exactly; and Amaury accordingly designed me a costume. Now, the turban was the most striking part of this costume, and, being rolled two or three times round the head, it passed round the neck and was tied at the point it started from. But the costume had to be made, and, as it was covered with embroidery and braid and lace, it took a fortnight to make.

At last, the evening arrived, and the dress was finished by eleven o'clock; by midnight I entered Madame Lafond's house. This costume of mine was then almost unknown in France: the jacket and leggings were of red velvet, embroidered with gold; the *fustanelle*, as white as snow, had not been robbed of a single inch of its proper width; the dazzling silver arms were marvellously wrought, and, above all, the originality of the head-dress drew all eyes upon me. I guessed I should make a triumphant sensation, but had no idea of the method in which it would be expressed. I had not taken ten steps into the room before a young woman, clad as a Roman priestess, crowned with verbena and cypress, made her apologies to her partner and left him to come to me. She then led me apart into a small boudoir and, making me sit down, remained standing in front of me and said—

"Now, Monsieur Dumas, you are going to teach me how to put on a turban like that; to-morrow I am acting Desdemona with Zucchelli and you know how those Italian devils array themselves; I should, at any rate, like him to have a head-dress like yours, it would work me up!"

The Roman priestess was Madame Malibran, of whom I shall soon have much more to say and of whom I have already spoken twice in connection with the first representation of *Henri III.*, where she hung over the edge of her box on the third tier throughout the fifth act; and also in connection with Dorval, into whose arms she ran to fling herself after a representation of *l'Incendiaire.* Yes, it was Madame Malibran, the incomparable artist, who alone, perhaps, of all artists, wedded the drama to song, strength to grace, joy to sadness, to a degree no one has ever attained. Alas! she too died young, and is now but a shadow on our horizon! Shade of Desdemona and of Rosine, of la Somnambule and of Norma, a dazzling, harmonious, melancholy shadow! that those who saw the living reality can still revive by the aid of memory, but who is merely a phantom for those who saw her not! She died when still young, but thereby she, at any rate, carried away with her into the tomb all the advantages that are to be derived from premature death; she died beautiful, loving and beloved, at the zenith of her triumph, girt with glory, crowned with laurels and enshrouded in fame! But theatrical artists leave nothing that can be transmitted to posterity, no traces of the purity of their singing, the grace of their movements or the passion of their gestures— nothing but a reflection which remains in the memory of their contemporaries. It therefore remains for us, painters or poets, who do leave something behind us after we have gone; to us, privileged children of Art, who possess the faculty of reproducing the form or the spirit of material and perishable things through the medium of our brushes and pens; to whom God has given a mirror for a soul, which remembers instead of forgets; it rests with us to make you live again, O brothers and sisters! to depict you as you were, and, if possible, to reflect your images even greater and more beautiful than they were in life!

Did my readers think when I began these volumes that my aim was merely egotistic, for the purpose of talking everlastingly of myself? No, indeed; I meant it to serve for a huge frame in which to depict all my brethren in Art, fathers or children of my century, the great spirits and charming personalities, whose hands, cheeks and lips I have pressed; those who have loved me, and whom I have loved; those who have been, or who still are, the ornament of our times; including those I may never have known, and those even who have detested me! The *Memoirs of Alexandre Dumas*—why, it would be absurd! What could I have become alone, as an isolated individual, a lost atom, a speck of dust amidst so many whirlwinds Simply nothing. But by associating myself with you, by pressing with my left hand the right hand of an artist, with my right hand the left hand of a prince, I became a link in the golden chain which connects the past with the future. No, I am not writing my own Memoirs, but those of all I have known; and as I have come in contact with the greatest and most illustrious people in France, it is really Memoirs of France I am writing.

I spent the best part of the night teaching Madame Malibran how to put on an Albanian turban, and the next day Zucchelli played Othello in a head-dress similar to the one I had worn on the previous evening. Madame Malibran was quite right. Othello's coiffure had its effect, for she had never been greater or more sublimely beautiful!

Farewell, Marie! Her name too was Marie, in common with Marie Dorval and Marie Pleyel—*au revoir!* I shall meet you again at Naples!

CHAPTER V

Why the Duc d'Orléans' recommendation on the subject of my croix d'honneur failed—The indemnity of a milliard—La Fayette's journey to Auvergne—His reception at Grenoble, Vizille and at Lyons—Charles X.'s journey to Alsace—Varennes and Nancy—Opening of the Chambers—The royal speech and the Address of the 221—Article 14—The conquest of Algiers and the recapture of our Rhine frontiers

Let us turn from an artistic to an aristocratic evening party, one which made quite a different sensation! I refer to the famous soirée at the Palais-Royal given, on 31 May 1830, by the Duc d'Orléans to his brother-in-law, the King of Naples. But first let us return to matters a little farther back.

Why did the recommendation of the Duc d'Orléans in the matter of obtaining a croix d'honneur for me carry so little weight? It was because, as his popularity grew day by day, so, in proportion, did his credit wane at the Tuileries. Because, daily growing emboldened and weighing in his mind the question he meant to put, so he has since told me, to a council and not to a prince of the blood, he let slip expressions against the Court which showed too open an opposition to its methods. Because, since M. de Polignac had been made a minister, since the occasion of the famous audience given to Victor Hugo when he was received by the king at Saint-Cloud, everybody was expecting a fresh revolution to break out. A revolution must have been universally expected, since I, in my own small turn, had replied to M. de Lourdoueix in the famous phrase "I will wait" (*j'attendrai*), and, had I waited, the matter would only have been postponed for six months.

On 2 March the Chamber re-opened. The king was present at the sitting, his mind made up for a revolutionary measure. Now a thousand things determined Charles X. upon taking such a course: his own travels in Alsace, M. de La Fayette's in the Auvergne, and other events that we will record in their proper places. General La Fayette, having gained possession of his indemnity money as a Royalist émigré, had made up his mind to travel through Auvergne as a Republican. In fact, the milliard of indemnity had just been distributed; and, strange to say, it was found to enrich more Liberals than Royalists. The Duc d'Orléans, for instance, received 16,000,000 francs. The Duc de Liancourt received 1,400,000 francs as his share. The Duc de Choiseul, 1,100,000 francs. General La Fayette, 456,182 francs. M. Gaëtan de La Rochefoucauld, 428,206 francs. M. Thiers, 357,850 francs. And lastly, M. Charles de Lameth, 201,696 francs.

Well, General La Fayette set out for Auvergne. General La Fayette, whom I knew intimately, and who was quite friendly in his inclinations towards myself, whom I hope to describe in his proper turn in the course of these Memoirs, without allowing the respectful homage of a young man and the sympathy of the friend to injure the impartiality of the historian—General La Fayette, I say, was born in 1757, at Chavagnac, near Brioude, and, some day before the close of the session of 1829, he had set out to visit the ancient land of the Arvernese. He had yielded to the wish of seeing his native land once more, a desire which moves our souls with such profound memories that it draws us to it throughout our whole life, and it is a remarkable fact that this attraction grows stronger as we near death, as though nature had implanted an imperious wish in man's heart to seek his burial-place near the spot where he was born. Now, General La Fayette was welcomed throughout that tour with joy and affection and respect, but without fanaticism. Banquets had been given him at Issoire and Clermont and Brioude; but none of them had had any sort of political significance until then: they were simply meetings of fellow-citizens, celebrating the return of one of their members, and nothing more. Suddenly, the news of a change of government became known, and the accession of M. de Polignac to power.

From the very moment that the news of the change of government arrived, La Fayette's journey assumed a different complexion: it bore the aspect of an influential protest, and an almost religious hopefulness of tone. The general was at Puy—a remarkable coincidence—in the same town where the ancestors of M. de Polignac had formerly held sway, when, a couple of hours before the banquet took place that was being prepared in his honour, the people heard of the formation of the Ministry of 8 August; immediately they rallied excitedly round the famous traveller, pressing up to him with shouts of "Vive La Fayette!" and, at the repast, two hours later, the following pretty revolutionary toast was drunk:—

"The Chambre des députés, the *one and only hope* of France!"

The general intended to go to Vizille to see his granddaughter, wife of Augustin Périer, who lived in a château built in olden times by the Constable of Lesdiguières, an ancient feudal manor house, which was later turned into a factory and workshop. To go to Vizille—a historic town whose Government, with that of Bretagne, in 1788 was the first to offer opposition to the royal decrees—he had to pass through Grenoble. Moreover, pass through it he would; the general was just the man to go two or three leagues out of his way in order to cull the flower of popularity, which quickly fades and which, after forty years, was springing up as fresh the second time as the first.

Grenoble is a great town for dissension: nowhere have the seeds of liberty produced more luxuriant crops than in this unsubmissive city, which, in 1815, out of reverence for Napoleon, burst the gates that would not open to him; which, in 1816, witnessed the guillotining of Didier, Drevet and Buisson, and the shooting down of twenty-two conspirators, including an old man of sixty-five and a child of fifteen! A couple of score of young men on horseback and several carriages came out to greet the general; they met him a league away from the town to form an escort; then at the gate of France the former mayor, deprived of his office, probably through the many political reactions of the times, awaited him, to present him with a crown of silver oak leaves. This wreath—*a token of the love and gratitude of the people*—was the outcome of a subscription at fifty centimes a head. At Vizille they outdid even this: they fired cannon. On 5 September it was the turn of Lyons to show the general sympathy by means of a reception that was quite an ovation in itself. A deputation was even appointed to receive him at the borders of the department of the Rhône; it was escorted by a troop of five hundred horsemen, by a thousand young folk on foot and by sixty carriages occupied by the leading merchants of the town. In the midst of these carriages came an empty barouche, drawn by four horses, which was intended for the general's use.

At the gate of the city the general was harangued by a former lawyer. We do not recollect the speech, except that it was ultra Liberal in tone, but we recall a few words of the reply from him to whom it was addressed. "To-day," the general replied, "after a long diversion of brilliant patriotism and of constitutional hopes, I once again find myself in your midst at what I should consider a critical moment, had I not observed everywhere during my journeyings, as also in this powerful city, the calm and even contemptuous steadfastness of a great people, which is aware of its rights, conscious of its strength and will remain faithful to its duties!"

This utterance, ten months beforehand, was prophetic of the Bretonne Association, the refusal of tax-paying and the Revolution of July.

The general's account of his travels was printed, and a hundred thousand copies of it were sold. "Those whom God would ruin He first deprives of reason." The Monarchy had, indeed, gone mad! A most influential paper, a monarchical one, published an article on this journey, of which the following few lines may serve as a specimen:—

"General La Fayette's journey is a revolutionary orgy, which is not so much the result of patriotic enthusiasm as of various combinations of party spirit. The Comité directeur and Masonic Lodges called them together, these parties being desirous of fêting the Revolution, in the person of the general, who, since 1789, has preached and defended similar principles in short, it is the actual Revolution elevated to high places."

It is now necessary for us to say a few words about the tour of Charles X. in Alsace; it will balance that of General La Fayette. Besides, any events that lead up to great catastrophes in history are of peculiar interest. Contrary to that of La Fayette, who, as we have seen, had excited the enthusiasm of the people wherever he went, the king's journey, following the usual custom of princely journeys, had only displayed an official and factitious loyalty, spread over the real hatred below, as the folds of a beautiful cloth cover up a worm-eaten table. It may be said to have done far more, it had brought to light some of those sinister omens which foretell great disasters. They had passed through Varennes (and one asks by what unlucky chance or forgetfulness had that town, fatal to the cause of monarchy, been chosen for the king's route?), and at Varennes they stopped to change horses, at the head of the bridge, at the entrance of the archway, exactly at the same spot where Louis XVI., the Queen, Madame Élisabeth, the Children of France and their governess, Madame de Tourzel, had been compelled to stop by Drouet's threats, to get down from the coach and to follow M. Sausse into his grocer's shop, which was to serve them as the antechamber to the Temple. Madame la Duchesse d'Angoulême, who had been one of the party on that first journey, was with the second. When she recognised the fatal spot, after a lapse of thirty-eight years, she shuddered, uttered a cry and would not allow the carriage time for a relay, but commanded the postillions to go on to the next posting-place. This time the postillions obeyed; they had refused on 21 June 1791. They did not, however, set off fast enough to prevent overhearing a few injudicious words which the duchess let fall; words that, borne on the winds of hatred, preceded her throughout the journey, to such effect that, when Charles X. and his family reached Nancy, the chief of Royalist towns, and showed themselves on the palace balcony to bow to the people, hissings were heard above the cheers, each time the king saluted: the people treated their princes just as one treats actors who have played their parts badly. The Duc d'Orléans lost sight of nothing; like a hunter on the watch for his prey, he lay in wait to take advantage of all the errors made by the royal quarry he was hunting down. Thus I, too, who was on a footing of intimacy in his household, could, so to speak, feel the pulse of his ambition beating, and had no doubt of the nature of his desires, which daily grew more and more hopeful in character.

I have mentioned that the Chamber opened on 2 March 1830. I was present at the opening session. Just as the king placed his foot on the first step of the throne, he caught it in the velvet pile carpet that covered the steps. He tripped and nearly fell. His cap rolled on the floor. The Duc d'Orléans sprang forward to pick it up, and returned it to the king. I nudged my neighbour—as far as I can recollect, it was Beauchesne.

"Before a year is out," I said to him, "the same thing will happen to the crown—only, instead of giving it back to Charles X., he will keep it for himself."

In the speech pronounced by Charles X., after he had set the cap on his head which the Duc d'Orléans had given him back, was the following noteworthy paragraph:—

> "I have no doubt of your co-operation in the good deeds I wish to carry out. You will reject with scorn all treacherous insinuations which malevolent feeling endeavours to propagate. Should evil machinations raise up against my rule obstacles which I neither will nor ought to foresee, I should find strength to overcome them through my resolution to maintain the public peace, in the just confidence of the French people and in the love they ever bear towards their king."

The Address of the 221 was the reply to this speech; to the above paragraph, the following was the answer:—

> "The Charter has laid it down as an indispensable condition of the regular working of public affairs, that there should be a permanent agreement of political views between your Government and the desires of the people. Sire, our loyalty and devotion compel us to tell you that such concurrence of opinion does not exist."

It was a declaration of war in perfect form.

Charles X. trembled in every limb whilst he listened to the reading of the Address. Then, when the deputation had quitted the Tuileries, he said—

"I will not suffer my crown to be dipped in the gutter!" And he dissolved the Chamber.

These were some of the events which thrilled through every heart, even in that of the *Journal des Débats*. It attacked the Government with most unusual violence.

> "Polignac, La Bourdonnaye and Bourmont," it exclaimed, "that is equivalent to saying Coblence, Waterloo, 1815! Those are the three principles, the three chief characters of

the Ministry. Press them hard, twist them and they will disgorge nothing but humiliations and misfortunes and danger!"

Charles X. read this article.

"Ah!" he said, "these people who invoke the Charter are not aware that it contains Article 14, which we can hold at their heads."

And, as a matter of fact, the Polignac Ministry had only been created in order to put into force that famous article, which Louis XVIII. had concealed in the Charter, as a sword of dissension, but of which he would never make use.

All the hopes of the king and M. de Polignac were vested in that very Article 14.

Thus, when M. de Peyronnet had been summoned to form a Ministry, M. de Polignac said to him—

"Remember, we want to put Article 14 in force."

"That is, indeed, my intention too!" M. de Peyronnet had said.

Everything was turning out for the best, since everybody was advising France to apply Article 14.

It only remained to be seen whether France would allow it to be put in force. They really hoped to turn the country's attention in another direction by two dazzling visions; then, whilst it was turned away, they meant to bandage its eyes and gag its lips. These two events were: the conquest of Algiers; and the restitution of our Rhine frontiers.

Our readers know all about the conquest of Algiers. Exasperated by our consul, the dey had struck him a blow across the face with his fan. This blow was followed by three years of siege; but, as the blockade really blockaded nothing, Hussein-dey, with Turkish logic, had concluded that, as in Turkey, insults were always revenged in proportion to the strength of the injured party, we could not be very strong since we did not take our revenge. Consequently, being blockaded as he was, he amused himself by shooting at a ship of truce, and also openly threatened to put our consul at Tripoli to death by empaling him; our consul not fancying a death of that kind, took refuge on board an English ship which deposited him one fine day at Marseilles. Now these insults were beyond toleration, and an African expedition was decided upon.

That good friend of ours, England, that precious ally, which I thinks it has a twofold right to meddle in all our affairs; which, every time that we put our foot on any shore, trembles for fear we mean to set up trade there; England, which, after having taken India from us, the West Indies, Antilles and the isle of France, would like to take away from us the two or three stations we have left, either in the Gulf of Mexico or in Oceania or in the Indian Ocean, was greatly disturbed at our projected expedition. Russia, on the contrary, rejoiced; it delighted at the thought of France encamped on the other side of the Mediterranean to keep an eye on Portugal and Gibraltar. Charles X. understood that Russia was his real ally, that we, the rulers of the West, had no disputed question to settle with her whose ambitions all looked Eastwards. Austria, on account of its Mediterranean coast-line, lent its aid to the expedition; Holland, whose consul had been put in chains by orders of the dey, approved; the King of Piedmont, who saw in it the safety of his commerce in respect of Genoa and Sardinia, rejoiced much; Greece, who saw in it the prospect of a fresh blow aimed at her old enemies, encouraged us to go ahead with our proceedings; Méhémet-Ali, who regarded it as a means of weakening the Porte, offered us his services; and, finally, all the powers of modern Italy, Tuscany, Rome, Naples and Sicily, applauded us! And it was a capital opportunity for once to send England about its business. M. d'Haussez, the Minister of Marine, took it upon himself to do this. One day, Lord Stuart, the English Ambassador in Paris, called upon him and, with that arrogant air peculiar to English ambassadors, demanded an explanation.

"If you wish a diplomatic explanation," M. d'Haussez replied, "M. le Président du Conseil will give it you; if a personal explanation will satisfy you, I will give it you: and it is this—we don't care a snap of the fingers for you."

I was at the house of Madame du Cayla the evening when M. d'Haussez related this heroic piece of brutality, and I should add that everybody applauded it, even the ladies present. Lord Stuart transmitted the reply to his Government, which, no doubt, found it satisfactory, since they left us alone.

History has recorded the various attempts that have been made to conquer Algiers; it was impregnable, a fact that had been proved, so people said, by the Charles V. expedition in 1541, by Duquesne's in 1662 and by Lord Exmouth's in 1816; all three attempts having failed or having been only partially successful. Happily, François Arago held very different views, when summoned for consultation on the point. François Arago knew Algiers, for he had been taken prisoner by a Corsair and had spent several months on board his ship. He declared that there were two things to be found in the neighbourhood of Algiers, namely wood and water, though their existence had been denied by the engineers. He convinced M de Polignac, who was ready enough to be convinced, and he, in his turn, convinced General Bourmont, who accepted the command of the land army, and Admiral Duperré, who accepted the command of the fleet. Then, when all the preparations had been energetically pushed forward, one hundred and three battleships, three hundred and seventy-seven transport ships, and two hundred and twenty-five vessels, carrying thirty-six thousand troops for landing, and twenty-seven thousand sailors, all set sail on 16 May from the port of Toulon and majestically advanced towards Algiers. So much for the conquest of Algiers, which, at the end of the month of May, the time we have reached, was in full swing.

Now let us pass on to the restitution of our Rhine frontiers. No accident had led up to this event as in the case of Algiers. It was a political combination, of which all the honour is due to M. de Renneval, for it was he from whom the idea first emanated. France and Russia entered into an offensive and defensive alliance against England. And, trusting to this alliance, France would take back her Rhine frontiers, and would, on her side, shut her eyes to the seizing of Constantinople by Russia. Turkey would cry out, but no one would care. Prussia and Holland would cry out, but Hanover would be taken from England and divided into two parts, of which one would be given to Prussia, the other to Holland. As to Austria, she would keep quiet, thanks to a slice of Servia, with which a cake would be kneaded and thrown to her as to Cerberus, not only to prevent her biting, but also to keep her from barking.

These were two fine schemes for a king of France to accomplish—that one man should abolish a barbarian power, the terror of the Mediterranean, and give back to France her Rhine provinces, performing, that is, a feat which Charles-Quint had failed in, winning back by diplomacy what Napoleon had lost by arms; he would be, at once, both a great military warrior and a great politician. What was to be feared, and who could upset the Monarchy in this double scheme? Two elements: the Ocean and the People!

CHAPTER VI

The soirée on 31 May 1830 at the Palais-Royal—The King
of Naples—A question of etiquette—How the King of
France ought to be addressed—The real Charles X.—M. de
Salvandy—The first flames of the volcano—The Duc de
Chartres sends me to inquire into the commotion—
Alphonse Signol—I tear him from the clutches of a soldier
of the Garde royal—His irritation and threats—The
volcano nothing but a fire of straw

It was in the midst of these events that the ball took place which I mentioned
at the beginning of the last chapter. As we have said, it was given by the Duc
d'Orléans to his brother-in-law, the King of Naples. The King of Naples was
that contemptible François, son of Ferdinand and Caroline, who in 1820 was
chosen by the patriots to represent them, and betrayed them; who, selected
in order to be a support to the Revolution, suppressed it. He was the ruler of
his citizens, decimated in 1798, and proscribed in 1820; but, sure of the
allegiance of his lazzaroni (the real pillar of strength upon which the throne
of the Two Sicilies rests), he came to visit France and to spend a short time
with his family. The regal travellers—the queen accompanied him—met with
a splendid reception at the Court, but so great was the aversion shown by
Paris to this betrayer, that the prefect of the Seine, much as he desired to give
a fête to him, dared not do it for fear the people would break his windows.
The Duc d'Orléans, however, under cover of the relationship, and relying
upon his ever growing popularity, ventured to do what the prefect of the
Seine had not dared. But there was one great question to be settled, or, rather,
a great favour to be obtained—and that was the presence at this fête of King
Charles X. I remember the stir that took place over it at the time, at the
Palais-Royal. The Duc d'Orléans, who knew Court etiquette as well as any
man in the kingdom, was fully aware that a King of France gives fêtes
himself, but does not accept invitations to any others. There was, indeed, a
precedent to this derogation from the usual custom: a century before, Louis
XV., on returning from a journey or fête, I forget which, spent three days
with the Prince of Condé; but it was *in the country*, at Chantilly, so it was of no
signification. It is also true, that in visiting the Duc d'Orléans you visited the
duchess, who was the daughter of a king and a *true Bourbon*, as Madame la
Duchesse d'Angoulême expressed it; which was not polite towards the
Orléans, who were then looked upon as *false Bourbons*; but the duke thought
it would be a fine thing to receive the king in his own house! So great an
honour would reflect glory upon the family escutcheon; and the duke closed
his eyes in order not to see the grimace that Madame la Dauphine made, shut

his ears in order not to hear the remarks made by Madame la Duchesse d'Angoulême and persisted in his request so respectfully, that Charles X. let himself be persuaded, on condition that a company of his guards should occupy the Palais-Royal an hour before his arrival. These questions of etiquette were very paltry matters compared with those which were being debated at the same time between the people and the Monarchy. As soon as the royal promise was obtained, the household of the Duc d'Orléans thought of nothing else but the forthcoming ball. It was resolved to display before the King of Naples all the best literary and artistic exponents of the world of France. King Charles X., who knew little or nothing about them, would see them at the same time, and so he could kill two birds with one stone. Apparently, I was looked upon as a spurious specimen, just as the Orléans were spurious Bourbons; for I had been forgotten, or, at all events, left out of the list. But that excellent youth, the Duc de Chartres, asked for a ticket for me, and was delighted to send me one. I hesitated to accept, since the man should see was the son of the king and queen who had poisoned my father. But not to reply to the invitation would have been to grieve the Duc de Chartres, both on account of my absence and because of the reason for that absence. I therefore decided to accept. The invitations said "Half-past eight"; the king, Charles X., was to arrive at nine. When the due d'Orléans caught sight of me, he came up to me—a mark of attention that astonished me much.

It was not that he had a favour to confer on me, but a piece of advice he had to give me. His Royal Highness, supposing me to be little versed in etiquette, wished to give me some tips to avoid tripping on the slippery floors of the Palais-Royal.

"Monsieur Dumas," the duke said, "if, by chance, the king does you the honour of addressing you, you know that, in replying to him, you should neither address him as *Sire* or *His Majesty*, but simply *the King*."

"Yes, monseigneur, I am acquainted with that fact."

"Ah! how do you know that?"

"I know it, monseigneur, and even the reason for the mode of address. The words *Sire* and *Majesty* were profaned directly they were given to the usurper, and true-born courtiers very wisely consider that they could no longer be given to a legitimate monarch."

"Very good!" the duke said, turning on his heel, and plainly indicating by the tone of his voice that he would much have preferred me to be less well informed in Court matters.

Ten minutes later, the drums beat to arms. The Duc d'Orléans took the duchesse by the arm and signed to Madame Adélaïde and to the Duc de

Chartres to follow him; he went at such a rate, to meet the royal visitor, that he lost his wife in the guard-chamber as Æneas had done three thousand years before on leaving Troy, and as, eighteen years later, the Duc de Montpensier was to do upon quitting the Tuileries. The duke reached the great entrance hall of the Palais-Royal just as Charles X. was stepping out of his carriage and putting his foot on the first step of the stairs that led up to it. We had rushed after our illustrious hosts, whom we saw reappear between a hedge of guards two deep, in the following order:—

King Charles X. walked first with Madame la Duchesse d'Orléans upon his arm. M. le Dauphin next, giving his arm to Madame Adélaïde. Then M. le Duc d'Orléans, with Madame la Dauphine; and, last, M. le Duc de Chartres, giving his arm to Madame la Duchesse de Berry. In front of them, ready to receive them at the door of the first salon, advanced the King and Queen of Naples.

It is quite twenty-two years since King Charles X. died in exile; the men of our generation saw him, but those of thirty, or young men of about twenty, did not see him and it is for their eyes we pen the following description. Charles X. was then an old man of seventy-six, tall and thin, with his head inclined a little on one side, adorned with beautiful white hair; his eyes were still vivacious and smiling; he had the Bourbon nose, and a mouth made ugly by the under lip drooping on his chin; he was most gracious and courteous, faithful and loyal, true to his friendships and to his vows; he possessed every kingly attribute except enthusiasm. In manner he possessed a regal air peculiar to his race. If Article 14 had not been in the Charter, he would certainly never have dreamt of making a *coup d'état*; for, to do so, meant breaking his oath, and had he forfeited his promise, he would, as he himself said, never again have dared to look at the portrait of François I. or the statue of King John. Furthermore, desiring absolutism from mere indolence, and tyranny from lack of activity, he used to say, apropos of tyranny and absolutism—

"You may pound all the princes of the house of Bourbon in the same mortar without extracting a single grain of despotism out of them!" And Louis Blanc has drawn him admirably in the lines: "As human as he was commonplace, if he desired to make his power absolute, it was in order to relieve himself of violent action; for there was nothing energetic about him, not even in his fanaticism; nothing really great, not even about his pride."

In conclusion, the precautions taken on my behalf by the Duc d'Orléans were unnecessary. The king never even looked at me; although I should add that I never took the least pains to put myself within range of his vision.

I felt a real antipathy towards the Bourbons of the Elder Branch of the family, and it was only when I thought of the dead, of the past and of those living in exile, that I could bring myself to do justice to them later.

When the king, the dauphin, the dauphiness and the Duchesse de Berry had arrived, the fête began.

M. de Salvandy has related, with regard to this fête, the whole of his conversation with the Duc d'Orléans. It began with these words, which made the political fortune of the author of *Alonzo*:—

"Monseigneur, this is a true Neapolitan fête, for we are dancing upon the edge of a volcano ..."

And, indeed, the volcano very soon began to show its fires. They proceeded from the Palais-Royal, the crater of 1789, which people thought had been extinguished thirty-five years before, but which was, in reality, only slumbering. I was there and saw it spring up, and can therefore give an account of the eruption that took place under my own eyes. I had gone out to cool myself on the terrace, and was meditating upon the strange coincidence of fate that made me, even in those days a Republican, almost an enforced witness of a fête given by the Bourbons of France, against whom my father had fought, to those Bourbons of Naples who had poisoned him, when all of a sudden loud cries were heard and bright lights were seen in the gardens of the Palais-Royal. A mass of flame, as though coming from a stack of wood, rose from one of the square lawns among the flower-beds which seemed to spring from the pedestal of the statue of Apollo. And this was what had happened. The numerous spectators of the princely fête that crowded in the Palais-Royal garden were anxious to have their share in the festivities, and, in contempt of the sentinels who guarded the lawns, a dozen young people had scaled the balustrades and, taking each other's hands, had begun a round dance, singing the old revolutionary *Ça ira*. During this time other young people had entertained themselves by piling up a pyramid of chairs and illuminating it by putting in the interstices of the chairs lamps taken from here and there. The leading builder of this tottering edifice and the principal actor in this revolutionary escapade was a young man whose death gave him a certain celebrity. He styled himself a literary man and his name was Alphonse Signol. Three days before, he had brought me a drama, entitled *le Chiffonnier*, and had asked me to read it. It certainly had some merit (we shall see later what became of it), but it was so far removed from my own style of writing of which, consequently, I was master, that it would have been impossible for me to render him any assistance, even in the way of advice. If only Signol had been content with putting the lamps on the chairs, all would have been well; but, instead, he took it into his head to place the chairs on top of the lamps, and all went wrong. The flame from a lamp reached the straw of one of the chairs and the whole pile flared up. Thence issued flames and cries, and women flying through the trees and under the arches of the stone galleries. This tumult quickly attracted the attention of the guests of the Duc d'Orléans. It was a serious matter to have shrieks and a fire in the garden of the Palais-Royal whilst Charles X. was within its precincts! I saw the Duc d'Orléans gesticulating wildly at a window; and whilst I was beginning to be far more taken up by what was passing inside than out of doors, I felt someone touch me gently on the shoulder. I turned round, and it was M. le Duc de Chartres, who had tried in vain to find out the meaning of all the disorder and smoke, and wanted to know if I had been more lucky in my inquiries than he. I replied in the negative, but offered at once to go and find out for him the cause and the upshot of the commotion; and as I could see he rejected my offer only from motives of discretion, in five seconds I was out in the hall and in another five in the garden. I arrived just in time to witness a struggle between a young man and a soldier, in which the youth was going to come off worst; when, thinking I recognised him, I sprang forward. I was so strong that I soon managed to separate the two combatants. I was right in my conjectures: the youth was Signol. The soldier was a corporal or sergeant belonging to the 3rd Regiment of the Guard. Signol had been pretty severely handled in the struggle; he was, consequently, furious, and although separated from the soldier, he still threatened to attack him again.

"Oh, you scamp!" he said, shaking his fist at him, "I don't want to have anything to do with you ... but the first officer of your regiment that I come across, I promise you, on my word of honour, I will box his ears for him."

I tried to quieten him down.

"No, no, no," he said; "when I promise I keep my word; and you shall be my second, will you not?"

I replied "Yes," to quieten him, and dragged him away into the rue de Valois. There, under pretext of inquiring the motive of his quarrel, I asked him what had taken place, and he told me what I have just related. In the midst of his recital he found a chance to ask me if I had read his drama. I replied in the affirmative.

"Very well, then," he said; "I will come and talk about it with you to-morrow."

And, as though he feared the tumult would calm down in his absence, he rushed back into the Palais-Royal garden. I did not restrain him, for I knew all I wanted to know—there had been no premeditated plot in this accident—it was nothing but a bit of tomfoolery. I went back into the palace and gave M. le Duc de Chartres an account of my expedition.

The narrative was so short and concise that, when it had been transmitted by the young prince to his father's illustrious guests, it immediately calmed the fears they appeared for a moment to have had. But, for greater safety, the crowd was made to leave the garden, and the fête continued, without further interruption, until daybreak.

At midnight the king and the royal family retired.

CHAPTER VII

A pressing affair—One witness lost, and two found—
Rochefort—Signol at the Théâtre des Italiens—He insults
Lieutenant Marulaz—The two swords—The duel—Signol
is killed—*Victorine* and *le Chiffonnier*—Death steps in

Next day I was awakened by Signol. A minute after his return to the garden
of the Palais-Royal, he had been compelled to leave it at the point of a
bayonet. He seemed to me to be, if possible, still more exasperated in the
morning than on the previous night. Now, he not merely thirsted to kill one
officer of the 3rd Regiment, but, like Han d'Islande, he desired to annihilate
the whole regiment. As I thought I detected incipient madness in this mania
for slaughter, I started the subject of his melodrama. Then the man's mood
changed: he had written the drama with the object of bringing some comfort
to his aged mother, and a whole year's hopes and happiness rested on that
work. If I did not keep it to re-read and did not offer to touch it up, or, at
any rate, advise him where to do so, he was conscious that, in its present state
of incompletion, it could not be acted and would be refused; then, good-bye
to the sweet light of hope which had shone for a brief space in the hearts of
both mother and son! I therefore promised to re-read *le Chiffonnier* and to do
my best to promote its success. After which promise I invited the author to
breakfast. We parted between noon and one o'clock. He went to the Théâtre-
Italien to claim a stall which he received as editor of some paper or other.

La Gazza ladra was being played that night. I myself had an appointment with
a very pretty woman, whom I had met at Firmin's house, a lady who played
in *les Mars* in the provinces; and it was a rendezvous of such an interesting
nature that I did not return home until the following noon. My servant told
me that the young man who had breakfasted with me the day before had
called to see me at seven in the morning and had seemed very vexed at not
finding me at home. He had asked for a pen and paper and written this
note—which Joseph (my servant) handed me:—

"Alphonse Signol, on very pressing business."

I thought it was about his drama, and, as I did not consider that business so
pressing as Signol did, and as I was very tired, I went to bed and told my
servant to tell any caller that I was not at home. Towards five o'clock I woke
and rang. Signol had returned and written another note, which, when brought
to me, contained these words:—

"DEAR DUMAS,—I fight a duel with swords to-morrow
morning with M. Marulaz, lieutenant of the 3rd Guards

Regiment. I told you I should ask you to be my second and I came this morning to beg you to render me that service. You were not at home, so I had to look for someone else. I have found a substitute. If I am killed, I bequeath *le Chiffonnier* to your charge; it will be the only source of income I have to leave to my mother.

"*Vale et me ama* "SIGNOL"

This letter filled me with sad thoughts for the rest of that day and night. I had no notion where Signol lived, or whether he had a home at all, so I could not send to him. I suddenly bethought me that I might possibly gain news of him at the café des Variétés, which he frequented most days; also, a month previous to this time, he had had a quarrel with Soulié, which had ended in the exchange of a couple of pistol shots. It was now nearly five o'clock in the afternoon. Rochefort (a friend of mine, a clever fellow who composed several original plays, one of them being *Jocko*, besides some delightful poems) was taking a glass of absinthe at one of the café tables. He rose when he caught sight of me.

"Ah!" he said, scratching his nose,'a habit he had, "you know poor Signol!..."

"Well?"

"He has just been killed!"

I heaved a sigh, although, really, it was no news to me, for my presentiments had already told me Rochefort's news. Here is an account of what had happened. When he left me two nights before, he had gone to get his stall ticket from the Théâtre-Italien. By ill-luck they gave him a stall in the orchestra. A second unfortunate coincidence decreed that an officer and soldiers of the 3rd Regiment of the Guard should be on duty that night at the Italiens. There was an empty seat in front of Signol, which an officer came and appropriated at the conclusion of the first act. He was the son of General Marulaz, now, I believe, himself a general. It was not really his turn on duty, but he had taken the place of one of his friends; his friend had a special engagement that night (notice the strange chain of circumstances!), he therefore begged Marulaz to be so good as to take his place. Marulaz consented, and had hardly sat down before he felt two hands leaning on the back of his stall. He did not think any rudeness was intended by the action, so he did not take any notice at first; but when the hands remained there for ten minutes, he turned round and saw that they belonged to Signol. Marulaz politely intimated that the back of his seat was not the right place for Signol's hands and, without replying, Signol withdrew them. The young officer thought the incident was accidental, and accordingly attached no significance to it. Five minutes later, on leaning back in his seat, he again felt the hands there. He did not wait this time, but turned round immediately.

"Monsieur," he said, "I have already intimated to you that your hands annoy me there; have the goodness to put them in your pockets if you have no other place for them, but please be so good as to take them off my seat!"

Signol withdrew them a second time. But, at the end of another two minutes, the young officer felt, not merely his irritating neighbour's hands but also his head upon his shoulder. This time he lost all patience, jumped up and turned round.

"Monsieur! monsieur!" he exclaimed, "if you are doing it on purpose to pick a quarrel with me, tell me so outright."

"Very well, then; it is done on purpose," Signol replied, rising too.

"Why?"

"On purpose to insult you, and if I have not done sufficient to that end already, take that!" And the angry madman gave Marulaz a blow across the face.

Thoroughly astounded at this incomprehensible conduct, the young officer mechanically drew his sword half out of its sheath.

"Look!" shouted Signol, "he is going to murder me!"

Marulaz pushed his sword back again into its scabbard and replied—

"No, monsieur; I will not assassinate you, but I will kill you!"

And, to avenge the insult he had thus gratuitously received, Marulaz, who was very strong, lifted Signol as though he had been a child right across from the one row to his own, and then placed him under his feet.

The incident caused a great commotion in the theatre, especially as even those close by did not know what it was all about: they had heard an altercation, seen the blow, and heard the words "He is going to murder me!" They had seen the flash of the drawn sword and its speedy return to its sheath; finally, they saw one man standing over another with his foot upon him. Not knowing precisely which was in the right or wrong of the quarrel, they took the part of the weaker, surrounded Marulaz, and pulled him off Signol, who, staggering and half suffocated, made for the corridor and street, and thence to the theatre café. Marulaz followed him there, and it became then a question of reparation, no longer one that could be settled by an immediate fight. They exchanged cards and fixed a meeting for the next day but one, in the bois de Vincennes.

The next day was to be spent by each combatant in choosing his seconds, and by the seconds in arranging the conditions of the duel. At two o'clock the following day, the four seconds met, conferred together and agreed upon swords as the weapons to be employed. Lieutenant Marulaz chose as one of his seconds the friend whom he had replaced on duty; this friend had duelling swords, and Marulaz examined them, pronounced them suitable and told him to bring them on the occasion.

"Agreed," said his friend; "but I warn you one of the two is an unlucky weapon: it has already served a similar purpose three or four times, and the combatants who used it were either killed or hurt."

"Plague take it!" Marulaz replied laughingly; "don't tell me which it is, then, and if I draw it I would rather not know."

The following morning they met in the bois de Vincennes. All had brought swords with them. They drew lots for them, and those brought by Marulaz' seconds won. Then they drew which should have the choice of these two swords. Marulaz again won the toss. He took the first that came to hand haphazard.

"Bravo!" his friend whispered to him; "you have drawn the right one!"

They stood to attention. At the second round, Marulaz disarmed Signol.

"Monsieur," he exclaimed, taking a step backwards, "I am disarmed!"

"So I see, monsieur," Marulaz coolly replied; "but since you are not wounded, pick up your sword and let us continue."

Signol picked it up, drew some string from his pocket, made surer hold of his sword, and, with a rapid attack, against the customary rules of duelling, stood on guard, lunged and wounded his adversary severely in the arm. When Marulaz felt the cold steel and saw the flow of blood he felt goaded to frenzy, sprang at his enemy and forced him to retreat twenty paces, bringing him up against a hedge where he lunged and passed his sword clean through the body. Signol uttered a sharp cry, stretched out his arms and died before he had time to fall to the ground.

"Messieurs," Marulaz said, turning to the four seconds, "have I fought fairly?"

All bowed in acknowledgment that he had. Had there been any recriminations to make in that fatal encounter, they would have been directed against the dead man. But no one thinks of laying blame on a corpse....

It will be remembered that I had now inherited Signol's manuscript, of which the manager of the Porte-Saint-Martin possessed a duplicate. Three or four months later, I was present at the first production of *Victorine, ou la Nuit porte conseil.* It was the skeleton idea of *Chiffonnier,* it is true, but encased in a delightful setting that was none of Signol's creation. One of its authors was Dupeuty, the others were Dumersan and Gabriel. I sought out Dupeuty, placed the MS. of *Chiffonnier* in his hands and asked him if he thought it fair to deprive Signol's mother of what I considered to be her share of the production. Dupeuty and his collaborators had no notion of the existence of an original manuscript, as the idea of their vaudeville had been supplied them by the manager of the Porte-Saint-Martin, and they had worked upon it; but when they learnt the true parentage, they spontaneously, generously and loyally agreed to include the poor mother in their success.

And that is the story of Signol's death and of the composition and production of *Victorine, ou la Nuit porte conseil.*

BOOK II

CHAPTER I

Alphonse Karr—The cuirassier—The medal of life saving and the Cross of the Légion d'honneur—Karr's home at Montmartre—*Sous les tilleuls* and the critics—The taking of Algiers—M. Dupin senior—Why he did not write his Memoirs—Signing of the Ordinances of July—Reasons that prevented my going to Algiers

The events we have just recorded in our last chapter bring us up to the 2nd of June.

As Charles X. looked up at the starry heavens from the top of the Duc d'Orléans' terrace he said—

"What splendid weather for my Algerian fleet!"

But he was mistaken: almost immediately the fleet had left port it had been scattered by a storm, and, when Charles made his comment, it was having the utmost difficulty in rallying at Palma.

As regards other matters, the Opposition was going ahead and great and small newspapers kept hitting at the Government, some with clubs and some with staves. We have mentioned how the *Journal des Débats* treated the Polignac Ministry upon its accession to power. If we had these little papers under our notice we might, perhaps, be able to prove that the banter of dwarfs can work as much mischief as insults inflicted by giants.

Le Figaro was among the number of the small journals which, at that time, were carrying on a skirmishing engagement with the Government. It was under the management of Bohain, and, as is well known, Janin, Romieu, Nestor Roqueplan, Brucker, Vaulabelle, Michel Masson and Alphonse Karr were among its most prominent contributors. Karr was, at that time, perhaps, the least known of that Pleiades of fighting men. He has since become one of our most distinguished literary artists—observe, I say literary artists and not literati or men of letters—but at that time he was fighting his maiden battles. He had been present at the reading of *Henri III.*, at Nestor Roqueplan's, where I became acquainted with him. According to our usual custom in the case of all the remarkable men of our day, let us select for particular comment, from his early efforts, that special faculty which has the power of giving to truth the charm of paradox. This truth, bare and undraped when treated by others, is always, on leaving the hands of Alphonse Karr, clad in a veil of gold. Without doubt Alphonse Karr has, since 1830, told the various Governments which have succeeded each other, as well as those who have flattered or attacked them, a greater number of truths than any other man. And, different from the supposed truths of others, those of Alphonse Karr are real and undeniable, the more they are probed the more they are proved to be true. Alphonse Karr was, in those days, a handsome young man of twenty-two or twenty-three, with regular features set in a frame of dark hair; he had adopted an eccentric form of dress, which he has always adhered to; he was extremely well made, strong physically, and an adept at all gymnastic exercises, especially at swimming and fencing. During the year 1829, when bathing in the Marne, he had rescued a cuirassier from drowning. The man was heavy and nearly as strong as Karr himself, so that it almost happened that, instead of Karr saving the cuirassier, the cuirassier drowned Karr. The act made sufficient of a stir for Karr to receive a medal from the Government, and I have occasionally seen him wear it. This medal was, in the hands of wags, the source of endless gibes, which Karr's reputation for bravery maintained, it is true, within the bounds of propriety, but which was never exhausted. There was no precedent for that famous medal, and I was reading something about it, only yesterday, in some newspaper rag or other. One day, at a great dinner at which I was present together with a host of people wearing decorations—not just ordinary medals but the Cross of the Légion d'honneur, which, at the present day, is distributed and conferred in a totally different manner from all the medals in the world—those jokes at Karr's expense, who was also one of the guests, broke out afresh. Karr, with his cool and habitual phlegm, called the waiter and asked for a pen, ink and paper. He cut the paper into as many round pieces as there were decorated guests at the table, wrote on each piece the reason for which the wearer had been decorated and passed each slip to its proper quarter. It completely silenced his scoffers.

Karr was born in Germany, in December 1808, and has only become a naturalised Frenchman since 1848. His father was one of the five or six German musicians who evolved the piano from the harpsichord. Three of his uncles died as captains in the French service. He was, besides, a nephew of Baron Heurteloup, and a cousin of Habeneck. In those days he wrote no political articles for the *Figaro*. He has more than once told me, in all seriousness, that he saw the Revolution of July, and even that of February, without knowing what they were about. But, later, he studied the subject of I revolutions very deeply; for, in 1848, he wrote on the subject—

"Plus cela change, plus c'est la même chose!" ("The more things change, the more do they remain the same!")

In 1829 he was an assistant professor in the Collège Bourbon and took to writing poetry, some of which he sent to the *Figaro*. Bohain opened all the letters received. Now Bohain was one of those plain-spoken men who openly professed a lofty scorn for poetry. His reply to Karr was—

"MY DEAR SIR,—Your lines are charming; but send me prose. I would rather be hanged than put a single line of poetry in my paper!"

Karr did not press the point: clever men are rare, and, as he did not wish Bohain to hang himself, he sent him prose instead. This was a great humiliation for the young poet to have to swallow. All the articles of a pastoral nature that were published by *le Figaro* at this period were by Alphonse Karr. Karr had made himself the oddest of dwelling-places. He had hired the old Tivoli at Montmartre, which had half tumbled in ruins into the quarries: there still remained a little wood and the cloakroom made of rushes. By night he slept in the cloakroom; by day he walked in the little wood. Here he began his first novel, *Sous les tilleuls*. He finished it in the rue de la Ferme-des-Mathurins, in the workshop of the two brothers Johannot, which he took after them. From Montmartre, Alphonse Karr only came into Paris about twice a month. He had a boat at Saint-Ouen, where he spent all the time he had left from his wood or the cloakroom.

Sous les tilleuls appeared in 1831, I believe. The book, worthy of notice, was accordingly noticed. That means it was attacked bitterly, as all things that show originality and power are attacked in France. They first accused the author of imitating a book of Nodier's that had appeared a fortnight after his; unfortunately, the date being on the title page, they had to withdraw that accusation. They next accused him of having translated it wholesale from the German, and even went so far as to give the title of the German original, *Unter den Linden* (Under the Limes), but it was soon seen that there was no book bearing such a title throughout the whole range of German literature, and that in nearly all the large towns was to be found a public promenade called thus—a fact Alphonse Karr did not deny. The author had placed as epigrams at the head of his chapters or letters verses of his own, no doubt those that Bohain had rejected, but which he had felt it his duty to adorn with the names of Schiller, Goethe and Uhland. The critics were taken in, and praised them at the expense of the prose. Prose and verse were both Karr's! Besides, a large number of the letters in the novel had been actually written to a young girl of whom Karr had been deeply enamoured. Karr did not receive his decoration until 1845 or 1846. One day he was told by Cavé that it was a question of giving the Cross to his father or himself. Marie-Louise had promised the Cross to his father, who, in 1840, was still waiting for it. Karr sought out M. Duchâtel, and, having satisfied himself that Cavé was quite correct in his statement, he said to the minister—

"Monsieur, when a father and son are both deserving of the Cross, the son does not accept it before his father."

And M. Duchâtel only gave the decoration to the father, whereas both father and son ought to have had it. When his father died, Karr received a decoration; he took the last ribbon his father had worn from his coat and put it on his own.

Early in June 1830, I met him in the street, arm in arm with Brucker. Brucker was a painter on china, and one of the most original workers in the journalism of 1830. I met them both at the very moment when the first of the hundred guns announcing the capture of Algiers were being fired.

"Listen!" Karr asked. "What is that? It sounds like the firing of guns."

"Doubtless Algiers has been taken," I replied.

"Bah! Have they been besieging it?" Karr replied.

Algiers was, indeed, taken; its surname of *la Guerrière* had not availed to save it. That nest of vultures which, as Hugo said, had been only half killed by Duquesne, was, at last, destroyed by M. de Bourmont. Directly the great news was received, the Minister for Marine, Baron d'Haussez, rushed off to the king. When he was announced, Charles X. sprang towards him with open arms; M. d'Haussez intended to kiss his hand, but Charles drew him to his breast.

"Come to my arms," he said; "to-day we all kiss one another."

And the king and his minister embraced.

However, amidst these apparent favours which Providence seemed to be piling on the head of the Elder Branch, clearsighted men could discern a yawning abyss.

"Take care!" M. Beugnot exclaimed, like a terrified pilot. "Unless you take care, the Monarchy will founder under canvas like a fully armed ship!"

"I should be much less uneasy were M. de Polignac a bit more so!" M. de Metternich remarked to our Ambassador at Vienna, M. de Renneval.

It must be confessed that even the Opposition, who were not so far-seeing as M. Beugnot and M. de Metternich, undertook to reassure the king, in the event of His Majesty feeling any anxiety. How, indeed, could they fear anything, when M. Dupin senior, one of the leaders of the Opposition, said, during the debate on the Address—

> "The *fundamental basis* of the Address is *a profound respect for the person of the King*; it expresses in the very highest degree *veneration for the ancient race of Bourbons*; it represents *legitimacy*, as a *legal truths* but, further, as a *social necessity*-a

necessity—now recognised *by all thoughtful minds*, the true outcome of experience and of conviction."

O good Monsieur Dupin! of sound mind and integrity of judgment, a shining light of the Bar, a fearless and blameless legislator; you who, pondering over the trial of Jesus, wrote these sublime lines on Pontius Pilate—

> "Pilate, seeing that he could not prevail over the spirit of the multitude, but that their excitement increased more and more, sent for water and washed his hands before the people, saying, 'I am innocent of the blood of this righteous man: see ye to it' (Matt, XXVII. 24); 'and he granted them their request' (Luke XXIII. 24), 'and delivered him into their hands to be crucified' (Matt, XXVII. 26). Wash thy hands, O Pilate! they are dyed with innocent blood. Thou hast given in through weakness, and art just as guilty as though thou hadst sacrificed him from wicked intention; generations have repeated it down to our times. 'The righteous man suffered under Pontius Pilate' (*passus est sub Pontio Pilato*). Thy name stands in history as a lesson to warn all public men, all pusillanimous judges, to show them the shame of yielding against their own convictions! The populace shrieked in fury at the foot of thy tribunal; perhaps thy own life was not safe, but what matter? Thy duty was plain, and in such a dilemma it is better to suffer death than to inflict it"—

O worthy Monsieur Dupin! advocate of Jesus Christ and of Béranger under the Restoration; President of the Chamber and Procurator-General under Louis-Philippe; President of the National Assembly, why do you not write your Memoirs, as I am writing mine? Why do you not, contrary to the cowardice and fear of Pontius Pilate, show yourself immovable in your convictions, unshaken in your duty, tenacious in your sympathies, immovable upon your bench as procurator-general, calm in your presidential chair, rigid on your curule chair of legislator? What instruction the world could have derived from the Memoirs of a man like yourself, who had such hosts of opportunities of showing proof of his faithful allegiance to the Elder Branch of the Bourbons on 29 July 1830, to the Younger Branch on 24 February 1848, and, finally, of his fidelity to the Republic on 2 December 1851! But you are too modest, good Monsieur Dupin! Modesty, combined with civil courage and a political conscience, is one of your greatest qualities, and it is only from modesty that you do not yourself dare to say what you think of yourself. But, never mind, for, every time that occasion presents, I shall do myself the honour of taking your place in the honourable task, my only regret being that I do not know more than I do, in order to speak out more fully and to treat you according to your deserts. What reason for fear had the legitimacy when the Society *Aide-toi! le ciel aidera*, at the Festival of the Gathering of the Grapes in Burgundy, declared that the king was the first power in the State, and drank toasts to the health of Charles X.? Why need they be afraid when M. Odilon Barrot, in another banquet given by six hundred electors, which was decorated with two hundred and twenty-one symbolic crowns, mingled the king and the law together in one single toast? O great statesmen, you who dig graves for kings and who bury monarchies, when, indeed, will the people, tired of your sham science, rub your faces, once for all, in the history which you are making, and which you do not see?

Thus, on 24 July, Charles X. called together a Council in absolute confidence. At this Council the fate of the Monarchy was again weighed in the balance, and it was decided to sign the Ordinances. But M. d'Haussez ventured to observe to the President of the Council that M. de Bourmont had extracted a promise from him to risk nothing during his absence.

"Bah!" the Prince de Polignac remarked, "what need have we of him? Am I not the War Minister during his absence?"

"But," M. d'Haussez asked, "how many men can you rely on in Paris? Have you, at the lowest computation, even as many as twenty-eight or thirty thousand?"

"Oh, more than that; I have forty-two thousand."

M. d'Haussez shook his head dubiously.

"Look, then, for yourself," the President of the Council said, and threw him a rolled document across the table.

M. d'Haussez unrolled it and added up the figures.

"But I can only find here thirteen thousand men, and that number on paper will mean scarcely seven to eight thousand men actually fit for war. Where do you get your missing twenty-nine thousand to complete your total of forty-two thousand?"

"Make yourself easy about the matter," M. de Polignac replied; "they are scattered round Paris and, in a few hours' time, if needed, could be all collected on the Place de la Concorde."

The Ordinances were signed the following day.

When signing, the king had the dauphin on his right hand and M. de Polignac on his left; the other ministers completed the circle round the green table. Each one signed in turn. M. d'Haussez again raised his objections.

"Monsieur," Charles X. said to him, "do you refuse to co-operate with your colleagues?"

"Sire," responded M. d'Haussez, "may I be allowed to put a question to the king?"

"What is it, monsieur?"

"Does the king intend to proceed, supposing one or more of his ministers should resign?"

"Yes," Charles replied with decision.

"Then, in that case," said the Naval Minister, "I will sign." And he did so.

Five minutes later, they all stood up and, as Charles X. passed by M. d'Haussez, he noticed that the minister's attentive gaze was fixed on the walls, and he asked—

"What are you looking at so attentively, Monsieur d'Haussez?"

"Sire, I was looking to see if by any chance I could find a picture of the Earl of Strafford."[1]

The king smiled and passed on.

These details became known afterwards; they were kept a profound secret at the time. Only two or three men were aware of what was happening. Casimir Périer, who was deeply attached to the Older Branch of the Bourbons, at that time, as were M. Dupin and M. Barrot and many others (we shall see presently how Périer did his utmost to quell the Revolution of July when it broke out) was dining at his country house in the bois de Boulogne, when he received a tiny triangular-shaped note. He opened, read it and grew pale, then livid, and his arms fell to his sides in despair. It announced that the Ordinances had been signed that very day. Who sent him the news never transpired. On the evening of the 25th or 26th, M. de Rothschild, who was speculating on a rise in stocks, received this simple statement from M. de Talleyrand:—

"I have just come from Saint-Cloud: speculate for a fall in prices."

But I, who was neither a M. Casimir Périer nor a M. de Rothschild nor yet a friend of M. de Talleyrand, I, who neither speculated upon rises or falls on the Stock Exchange, knew absolutely nothing of what was going on, and I was about to start for Algiers. Algiers would be a really fine sight during the early days of its conquest. I had taken my seat on the mail coach for Marseilles and packed my luggage; I had exchanged three thousand francs in silver for three thousand francs in gold, and I was to have set out at five in the evening of Monday the 26th, when, at eight on Monday morning, Achille Comte entered my room and said—

"Have you heard the great news?"

"No."

"The Ordinances are announced in the *Moniteur*. Shall you still go to Algiers?"

"I shall not be so foolish. We shall see stranger events here at home than out there!"

'Then I called my servant.

"Joseph," I said, "go to my gun-maker's and bring me back my double-barrelled gun and two hundred bullets of twenty calibre!"

---

[1] See the passage wherein Louis Blanc admirably describes this scene in his *Histoire de dix ans*.

CHAPTER II

The third storey of No. 7 in the rue de l'Université—The first results of the Ordinances—The café du Roi—Étienne Arago—François Arago—The Academy—La Bourse—Le Palais-Royal—Madame de Leuven—Journey in search of her husband and son—Protest of the journalists—Names of the signatories

My servant returned with the necessary articles a couple of hours later. I carefully locked up gun and ammunition and went out to take a breath of air in the streets. It was ten o'clock in the morning, and the face of Paris looked as quiet as though the *Moniteur* had announced the beginning of the shooting season, instead of having published the Ordinances. Comte laughed at my forebodings. I took him to breakfast on the third floor of No. 7 rue de l'Université. It was then occupied by a very pretty woman, who had taken such a warm interest in my intended departure for Algiers that she meant to accompany me as far as Marseilles. I went to tell her that, for the time being, at all events, I had given the journey up and that, consequently, if she had packed her trunks, she could unpack them. She had not been able to take in the fact that my real motive for my African trip was curiosity; she could not understand any more clearly my reasons for staying in France, which were entirely from curiosity. She considered I ought to have found more adequate reasons both for my going and for my staying.

My readers who have been good enough to follow the different phases of my life in these Memoirs must have noticed that I have been careful to avoid details of the kind just hinted at above; but I shall have occasion to refer more than once to this friendship, which was to be the means, by God's providence, of bringing me much happiness, in dark days turning sadness to joy and tears to smiles.

I owed the acquaintance to Firmin. He had been acting Saint-Mégrin in the provinces and, one day, he came to my rooms, bringing with him a magnificent "Duchesse de Guise," on whose behalf he solicited all the influence I could bring to bear in theatrical circles. I began by asking Firmin what amount of interest and what kind of interest he took in his protégée. I have ever been careful to respect the various protégées of my friends; and the question was of some importance with reference to this beautiful woman.

Firmin replied that his interest in her was entirely artistic, and that my own might assume what form I pleased.

I had then only gone so far as to notice the beautiful duchesse from the point of view of her stage qualifications. Her hair was jet black, and her eyes were a deep blue, her nose as straight as that of the Venus de Milo and her teeth like pearls. I need hardly say that I placed myself entirely at her disposal. Unfortunately, or fortunately, the time for entering into theatrical engagements was over, this takes place in April, and Madame Mélanie S was only presented to me in the month of May. I was therefore unsuccessful in my introduction on her behalf; but, as the beautiful duchesse saw that it was through no fault of mine, she did not take umbrage at my failure. I even persuaded her to remain on in Paris: she was young and could wait; opportunities were sure to come her way if she were on the spot and ready to seize them; moreover, if such occasion did not come unasked, I would arrange to bring them about. I had already at that time sufficient reputation to get the doors of a theatre opened wide for any man or woman to whom I handed a signed note addressed to the manager.

Meanwhile, following the example of the Abbé Vertot, I began my siege. I thought for the moment that I was to have nine years, as Achilles before Troy! But I was mistaken; it only lasted three weeks, as did the siege of the Duc d'Orléans before Anvers. If my readers be frank, they will admit that which our French engineers have admitted loudly in their praises of General Chassé's tactics: a resistance of three weeks is an honourable one; there are but few places, no matter how strongly fortified, that can hold out so long. Now, mine had held out as long and, as it had only been taken by surprise in the end, it had not therefore been stipulated among the articles of capitulation, that I should be forbidden to leave Paris merely on the grounds of curiosity. I have already stated how great my curiosity had been to see Algiers just after its capture, and how a still stronger feeling of curiosity induced me to alter my plans. Then, too, I ought to confess another thing, which I remember, far off though that day is from the time during which the events I am relating happened, namely, that my insatiable curiosity to see Algiers came over me in a moment of ill temper; that, directly the mood passed, I was equally pleased to find an excuse for staying in Paris, as I had been, at the time, for going.

Achille Comte and I came down at one o'clock and took a few turns together along the quays; then, as there seemed no appearance of any excitement, he left me, and we arranged to meet again next day. I went to the Palais-Royal, where I hoped to have gained intelligence; but nothing was known there: the Duc d'Orléans was at Neuilly and the Duc de Chartres at Joigny, at the head of his regiment; M. de Broval was at Villiers, and nobody had seen anything of Oudard. So I went to the café du Roi. Its principal frequenters were, it will be recollected, the editors of the *Foudre*, of the *Drapeau blanc*, and of the *Quotidienne*, all Royalist journals. They applauded the measure highly.

Lassagne alone appeared anxious about it. I did not join much in the conversation, as all these men, Théaulon, Théodore Anne, Brissot, Rochefort and Merle held different views from my own, but were my personal friends. I have a perfect horror of disputing with my friends, and much prefer to fight a duel with any of them. For I always held the conviction that, before twenty-four hours had gone, such dispute would end in pistols.

Whilst I was in the café du Roi Étienne, Arago entered. Our friendship dated, as I have mentioned, from the time when he took notice of my *Ode au général Foy* and my *Nouvelles contemporaines*, in *la Lorgnette* and *le Figaro*. But on this particular day there was another reason for our seeking one another—our political opinions were the same. We went out together at half-past one and, at two o'clock, his brother François was to make a speech at the Academy. As Étienne had a spare ticket, he proposed I should accompany him. I had never seen more of the *Institut* than its exterior, and thought it might be a long while before I had such a good chance again of seeing the inside of it, so I accepted his invitation. At the beginning of the Pont des Arts we met a barrister friend of ours—Mermilliod, I think. At the first news of the Ordinances, five or six journalists and as many deputies had assembled at the house of Maître Dupin to ask the famous lawyer if there were any means of publishing newspapers without authority; but, instead of solving the problem, the lawyer contented himself with answering—

"Messieurs, the Chamber is dissolved—I am therefore no longer a deputy...."

And no matter how they tried, the journalists and deputies could not get any more out of him. The journalists had gone away in a furious rage; the editors of the *Courrier français, Journal du Commerce* and the *Journal de Paris* declared they would appeal, in the first instance, to M. de Belleyme, President of the Tribunal, for an order calling upon the printers to lend their presses for the printing of the unauthorised newspapers. But it seemed pretty hopeless to expect M. de Belleyme to issue any decree, when M. Dupin had refused to grant even a simple consultation touching the event of the moment! Nevertheless, all these proceedings clearly indicated the beginning of resistance. Étienne, for his part, asserted that his brother would not now give his lecture, urging the gravity of the political situation as the reason for his abstention.

The courage and patriotism of François Arago were too well known for this opinion (which was put forth by his brother) to be thought extraordinary. When we reached the *Institut* we found a great commotion and excitement among the usually calm and collected immortals, in their blue coats braided with green. Their meeting had not yet begun. A rumour had spread abroad that Arago would not speak, and some of the Academicians said that he would, because he was much too straightforward a man to compromise the Academy by his silence.

"Will he speak or will he not?" I inquired of Étienne.

"We will find out," he replied. "There he is, out there."

"Ah!" I said, "isn't he talking to the Duc de Raguse?"

"Yes; the Duc de Raguse is one of his oldest friends."

"Let us push forward, then.... I am very anxious to know what the subscriber to the capitulation of Paris has to say about the subscribers to the Ordinances."

"By Jove!" Étienne replied, "he will say that they have undone to-day, 26 July 1830, all he did on 30 March 1814!"

We continued our course, but it was no easy matter to thread our way through the midst of an illustrious crowd, to whom one had to offer at least one apology for each push of the elbow. By the time we reached François Arago, the duke was already some distance away from him.

"You have just left Marmot," Étienne asked; "what does he say?"

"He is furious! He says they are the type of people who fling themselves in the very teeth of ruin, and he only hopes he won't be obliged to draw swords on their behalf."

"Good!" I said; "he only needs to do that to make himself popular."

"And what have you to say about it?" Étienne asked his brother.

"I? Oh! I should not speak."

Cuvier was going by. He had just happened to catch these words in passing, and he stopped.

"What! you won't speak?" he exclaimed.

"No," Arago replied,

"Quite right, too!" interpolated Étienne.

"Look here, my dear fellow, come aside with me and let us talk reasonably," said Cuvier.

He drew François Arago away to a distance from us. We could judge, from the spot where we stood, of the animated discussion that ensued by the vivacity of their gestures. M. Villemain joined the two speakers and seemed to be taking Cuvier to task. Several other Academicians, whom I did not know by sight, and, perhaps, not even by name, surrounded Arago, and, contrary to M. Villemain, seemed to be insisting with Cuvier that Arago should speak. After a quarter of an hour's discussion, it was settled that Arago should speak. Now, this decision had been arrived at by a majority of votes, so to speak, and it would have been impossible for the famous astronomer to withstand the wishes of the majority of his confrères, who all loudly declared that they would regard his silence as contentious. He passed by us as he went to his place.

"Well, you are going to speak after all?" Étienne said to him.

"Yes, but set your mind at rest," he replied; "I assure you, by the end of my speech, they will think it would have been as well if I had not opened my mouth."

"What the dickens can he find to say about Fresnel?" I asked Étienne.

It was in praise of Fresnel that he was to speak.

"Oh!" replied Étienne, "I am not alarmed on that score. If it were about the Grand Turk, he would manage to squeeze in what he wanted to say."

And Arago, taking as his subject the clever engineer of bridges and embankments, the learned physician, the severe examiner of the École polytechnique, the famous inventor of lenticular lighthouses, actually found means of throwing fiery allusions upon the burning political situation, which were received by the assembly with frantic applause.

Cuvier and the other Academicians who had insisted that Arago should speak were right; only, they were right according to our point of view, not from their own.

Arago's lecture was a splendid triumph. Indeed, it is impossible for any speaker to be more picturesque, grander or more striking than François Arago in the tribune when carried away by genuine passion; he would throw up his head and shake back his locks—locks dark in colour in 1830, grey in 1848. Whether he were attacking the violators of the Royalist charter or defending the Republican constitution, he was ever the same eloquent orator, ever the inspired poet, the same convinced legislator. For Arago is not only science, he is conscience itself; he is not only genius, but the soul of honour. Let us state this in passing; though I know that plenty of others will say the same, yet I should like to be among their number.

When I left the Institut, I went upstairs to see Madame Chassériau, who lived at the Academy, owing to the position which her father, M. Amaury Duval, occupied there. Madame Chassériau, who, later, was called Madame Guyet-

Desfontaines, was one of my oldest friends: I think I have already spoken of her and said that at her house, as well as at those of Nodier and Zimmermann, I always felt in the best intellectual form. Do not let me be misunderstood: I am not paying myself a compliment, I am only rendering justice to Madame Guyet-Desfontaines. She was so good and kind and affable, and laughed so prettily, had such lovely teeth, one would be a downright idiot not to show in her company a wit at least equal to her own. She, too, like everybody else, was full of the events taking place: she would soon receive news, as M. Guyet-Desfontaines had gone to consult that great testing thermometer of the Parisian mind, the Bourse. The Bourse was in a state of uproar, Three Per Cents, had fallen from seventy-eight francs to seventy-two. Was it not curious that, on the same day and at the same moment, the Academy and the Stock Exchange, knowledge and money, should both cry "Anathema" and be of the same opinion?

I went to dine at Véfour's. As I crossed the gardens of the Palais-Royal, I noticed some excitement going on among a group of youths who were mounted on chairs reading the *Moniteur* aloud; but their imitation of Camille Desmoulins did not meet with much success. After my dinner, I ran to Adolphe de Leuven, whose father was, as my readers know, one of the principal editors of the *Courrier.* Madame de Leuven was very uneasy about her husband, who had left home at two o'clock in the afternoon and had not returned by seven in the evening. She had sent Adolphe to find out about him, but, like the raven from the Ark, he too had not returned. So I, in my turn, went in pursuit of Adolphe. M. de Leuven had not come in because there had been a meeting at the office of the *Courrier français*, and Adolphe had not come back because he had been sent to Laffitte's. They were drawing up a protest in the name of the Charter, in the offices of the *Courrier*, which was to be signed by all the journalists. With regard to the form resistance was to take, they, at present, merely talked of refusing to pay the taxes. Suddenly Châtelain came in triumphant. M. de Belleyme had just issued a decree bidding the printers to print the suspended newspapers. Everyone in the political world was acquainted with Châtelain; he was one of the most honourable men on the press, and one of the rare number who held Republican views in 1830. He formally declared that the *Courrier français* would appear next morning, even if on his own responsibility alone. Adolphe de Leuven was the next to enter: he had found Laffitte's doors closed. I returned to give this news to Madame de Leuven; unfortunately, it was not such peaceful information as that of the dove, and I was bringing anything but an olive branch back with me; but I was able to reassure her about her husband and son: both were safe and sound and would return home as soon as the protest had been drawn up. We say *drawn up*, instead of *signed*, because the question whether the protest should be signed or not was debated for a long time. Some asserted that there was an unplumbed force in the press which was increased by a mystery. These urged that it should not be signed. Others, on the contrary, declared that it would be much better to make the act of opposition a public one, and to sign the protest with names in full. It was a singular thing that it was MM. Baude and Coste, two bold sportsmen, who wanted to preserve anonymity; and M. Thiers, the cautious politician, who wished it to be signed openly. The opinion of M. Thiers carried the day. By midnight the last page of the protest was covered with forty-five signatures. They were those of MM. Gauja, Thiers, Mignet, Carrel, Chambolle, Peysse, Albert Stapfer, Dubochet and Rolle, of the *National*; Leroux, Guizard, Dejean and de Rémusat, of the *Globe*; Senty, Haussman, Dussart, Busoni, Barbaroux, Chalas, Billard, Baude and Coste, of the *Temps*; Guyet, Moussette, Avenel, Alexis de Jussieu, Châtelain, Dupont and de la Pelouze, of the *Courrier français*; Année, Cauchois-Lemaire and Évariste Dumoulin, of the *Constitutionnel*; Sarrans junior, of the *Courrier de Électeurs*; August Fabre and Ader, of the *Tribune des départements*; Levasseur, Plagnol and Fazy, of the *Révolution*; Larreguy and Bert, of the *Journal du Commerce*; Léon Pillet, of the *Journal de Paris*; Bohain and Roqueplan, of the *Figaro*; Vaillant, of the *Sylphe*.

Lest my readers should be surprised at my giving here all the forty-five names, I would point out that they were the names of forty-five men all of whom risked their heads by signing. While I, who risked nothing at all, but would have asked nothing better than to run some such risk, simply returned to my rooms at eleven o'clock, after first taking care to go and give news of myself at No. 7 rue de l'Université. They thought I had left for Algiers!

CHAPTER III

The morning of July 27—Visit to my mother—Paul
Foucher—*Amy Robsart*—Armand Carrel—The office of
the *Temps*—Baude—The Commissary of Police—The
three locksmiths—The office of the *National*—Cadet
Gassicourt—Colonel Gourgaud—M. de Rémusat—
Physiognomy of the passers-by

I returned home in order to keep my entire freedom of action for the
morrow. I meant to visit my mother first thing in the morning: I had not
seen her for two days and feared she would be uneasy, especially if she had
heard what was happening outside. My poor mother, at that time, was living
in the rue de l'Ouest. I think I have previously stated that we chose this new
home for her so that she could be nearer to the Villenave family, who had
left the rue de Vaugirard, and were living next door to her. But, unluckily,
just when my mother had needed neighbourly help the most, Madame
Villenave and Madame Waldor and Élisa (my mother's most faithful
companion, with her cat, Mysouf) had gone to la Vendée, where they owned
a little country place called la Jarrie, three leagues from Clisson. I found my
mother in the most perfect state of tranquillity of mind and body; no rumour
of passing events had yet penetrated into that Thébaïd called the quartier du
Luxembourg. I breakfasted with her, kissed her and left her in her sweet,
undisturbed quiet.

As I went away, I ran across Paul Foucher. He was returning from his
brother-in-law, Victor Hugo's, who lived in the rue Notre-Dame-des-
Champs, and to whom he had been to announce that he had to give a reading
the following day, of what play or at what particular theatre, I know not. Paul
Foucher was then the same short-sighted, absent-minded fellow that he still
is, knocking indifferently into passers-by, posts and trees, on which he always
seemed to be looking for the bills of the theatres where his pieces were being
played; absorbed in the train of thought that preoccupied him at the moment
you met him, and incapable of entering into yours, or of coming out of his
own, into which he would lead you back again and again. His dominant
thought when I met him that morning was the reading he was to give next
day. Paul Foucher, young though he was, had made quite a sensational entry
into the dramatic life. The year before, a piece of which he was said to be the
author had been played at the Odéon, but its great beauty, a beauty of an
eccentric character and ill adapted to the stage, had hastened its failure, and
the failure, though great, was glorious, the kind of failure that brings to light
a man's qualities, just as certain defeats reveal the character of a nation. Paul

Foucher had had his Poitiers, his Agincourt and his Crécy, and could take his stand accordingly. The play was called *Amy Robsart*, and was taken from, or, rather, inspired by, Walter Scott's romance of *Kenilworth*. The day after its failure, Hugo proclaimed himself its author; but the honour of the only representation it had was none the less inseparably associated with Paul Foucher. The play was never printed. Hugo made me a present of the manuscript later; I daresay I have it still in my possession. I tried in vain to get any information out of Paul: he knew but one piece of news, and did not consider either the political or literary world needed to know any other. This news was that next day he was to read a play in five acts. I saw the moment coming when he was about to anticipate the right of the Committee and read me his play. But the reading of the finest drama the world ever saw would not have consoled me for losing the smallest detail of the play which Paris was at that moment putting on the stage. I leapt into a cab and escaped from the reading. I gave the driver Carrel's address.

Since the present crisis had arisen, Carrel was looked upon by the younger members of the Opposition as their leader, elected, if not publicly, at least by tacit consent. I had become acquainted with Armand Carrel at M. de Leuven's, who, since the return to France of the young political exile, after the coronation of Charles X., had placed him on the editorial staff of the *Courrier*; he lived, if I remember rightly, in the rue Monsigny or near by. As he died in 1836, he is already, to the young generation of between twenty and twenty-five years of age, but a historical figure. At the time of which we are now speaking, he was a man of twenty-eight, of medium height, with a calm and retreating forehead, dark hair, small, lively, flashing eyes, a long sharp nose, thin and rather pale lips, with white teeth and a bilious complexion. Although Carrel professed the most advanced of Liberal opinions, as is often the case with men of great intellect and of refined organisation, he had the most aristocratic habits imaginable, and this made the contrast between his words and his appearance very strange. He almost invariably wore patent leather boots, a black cravat tied tight round his neck, a black frock-coat buttoned up all but the last button, a waistcoat of white piqué or of chamois leather and grey trousers. His whole get-up revealed the military style of the former officer. This warlike quality had, to some extent, passed from Carrel's body into his mind. Charlemagne signed his treaties with the pommel of his sword and enforced them with its point; and so with Carrel: his articles always seemed to have been written with a steel point, similar to those used by the ancients, which left deep traces of sharpness on their tablets of wax. But Carrel's polemical style of writing was very fine, noble and frank; he boldly showed his front to his enemies: it was in some way similar both to Pascal's and Paul-Louis Courier's. He had received but little historical education, except about our neighbours across the Channel; he was secretary to Augustin Thierry while he wrote his fine book on the Conquest of England by the Normans (*Conquête de l'Angleterre par les Normands*). Carrel, with his usual earnestness, had picked up the crumbs that fell from that sumptuous table, and had compiled an abridged History of England. We were good enough friends, although, perhaps, we were not quite just to one another; he looked upon me as too much of a poet, and I looked upon him as too much of a soldier. I found him quietly engaged eating his breakfast. He had signed the protest as a duty; risking his head as coolly at the point of the pen as he had already done several times at the point of the sword, though believing in nothing but lawful methods of resistance. As for armed resistance, he would have nothing to do with it. He had meant to stay at home all day to work; but, upon my entreaties, and, owing to my telling him I thought I had seen some rising excitement in the streets, he decided to go out with me. He put a pair of small pistols in his pocket, of the kind called pocket pistols, took a little whalebone cane in his hand as flexible as a horsewhip, and we went down together towards the boulevards. Doubtless cooled by his action at Béfort and Bidassoa, he hesitated to put himself forward when so many people were seen to hang back. We tramped the boulevards from the rue de la Chaussée-d'Antin to the rue Neuve-Vivienne, and then we went along the Place de la Bourse. People were rushing in the direction of the rue de Richelieu. They reported that the offices of the *Temps* were invaded, and being sacked by a detachment of mounted police.

Of course, needless to relate, we, too, followed the crowd; there was, as usual, but a portion of truth in the rumour. A score of police were drawn up in line in front of the building where the printing was carried on, which stood at the bottom of a very large courtyard. The street door was closed and, before they could invade the workshops, they were waiting for the arrival of the Commissaire de Police. When he arrived, Baude, one of the editors of the *Temps*, and signers of the protest, gave orders to close the workshop door and to open the one on the street. The Commissaire, wearing his white scarf of office, knocked at the door exactly as it was being opened, and Baude and he stood face to face. The Commissaire stepped back before the formidable apparition. Baude was a magnificent figure of a man, not only in general appearance but in every detail of his person. He was a giant of five feet eight or ten inches, with thick black hair which floated round his head like a mane; his eyes were brown and deeply set beneath dark eyebrows: they seemed, at certain moments, to shoot out lightning; he had a rough, tremendous voice which, heard amid the noise of a revolution, sounded like thunder in a storm. Baude was followed by other editors and by employés and workmen, who formed up behind him in a body of thirty persons. When they saw the bare-headed, pale-faced leader and the set faces of the workmen, they guessed that, beneath the legal resistance which Baude had called to his aid, lay a very real and material resistance, namely, one that meant resistance with arms. I squeezed Carrel's arm; he was very pale and seemed greatly moved, but he kept quite mute and shook his head in sign of disapproval. There was such a dead silence throughout the street, filled with, perhaps, a couple of thousand people, that a child's breathing could have been heard. Baude was the first to speak and to question the Commissaire.

"What do you want, monsieur? and why have you presented yourselves before our printing house?"

"Monsieur," stammered the Superintendent of Police, "I have come in consequence of the Ordinances...."

"To break up our presses, I suppose?" Baude questioned. "Well, then, in the name of the Code, which is both anterior and superior to your Ordinance, I call upon you to respect them!"

And Baude stretched forth a copy of the Code opened at the article on *Effraction* (Housebreaking). This weapon was, certainly, of a more alarming and terrible nature than the presenting of pistols or swords, but the Superintendent's orders had been perfectly clear.

"Monsieur," he said, "I am obliged to do my duty"; and, turning to one of his men, he said, "Send somebody to find a locksmith."

"All right! I will wait till he comes," said Baude.

A murmur ran through the crowd. They began to understand that there, in the open street, before the eyes of the crowd, under the gaze of Providence, was going to take place one of the grandest spectacles that it is given to human sight to behold—the resistance of law to arbitrary force, of the individual to the crowd, of conscience to tyranny.

Not a man among the spectators had said to Baude, "You can count on my support"; but it was apparent that he felt he could reckon on all.

The locksmith arrived; and, at the order of the Superintendent, he was just going to cross the threshold of the street door, in order to go and open the doors of the printing house with his tools, when Baude, stopping him, by gently taking hold of his arm, said—

"My friend, you probably do not know what risks you are running by obeying the orders of the Superintendent of Police? You are running the risk of being sent to the galleys." And he read in a loud voice the following lines:—

> "Any person will be punished with penal servitude who is guilty of, or accomplice in, theft committed by means of breaking into a house or room or lodging dwelt in or serving as a dwelling-house by means of breaking in from without by scaling or by using false keys, whether he assume the rank of a public functionary or of a civil or military officer,

or after having put on the uniform or dress of a public functionary or officer, or alleging a false order of the civil or military authorities."

As Baude read on, the locksmith raised his hand to his cap and, by the end of the article, he was listening to the reader with bared head. At this token of respect shown to the law by a man of the people the crowd broke out into immense applause. The Commissaire insisted, and the locksmith, obeying his authoritative commands, made an attempt at entrance. Baude drew back and made way for him.

"Do it!" he said, "but you know that it will mean the galleys for you."

The locksmith again stopped and the cheering redoubled. The Superintendent renewed his orders to pick the locks of the doors.

"Messieurs," Baude cried in a loud voice, "I appeal against M. le Commissaire to a jury, and from the Ordinances to the Assizes.... Who will give me their names as witnesses of the outrage offered to me?"

Five hundred voices simultaneously responded. Pencils and papers were instantly circulated among the crowd with wonderful eagerness and unanimity; each took the pencil in turn and wrote down his name and address on the paper. Then all were handed in to Baude.

"You see for yourself, monsieur," he said to the Superintendent of Police, "I have plenty of witnesses."

"Upon my word, Monsieur le Commissaire," the locksmith finally said to that officer of the law, "get somebody else to do your job, I back out of it."

And, putting his cap on his head, he withdrew. He was accompanied by vivats and more applause.

"Force, however, still must rest with the law!" retorted the Superintendent.

"I am beginning to believe, indeed, that it will," Baude replied ironically.

"Oh, I know my business," the officer replied. "Call another locksmith."

An official in black appeared from the crowd as before, and returned with a locksmith carrying a bunch of picklocks at his waist. The applause that had accompanied the retreat of the other man changed quickly to groans as this fresh one appeared. The locksmith was frightened.

As he made his way through the crowd he slipped his bunch of picklocks into the hand of one of the spectators, who passed it on to the next man, and so on through the crowd. When he had reached the door, the order previously given to his colleague was renewed.

"Monsieur le Commissaire," he said, pointing to his empty girdle, "I cannot do it: my tools have been stolen from me."

"You lie!" exclaimed the Commissaire, "and I will have you arrested!"

The hand of one of his men was stretched out to seize him, but the crowd opened a way for him and then closed up after him, wrapped him in its folds and engulfed him completely in its stream. He disappeared literally as though he had been devoured!

They then summoned the blacksmith whose duty it was to rivet the convict's fetters. But, as the opposition of the crowd began to assume a grave character, and looked dark and threatening, the street was cleared with the help of the police.

The crowd withdrew by way of the place Louvois and the arcade Colbert, and by the rue de Ménars, shouting—

"Vive la Charte!"

Men climbed upon posts, waved their hats and cried out to Baude—

"You may rely on us—you have our addresses. We will be witnesses for you. *Au revoir! au revoir!*"

A reinforcement of police seen coming from the direction of the Palais-Royal completed the clearing of the street. But what did that matter? The moral victory remained with the Opposition, and Baude had played as great a part as any ghostly Revolutionist of 1789.

Carrel and I left the rue de Richelieu and went to the *National* offices. The *National* had scarcely been in existence a year then; it had been started by Thiers, Carrel and the Abbé Louis, at the château de Rochecottes, at the feet of Madame de Dino, under the eye of M. de Talleyrand. The Duc d'Orléans, who had lent the necessary funds, paid, as it were, for the nursing of this infant Hercules, which, eighteen years later, was to seize him round his waist and suffocate him. These offices were situated in the rue Neuve-Saint-Marc, at the corner of the place des Italiens. We found it a hotbed of news. The evening before one of the editors had come in, out of spirits and broken down: he had been scouring the poorest quarters, which are always the easiest to stir up, and, shaking his head, he had pronounced these discouraging words:—

"The people will not be moved!"

And when we entered the *National* offices at two o'clock the people were still quiet; but one could feel that kind of shiver of excitement in the air which made people hurry in their walk and grow paler, they knew not why; like the deep, instinctive terror felt by animals at the approach of an earthquake.

From whence arose this shuddering, which was but yet, as it were, upon the surface of society? It is easy to make a guess. The motion of M. Thiers, which had borne forty-five signatures at the foot of the journalists' protest (it had been published in the *Globe*, the *National*, and the *Temps*, and a hundred thousand copies had, perhaps, been printed and distributed in the streets), this motion, we say, had compromised forty five persons. Now, these forty-five individuals made up a compact body working upon the masses, and each also was a separate force, working upon individual members of society. Each signature was the centre of a more or less wide circumference of friends, employés, clerks, workmen, compositors, journeymen and printers' devils. Each one stirred up his own particular circle, and each individual member of this circle, however humble, was himself an agent and used his influence on his subordinates; therefore, as soon as the impulse was given, it was communicated from great centres to small, the wheels began to turn, and one felt society tremble under the throbbing of an invisible machine, almost as one feels a windmill quiver from the revolution of its sails or a steamboat from the beating of its paddles. Carrel was invited to three different meetings, all for the purpose of organising opposition. One was purely of a Liberal character, bordering on Republicanism, and was held in the rue Saint-Honoré in the house of the chemist Cadet de Gassicourt; the principal members were Thiers, Charles Teste, Anfous, Chevalier, Bastide, Cauchois-Lemaire and Dupont; at this one they discussed a motion as to creating a committee of resistance in every arrondissement (ward), with power to put itself into direct communication with the deputies. The second was Bonapartist, and was held at the house of Colonel Gourgaud. It was chiefly composed, first and foremost, of the master of the house, then of Colonels Dumoulin, Dufays and Plavet-Gaubet, and of Commandant Bacheville. Their object was to try and promote the affairs of Napoleon II., but, as all these men were more men of action than of thought, nothing was settled, and they fixed another meeting for the next day at the place des Petits-Pères. The third meeting took place in the *Globe* offices and was composed of Pierre Leroux, Guizard, Dejean, Paulin and Rémusat, and of several persons who had nothing to do with the staff of the paper. Here, the most conflicting counsels were put forth: some wanted to appeal to arms on the morrow, others were horrified at the pace at which, as soon as any movement is started, it descends, in spite of everything, down the path that leads to revolution.

M. de Rémusat was one of the scared.

He exclaimed, in despairing tones, "Where are you going? Where are you urging us? It must on no account lead us to revolution—that is not what we desire: legal resistance, well and good—but nothing beyond."

Of course, this meeting did not decide on a course of action any more than the others, unless it drove M. de Rémusat to his bed with the fever which seized him afterwards.

Carrel did not attend any of these three meetings. He was in favour of lawful resistance stretched to its widest limits, but of lawful resistance only. He did not believe in any good arising out of any conflict between citizens and soldiers: he understood the meaning of pretorian revolutions and demanded of those who talked of resorting to arms—

"Have you any regiment you can safely count on?"

No one had regiments ready, seeing that no plot had been prepared. But there was, none the less, a great and formidable general conspiracy afoot, namely public opinion, which accused the Bourbons of being responsible for the defeat of 1815 and wanted to avenge Waterloo in the streets of Paris.

This conspiracy was visible in the eyes, gestures, words and even in the very silence of the people whom one passed, the groups one met, the solitary individuals who stopped, hesitating whether to go to the right or left, as though saying to themselves, "Where is anything going on? Where are they doing anything? I must go and do just what the rest are doing."

CHAPTER IV

Doctor Thibaut—The Government of Gérard and
Mortemart—Étienne Arago and Mazue, the
Superintendent of Police—The café Gobillard—Fire at
the guard-house in the place de la Bourse—The first
barricades—The night

We went back to the boulevards again from the office of the *National.* At the
top of the rue Montmartre we heard what sounded like firing, in the direction
of the Palais-Royal. It was nearly seven o'clock in the evening.

"Hah! What is that?" I asked Carrel.

"By Jove!" he answered, "it was a volley being fired."

"Well, will you come along and see?"

"Good gracious no!" he replied. "I shall turn in home."

"I mean to go," I said.

"Go, then; but don't be fool enough to get drawn into things!"

"No fear. Adieu!"

"Adieu!"

Carrel walked away with his calm and measured step, along the faubourg
Montmartre, whilst I dashed off at a run for the place de la Bourse. I had not
gone fifty yards before I met Dr. Thibaut. He looked very important.

"Ah! it is you, dear friend?" I said. "What is the news?"

Thibaut, who had adopted great gravity of expression, claiming that no
doctor could make his way in the world without it, was, on this occasion,
more than grave: he was gloomy.

"Bad news!" he replied; "things are getting horribly complicated."

"But are they fighting?" I said,

"Yes; one man has been killed in the rue du Lycée and three more in the rue
Saint-Honoré.... The Lancers charged in the rue de Richelieu and upon the
place du Palais-Royal.... A barricade was being run up in the rue de Richelieu,
but it was taken before it was finished."

"Where are you bound for?"

"You will hear that to-morrow, if I am successful," he said.

"Upon my word, my dear fellow, you assume the airs of a diplomatist."

"Who knows?—I may be going to form a new Government!"

"In your calling as a doctor, my dear friend, I would invite you to give your whole attention to the old Ministry, for it seems to me deuced ill!"

Two young people passed us by rapidly at this moment.

"A tricoloured flag?" said one. "Surely it is not possible!"

"I tell you I saw it myself," the other replied.

"Where?"

"On the quai de l'École."

"When?"

"Half an hour ago."

"What did they do to the man who was bearing it?"

"Nothing ... they just let him pass."

"Let us go there, then."

"All right."

And they ran off down the rue Notre-Dame-des-Victoires.

"You see, my dear fellow," I said to Thibaut, "things are getting warm! Go off to your Ministry, my friend."

"I am going."

He went away in the direction of the boulevard des Capucines.

Thibaut had not deceived me. He was actually engaged in forming a Ministry; only, his Ministry was not destined to die of longevity. It was the Ministry of Gérard and Mortemart, which had its counterpart in the Thiers and Odilon Barrot Ministry of the Revolution of 1848. But, it will be urged, how could Dr. Thibaut form a Ministry? As for that—well, I will tell you.

It will be remembered that, in 1827 or 1828, Madame de Celles, daughter of General Gérard, who was suffering from a chest complaint, had asked Madame de Leuven to tell her of a young medical man who could accompany her to Italy, and that Thibaut's name had been given her. He had made the journey with the beautiful invalid, and the combined results of travel and doctor worked wonders in her health. On their return, the general was so grateful for the care Thibaut had bestowed upon his daughter that he admitted him into personal intimacy in his household. Thibaut, when I met him, was on his way to call upon M. le Baron de Vitrolles, on behalf of General Gérard, to try and persuade him to urge conciliatory measures upon M. de Polignac and, if that failed, upon the king himself. Serious-minded people were evidently beginning to realise the gravity of the situation. This was the information which Thibaut could not tell me when we met, but which he divulged to me later.

Eight o'clock chimed out from the Bourse clock; I wanted to get back to my faubourg Saint Germain; but, as I entered one end of the rue Vivienne, I saw bayonets at the other. I could have gone by the rue des Filles-Saint-Thomas, but curiosity kept me back. I beat a retreat as far as the café of the théâtre des Nouveautés. As far as I can recollect, it was kept by a man named Gobillard, an excellent fellow, a favourite with us all. The troop advanced with regular step, taking up the whole width of the street, pushing men, women and children before them. The people, driven by the soldiers, gave way and walked backwards, shouting—

"Vive la ligne!"

Women waved their handkerchiefs from the open windows, crying—

"Do not fire on the people!"

There was a certain type among the men whom the soldiers were driving aside which is only to be seen at special hours of the day—the kind of men who start riots and revolutions, men whom one might style the pioneers of disorder. When the troops reached the place de la Bourse they deployed, but, as they could not cover the whole width of the square, a portion of those who were being pushed along by the soldiers overflowed on both sides and swept back after them. Now, there was near the Bourse a rickety old wooden shanty which was used as a guard-house. The regiment left about a dozen soldiers there as in a block-house and disappeared down the rue Neuve-Vivienne in the direction of the Bastille. The regiment was scarcely out of sight when some boys from the crowd came up to the soldiers who were left in the guard-house, shouting—

"Vive la Charte!"

Whilst these lads did no more than shout, the soldiers kept their patience, but stones soon followed the shoutings. A soldier, hit by a stone, fired, and a woman fell—a woman of about thirty. Cries of "Murder!" went up and, in a second, the square was emptied, lights were extinguished and shops closed. The théâtre des Nouveautés alone remained lighted and open,—they were playing *la Chatte blanche*,—and those inside the house had no idea what was going on outside. A small troop of about twelve men appeared, at that moment, from the rue des Filles-Saint-Thomas. It was headed by Étienne Arago and was shouting—

"Stop the play! Close the theatres! They are killing people in the streets of Paris!..."

It stumbled against the body of the woman who had been killed.

"Carry this corpse to the steps of the peristyle, so that everybody can see it," said Étienne; "I am going to have the theatre emptied."

And, as a matter of fact, the place was emptied an instant later, the stream of spectators, on coming out, spreading apart as a torrent does before a rock, so as to avoid trampling upon the body. I ran to Arago.

"What are they doing," I asked. "What has been decided?"

"Nothing yet.... Barricades are being erected ... and women killed and theatres closed, as you see."

"Where shall I find you again?"

"To-morrow morning at my house, No. 10 rue de Grammont."

Then, turning to the men who were with him—

"To the Variétés, my friends!" he said; "to close the theatres is to hoist the black flag over Paris!"

And the little crowd disappeared with him down the rue de Montmorency. It had passed before the sentinel and the barracks without producing any sign. And this was how the movement had begun and from whence the firing had come that Carrel and I had heard.

Étienne Arago (I hope I may be pardoned for always quoting the same name, but I will engage to prove, beyond exception, that Étienne Arago was the mainspring of the insurrectional movement), Étienne Arago, I say, had just been dining with Desvergers and Varin and had returned with them to the Vaudeville theatre, which was then in the rue de Chartres, when a mob barred their way in the rue Saint-Honoré, in front of the Delorme passage. They were saying that a man had been killed in the rue du Lycée. A cart, loaded with rubble, was waiting to pass, as soon as the mob had dispersed; four or five carriages, stopped by the same obstruction, were waiting too, in file.

"Excuse me, my friend," Étienne said to the driver, unharnessing the horse from the shafts; "we require your cart."

"What for?"

"To make a barricade with, to be sure!"

"Yes, yes, barricades—let us have barricades!" exclaimed several voices.

And, in the twinkling of an eye, the horses were detached, the cart thrown on its side and the contents piled up across the street.

"Good!" said Arago. "Now you won't need me any more; I am wanted elsewhere."

And, leaving the barricade to be guarded by those who had helped in its construction, he crossed the Delorme passage, went along the rue de Rivoli and reached the Vaudeville. People were just going in.

"There shall be no play while fighting is going on!" he said; "give the people back their money!"

Then, to those who persisted in going in—

"Pardon, messieurs," he said—"there shall be no laughing at the Vaudeville whilst Paris is in tears."

And he began trying to shut the gate.

"Monsieur," a voice asked, "why are you closing the Vaudeville?"

"Why?... Because I am the manager of the theatre and choose to close it."

"Yes, but the Government does not choose to do so: in the name of the Government I order you to leave it open!"

"Who are you?"

"Heavens! you know me well enough."

"Possibly, but I want those who are listening and taking part in this debate to know who you are too."

"I am M. Mazue, Superintendent of Police."

"Well, then, Monsieur Mazue, Police Superintendent, look out for yourself!" replied Arago, pushing against the grating; "those who do not go will soon be crushed."

"Monsieur Arago, to-morrow you will be no longer manager of the Vaudeville!"

"Monsieur Mazue, to-morrow you will no longer be the Superintendent of Police."

"We shall see about that, Monsieur Arago!"

"I hope so, Monsieur Mazue!"

With the help of two scene-shifters, Étienne closed the grille, in spite of the efforts of the police officers; then, leaving by the stage door, he began the work of closing the other theatres—an act that had an immense influence upon that evening's proceedings and upon those of the next day.

All these details were related to us behind the carefully closed doors of the café Gobillard. We were there to the number of three or four and, as we had been rushing about the whole day, we were dying with hunger. We ordered supper. The topic of our conversation can easily be guessed. Some said that the agitation of the hour was of not more significance than that of 1827, and that the riot had not strength to rise to the proportions of a revolution, but would fail in like manner. Others, and I among them, believed, on the contrary, that we were but at the prologue of the comedy and that the morrow would show a different state of things altogether. We were in the full flow of this discussion when the sound of firing startled us and made us shudder. It was fired in the square. Almost immediately there was a cry of "To arms!" followed by a noise like that of a hand-to-hand combat.

"You see," I said, "the drama begins!"

It was now twenty minutes to ten by the café clock. We ran upstairs to the first floor to look out of the windows. The guard-house had been surprised, surrounded and attacked by a score of men. A struggle was proceeding in the darkness, of which we could not make out any details—nothing beyond a confused mass. The soldiers were defeated and disarmed. Their guns, cartridge-pouches and swords had been taken from them and they were sent away by the rue Joquelet; then some fifteen were detached from the main body and picked up the corpse of the woman, which still lay on the theatre steps, placed it on a litter and went away down the rue des Filles-Saint-Thomas crying, "Vengeance!" Three or four who were provided with a torch remained behind the rest and, with this torch, lighted a bonfire of straw in the middle of the guard-house; then they kicked down and broke up the planks it was made of and let them fall into the bonfire. Of course, the planks ignited very rapidly, and instantly the barrack was one vast blazing mass; the three or four laggards left it to its fate and rejoined their companions. The fire threw a lurid illumination over the square and burned half the night without anyone attempting to extinguish it. We went down and finished our supper, our thoughts very full of what we had just witnessed. We separated towards midnight, and I took the rue Vivienne; the Perron passage being closed, I went along the rue Neuve-des-Petits-Champs and the rue de Richelieu. In the rue de l'Échelle, moving about through the darkness, were shadows which, when I approached, cried, "Qui vive?" I replied, "A friend!" and walked straight on. It was a barricade that was being silently raised, as though built by some spirits of the night. I shook hands with several of these nocturnal workmen and gained the Carrousel. Behind the château gates I could see two or three hundred men camped in the court of the Tuileries. I thought it must have been almost the same as this on the night of the 9th to 10th of August 1790. I tried to peep through the gates, but a sentinel cried "Keep off!" and I went on my way. On the quays everything was resuming its normal appearance. I reached the rue de l'Université without having met a single person either upon the Pont Royal or in the rue du Bac. As soon as I reached my lodgings, I opened my window and listened: Paris seemed silent and deserted; but this tranquillity was but superficial, one felt that the solitude was peopled and the silence alive!

CHAPTER V

I was awakened, as on the 26th, by Achille Comte.

"Well?" I asked, rubbing my eyes.

"Oh, it is going ahead!" he said. "The Quartier des Écoles is in a state of open insurrection, but the students are furious."

"Against whom?"

"Against the principal leaders—Laffitte, Casimir Périer and La Fayette.... They called upon these persons yesterday: one told them to keep quiet, whilst others did not even see them.... But Barthélemy and Méry will give you full details; they were there, with their pockets full of gunpowder which they had bought of a grocer."

I dressed, took a carriage to go and call on my mother and found her as calm as if nothing extraordinary was happening in Paris. I had given orders that she should be kept in ignorance, and they had been carefully executed. When I left my mother, I drove to Godefroy Cavaignac, who lived in the rue de Sèvres. He had gone out, but I was told I should find him either at Joubert's the bookseller's, in the passage Dauphine, or at Charles Teste's, at *la Petite-Jacobinière*, in the place de la Bourse.

Joubert, who was afterwards aide-de-camp to La Fayette, I believe lieutenant-colonel, was a former Carbonaro and a friend of Carrel; condemned to death as the latter was, after the affair of Béfort, he had escaped from the prisons of Perpignan by the help of a nun and two of his friends, Fabre and Corbière.

Charles Teste, whom we all knew well, had built a bookshop in the place de la Bourse, which was dubbed with the expressive name of *Petite-Jacobinière*, because of the opinions of those who frequented it. Charles Teste was one of the worthiest and noblest characters it was possible to meet with. Being poor, he had quarrelled with his richer brothers. During the reign of Louis-Philippe he would not take up any profession, and goodness knows how he managed to live! When his brother was condemned by the Court of Peers, he placed himself entirely at his disposition, and became his support and comfort and strength. Then, after the Revolution of 1848, all his old friends came in to power, but he declined the posts that were offered to him, and the only favour he asked was that his brother might be removed from prison to a sanatorium. Charles Teste died, I think, eighteen months or two years ago; when he drew his last breath France lost one of her greatest citizens.

I drove first to the passage Dauphine, but Cavaignac had been there and had gone out with Bastide, and it was thought that both had gone to *la Petite-Jacobinière*. So I dismissed my cab, as I had a call to make at No. 7 rue de l'Université. Here I had drawn no preventive cordon, as in the case of my mother, and everything was known. I promised to regard things from a spectator's standpoint and not to mix myself up in the disturbance: on those conditions, I was allowed leave.

There was a large gathering in the rue de Beaune, at the house of a chemist whose name was Robinet; it was composed of electors and members of the National Guard of the 10th and 11th Arrondissement. All they wanted was to start out on the warpath, but no one possessed arms.

"No arms?" asked Étienne Arago, who entered at this juncture. "If you have no arms, there are plenty to be had at the armourers'!"

It was known at the *National* offices and at *la Petite-Jacobinière* that a meeting was going on in Robinet's house, and they had sent Arago as a deputy. He had not wasted his time since the morning.

"No arms!" was the general cry at the *Petite-Jacobinière* as elsewhere.

Le Sergent Mathieu was then being played at the Vaudeville theatre, and, consequently, there were about a score or so of rifles, swords and powder-wallets lying among the property stores. Gauja and Étienne ran off to the Vaudeville and put the weapons in wicker baskets which they covered with sheets; they recruited porters and scene-shifters, whilst they followed the procession, clad beneath their long coats in the uniform of officers of the Imperial Guard. The place du Palais-Royal was crowded with troops. A captain stepped out of the ranks and asked the commissionaires: "What are you carrying there?"

"A wedding breakfast from Parly, Captain," Arago replied.

The captain began to laugh: the points of the swords and bayonets were sticking through the basketwork. But he only turned his back on what he saw, and returned to the ranks. Guns, swords and powder-flasks arrived safely at *la Petite-Jacobinière*, where they were distributed. It was as a consequence of this distribution of arms that Étienne had been sent to Robinet's.

"At his words, "If you have no arms, there are plenty at the armourers'!" everybody went out. Étienne ran to the nearest armourer with Gauja and a man named Lallemand. The armourer lived in the rue de l'Université. When I had pointed out to Étienne his shop, which was on the left side of the rue de Beaune, I turned to the right, to fetch my own gun. Étienne and Lallemand rushed in to the armourer's shop, which was just being closed. Étienne was more lucky with the armourer than he had been the previous day with the Superintendent of Police, and he managed to enter the shop.

"My friend," he said, "do not be alarmed; we have not come to seize your arms, but to purchase them."

He took five or six rifles, and kept one for himself, one for Gauja and one for Lallemand, giving away the remainder. Then he emptied his pockets, which contained 320 francs and, for the surplus expenditure, he gave a draft on his brother François, of the Observatoire, who paid religiously. Lallemand endorsed the bill. This Lallemand was a well educated and highly cultivated young fellow whom we nicknamed *le Docteur*, because he always talked so much Latin. I make this explanation in order to avoid confusion with Professor Lallemand. They also took powder and bullets from the same armourer and, as we shall see, it was not long before they were required.

I had gone back home, called my servant Joseph and told him to put me out my complete shooting costume. It was the most suitable and convenient for the form of exercise to which we were going to apply our energies; also, more important still, it was the least conspicuous. I was half-way through my toilet when I heard a great uproar in the rue du Bac and rushed to my window: it came from Étienne Arago and Gauja, who were calling the people to arms. It will be remembered that I lived above the café Desmares; but I forgot to mention that three of my windows looked into the rue du Bac. At that moment, two mounted policemen appeared from the bridge side, at the entrance of the street. Why had they come there? What chance had brought them? We did not know at all. When the crowd which filled the street caught sight of them, loud cries were set up. Thereupon, the policemen seemed to confer together; but, if they hesitated, it was only for a moment: they took their bridles between their teeth, drew their sabres in one hand and held their pistols in the other. The crowd was unarmed and ran into side alleys or open shops or made off down the rue de Lille. Arago and Gauja hid in corners of the street: one of them (I do not know which) cried to the other—

"Come! it is time to begin!"

At the same moment, the two policemen pounced upon them at full gallop. Two reports and flashes of firing came simultaneously from Étienne and Gauja. Both had aimed at the same man and he fell pierced by both bullets. They rushed to the gendarme stretched on the ground. He was dying. The other policeman turned back. The riderless horse went its own way and disappeared down the rue du Bac. They took his sabre, pistol and powder-box from him and carried him to la Charité. When it was seen that a wounded policeman was being brought into the hospital and they learnt that he had been wounded because he charged at the people, the patients were for finishing him off.

The spirit of revolution had actually penetrated into the hospitals!

Meanwhile, I had put on my jacket, picked up my gun, game-bag and powder-horn, stuffed my pockets with shot and I gone downstairs. Arago and Gauja had both disappeared. I was known in the district and people collected round me.

"What must be done?" they inquired.

"Put up barricades!" I replied.

"Where?"

"One at each end of the rue de l'Université; the other across the rue du Bac."

They brought me a crowbar and I set to the task by beginning to unpave the street. Everybody clamoured for arms.

While this was going on drums were beating in the Tuileries garden. Three soldiers of the Garde Royale appeared at the ii top of the rue du Bac, from the direction of the rue Saint-Thomas-d'Aquin.

"Look here!" I said to those surrounding me, "you are asking for arms? Nothing could be more opportune. See! here are three rifles coming towards you; the only thing you have to do is to take them...."

"Oh, if that is all!" they said.

And they rushed towards the soldiers, who pulled up. I was the only man armed in the crowd.

"My friends," I shouted to the soldiers, "give up your guns and no harm shall be done you!"

They consulted for a moment, then gave up their guns. I kept the soldiers covered with mine, prepared to kill the first man who should make any hostile demonstration. The people took the guns, but these were actually not loaded: hence, of course, arose the poor devils' readiness to give them up. The people uttered loud shouts of triumph, the battle had begun with a victory: one gendarme killed and three soldiers of the Royal Guard made prisoners! True, we had to let our captives go, because we did not know what to do with them.

We now went on with our barricades. A little group of students arrived from the top of the rue de l'Université; a tall fair young man marched at its head, dressed in an apple-green frock-coat. He was the only one of the party who possessed a service gun. We fraternised and they joined with us to work at the barricades. The close vicinity of the barracks of the Gardes du Corps on the quai d'Orsay made us fearful of an attack. It was quite impossible for the sentinel not to have heard the two reports of a gun, not to have seen the police fly and not to have raised the alarm. I was tired of turning up paving-stones, so gave my pickaxe to the tall fair youth. He began to pick up the intermediate space, but the crowbar was heavy, fell out of his hands and struck me on the leg.

"Ah! monsieur," he cried, "I beg your pardon most profoundly, for I am sure I must have hurt you badly!"

It was true enough, but there are moments when one does not feel pain.

"Never mind," I said to him; "it is on the bone."

He raised his head. "Do you happen to possess a ready wit?"

"By Jove!" I replied, "that's a fine question:' it is my business to have one!"

"Would you favour me with your name?"

"Alexandre Dumas."

"Oh! monsieur!" (He held out his hand to me.) "My name is Bixio ... Profession—medical student. If I get killed, here is my card; have the goodness to see that I am carried home. If you are wounded, I will put my scientific knowledge at your disposal."

"Monsieur, I hope that neither your card nor your knowledge will be required; but, all the same, I will take the one and accept the other. Take care to remember my name, if you please, as I will remember yours!"

We shook hands, and our friendship dated from that meeting.

The barricades finished, we left them to be guarded by those who had helped to make them.

"Now, then," I said to Bixio, "where are you going?"

"I am going in the direction of Gros-Caillou."

"In that case, I will accompany you as far as the Chamber.... I want to go and see what is happening at the *National*."

"What!" Bixio exclaimed. "Are you going like that, with your gun, through the streets?"

"Certainly!" I replied; "you seem to me to be going to do just the same."

"Yes, but only on this side of the Seine."

"Bah! I am in a shooting costume and not a fighting one."

"But shooting hasn't begun yet."

"All right, then; I will open the season."

However, as will be seen, I did not venture to cross the Tuileries with my accoutrements: I went round by the place de la Révolution, I crossed it without hindrance and went down the whole length of the rue Saint-Honoré. The barricades in the rue de l'Échelle and the rue des Pyramides had been broken down. When I reached the rue de Richelieu and saw a regiment at the top of the place Louvois, from the other side of the Palais-Royal a dense line of troops was visible, and a squadron of Lancers was stationed in the place du Palais-Royal. There was no passage left me unless I went back the way I had come. I found I was nearly opposite my old offices, No. 216. So I went in and upstairs to the first floor. There I found Oudard. He looked at me, hesitating whether to recognise me.

"What! is that you?" he asked.

"No doubt about that."

"What are you doing here to-day?"

"I have come to see if I cannot meet the Duc d'Orléans."

"What do you want with him?"

I began to laugh.

"I want to address him as *Your Majesty*," I replied.

Oudard uttered a lamentable cry of distress.

"Unlucky fellow!" he said, "how can you utter such words? Suppose anybody heard you!"

"Yes, but nobody will hear me—the duke least of all." "Why so?"

"Because I presume he is at Neuilly."

"The Duc d'Orléans is in his right place!" Oudard replied magisterially.

"My dear Oudard, as I am much less well versed in matters of etiquette than yourself, allow me to inquire where the right place is?"

"Why, by the king's side, I suppose."

"Then," I said, "I present my compliments to His Highness."

At this moment drums began beating at the corner of the rue de Richelieu, turning by the rue Saint-Honoré, and advancing towards the Palais-Royal. Behind them came a general, surrounded by his staff of officers. I could see them plainly through the chinks of the outside blinds.

I felt a great desire to make Oudard sick with fear.

"Look here, Oudard," I said, "I am strongly of opinion that if I picked off the general who is just passing it would considerably advance the affairs of M. le Duc d'Orléans ... who is so near the king."

And I covered the general with my gun. Oudard became as pale as death and flung himself upon my gun, which was not even cocked. I laughingly showed him the hammer lowered on the nipple.

"Oh!" he said, "you will leave this place, will you not?"

"You must wait till the soldiers have filed past.... I cannot reasonably attack, singlehanded, two or three thousand men."

Oudard sat down, and I laid my gun in a corner and opened the window wide.

"What are you up to next?" he asked.

"I am going to amuse myself by watching the military pass by"; and I watched them from beginning to end.

They went to the Hôtel de Ville, where warm fighting had begun. The general in command, whom I had picked out to Oudard's extreme terror, was General Wall.

I went back by the rue de Richelieu, behind the last ranks, with my gun on my shoulder, as quietly as though I were going to the opening of the shooting season, on the plains of Saint-Denis.

CHAPTER VI

The aspect of the rue de Richelieu—Charras—L'École polytechnique—The head with the wig—The café of the Porte Saint-Honoré—The tricoloured flag—I become head of a troop—My landlord gives me notice—A gentleman who distributes powder—The captain of the 15th Light Infantry

The rue de Richelieu wore a very strange aspect. Hardly had the troops left the street before the insurgents audaciously entered it, or, rather, issuing from every door, reigned there supreme. In all directions the fleurs de lys were blotted out along with the royal monogram, whilst everywhere the mottoes were daubed with mud. To the cries of "*Vive la Charte!*" began to succeed those of "*À bas les Bourbons!*" Armed men appeared at the street corners, looking as though in search of some centre of resistance or field of battle. From time to time a shop door would open and, through the half-opened space, a soldier of the Garde National in his uniform could be seen, still hesitating to come out, but only awaiting the right moment to join in the vast tumult. Women waved handkerchiefs out of the windows and cried bravo to every man who appeared with a gun in his hand. Nobody walked with his usual step, all ran. No one spoke as usual, they jerked out half-finished expressions. A universal fever seemed to have seized the population: it was a wonderful sight! The coldest and most unsympathetic being would have been compelled to join in the general excitement abroad.

I reached the *National* offices and, at the door, I met Carrel in conversation with Paulin.

"Ah!" I exclaimed, "there you are!... good. They told me you had left Paris and were in the country with Thiers and Mignet, they even said that you were in the valley of Montmorency."

"Who told you that?"

"As though I could remember!..." And, indeed, I could not have said who had told me this bit of news, which had been given me, moreover, by way of proving to me what little effect the leaders of the movement were themselves having upon the so-called Revolution which was going on.

"There is some truth in the rumour," he said. "I really did go into the country with Thiers, Mignet and another person whom I wished to place in safety."

"Élisa?" I said heedlessly.

"Yes, my wife Élisa," Carrel emphasised; "but directly she was in a place of safety I returned, and here I am."

Carrel was quite sincere in the few words he had just uttered. Those who lived in intimate intercourse with Carrel knew the person I had just called Élisa, whom, by way of reading me a lesson, he had called his *wife*. He adored this lady, who was indeed adorable and the best and most devoted of women! There existed between them one of those liaisons that society proscribes but the heart respects—a love which redeems the fault committed by such virtue that out of a sinner it creates a saint. What became of this poor noble creature after Carrel's death? I have no idea; but I know that when I heard of the terrible accident I thought far less of him who had died than of her who was condemned to live.

I ask the forbearance of my readers for so often digressing from my subject to speak of affairs of the heart such as this, but I am writing my Memoirs and not a history; my impressions, and not a compilation of dates: as my impressions recur to my memory, so do they cause a dark or a golden cloud to float between my eyes and my paper, according as they are sad or joyful.

We were now joined by a fine, handsome lad of between twenty and twenty-two. Carrel held out his hand to him.

"Oh! so it is you, Charras?" he said.

"Yes. I have been looking for you."

"For what purpose?"

"To ask you where they are fighting."

"Is there fighting anywhere?" Carrel questioned.

"My goodness! Of course there is!"

"Well! no matter; but I should never have thought it was so difficult a matter to get one's head broken.... Since yesterday night I have been running all over the place with that object in view and I haven't yet got my desire!"

Charras, one of the bravest officers in the African army and one of the staunchest characters of the Revolution of 1848, had been driven out of the École polytechnique, at the beginning of 1830, for having sung "La Marseillaise" and cried "*Vive La Fayette!*" at a dinner. One of these two offences would alone have been enough to have expelled him, but, as they could not turn him out twice, they had to be content with turning him out once for all. Since that time, he had lived at No. 38 rue des Fossés-du-Temple, at Fresnoy the actor's, who kept a furnished hotel, being also, at the same time, a manager of the Petit-Lazari theatre of marionnettes, which the protection and influence of his tenant changed into a theatre of living, speaking actors, a week after the Revolution of July. Since the 26th, Charras had been planning what part his old comrades the students of the École polytechnique could play in the insurrection; consequently, he at once put himself into communication with them, and, on the 27th, he had managed to distribute among them the Opposition journals that had appeared, the *Globe*, the *Temps* and the *National*. The printer of the *Courrier français* had declined his presses, and the *Constitutionnel* and the *Débats* had not dared to appear. At two o'clock, the graduate students, sergeants and sergeant-majors, who had the right to go out as they liked, had rushed into the streets, and had drawn all the quarters seething with revolt, returning to the École saying, after what they had seen, that a collision was imminent. At this piece of news the excitement became intense. About seven o'clock they heard musket shots in the rue du Lycée and volley firing in the rue Saint-Honoré. The students were soon collected in the billiard-room, and there they decided that four of their members should be sent to Laffitte, to La Fayette and to Casimir Périer to tell them the feeling of the École and that the students were ready to throw themselves into the insurrection. The École numbered between forty to fifty Republicans, as many, perhaps, as Paris contained among her twelve hundred thousand inhabitants. The four students chosen were MM. Berthelin, Pinsonnière, Tourneux and Lothon. The authorities tried to keep them in, but they broke out without leave and arrived at Charras's lodgings at nine o'clock in the evening. Charras was busy burning down the guard-house in the place de la Bourse, and did not return home until half-past eleven. But that did not matter, and it was decided they should go at once to Laffitte's house. They left the rue des Fossés-du-Temple at midnight and reached the door of his hotel at twenty minutes past. They rang and knocked at the same time, so great was their haste to gain an entrance. Moreover, in the innocence of their hearts, the five youths imagined that Laffitte was in as great a hurry to accept their lives as they themselves were to offer them. An ill-tempered concierge opened a wicket-gate.

"What do you want?" he asked.

"To speak to M. Laffitte."

"What about?"

"About the Revolution."

"Who are you?"

"Students from the École polytechnique."

"M. Laffitte has gone to bed."

And the porter shut the door in the faces of the five young fellows.

Charras had a great mind to force open the door and even went so far as to propose it, but, being dissuaded by his companions, he merely heaped abuse upon the concierge.

The manner of their reception at Laffitte's did not encourage them to pay the other calls they had planned to make: they agreed to call next day on La Fayette and Casimir Périer, but in the meanwhile they would return to the rue des Fossés-du-Temple. They therefore went back to the Hôtel Fresnoy and accommodated themselves as best they could on mattresses, on chairs, or on the floor. Next day, at dawn, they went to a professor of mathematics, named Martelet, who coached for the École examinations. M. Martelet lived at No. 16 rue des Fossés-du-Temple. They wanted to procure themselves civilian's dress—the king's highway not being safe in open daylight for the students who wore the École uniform. The five friends found all, they required at M. Martelet's house. Then, as they feared that if they called upon La Fayette too early, the same thing would happen as when they called too late at Laffitte's, they set to work to build a barricade in order to pass the time of waiting.

A wigmaker was busy in a house opposite that of M. Martelet, curling and powdering a wig: the young men invited him to join them; but, whether the wigmaker's political opinions differed from the makers of the barricade, or whether he was too much engrossed in his art and thought his time was better employed in powdering and curling wigs, he refused. By chance the barricade and the wig were both finished at the same moment. As there was nobody to guard the barricade, they took a model of a head with its pedestal from the wigmaker's shop, placed it behind the paving-stones, dressed it up in the freshly powdered and curled wig, rammed a three-cornered hat jauntily on the top and confided the protection of the barricade, to the mannikin, forbidding the wigmaker under pain of death to dare to make any change in the strategic arrangements. After which they directed their course to La Fayette's dwelling-place. La Fayette was not at home. The young people left their names with the concierge, and were about to resume their Odyssey by going to knock at the door of Casimir Périer. But Charras thought two fruitless attempts were enough, and left his comrades to fulfil their third attempt by themselves, which proved as barren as the first two. He sought out Carrel to inquire where fighting was taking place. But nobody seemed to know. There was a general idea that there was fighting going on near the Hôtel de Ville, and, at certain moments, the great bell of Notre-Dame could be heard ringing. As Charras had no arms he was able to take a direct course by the Palais-Royal and the Pont des Arts or by the Pont Neuf; whilst I, who had my gun, was obliged to retrace my steps the way I had come, by the faubourg Saint-Germain, the place de la Révolution and the rue de Lille.

Charras went his way and I mine. We shall find Charras again later. Carrell went to the *Petite-Jacobinière* and I went back again into the streets.

The spirit of hatred was still spreading: people were no longer satisfied with effacing the fleurs de lys from the signboards, they now dragged them in the gutters.

I called at Hiraux's for a few minutes (the reader will recall the son of my old violin master, who kept and still keeps the café de la Porte Saint-Honoré). I went in there first of all to see him, and secondly, because there seemed a great agitation going on inside his house. It was caused by a piece of news which was being spread abroad and which exasperated people. It was said that the Duc de Raguse had offered his services to the king, to take command of the armed forces in Paris. If this news sounded odd to the world at large, it surprised me still more: only two days before, had I not heard the Duc de Raguse, at the Academy deploring the Ordinances and asking François Arago not to speak? And, as a matter of fact, he had had no thought of offering his services for the post until Marshal Marmont, who was in a state of despair, had received that very morning, from the Prince de Polignac, the order appointing him to the command of the first military division. He had been upon the point of refusing, but his evil genius had prevented him from doing so. There are men predestined to do fatal acts! This news probably threw five hundred more combatants into the streets.

When I reached the Pont de la Révolution, I stopped short in stupefaction to rub my eyes, for I thought they must have deceived me: the tricolour was floating from Notre-Dame! I must confess that I experienced a strange feeling of emotion at the sight of that flag, which I had not seen since 1815 and which recalled so many noble memories of those Revolutionary times and so many glorious recollections of the Imperial rule. I leant against the parapet with outstretched arms and my eyes filled with tears, rivetted upon the sight.

From la Grève side a lively fusillade burst forth, the smoke rising in dense clouds. The sight of my gun brought a dozen people round me. Two or three were armed with guns, others had pistols or swords.

"Will you lead us?" they said. "Will you be our chief?"

"Indeed I will!" I replied. "Come along."

We went across the Pont de la Révolution and we took our way through the rue de Lille, to avoid the Orsay barracks, which commanded the quay. The drums of the National Guard were beginning to beat the *rappel* and, our little company forming a nucleus, I had fifty men round me, with two drums and a banner, by the time I reached the rue du Bac. As I passed my rooms, I wished to go upstairs to fetch some money, as I had gone out in the morning without troubling to look to see what I had upon me, and I found I had only fifteen francs; but the landlord had come and had given the porter orders not to admit me. My conduct that morning had given rise to scandal: I had, myself, with nineteen others, disarmed three soldiers of the Royal Guard, and, with nine others, I had made three barricades; finally, as they evidently thought I was so rich that they could risk lending me something, they added to the charges against me the murder of the gendarme by Arago and Gauja. My troop made me the same offer that Charras had made to his comrades, the night before; they offered to break in the door, but I was fond of my lodgings, they were very comfortable and I had not any desire that my landlord should turn me out, so I restrained the enthusiastic zeal of my men.

We resumed our journey along the rue de l'Université. At that moment, I had nearly thirty men with me who were armed with rifles; when we got to the top of the rue Jacob it occurred to me to ask them if they had ammunition. They had not ten cartridges between them; but this fact had not prevented their marching to face fire with that naïve and sublime self-confidence which characterises the people of Paris during periods of insurrection.

We went into an armourer's shop whose arms had all been seized, to ask him if he could tell us where to find some cartridges. He told us that we should find a *monsieur* at the small gate of the Institut, in the rue Mazarine, who was distributing powder. Now, although it was highly improbable that such a *monsieur* existed, we went off to the address indicated.

The information was perfectly correct: we found the little door of the Institut, and the *monsieur* who was distributing powder. Who was the gentleman and where did he hail from? And on whose behalf did he distribute this powder? I know nothing about it and shall certainly not put myself out about the question now, as I did not allow it to trouble me at the time. I simply state the bare facts. A queue had been formed, as you may suppose. Each man armed with a gun received a dozen charges of powder; every man with a pistol received six. The *monsieur* did not keep bullets; and these I hoped to procure at Joubert's, in the Dauphine passage. I left my men in the street and went alone to Joubert's, for fear of alarming those who lived down the passage. Joubert had gone off with Godefroy Cavaignac and Guinard. Cavaignac and Guinard had quarrelled; but, when they met by chance at Joubert's, guns in hand, they fell into one another's arms and made it up. In spite of the absence of the master of the house, they gave me fifty bullets, which I took away to my men. This hardly allowed us two balls to each gun; but we pursued our way, putting our trust in Providence.

As we were going to the place de Grève, we went by the rue Guénégaud, the Pont Neuf and the quai de l'Horloge. It seemed there was to be no opposition to our march, which was hastened by the sound of musketry and cannon;

until, on arriving at the quai aux Fleurs, we found ourselves face to face with a whole regiment. It was the 15th Light Infantry. Thirty rifles and fifty rounds of ammunition were scarcely enough with which to attack fifteen hundred men. We pulled up. However, as the troop did not assume an aggressive attitude towards us, I made my men halt, advanced to the regiment with my gun erect and indicated by signs that I wished to speak with an officer. A captain came out to meet me.

"What is your business, monsieur?" he asked.

"A passage for myself and men."

"Where are you going?"

"To the Hôtel de Ville."

"What to do?"

"Why, to fight," I replied.

The captain began to laugh.

"Really, Monsieur Dumas," he said to me, "I didn't think you were as mad as that."

"Ah! you know me?" I said.

"I was on guard one night at the Odéon when *Christine* was being played and I had the honour of seeing you."

"Then let us talk like two good friends."

"That is indeed what I am doing, it seems to me."

"Why am I a madman?"

"You are a madman, first of all, because you risk getting yourself killed, when it is not your calling to get killed; secondly, you are mad for asking us to allow you to pass through, because you know very well we shall not do so.... Besides, look what will happen to you if we grant your request—the same that has happened to these poor devils who are being brought in...."

And he showed me two or three wounded, returning leaning upon the shoulders of their comrades or laid on stretchers.

"Oh, ah! but you yourself? What are you doing here?" I asked him.

"A very sad thing, monsieur,—our duty. By good luck, the regiment has, so far, received no orders beyond the prevention of traffic. We are restricting ourselves, as you see, to the execution of that order. So long as no one fires on us, we shall fire on no one either. Go and tell that to your men and let them turn back quietly, and if, to go further still, you have enough influence over them to persuade them to return to their homes, you will be doing the very best deed possible!"

"I thank you for your advice, monsieur," I said, laughing in my turn; "but I doubt whether my companions will be disposed to follow the latter part of it."

"Then it will be so much the worse for them, monsieur!"

I bowed and turned to go away.

"By the bye," he said, "when will *Antony* appear? Is not that the title of the first play you mean to have performed?"

"Yes, Captain."

"When?"

"When we have accomplished the Revolution, seeing that the Censorship has suppressed my play, and that it needs nothing less than a Revolution to permit the performance of it—so they have told me at the Ministry of the Interior."

The officer shook his head.

"Then I am very much afraid, monsieur, that the play will never see daylight."

"You are afraid of that?"

"Yes."

"All right—here's to the first representation! And if you would like seats at it, come to No. 25 rue de l'Université and ask me for them."

We bowed. The captain returned to his company, and I rejoined my troop, to whom I related all that had passed. Our first care was to retire beyond gunshot, in case our advisers should change their views for less pacific ones. Then we held counsel together.

"Upon my word!" one of my men remarked, "the matter is easy enough. Do we or do we not wish to go where there is fighting?"

"We do."

"Well, then, let us go down the rue du Harlay, the quai des Orfèvres and return to the Pont Notre-Dame by the rue de la Draperie and the rue de la Cité."

This proposition was unanimously adopted: our two drums began to beat again, and we reascended the quai de l'Horloge to put our fresh strategic plan into execution.

CHAPTER VII

The attack on the Hôtel de Ville—Rout—I take refuge at
M. Lethière's—The news—My landlord becomes
generous—General La Fayette—Taschereau—Béranger—
The list of the Provisional Government—Honest mistake
of the *Constitutionnel*

We kept strictly to the route agreed on. A quarter of an hour after our
departure from the quai de l'Horloge, we issued forth by the little street of
Glatigny. We arrived in the nick of time: they were going to make a decisive
charge upon the Hôtel de Ville by the suspension bridge. Only, if we wished
to join in the attack, we must hurry on. Our two drums beat the charge and
we advanced at quick pace. We could see about a hundred men in the
distance (who composed pretty nearly the whole of the insurgent army)
boldly marching towards the bridge, a tricolour standard at their head, when,
suddenly, a piece of cannon was pointed and fired in such a way as to rake
the whole length of the bridge.

The cannon was charged with grapeshot and the effect of the discharge was
terrible. The standard disappeared; some eight or ten men fell and a dozen
to fifteen took flight. But the fugitives rallied again at the outcries of those
who remained unmoved on the bridge. From the point where we were
sheltered by the parapet, we fired on the place de Grève and upon the
gunners at the cannon, two of whom fell. They were instantly replaced, and
with indescribable rapidity the cannon was reloaded and fired a second time.
There was frightful confusion on the bridge; many of the assailants must
have been killed or wounded, to judge by the gaps in their ranks. One of us
shouted—

"To the bridge! To the bridge!"

We soon sprang forward; but we had not cleared a third of the distance when
the cannon thundered forth a third time, and at the same moment the troop
advanced upon the bridge with fixed bayonets. Hardly twenty combatants
survived that third discharge; forty or so lay dead or wounded on the bridge.
Not only was there no longer any means of attacking, but, further, we could
not dream of defending ourselves—four to five hundred men were charging
us with fixed bayonets! By good fortune we only had to cross the quay in
order to reach the network of little streets which were buried in the heart of
the city. A fourth discharge of the cannon killed three or four more of our
men and hastened our retreat, which, from that moment, might be more

accurately described as a rout. This was the first time I had ever heard the whistling of grapeshot, and I confess I shall not believe anyone who tells me he has heard this sound for the first time unmoved. We did not even attempt to rally, and, with the exception of one of the drummers whom I met upon the square in front of Notre-Dame, my whole troop had vanished like smoke. But, five minutes later, we met each other again, some fifteen of us, who all arrived by different streets from the bridge. The news they brought was disastrous: the standard-bearer, whom they asserted was called Arcole, had been killed; Charras, they said, was mortally wounded; finally, the bridge was literally strewn with dead. I thought I had done enough for one day, considering I was a novice in my military career; also, cries round us announced the approach of soldiers: they were coming to take down the tricoloured flag from the tower and to stop the ringing of the great bell of Notre-Dame, which boomed on with admirable persistence, dominating all other sounds, even that of the cannon. I regained the quai des Orfèvres and the same street, rue Guénégaud, by which I had passed triumphantly at the head of my fifty men only an hour before; I went down the rue Mazarine and, by the same door from which the *monsieur* had distributed powder, I entered the house of my friend, Lethière. I was received just as cordially as usual, even more so, perhaps: M. Lethière held strong Liberal views, Mademoiselle d'Hervilly was almost Republican. They gave me some of that famous rum-arrack which comes directly from la Guadeloupe, of which I was inordinately fond! Upon my word, it was good, after listening to the whistle of grapeshot and seeing fifty men mowed down, to find oneself among warm friends who embraced and shook hands with one and poured one out arrack!

It was almost three o'clock: M. Lethière declared that he had got me and did not mean to let me go again that day. I asked nothing better than to be kept back compulsorily, and remained to dinner. At five, Lethière's son came in, bringing news with him. Fighting was going on, or had gone on, in every quarter of Paris. The boulevards were on fire from the Madeleine to the Bastille; half the trees were cut down and had been used in the making of upwards of forty barricades. The Mairie of Petits-Pères had been taken by three patriots, whose names were already known—MM. Degousée, Higonnet and Laperche. In the faubourg and in the rue de Saint-Antoine the enthusiasm had been extraordinary: they had crushed the soldiers, who were coming from Vincennes, beneath furniture which was flung on them from the windows. Nothing had come amiss as arms: wood from bedsteads, cupboards, chests of drawers, marble, chairs, firedogs, screens, cisterns, bottles—even a piano had been thrown down! The troops were completely decimated. The attack in the Louvre district had advanced as far as the place Saint-Germain-l'Auxerrois. A column of twenty men had marched to battle headed by a violin which played *Ran tan plan tire lire!* And, more than this: the members of the Chamber were beginning to rouse themselves. They met at the house of Audry de Puyraveau, and talked much but did little. That was better than nothing! Finally, they decided that five deputies should wait upon the Duc de Raguse to lay certain propositions before him, and to treat with him if necessary.

"Four millions," Casimir Périer said, "would, according to my thinking, be well spent in this matter."

The five deputies repaired to the headquarters in the square, where the marshal was: they were MM. Laffitte, Casimir Périer, Mauguin, Lobau and Gérard. They had been shown in at Marmont's house, where they found François Arago, who had preceded them on the same errand; but neither the one nor the other had had the slightest success whatever. While they were waiting at the marshal's, a lancer, with his chest horribly lacerated by a gunshot, had been carried into the next room to the one in which the conference was being held. They could not at first tell what kind of projectile the wound could have been made with: the surgeon thought it must have been shot used for killing hares. But it was with printer's type! The men whose presses had been broken were taking their revenge. This is only a detail, but it was one which indicated how each person used whatever means he had at hand in default of proper arms.

The news, as will be seen, was not bad, but there was nothing decisive about it yet. The people, the bourgeoisie, young lads, had flung themselves passionately into the insurrection; it was the financial circles and those in high places in the army and the aristocracy who hung back. M. Dumoulin had been seen in his plumed hat, with his great sword by his side, haranguing in the rue Montmartre; and Colonel Dufys, dressed as one of the people, with a scarf round his head, had been seen urging on the insurgents; but M. de Rémusat was still suffering from a feverish attack at the *Globe* offices, and M. Thiers and M. Mignet were at Montmorency, at the house of Madame de Courchamp, whilst M. Cousin talked of the white flag as the only one that could save France; M. Charles Dupin, meeting Étienne Arago under one of the pavilions by the Institut, had exclaimed, with tears in his eyes, seeing him with a gun in his hand—

"Oh! monsieur, has it come to this, that soldiering is your work now?"

M. Dubois, chief editor of the *Globe*, had given up his editorship; M. Sebastiani was for keeping in orderly legal ways; M. Alexandre de Girardin protested that it suited France best to have the Bourbons without the Ultras; Carrel loudly condemned the folly of those citizens who attacked the military; then, finally, when the people and bourgeoisie and the youths from the colleges were shedding their blood freely and without stint, MM. Laffitte, Mauguin, Casimir Périer, Lobau and Gérard were satisfied with trying to draw up a measure of conciliation with the man who was firing grapeshot over Paris!

If, next day, things did not settle themselves more favourably, they would certainly become worse. There were not really more than from twelve to thirteen thousand men in Paris; but there were fifty thousand within a radius of twenty-five to thirty leagues, and the semaphores, which flourished their huge, mysterious arms in the eyes of all, showed that the Government had a thousand things to tell the provinces which it was particularly anxious that Paris should not know.

The upshot of all this was that it was quite possible that on the next day, the 29th, the heroes of the 27th and 28th would be obliged to clear out of the capital, if not out of France itself. With a view to this eventuality, M. Lethière inquired the state of my finances, and offered to help me in case of need (it was not the first time he had done me a similar service), but I was quite rich, for, when I was ready to start for Algiers, I had called in all my theatrical payments and was in possession of something like a thousand crowns. But M. Lethière, who knew my way of economising, declined to believe in this fortune and suspected me of boasting. It was true my fortune was under sequestration, on account of the orders my landlord had given forbidding me to enter my rooms. But this ban could not also include my friends. Therefore, as much to relieve the mind of the excellent man who offered to lend me money as to put myself in possession of my own fortune, I deputed M. Lethière's son to take a message to my servant; giving him the key of the place where I kept the purse containing my three thousand francs and my passport,—two things each equally necessary at that moment,—I begged my obliging commissionaire to effect an invasion of my premises, whether by fair means or foul, and to bring me back my purse. He was also to bring some forty bullets which he would find deposited in a cup on my bedroom mantelpiece, to replace those I had made use of during the day. He was also to be so obliging as to leave a letter at No. 7 rue de l'Université, as he passed: the letter told the person to whom it was addressed to be quite easy on my account; it also told her I was in safety, and I promised not to commit any follies. This pledged me to nothing, since it left me free to place my own limits as to what things were prudent and what were rash. Half an hour later, Lethière returned with all the commissions executed. He had not only not experienced any trouble at the hands of the concierge, but the landlord had relented—no doubt on account of the way he saw that things were turning out: he had given me permission to return on condition that I would give my word of honour not to fire from the windows of his rooms. The insurrection had wrought one great moral victory, at any rate.

I left my good, worthy friend Lethière at nine o'clock and returned home, first giving the concierge the requisite promise. He had run round the whole of the faubourg Saint-Germain, and the result of his exploration, ordered by the landlord himself, was that the whole quarter was in a state of insurrection. There was talk of a great meeting to be held next morning, in the place de l'Odéon, as a suitable centre from which they could set out to attack the various barracks or guard-houses, which usually play the same part in the midst of an insurrection that fortified places do during an invasion.

I returned, but not to go to bed, only to deposit my gun, powder and balls; I meant to spend a good part of the night in gleaning information. I felt it was urgently needful to implicate, by some means or other, those great leaders of the Opposition who had been waiting for fifteen years, and I desired to know if our friends were busy over this little piece of work. I dressed myself, therefore, for the occasion, and tried to cross the bridges. The sentries on duty at the gates of the Tuileries and the Carrousel were expressly forbidden to allow anyone whomsoever to enter without the password. Through the stone arcade could be seen the court of the Tuileries and the square of the Carrousel transformed into a vast, dark, dreary camp, silent and almost motionless. The soldiers looked more like phantoms than like men. I went along the quay, and by the place de la Révolution and the rue Saint-Honoré, as I had done in the morning. All the shops were shut, but there were lamps in most of the windows. Foot passengers were scarce and, as the noise of traffic had nearly ceased, on account of the obstruction caused by the barricades, the lugubrious, ceaseless ringing of the bell of Notre-Dame could be heard in the air, like the sound of a flight of bronze birds. As I went down the quay, I remembered Paul Fouché and his play, and I felt curious to know if he had read it to the Committee and if his drama had been received or rejected. I have already said that I knew General La Fayette. I attempted what Charras and the students of the École polytechnique had failed in—I went to call upon him. They told me he was out, which I doubted at first, and I went inside the porter's lodge and told him my name; but the honest man repeated there what he had already said to me through his little grating. I was going away very much disappointed when I saw three or four men walking in the darkness, and in the middle figure I thought I recognised that of the general. I went forward and it was he. He was leaning upon M. Carbonnel's arm; M. de Lasteyrie, I believe, came behind, talking to a servant.

"Ah! General," I exclaimed; "it is you!"

He recognised me.

"Good!" he said. "I am surprised that I have not seen you before now."

"It is not easy to gain access to you, General"; and I related all that Charras and his friends had gone through in their attempt.

"True," he said; "I found their names and ordered that they should be admitted if they returned."

"General, I cannot say whether the others will do so, but I doubt if Charras will."

"Why not?"

"Because I hear he was killed over in the direction of la Grève."

"Killed?" he exclaimed. "Ah! poor young fellow!"

"It is not surprising, General;... there was warm work there!"

"Were you there?"

"Yes, indeed! but only for a short time."

"What are you intending to do to-morrow?"

"I confess, General, that was the very question I was going to put to you."

The general leant on my arm and took a few steps forward, as though to get out of sight of his two companions.

"I mean to leave the députies," he said; "there is nothing to be done with them."

"Then why not move without them?"

"Let people drive me to it and I am ready to act."

"Shall I repeat that to my friends?"

"You may."

"Adieu, General!"

He kept hold of my arm.

"Don't get yourself killed...."

"I will try not."

"In any case, no matter how things turn out, manage to let me see you again."

"I can't promise you that, General, unless...."

"Come, come," the general said; "*au revoir!*"

And he went into his house.

I ran off to Étienne Arago, No. 10 rue de Grammont. All the Revolutionary leaders were gathered at his house. The day had been a hard one, but, thanks to Joubert's library, to Charles Teste's *Petite-Jacobinière* and to Coste, who had spent between three and four thousand francs in buying bread and wine to distribute among the fighters, the insurrection had spread to all parts of the town. I told Étienne I had seen the general and reported what he had said, word for word.

"Come, let us go to the *National*!" he said.

And to the *National* we went.

Taschereau was busy preparing to make a sublime forgery: he and Charles Teste and Béranger concocted a Provisional Government composed of La Fayette, Gérard and the Duc de Choiseul. He did still more: he issued a proclamation which he signed with their three names. He had first chosen Laffey de Pompières as the third member of their Government, but Béranger had had this name erased in order to substitute that of the Duc de Choiseul in its stead. Thus, besides preparing the Revolution by his chansons, Béranger took an active part in it personally. We shall soon see that he was the principal agent in its denouement.

Next day, the list of the Provisional Government was to be stuck up on all the walls of Paris, and the first proclamation of this Government was to appear in the *Constitutionnel*. I need hardly say that the honest *Constitutionnel* was sincere, and that it thought Taschereau's three calligraphic attempts were authentic and legal signatures. Thereupon, I entered my lodgings with an easier mind: as I was quite knocked up with my day's work, I slept as sound as a top through the tolling of Notre-Dame and the intermittent popping of belated stray shots.

CHAPTER VIII

Invasion of the Artillery Museum—Armour of François I.—Charles IX.'s arquebuse—La place de l'Odéon—What Charras had been doing—The uniform of the École polytechnique—Millotte—The prison Montaigu—The barracks of l'Estrapade—D'Hostel—A Bonapartist—Riding master Chopin—Lothon—The general in command

---

I was awakened next morning by my servant Joseph. He was standing by my bedside calling me with ever increasing loudness.

"Monsieur!... Monsieur!!... Monsieur!!!..."

At the third *Monsieur*, I groaned, rubbed my eyes and sat up. "Well," I asked, "what is the matter?"

"Oh, don't you hear, monsieur?" Joseph exclaimed, holding his head with his hands.

"How should I hear, you idiot? I was asleep."

"But fighting is going on all round us, monsieur!"

"Really?"

He opened the window.

"Listen! it sounds as if it were in the courtyard."

And, indeed, the firing seemed to me to come from no very distant point.

"The deuce!" I said, "where does it come from?"

"From Saint-Thomas-d'Aquin, monsieur."

"What! from the church itself?"

"No, from the Artillery Museum.... Monsieur knows that a post is stationed there."

"Ah! true," I exclaimed, "the Artillery Museum! I will go there."

"What! Monsieur will go there?"

"Certainly."

"Oh, good Heavens!"

"Quick, help me!... A glass of Madeira or Alicante wine!... Oh! the wretches! they will pillage everything!"

That, indeed, was the thought which preoccupied my mind, and that was what made me run to the place where I heard the firing going on. I remembered the archæological treasures that I had seen and handled, one after another, in the studies I had written on Henri III., Henri IV. and Louis XIII., and I saw them all being scattered among the hands of people who did not know their value: marvellous rich treasures of art being given to the first comer who would exchange them for a pound of tobacco or a packet of cartridges. I was ready in five minutes and darted off in the direction of Saint-Thomas-d'Aquin. For the third time, the assailants had been repulsed. This was easily explained: they were madly attacking the Museum by the two openings made by the rue du Bac and the rue Saint-Dominique. The firing of the soldiers raked the two streets and swept them clean with deplorable facility. I looked at the houses in the rue du Bac, which on both sides formed the corner of the rue Gribauval, and I judged that their backs must look upon the place Saint-Thomas-d'Aquin, and that from their upper storeys one could easily dominate the post of the Museum of Artillery. I confided to the combatants the plan suggested to me by the view of the position: it was instantly adopted by them. I knocked at the door of one of two houses, No. 35 rue du Bac, and it was opened after a long wait; still, it did open, in the end, and eight to ten armed men entered with me and we rushed upstairs to the higher storeys. I and three or four other fellows reached an attic, which was rounded off at the top to fit the shape of the roof above it, and here I established myself with as much safety as if I had been behind the parapet of a bastion.

Then firing began, but with quite different results. In ten minutes the post had lost five or six of its men. Suddenly, all the soldiers disappeared, the firing died down. This must, we thought, be some kind of ambuscade, so we hesitated before quitting our intrenchments. But the porter of the Museum soon appeared at the door making unmistakable signs of peace So we went down. The soldiers had scaled the walls and run away over the surrounding courts and gardens. A portion of the insurgents was already crowding up the corridors when I reached the Museum.

"For God's sake, friends," I cried, "respect the armour!"

"What! Why should we respect it?"

"I like that joke," replied one of the men to whom I addressed myself. "Why, to take the weapons is the very reason we are here!" he said.

It then occurred to me that, of course, this must have been the sole object of the attack, and that there would be no means of saving the magnificent collection from pillage. I considered: the only thing left to do was to take my share of the most valuable of the armour.

One of two things would happen: either they would keep the arms or bring them back to the Museum. In either case, it was better that I should take charge of the precious things, rather than anyone else. If I kept them, they would be in the hands of a man who knew how to appreciate them. If they were to be restored, they would be in the hands of one who would give them up. I ran to the best place, where there was an equestrian trophy of the Renaissance period. I seized a shield, a helmet and a sword which were known to have belonged to François I., also a magnificent arquebuse which had belonged, according to the same tradition, to Charles IX., and had been used by him to fire upon the Huguenots. This tradition has become almost historic, on account of the quatrain which the arquebuse carries, inlaid in silver letters, on its barrel, forming one single line from the breech to the sighting-point:—

"Pour mayntenir la foy,
Je suis belle et fidèle;
Aux ennemis du Roy
Je suis belle et cruelle!"

I put the helmet on my head, the shield on my arm; I hung the sword by my side, put the arquebuse on my shoulder, and so made my way, bending under their weight, to the rue de l'Université. I nearly fell when I reached the height of my fourth floor. If these were, indeed, the very shield and buckler that François I. had worn at Marignan, and if he remained fourteen hours in the saddle with these in addition to his other armour, I could believe in the prowess of Ogier the Dane and Roland and the four sons of Aymon.

"Oh! monsieur," Joseph exclaimed, when he caught sight of me, "where have you been, and whatever is all that old iron?"

I did not attempt to correct Joseph's ideas with respect to my booty; it would only have been waste of time. I simply told him to help me to take off the helmet, which nearly suffocated me. I laid them all down on my bed and rushed back for more of this splendid quarry. I brought back next the cuirass, axe and the bulk of the arms. I gave all my fine trophies back, later, to the Artillery Museum, and I still possess the letter of the former Director, thanking me for their restitution, and giving me free entry on days not open to the general public. It was a curious spectacle to see that huge removal of the Museum. Everyone took what suited him best, but it is only fair to say that these worthy fellows were much more careful to select arms they thought most suitable to fight with than sumptuously wrought ones. So nearly the whole of the collection of old muskets, flint and percussion caps, from the time of Louis XIV. to our own day, disappeared. One man took away a rampart gun that must have weighed at least a hundred and fifty pounds; four others dragged a piece of iron cannon with which they meant to attack the Louvre. I found the man who had taken the rampart gun, a couple of hours later, lying unconscious upon the quay. He had rammed his gun with two handfuls of powder and from twelve to fifteen balls; then, from one side of the Seine, leaning it up against the parapet, he had fired upon a regiment of cuirassiers which was marching along by the Louvre. He had made some cruel gaps in the regiment, but the recoil of the gun had flung him ten feet backwards, dislocating his shoulder and breaking his jaw. Before I found him, I had witnessed several scenes characteristic enough to be worth putting down here. Intoxication from wine, brandy or rum is nothing to that caused by the smell of powder, the noise of firing and the sight of blood. I can understand a man flying at the first shot of gun or cannon, but I cannot understand anyone who has once tasted fire leaving before it ceases. At all events, this was the effect it was beginning to have upon myself.

Delanoue, whom I met, who was hunting all over the place for a gun, told me there was going to be a rallying of forces on the place de l'Odéon. I had already heard of this gathering the day before. Unfortunately, I had only my gun with me and I did not wish to part with it; I therefore mentioned to Delanoue the Artillery Museum as a place where he might find what he was in search of, and then I set off at a run down the rue de Grenelle. The place de l'Odéon was blocked and there must have been something like five or six hundred men there. Two or three pupils from the École polytechnique were in command of some companies. In one of these uniforms, I recognised Charras, whom I had seen dressed the previous day as a civilian.

So he was neither killed nor wounded. This is the story of what happened, which had made people believe he was dead.

As will be seen, he had not wasted his time since the day before, and particularly since the morning. When he had parted from Carrel and me, he went through the faubourg Saint-Germain, where he had done his utmost to procure a gun; but, on 28 July 1830, a gun was as scarce as Juvenal's *rara avis*. He had heard of, the *monsieur* who was giving away gunpowder at the small door of the Institut and had gone to have an interview with the worthy citizen. The *monsieur* not only refused to give him a gun, but went still further and refused him any powder because he had no gun.

Charras next made this sapient observation—

"I will go where there is fighting, I will put myself in the midst of the fighters, I will constitute myself the legatee of the first man who falls dead and take possession of his gun."

In consequence of that resolution, he had gone along the quai des Orfèvres and met the 15th Light Infantry, with whom he held a conversation; perhaps they were the very same I had talked with; but, as he was alone, unarmed and had kept his hands in his pockets, they had let him pass through. When through, Charras gained the Pont Notre-Dame and, from thence, the suspension bridge. Now we know that the insurrection was raging furiously on the latter bridge. Charras arrived half an hour earlier than I did and waited. He did not have to wait long, for a man was soon struck in the eye by a bullet, and rolled at his feet. Charras seized the dead man's gun. A street urchin, who was probably watching for the same opportunity, also ran up, but was too late. Armed with his gun, Charras was still not much better off, for he had neither powder nor shot.

"I have some," the urchin said, and he drew a packet of fifteen cartridges from his pocket.

"Let me have them," said Charras.

"No.... We will divide them, if you like."

"All right, we will."

"Here are seven, then; but let me use the gun after you?"

"I suppose so, since that was our agreement."

Charras scrupulously fired only his seven cartridges, then honourably passed the gun to the urchin and withdrew behind the parapet; from actor he became spectator and, in the latter capacity, he sheltered himself as best he could. The street lad fired four cartridges, and then the charge came that we had witnessed from a distance. The lad rushed on the bridge with the rest, and Charras, although unarmed, followed the stream. I have previously described the effect of the three successive discharges. Charras was spun round under the blast of that whirlwind of iron, and clung on to his neighbour to keep himself from falling; but the man had been mortally wounded and fell, dragging Charras with him. Hence had arisen the rumour that he was killed. By good fortune, however, he escaped safe and sound, but, not feeling too sure of the fact, he tested it by reaching the other side of the quay and threading his way through a little street in the shelter of which he was able, without interruption, to feel himself all over. As for the urchin and his gun, he had to accept the inevitable: the lad had disappeared like Romulus in the storm, or Curtius in the gulf, or Empedocles in the volcano! Charras then began to wonder what possible use a man could be without a gun, or who did not know where to procure one. A band of patriots, unarmed, like himself, happening to pass at the same moment, seemed to have come for the express purpose of answering his question.

"Well, citizen," one of the men said, "will you come along with us to sound the tocsin from Saint-Séverin?"

"All right!" Charras replied, it being a matter of indifference to him where he went, so long as he took some part in being useful to the cause. And he went with them to Saint-Séverin. The doors were shut; they knocked at all, little and great, from the door for marriages and baptisms down to the door of the last Sacrament. In cases like this, decisions are quickly arrived at: they decided to burst the doors open, as they would not open of their own accord; they tore away a beam from a house that was being built and a dozen men carried it to serve as a battering-ram. At the third charge delivered by this huge implement against the door, the locks and bolts gave way. The sacristan arrived upon the scene and opened the door altogether, just as a fourth blow was going to break it in. When the door was opened, they soon set the bell ringing, and Charras's work at Saint-Séverin was concluded. He went to join a party of friends in the Latin Quarter, with whom he spent the night constructing a plan.

Now, the uniform worn by the students of the École polytechnique had been very much looked down upon before the insurrection was declared, but had gone up in reputation very considerably as the insurrection advanced. The plan made during the night was to go at daybreak in search of uniforms of the École polytechnique. So, about four in the morning, Charras, with a friend of his, called Lebeuf, rang at the porter's gate. The rise in sentiment had made its way even to the École, and both porter and professors gave the two rebels a warm reception, shaking hands with them and giving them the clothes they asked for.

I remember one small incident: Charras, having found a coat, apparently was not able to find trousers to match; for, with a blue coat, he wore grey trousers, which, as a uniform, was rather meagre. The two friends thus being fitted with uniforms and particularly with hats—the hat always plays an important rôle in insurrections—they made their way to the place de l'Odéon. They heard, *en route*, that guns were being distributed in the rue de Tournon. Indeed, the barracks of the Gendarmerie had just been captured, and muskets, pistols, sabres and swords were being distributed in a fairly orderly manner.

Charras and Lebeuf joined the queue, but, when they reached the office, those in the barracks would only give them swords, because they said that students from the École polytechnique were all officers by right and, in that capacity, were destined to command detachments; they ought, therefore, to receive swords and not guns.

Not even the most earnest entreaties of these two young people were able to change the programme—they would only give them swords and no other arms. But a student of colossal stature and herculean strength did not accept this improvised lawmaking so easily as Lebeuf and Charras had done: he seized the distributor by the throat and began to strangle him, telling him he would not let him go until he had a gun. The distributor seemed to consider the argument sound, for he hastened to give a gun to the merry blade who could put into action so sensible an application of that branch of philosophy we call logic; and the student went away armed to his own liking. This was Millotte who, afterwards, became a representative of the People and who sat in the Legislative Assembly with Lamartine and our friend Noël Parfait. Millotte is now one of our most respected exiles. In virtue of his uniform, his sword and the rights possessed by the students of the École to become officers, Charras took the command of a troop of a hundred and fifty men. A drummer and standard-bearer put the finishing touch to this troop. Then the question was where to go? A voice shouted—

"To the prison Montaigu, place du Panthéon!"

So Charras and his troop started for that destination.

Revolutions have their mysterious winds which blow men to one point or another without any apparent reason; they are the waterspouts that blow up from under the ocean and they go south or north, east or west, how or why nobody knows. It is the breath of God which guides them. At the prison Montaigu, they found a hundred and fifty men under arms, ready to defend themselves. A brewer from the rue Saint-Antoine, named Maes, was there—another Santerre—with some sixty insurgents. He was on horseback and wore the old uniform of the National Guard. The struggle had threatened to become hot, and they were trying to come to terms.

"Hulloa! Captain," cried Charras, "will you come to me, or would you rather I came to you?"

"Come to me, monsieur," the captain replied.

"I have your parole?"

"Yes."

Charras then approached him, and there ensued a dialogue between them, the offspring of their peculiar situation, which could not have taken place under other circumstances—a dialogue in which Charras tried to prove to the captain that it would be far more advantageous and honourable and patriotic for him to join the people's side or, at the very least, to lend them guns. The captain did not seem to understand Charras's logic so well as the distributor of muskets in the rue de Tournon had understood that of Millotte. Charras redoubled his eloquence, but made no headway; yet if he failed to advance, his men did not: they came up nearer, little by little.

The reader knows the true Parisian, who never gives up his end but presses towards it out of curiosity or passion; he slips through the hands of police, sentries and squadrons, dragging one foot after the other, with honied tones and wooing gesture, part cat, part fox; then, if you want to keep him back, he is soon far away! When you want to stop him, he is already past you! And, as soon as he feels himself out of your reach, his sole answer to your reproaches is a mocking gesture or a sarcastic remark.

In such fashion had Charras's men slipped past the sentinels and come up imperceptibly to their commander, and, consequently, nearer to the soldiers; so effectively was this movement executed that, in five minutes' time, before Charras had himself perceived them, they were within ten paces of their adversaries and ready for a hand-to-hand tussle with them. Whether it was the mingling of the forces or the names of Jena, Austerlitz and Marengo of which Charras reminded them; whether it was the tricolour ribbons, with their stirring tones of colour, that floated before his eyes; or whether he really felt a brotherly sympathy extended to him, which decided the officer to capitulate, Charras did not know; but he realised that a capitulation was arrived at, that his troop obtained fifty guns and the captain's word of honour that he and his soldiers would remain neutral. True, the captain was inexorable in his refusal of cartridges; but Providence did not stop thus half-way: it had given the guns, it was also to bestow the requisite cartridges.

The fifty guns were distributed among those of Charras's men who had no firearms, and among those of a fresh troop that had come up meanwhile, who were in the same plight. This new troop was commanded by another student of the École polytechnique called d'Hostel. The division made, again the question arose as to where they were to go.

"To the Estrapade!" cried a voice.

"To the Estrapade!" all the voices repeated in unison.

So off they rushed towards the Estrapade.

Our Parisian readers will know the position of the barracks of the Estrapade, and that they are approached by a narrow street which is easily defended. There were nearly four hundred men; quite enough, in like circumstances, to attack Metz or Valenciennes or Mont-Saint-Michel; but they were so elated with their recent negotiations at the place du Panthéon that they decided to try the same tactics in the rue de l'Estrapade. This time d'Hostel proposed himself as negotiator; for, he said, he had accomplices inside the place. He advanced with a handkerchief in his hand, leaving his gun with one of his men. They held a parley between the street and the first floor; but this was too high up to be heard, so d'Hostel cleared the distance between himself and his interlocutors by suddenly climbing up the wall. How did he do that? It was a miracle to those who watched his ascent! D'Hostel was extremely adroit, and renowned at the École for his gymnastic feats. In an instant, he had reached one of the windows on the first floor, he was lifted in by his arms and found himself inside the barracks, where he was swallowed up like the fiends in English theatres which disappear through trap-doors. Ten minutes later, he reappeared, clad in the coat and leather cap of the officer, whilst the latter wore the uniform of a pupil of the École polytechnique, with the three-cornered hat in his hand, and bowed to the people. The game was won! The square resounded with vivats and applause. The soldiers abandoned the barracks and surrendered a hundred of their guns. This ruse, executed by Charras and d'Hostel, was worthy of winning them the posts of ambassadors to London and St. Petersburg! But, unluckily, the deed either did not reach the ears of the Government or was not properly appreciated by it, so they sent instead, to those two cities, M. le Prince de Talleyrand and M. le Maréchal Maison, who confined themselves to committing stupid acts.

Full of pride at this second triumph of theirs, Charras and d'Hostel reached the place de l'Odéon. I was struck with the ease with which drums seem to multiply during a time of Revolution; they appear to ooze out of walls and rise out of the pavements—Charras and d'Hostel had about fifteen between them. At the same time that we reached the place de l'Odéon, a piece of cannon that had been taken from the post was being drawn through the rue des Fossés-Monsieur-le-Prince by five men, three of whom were firemen; next came a carriage, containing three barrels of powder from the powder magazine at the Jardin des Plantes; I think it was driven by Liédot, who has since become an artillery captain. The barrels were broken open and the distribution of their contents begun. Everybody had some, either in his coat pocket or handkerchief or cap or tobacco pouch. They were smoking amidst all this, incredible as it may appear. How Jean Bart would have shuddered from head to foot! But they very soon discovered that all this powder was useless and that the best thing to do with it would be to make it into cartridges. This was the more feasible since they had just received two or three thousand bullets from the passage Dauphine. Four men were occupied in moulding them out of the lead of the gutters, in a tavern to the left of the square as you come to it from the rue de l'Odéon. The only thing they lacked was paper. However, all the windows facing the square were wide open and they only had to cry out "Paper is wanted!" and soon the air was flecked with projectiles of every shape and description, but of the same material: paper fell in exercise-books, in reams and in volumes. I was very nearly knocked down by a *Gradus ad Parnassum!*

Amongst the crowds were about a hundred old soldiers, who set to work and, in less than an hour made and distributed three thousand cartridges. The spectacle must have been seen in order to realise the animation, high spirits and gaiety that prevailed. Everybody called out something, whether "Vive la République!" or "Vive la Charte!" One man of Charras's band made himself hoarse with shouting "Vive Napoléon II.!" The oft-repeated cry at length exciting Charras, who was already, at that period, a strong Republican, he went to this Bonapartist and said—

"Look here, do you suppose we are fighting for Napoleon II.?"

"You can fight for whom you like," the man replied, "but that's the man I mean to fight for!"

"You have the right to, if you wish it, of course.... But if you fight for him you must enlist in some other troop than this."

"Oh! that will suit me all right," said the man: "there are plenty of engagements going on nowadays!"

He therefore left Charras's ranks and went to seek service in a troop led by a chief who was of less decided opinions.

At this very moment, by some strange coincidence, a man called Chopin, who owned the stables of the Luxembourg, arrived at a gallop at the place de l'Odéon; he was clad in a buttoned-up frock-coat, wore a three-cornered hat and rode a white horse. He pulled up in the very centre of the square, with one hand held behind his back. The resemblance to Napoleon was so striking and extraordinary that the whole crowd, not a single member of which had taken sides with the expelled Bonapartist, began to shout with one accord and simultaneously, "Vive l'Empereur!" One good woman of seventy took the joke quite seriously and fell on her knees, making the sign of the cross, and exclaiming—

"Oh! Jesus! I shall not die, then, before I have seen him once more!..."

If Chopin had desired to put himself at the head of the six to eight hundred men there present, it is probable that he could have marched straight off to Vienna.

Charras was furious, whilst I completely forgot the political situation of the moment and became solely a philosophic student of humanity. I only needed a tub and Laïs and I could have established myself there for ever in the place de l'Odéon, as Diogenes established himself in the gymnasium of Corinth.

But a serious discussion drew me from my dreams. They wanted to make Charras general-in-chief and he would not take the position. He offered the citizens Lothon, a tall, fine young fellow, a combination of Hercules and Antinous, as a suitable candidate, instead; his principal reason being that he was on foot while Lothon rode on horseback; therefore, he considered Lothon had far more claim to the generalship. And, in truth, no general-in-chief was ever seen afoot. But Lothon excused himself fiercely from being appointed to this high post. For all this, he was on the point of being obliged to yield, when a gentleman came up to him and whispered—

"Oh! monsieur, if you will not be general-in-chief, let me take your place.... I am an ex-captain and I think I have a right to this honour."

Never did ambition display itself at a more fitting opportunity.

"Oh! monsieur," Lothon replied, "you will indeed render me a welcome service!"

Then, addressing the crowd, he asked—

"You want a general-in-chief?"

"Yes, yes!" was repeated on all sides.

"Well, then, I introduce this gentleman to you ... he is an ex-captain who is *covered with wounds* and who would much like to be your general-in-command."

"Bravo!" a hundred voices shouted.

"Pardon me for covering you with wounds, my dear monsieur," said Lothon, as he stepped to the ground and presented his horse to the newly elected chief; "but I thought it the surest method of getting you promoted above the intermediate ranks."

"Oh! monsieur," the delighted captain said, "there is no harm done!"

Then he addressed the crowd—

"Well," he asked, "are we ready?"

"Yes! yes! yes!"

"Then forward, march! Beat drums!"

And the drums began to beat, and they all went down the rue de l'Odéon singing *la Marseillaise*. At the Bussy crossing, from some strategic manœuvre unknown to me, the troop divided itself into three. One part went towards the rue Sainte-Marguerite, another to the rue Dauphine and the third went straight on: I was among the latter. We had to approach the Louvre by the Pont des Arts, in order to take the bull by the horns. It was on coming out on the quay that I found the man with the rampart gun leant up against the wall, groaning, both his shoulder and his jaw dislocated.

Oh! I must not forget to say that at every street-corner I had seen stuck up on the walls bills announcing the nomination of the Provisional Government and the proclamation by MM. La Fayette, Gérard and de Choiseul calling the people to arms. What a singular effect it would have produced on those three gentlemen if they had been in my place and read what I read!

CHAPTER IX

Aspect of the Louvre—Fight on the Pont des Arts—The
dead and wounded—A cannon ball for myself—Madame
Guyet-Desfontaines—Return from the Babylone
barracks—Charras's cockade—The taking of the
Tuileries—A copy of *Christine*—Quadrille danced in the
Tuileries court—The men *who made the Revolution of 1830*

It was thirty-five minutes past ten in the morning by the Institut clock. The
Louvre presented a formidable appearance. All the windows of the great
picture galleries were open, and at each window there were two Swiss Guards
armed with guns. The Charles IX. balcony was defended by Swiss who had
made a rampart with mattresses. And then, behind, through the gratings of
the two gardens that are, I believe, named the garden of the Infante and the
garden of the Queen, we could see drawn up a double line of Swiss. In the
foreground, a regiment of cuirassiers wound in and out along the parapet,
like a great snake with scales of steel and gold, whose head had already
entered the Tuileries gate, whilst its tail still trailed along the quai de l'École.
In the background, away in the distance, stood the Louvre Colonnade,
almost invisible from the cloud of smoke which arose by reason of the attack
made upon it from the small streets surrounding the church of Saint-
Germain-l'Auxerrois. On the right, the Tricolour was floating from Notre-
Dame and the Hôtel de Ville. And the breezes carried the trembling
vibrations of the tocsin. A fiery sun burned high in the white, hot sky. They
were firing all along the quay, especially from the windows and door of a
little guard-house, situated by the river-side, opposite the point where the rue
des Saints-Pères runs into the quay Malaquais. However, both attack and
defence were weak: everyone seemed to be there because he thought it was
his duty, and people were mauling one another to pass the time, till some
leader came along to organise sides.

Our arrival created a diversion just when interest had begun to flag. There
were about a hundred and twenty of us. We divided ourselves in half
(*Égaillâmes*, as they say in the Vendean patois), one part going back by the
Pont Neuf side and the other going along by the Palais Mazarin, as far as the
small guard-house already referred to. I first of all settled myself under one
of the turnstile shelters, but I soon saw that I should be constantly disturbed
by people coming and going past. I therefore made for the fountain and
installed myself behind the bronze lion that was nearest to the rue Mazarine.
I had the great entrance gate of the palace, therefore, on my right, which, like
that of the Jubilee at St. Peter's in Rome, is only opened once in fifty years. I

had the small door leading to the apartments of persons who lodged at the Institut on my left. Thus, in front of me was the Pont des Arts, which presented an object to my view that inspired me with some disquiet, for it looked very like a piece of cannon in position. It had a magnificent target before it: no less than a whole regiment of cuirassiers presenting its flank! And, behind these, the Swiss in their red coats with their white lace facings, not two hundred yards off. The mere thought of the situation made one's mouth water; to dwell on it made the perspiration stand out on one's forehead.

I have elsewhere described my sensations when confronted with danger—I approach it at first reluctantly, but very quickly familiarise myself with it. Now, my apprenticeship of the previous day upon the quay Notre-Dame, and of the morning following at the Artillery Museum, had removed my first feelings of fear. Moreover, I ought to say that my position was a good one and that it would take either a very extreme chance, or a very clever marksman, for a bullet to find me out behind my lion. I therefore watched with much coolness the scene I am about to describe.

Out of the hundred or hundred and twenty combatants, the uniforms of two soldiers of the National Guard were hardly noticeable. Most of the men who composed the gathering in the midst of which I found myself were of the lower classes—shopmen and students and street lads. All were armed with muskets or fowling-pieces, the latter in the proportion of one to fifteen. The street boys had either pistols or sabres or swords, and one of the most zealous of them had only a bayonet. Usually, it was the street lads who marched in front and were the first in any row; whether from recklessness or ignorance of danger I cannot say. Probably it was the influence of young hot blood, which from the age of eighteen pulses in the veins of man at the rate of from seventy-five to eighty-five beats to the minute; then gradually calms down, but, with each expiring pulsation, deposits at the bottom of every heart a shameful vice or an evil thought.

While the regiment of cuirassiers was passing, the fusillade from the Royal troops was mild and, although very active on our side, it must be confessed it was without much effect. They were hampered by the line of horse soldiers which was passing between them and us. But the last rider had scarcely passed the second garden gate before the real music began. The heat was insupportable and there was not a breath of air stirring. The smoke from the guns of the Swiss Guards, therefore, only cleared away very slowly; soon the whole of the Louvre was surrounded by a girdle of smoke which hid the Royal troops from our eyes as completely as the painted clouds, which rise from the wings of a theatre at the epilogue to a drama, hide the apotheosis being prepared at the back of the stage from the gaze of the spectators. It was only wasting shot to attempt to pierce that curtain of smoke. Every now and then, however, a hole was made, and one could catch a glimpse, through the clearing, of the white facings on the red coats and the gilded plates on the bearskin caps of the Swiss Guard.

This was the opportunity the true marksmen waited for, and it was very seldom that one did not see two or three men totter and disappear behind their comrades. From our side, during the first attack, we had one man killed and two wounded. The man that was killed was hit in the top of the forehead whilst kneeling behind the parapet to take aim. He leapt up as though on springs, took a few steps backwards, dropped his musket, turned round twice, fighting the air with his arms, then fell on his face. One of the two who were wounded was a street lad. His injury was in the flesh of the thigh. He had not hid behind the parapet, but had danced on top of it with a pocket pistol in his hand. He went off, hopping away upon one leg, and disappeared down the rue de Seine. The other man's wound was more serious. He had received a ball in the stomach. He fell in a sitting posture, with both hands pressed on the wounded part, which scarcely bled at all. The hæmorrhage was probably internal. He was seized with thirst in about ten minutes and dragged himself towards me, but, when he reached the fountain, he had not sufficient strength to get to the basin and he called me to his assistance. I gave him a hand and helped him to climb up. He drank more than ten mouthfuls in as many minutes; and between the drinks he said—

"Oh! the beggars! They have not missed me!"

And when, from time to time, he saw me put my gun to my shoulder, he added—

"Be sure you don't miss them!"

Finally, at the end of half an hour, this useless fusillading was discontinued. Two or three men exclaimed—

"To the Louvre! To the Louvre!"

It was madness, for it was evident enough that there were only a hundred men or so to deal with two or three hundred of the Swiss Guard. But, under circumstances like those I am describing, people do not stop to think of the most reasonable things to be done; since the very work they are engaged in is almost itself an act of insanity, it is generally some impossible feat they determine to attempt.

A drummer beat the charge and was the first to dash upon the bridge. All the street lads followed him, shouting, "Vive la Charte!" and the main body followed them. I ought to confess that I formed no part of the main body. As I said, from my slightly elevated post I could distinguish a gun in position. Now, while it could do nothing but scatter grapeshot haphazard, it had kept perfectly quiet; but, directly the assailants debouched on to the bridge, it was unmasked: it showed itself in its true colours.... I saw the smoking match approach the touchhole, I effaced myself behind my lion, and, at the same instant, I heard the sound of the explosion and the whistle of grapeshot as it splintered the façade of the Institut. The stone broken by the projectiles fell in a perfect shower round me. Identically the same thing happened on the Pont des Arts as took place on the suspension bridge. All the men who were stationed in the narrow space whirled round; only three or four continued their march forward and five or six fell, twenty-five or thirty stood firm and the rest took to their heels. A platoon fire succeeded the cannon, and bullets sang all round me; soon, my wounded comrade uttered a sigh: a second bullet had finished him off. Almost immediately after the platoon firing, the cannon roared out again and the storm of shot passed over my head a second time. At the second charge, there was no further thought of advancing, and two men, regarding the water as safer than the planks of the bridge, leapt into the Seine and swam to the quay of the Institut. The rest came back with lightning speed, like a flock of frightened birds, and rushed down the rue Mazarine, the rue des Petits-Augustins and the sort of blind alley which skirts the Mint.

The quay was instantly deserted, and, though I am by no means vain, I may state that this third cannon-shot was fired for me alone. I had a long time previously formed my plan of retreat, and I based it on the small door of the Institut, which was on my left. Scarcely had the gun been fired a third time, before the smoke had dispersed and allowed my manœuvre to be seen, I rushed out and knocked at the door with loud blows with the butt-end of my gun. It opened without keeping me long waiting: I will pay that much justice to the porter, though, generally, in Revolutionary times, porters are not so smart. I slipped in through the half-opened doorway into shelter. As the porter was shutting the door, a bullet pierced it, but without wounding him. When inside, I had quite a choice of friends: I went upstairs to see Madame Guyet-Desfontaines. I should mention that, at first sight, my appearance did not produce the effect I expected. They did not immediately know me; then, when they had recognised 'me, they considered me pretty badly dressed. My readers will recollect how I had arrayed myself for the occasion. I went and fetched my gun, which I had left outside the door for fear of frightening Madame Guyet and her daughter. The gun soon explained matters. Directly she recognised me, Madame Guyet became her charmingly sprightly, animated self, in spite of the gravity of the situation: she is, in this respect, quite incorrigible. I was nearly dead with hunger, and especially with thirst; I thereupon unaffectedly made my wants known to my hosts. They brought me a bottle of Bordeaux, which I drank almost at one draught. They also brought me a huge bowl of chocolate, and that disappeared also. I believe I must have eaten everyone else's breakfast!

"Ah!" I said, parodying Napoleon's remark on his return from Russia, as I stretched myself in a big arm-chair, "it is much better here than behind the Institut lion!"

Of course, I had to give an account of my Iliad, which, up to then, consisted of one victory and two retreats. True, the last retreat—with the exception of the embarrassment of having ten thousand men under me—might be likened to that of Xenophon. But, on the other hand, the first might be compared with a Waterloo. I made honourable mention of the lion, which had probably saved my life, and which possessed, under the circumstances, that superiority over Androcles' lion, that it was not repaying a kind act done to it. The upshot of the delightful welcome I received (the minutest details whereof I can still remember, after the lapse of more than twenty-two years) was that Madame Guyet-Desfontaines' house all but became to me what Capua was to Hannibal two thousand years before. However, with a little moral courage, I had the advantage over the conqueror of Trebia, Cannes and Trasimène of tearing myself away in time from the delights that were spread before me.

I went away by the little gate opening into the rue Mazarine and regained my lodgings in the rue de l'Université. This time I was received by my porter as a hero; the position of affairs soon declared itself. Instead of showing me the door, it was now a question of raising an Arc de triomphe for me! Joseph was rubbing up the armour belonging to François I.

"Ah! monsieur," he said, "how beautiful it is! I had not discovered all the little absurdities that there are on it."

He meant the battle scenes.

I went home to change my shirt (pardon this detail, it will be seen, later, that it was not without importance in my story), and also to renew my stock of powder and bullets. But I had not had time to take off my jacket before I heard a great uproar in the street outside. It was made by Charras and his troop returning from the barracks in the rue de Babylone. There had been a frightful slaughter: after half an hour's siege, they had been obliged to set fire to the barracks, to dislodge the Swiss Guard. They carried the red coats of the vanquished enemy at the point of their bayonets as victorious trophies. Charras (he must remember the circumstance well enough to-day, for he is not one of those who forget) wore a sleeve from some Swiss Guard's coat in place of the cockade, which was fastened to the top of his three-cornered hat and fell coquettishly over his shoulder. They were all marching upon the Tuileries, with drums to the fore.

At the same moment, the cries increased, coming from the direction of the château. I turned my eyes in the direction whence they came and, from my window, which looked out on the rue du Bac, I saw thousands of letters and papers fluttering into the Tuileries garden. It looked as though all the wood pigeons about the place were taking flight. It was the correspondence of Napoleon, of Louis XVIII. and of Charles X. being scattered to the winds. The Tuileries had been taken. Although I was not Crillon, I was seized with a sudden desire to go and hang myself. Now, a man in that state of mind does not think it worth while changing his shirt. So I replaced my jacket and rushed downstairs. I rejoined the tail of the column just as it entered the Tuileries by the gate at the water-side. On the pavilion in the centre, the Tricolour had replaced the White standard. Joubert, the patriot of the Dauphine passage, had planted it on the roof and had then fainted away, from fatigue or joy, or probably both combined. The gates of the Carrousel had been forced open and people were rushing in by every door, among them hundreds of women: where did they spring from? No one who witnessed the spectacle will ever forget it. One student of the École polytechnique, named Baduel, was being drawn in triumph on a cannon. Like Achilles, he had been wounded in the heel, but, in his case, by grapeshot, and not by a poisoned arrow. Neither did he die, although he expected he should. Had he lost his life on that occasion it would not have been from his wounds, but from brain-fever, consequent on fatigue, heat and the exhaustion he had felt during the triumph they had compelled him to submit to, in spite of his remonstrances, by reason of the high courage he had shown. Another student, with a bullet through his chest, was lying on the staircase: they took him up in their arms, carried him to the first storey and laid him upon the throne embroidered with fleurs de lys, where over ten thousand of the populace seated themselves in turn, or several at a time, throughout that day. Through the windows that looked out on the garden, one could see the tail end of a regiment of Lancers, as they disappeared under the great trees. A cab was trying to catch them up; the horse was galloping fast, for, no doubt, the driver wanted to put himself under protection of the regiment.

The Tuileries was crowded: people were recognising their friends among the crowd and embracing and questioning one another—

"Where is such and such a person?"

"He is over there!"

"Where?"

"There!"

Another was wounded—or dead!

And each made a gesture as funeral oration, signifying, "It is a pity! but, bless me, he died on a grand day!"

And on they would go, from the throne-room to the king's private study, from there to the king's bedroom. The king's bed, by the way, must have been out of the common, although I never knew what went on in that room; for, to judge by the number of spectators that surrounded it and by their shouts of laughter, something outrageous must have taken place round it. Perhaps a mock wedding of Democracy with Liberty! And again the crowd moved on, each individual mingling his voice and gesticulations with those of the multitude. On they went, following those who walked ahead, pushed forward by the crowds behind. They reached the Marshals' Hall. I had never seen these rooms before, and did not see them again until the fall of King Louis-Philippe, in 1848.

During the eighteen years' reign of the Younger Branch I never set foot in the Tuileries, except to visit the Duc d'Orléans. But, be it understood, the Marsan pavilion is not in the least degree part of the Tuileries, and it was very often a reason for not going to the Tuileries if one were sent for to the Marsan pavilion. Forgive the digression, but I am glad to flout those who might say they had seen me with the king.

The crowd had, as I say, reached the Salle des Maréchaux. The frame of the portrait of M. de Bourmont, who had recently been made a marshal, already occupied its position on one of the panels; but although the name had even been printed on the frame, the portrait had not yet been inserted. In place of the canvas, by way of substitute no doubt, there was a large piece of scarlet taffetas. This was torn down and used to make the red portion of the tricolour favours which each person wore in his buttonhole. I detached a morsel which had been diverted to this end. As I was disputing with my neighbours over this strip of stuff, I heard the sound of several gunshots. They were shooting at the portrait of the Duc de Raguse in lieu of the original. Four balls had pierced the canvas, one through the head, two in the breast and the fourth through the background of the picture. A man of the people climbed up on the shoulders of a comrade and, with his knife, cut out the portrait in the shape of a medallion; then, passing his bayonet through the breast and head, he carried it as the Roman lictors used to carry the S.P.Q.R. at their triumphs. The portrait had been painted by Gérard. I went up to the man and offered him a hundred francs for his trophy.

"Oh! citizen," he said, "I would not let you have it if you offered me a thousand."

Alophe Pourrat next went up to him and offered him his gun in exchange and got the portrait. He probably has it still.

As I entered the library of the Duchesse de Berry, I noticed a copy of *Christine*, bound in purple morocco and stamped with the duchess's arms, lying upon a little work-table. I thought I had a right to appropriate it. I afterwards gave it to my cousin Félix Deviolaine; who has probably lost it. I had gone in by the pavilion de Flore and I went out by the pavilion Marsan. In the courtyard there was a quadrille of four men, dancing to the piping of a fife and a violin: it was an early Cancan that was being danced. They were dressed in court dress, with plumed hats, and the wardrobes of Mesdames les Duchesses d'Angoulême and de Berry had furnished the costumes for the masquerade. One of these men had a cashmere shawl on his shoulders worth quite a thousand crowns. It would have been perfectly safe to bet that he had not a five-franc piece in his pocket. By the end of the country dance the shawl was in tatters.

Now, how did it come to pass that the Louvre and the Tuileries and Carrousel, with their Cuirassiers and Lancers and Swiss, their Royal Guard and artillery, with three or four thousand men in garrison besides, had been taken by four or five hundred insurgents? This is what happened.

Four attacks were directed upon the Louvre: the first by the Palais-Royal; the second from the rue des Poulies, the rue des Prêtres-Saint-Germain-l'Auxerrois and the quai de l'École; the third by the Pont des Arts, and the fourth by the Pont Royal. The first was led by Lothon, whom, as it will be remembered, we left at the top of rue Guénégaud. He had been hit in the head by a bullet and had fallen unconscious in the place du Palais-Royal. The second was conducted by Godefroy Cavaignac, Joubert, Thomas, Bastide, Degousée, Grouvelle and the brothers Lebon, etc. It was they who took the Louvre, as will be seen presently. The third was that which had taken place by the Pont des Arts—the result is known. The fourth, that of the rue du Bac, did not cross the bridge in reality, until the Tuileries was taken.

We have given an account of the second attack which captured the Louvre. This success was due, in the first case, to the admirable courage shown by the assailants and, afterwards, it must be confessed, by chance, to a false manœuvre: we will call it so in consideration of the feelings of those who decline to recognise the intervention of Providence in human affairs.

One anecdote will be sufficient to give an idea of the courage of the assailants. A child of twelve had climbed, like a chimney-sweep, up one of the wooden shafts which are erected against the Colonnade to put rubbish in, and he had planted a tricolour flag on the Louvre in the face of the Swiss. Fifty shots had been fired at him and he had been lucky enough to escape without a single one disturbing him! Just at this moment, as enthusiastic shouts greeted the successful issue of the child's mad feat, the Duc de Raguse, who had concentrated his forces round the Carrousel for a last struggle, learnt that the soldiers stationed on the place Vendôme had begun to enter into communication with the people.

The capture of the place Vendôme meant the occupation of the rue de Rivoli, of the conquest of the place Louis XV.,—meant, in a word, that retreat on Saint-Cloud and Versailles was cut off. The Louvre was especially guarded by two battalions of Swiss. One alone would have been enough for its defence. So the marshal conceived the notion of replacing the troops on the place Vendôme (who, as we have just said, were threatening defection) by one of these two battalions of Swiss. He despatched his aide-de-camp, M. de Guise, to M. de Salis, who was in command of the two battalions. M. de Guise carried orders to bring back these two battalions. M. de Salis, on receipt of this order, saw no objection to carrying it out. He was the more ready to follow it, as one single battalion was enough to defend the Louvre, and that one had, indeed, been defending it successfully since the morning. The other battalion had been standing in the courtyard with arms at rest. M. de Salis next conceived the very natural idea of sending the Duc de Raguse, not the reserve battalion stationed in the courtyard, but the one which had been fighting since the morning from the balcony of Charles IX. and the windows of the picture galleries, on the Colonnade du Louvre side. He therefore commanded the fresh battalion to the place of the fatigued one. But he made this mistake—instead of ordering the fresh battalion to come up, he first ordered the tired battalion to go down. This manœuvre was executed just at the moment of the highest enthusiasm and the greatest efforts of the assailants. They saw the Swiss retire, the firing grow feebler and then cease altogether; they believed their enemies were beating a retreat and they sprang forward. The movement was so impetuous that, before the second battalion had taken the place of those who were being withdrawn, the people had entered by all the wicket gates and gratings, had spread over the deserted rooms on the ground floor and were firing from the windows on the court.

When the Swiss saw the flames and smoke, they thought the awful and bloody scenes of the 10th of August were about to be repeated. Uneasy, surprised and taken unprepared, not knowing if their comrades had retired by superior orders or were beating a retreat, they recoiled and tumbled hurriedly over one another, never attempting even to return the fire that was decimating their ranks; they crushed through the door leading out on the place du Carrousel, suffocating and treading one another down and flying in complete rout as soon as they were through the gateway. The Duc de Raguse vainly flung himself into their midst to try to rally them. Most did not understand French, so could not tell what was said to them; moreover, fear had turned to terror and fright to panic. You know what the angel of fear can do when he shakes his wings over the mob: the fugitives drove everything before them,—cuirassiers, lancers, police,—crossed that huge space, the place du Carrousel, without stopping, cleared the Tuileries gate and scattered themselves in every direction over the garden. Meanwhile, the assailants had reached the first landing, rushed through the picture gallery, which they found without defenders, and proceeded to break in the door at the end of the galleries that leads from the Louvre to the Tuileries. After that, resistance was no longer possible: the defenders of the château fled as best they could; the garden and both the terraces were crowded; the Duc de Raguse was among the last to withdraw and left the gate de l'Horloge just when Joubert was planting the Tricolour above his head, and when the people were raining down from the windows papers from the king's study. The marshal found a piece of cannon being taken away at the top of the jardin d'Hippomène and d'Atalante; and, at his command, it was replaced in its battery and a final volley was fired from it towards the Tuileries, which had ceased to be the dwelling-place of kings and had become the people's prize; one of its bullets, a posthumous present from Monarchy, as it were, cut one of the charming little grooved pillars on the first floor in two. This last cannon shot did no harm except to Philibert Delorme's masterpiece, but seemed as though it saluted the Tricolour which was waving over the pavilion de l'Horloge.

The Revolution of 1830 was accomplished. Accomplished (we will repeat it, print it, engrave it if necessary on iron and brass, on bronze and steel), accomplished, not alone by the cautious actors of the past fifteen years' comedy, who hid, as it were, behind the wings, whilst the people played that Three Days' bloody drama; not only by Casimir Périer, Laffitte, Benjamin Constant, Sébastiani, Guizot, Mauguin, by Choiseul, Odilon Barrot and the three Dupins. No! those actors were not even behind the wings; that would have been too near the stage for them! They kept at home, carefully guarded, hermetically sealed. With such as they, there was never any mention of resistance other than one legally organised, and, when the Louvre and Tuileries were being taken, they still went on discussing in their drawing-rooms the terms of a protest which many of them yet considered too risky a step to forward. The people who accomplished the Revolution of 1830 were those I saw at work, and who saw me there in their midst; those who entered the Louvre and the Tuileries by the broken doors and windows were, alas! (I may be pardoned this mournful exclamation, since most of them are now either dead or prisoners or exiled), Godefroy Cavaignac, Baude, Degousée, Higonnet, Grouvelle, Coste, Guinard, Charras, Étienne Arago, Lothon, Millotte, d'Hostel, Chalas, Gauja, Baduel, Bixio, Goudchaux, Bastide, the three brothers Lebon (Olympiade, Charles and Napoleon: the first was killed and the other two wounded in the attack on the Louvre), Joubert, Charles Teste, Taschereau, Béranger and others whose forgiveness I ask if I have either forgotten or not named them. I also ask pardon of some of those whom I name and who would perhaps prefer not to have been mentioned. Those who accomplished the Revolution of 1830 were the fiery youths of the heroic Proletariat which, it is true, lit the fires, but extinguished them with their own blood; those men of the people who are scattered when the work is achieved, and who die of hunger after having mounted guard by the Treasury gates, who stand on tiptoe with bare feet, in the streets, to watch the convivial parasites of power admitted to the care of offices, to the plums of good posts and to a share in all high honours, to the detriment of their less fortunate brethren.

The men who made the Revolution of 1830 were the same who, two years later, were killed at Saint-Mery for the same cause. But, this time, a change of name was given them just because they themselves had not changed their principles, and, instead of being called "heroes," they were styled "rebels." Only those renegades who change their opinions to suit the times can avoid the epithet of rebel, when different powers succeed one another.

BOOK III

CHAPTER I

I go in search of Oudard—The house at the corner of the rue de Rohan—Oudard is with Laffitte—Degousée—General Pajol and M. Dupin—The officers of the 53rd Regiment—Interior of Laffitte's salon—Panic—A deputation comes to offer La Fayette the command of Paris—He accepts—Étienne Arago and the tricoloured cockade—History of the Hôtel de Ville from eight in the morning to half-past three in the afternoon

Now would you like to know what was going on at M. Laffitte's, in the same drawing-room where, two days later, a King of France, or rather, a King of the French, was to be created, just at the moment that the Tuileries had been taken? I can tell you: and this is why. When I left the Tuileries, I had been seized with a burning desire to find out whether Oudard was still, on the evening of 29 July, of the same opinion as on the morning of the 28th, with respect to the Duc d'Orléans' devotion to His Majesty Charles X. So I went to No. 216 rue Saint-Honoré. At the place de l'Odéon I had been very nearly knocked down by a *Gradus ad Parnassum*; and, as I approached No. 216, I was also nearly knocked down by a dead body. They were throwing the Swiss out of the windows at the corner of the rue de Rohan. This was happening at a hatter's, the front of whose house was riddled with bullets. A post of Swiss had been placed by it as an advance guard and they had forgotten to relieve them, but the guards had kept their post with true Swiss courage, and no higher praise than that could be given. The house had been carried by storm, a dozen men had been killed and the bodies were being thrown out from the windows, as I have said, without even a warning cry being given to the passers beneath. I went up the stairs to the offices of the Palais-Royal. Now, my rifle, that had caused such consternation on the previous day, was received with acclamation. I found the office-boy busily occupied in putting things a little straight in our establishment. That portion of the palace having been invaded, they had fired from the windows, and this had not been done without causing some disorder among the papers. But there was no sign of Oudard! I inquired after him from the office-boy and learnt, in confidence, that I should, in all probability, find him at Laffitte's house. I have said already how I had made acquaintance with the famous banker through the service he had rendered me. I therefore made my way to his mansion, where I felt sure I should not altogether be looked upon as an intruder. It took me more than an hour to get from the Palais-Royal to the Hôtel Laffitte, so crowded were the streets and so many acquaintances did one meet on the way.

At the door I ran into Oudard.

"Ah! by Jove!" I said, laughing, "you are just the man I am looking for!"

"I! what do you want with me?"

"To know whether your views on the present situation are unchanged."

"I shall not express any opinion until to-morrow," he replied.

And, making a sign of farewell, he disappeared as fast as he could. Where was he off to? I did not know until three days later: he went to Neuilly to carry this short ultimatum to the Duc d'Orléans:—

"Choose between a crown and a passport!"

The ultimatum was drawn up by M. Laffitte.

I had flattered myself with vain hope in believing I should be able to enter Laffitte's house: courts, gardens, antechambers, drawing-rooms were all crammed; there were even curious spectators on the roofs of the houses opposite that looked down over the Hôtel courtyard. But it must be said that the men gathered together there were not all in a state of enthusiasm and appreciative of the situation. Certain stories of what was passing inside filtered through to the crowd outside, at which they grumbled loudly as they listened. One story will give an idea of the cautious prudence of the deputies assembled at Laffitte's house.

When Degousée had, that morning, seen the Hôtel de Ville fall into the hands of the people, he left Baude installed there and rushed off to General Pajol to offer him the command of the National Guard. But General Pajol replied that he could not take any such decided steps without the authorisation of the deputies.

"Then where the devil are there any deputies?" asked Degousée.

"Look for them at M. de Choiseul's," General Pajol replied.

So Degousée went there. M. de Choiseul was at his wits' end: he had just learnt that he had been made a member of the Provisional Government the night before, and that, during the night, he had signed a seditious proclamation. M. Dupin, senior, was with the duke, doubtless having a consultation upon this unexpected bit of French legislation. The idea proposed by Degousée of reorganising a corps that could not fail to become a Conservative power delighted M. Dupin immensely. He took a pen and wrote these words:—

"The deputies assembled in Paris authorise General Pajol to take the command of the *Parisian Militia*."

"*The Parisian Militia!*" Degousée repeated. "Why do you call them by that name?"

"Because the National Guard has been legally dissolved by the Ordinance of King Charles X.," was M. Dupin's reply.

"Come, come," Degousée went on to say, "don't let us quibble over terms. Sign this quickly and kindly tell me where I shall find your *deputies assembled in Paris.*"

"At the house of M. Laffitte," M. Dupin replied.

And he signed the authorisation without making any further difficulties.

The deputies were, indeed, assembled with Laffitte. And Degousée, more fortunate than I, thanks, no doubt, to the paper which he carried, had been able to reach the room where the deliberations were going on. The deputies looked at the afore-mentioned three lines and, seeing M. Dupin's signature, signed in their turn; but they had no sooner done so than they were seized with terror: Degousée, who never let the grass grow under his feet, and who, besides, was aching to be at the assault of the Louvre, had already reached the street door when a deputy caught him up.

"Monsieur," he said, "will you permit me to look at that paper once again?"

"Certainly," Degousée replied unsuspectingly.

The deputy stepped aside and tore off the signatures, then returned the paper, folded up, to Degousée, who took it, not discovering the missing signatures subtracted by the clever conjurer, until he reached General Pajol's door.

My readers remember La Fontaine's fable of *le Lièvre et les Grenouilles* (The hare and the frog)? The worthy man foresaw everything, even that which was thought almost impossible, namely, that M. Dupin would find a greater coward than himself! That was the story going the round of the knots of people standing about outside.

But let us hasten to add that La Fayette had not yet arrived at the Hôtel Laffitte when the incident took place that we have just related. He arrived as a man of the populace, gun in hand and face blackened with powder, was running in to announce the taking of the Louvre. A sergeant of the 53rd Regiment of the line had made such good use of his feet and hands that he had got into the drawing-room, where he announced that that regiment was on the point of fraternising with the people. The officers only asked that some person of high position might be sent them in order that their going over to the Revolutionary cause might not look like an ordinary defection. They sent Colonel Heymès, in civilian dress, and M. Jean-Baptiste Laffitte, with several members of the National Guard, whom they had recruited as they came along the boulevard. The regiment was arriving just as I came: five officers entered the council hall and I with them. M. Laffitte was near the garden window, which was open, although the outside blinds were closed; he was seated in a large arm-chair with his leg resting on a footstool. He had sprained his foot the morning before. Behind him was Béranger, leaning upon the back of his chair, and, on one side, stood General La Fayette, inquiring after his health; in the recess of a second window, Georges La Fayette was talking with M. Laroche, M. Laffitte's nephew. Thirty or forty deputies conversing in groups filled up the rest of the drawing-room. Suddenly, a fearful sound of firing was heard and the cry resounded—

"The Royal Guard is marching towards the Hôtel!"

I have seen many spectacles, from that of *Paul et Virginie*, at the Opéra-Comique, the first I ever saw and admired, down to *la Barrière de Clichy*, at the Cirque, one of the latest I have managed, but I never saw such a change of scene as that! One could have imagined that every deputy had been on a trap-door and had disappeared at a whistle. In the turn of a hand there was absolutely not a single person left in the salon but Laffitte, who remained still seated, without a trace of emotion apparent in his face; Béranger, who remained steadfast where he stood; M. Laroche, who came to his uncle's side; La Fayette, who raised his noble and venerable head and took one step towards the door, which meant facing danger; Georges La Fayette, who rushed towards his father; and the five officers who formed a bodyguard round M. Laffitte. All the others had disappeared by the private doors or had jumped out through the windows. M. Méchin had distinguished himself by being among the latter. I was intending to take advantage of the situation to present my compliments to the master of the house, but General La Fayette stopped me on the way.

"What the deuce is the matter?" he asked me.

"I have no idea, General," I replied; "but I can confidently affirm that neither the Swiss nor the Royal Guard are here.... I saw them leave the Tuileries, and, at the rate they were going, they must, by this time, be nearer Saint-Cloud than the Hôtel Laffitte."

"Never mind! try and find out what it is all about."

I was advancing towards the door when an officer came in and brought the solution to the riddle.

The soldiers of the 6th Regiment of the line had met those of the 53rd and had followed the example of the latter in siding with the popular cause; in sign of their joy they had discharged their rifles in the air. This explanation given, we went in search of the missing deputies whom we at last found here, there and everywhere. Only two failed to answer the roll-call. However, by dint of further hunting, they were discovered hiding in a stable. If you wish it, I am quite ready to give their names. A deputation was introduced a few minutes later; Garnier-Pagès was of its number, if I remember rightly. This deputation had taken Taschereau's placards and proclamation as genuine, and had come to entreat Generals La Fayette and Gérard to enter upon their duties. General Gérard, who had but just arrived, eluded the proposition. Gérard's dream was to become a minister of Charles X. with M. de Mortemart, and not a member of a temporary and Revolutionary Government. La Fayette's response to the deputation was nearly the same that he had given me the night before.

"My friends, if you think I can be useful to the cause of liberty, make use of me"; and he placed himself in the hands of the deputation.

The cry of "Vive La Fayette!" echoed through the salons of the Hôtel Laffitte and were taken up in the street outside. La Fayette turned towards the deputies.

"You see, gentlemen," he said, "I am being offered the command of Paris and I think I ought to accept it."

It was not the moment for dissent, and adherence was unanimous. Everybody present, including even M. Bertin de Vaux, went up to La Fayette to offer him congratulations, but I could not catch the words. I was already in the antechamber, courtyard and street shouting—

"Make room for General La Fayette, who is going to the Hôtel de Ville!"

The unanimity of the shouts of "Vive La Fayette!" proved that the hero of 1789 had not lost an atom of his popularity in 1830.

What a splendid thing is Liberty! an immortal and infallible goddess! The Convention had its day, the Directory, the Consulate, the Empire and the Restoration all passed away too and heads and crowns fell with them; but the man whom Liberty had consecrated King of the people in 1789 found himself once more King of the people in 1830.

La Fayette went out, leaning upon Carbonnel, accompanied by a deputy, whose name I did not know until I inquired: it was Audry de Puyraveau. Everybody, men, women and children, formed a procession after the illustrious old man, whom we honoured and glorified because we knew that in his person he embodied the chief principle of Revolution. And yet, although he was so advanced in his views, he was then far out-distanced by those of younger people!

At the door of the *National* offices in the rue Neuve-Saint-Marc, La Fayette caught sight of Étienne Arago, wearing a tricolour cockade. "Monsieur Poque," he said, addressing one of the persons who accompanied him, "go and beg that young man to take off his cockade."

Arago came to La Fayette.

"I ask pardon, General," he said, "but I do not think I can have understood."

"My young friend, I beg you to take off that cockade."

"Why, General?"

"Because it is a little premature.... Later, later we will see."

"General," replied Étienne, "I have been wearing a tricolour in my buttonhole since yesterday, and in my hat since this morning. There they are and there they will remain!"

"Obstinate fellow!" murmured the general, as he went on his way.

They suggested he should have a horse from Pellier's livery stables, but he refused. So it took nearly an hour and a half to go from the rue d'Artois to the Hôtel de Ville. He reached it about half-past three.

But I must give the history of the Hôtel de Ville from eight that morning, when it had been definitely taken by the people, to the moment when General La Fayette came to occupy it at half-past three. About seven in the morning, the people noticed that the Hôtel had been evacuated by the troops. The news was instantly carried to the *National* offices. It was important that possession should be taken of it, so Baude and Étienne Arago went. At nine o'clock they were installed inside. From that very moment, and visionary as it was, the Provisional Government was installed in office. A man had risen up who did not shrink before the terrible responsibility which made so many people hang back. That man was Baude. He constituted himself Secretary of a non-existent Government. He issued numberless orders, proclamations and decrees, which he signed

"BAUDE, *Secretary to the Provisional Government.*"

We said that he had entered the Hôtel de Ville at nine o'clock. By eleven, the municipal safe was examined and found to contain five million francs. At eleven o'clock, the master bakers were summoned, and they declared on their own responsibility that Paris was provisioned for a month. Moreover, at eleven o'clock, commissions were set up in all the twelve arrondissements of

Paris, with instructions to put themselves into communication with the Hôtel de Ville. Five or six devoted patriots rallied round Baude and were sufficient for his working staff. Étienne Arago was one of these. Reports, orders, decrees and proclamations were placed between the barrel and the ramrod of Arago's rifle and carried to the *National* offices. He went by way of the rue de la Vannerie, the market of the *Innocents*, and the rue Montmartre. From ten that morning not a single obstacle had impeded his course. In accordance with Marshal Marmont's order the whole of the troops had concentrated round the Tuileries.

While Étienne was carrying off the proclamation announcing the downfall of the Bourbons, signed "BAUDE, *Secretary of the Provisional Government*," he met a former actor named Charlet, in the market of the Innocents, who was walking in front of an immense crowd of people which filled up the whole of the square. The two principal personages in that crowd, those who appeared to be conducting it or to be conducted by it, were a man dressed as a captain, and another in the uniform of a general. The man in captain's uniform was Évariste Dumoulin, the editor of the *Constitutionnel*, to whom I have referred apropos of Madame Valmonzey and *Christine*. The man in the general's uniform was General Dubourg. Nobody knew who General Dubourg was or where he sprang from, or whether he had been to an old-clothes shop and either borrowed or hired or bought his general's uniform. But the epaulettes were wanting, and this was too important an accessory to be neglected. Charlet, the actor, went and fetched a pair of epaulettes from the property stores of the Opéra-Comique and brought them to the general. And, thus complete, he set off at the head of his procession.

"What is all this crowd? Étienne asked of Charlet.

"It is General Dubourg's procession starting for the Hôtel de Ville."

"Who is General Dubourg?"

"General Dubourg is General Dubourg," said Charlet.

And there was indeed no other explanation to be offered.

General Dubourg had presented himself before Higonnet and Degousée at the Mairie des Petits-Pères the previous day.

"Gentlemen," he asked, "do you require a general?"

"A general?" Degousée repeated. "In Revolutionary times it only needs a tailor to make anything or anybody—and, given sufficient tailors, there will be no lack of generals."

The general made a mental note of the expression, but, instead of applying to a tailor, he did what was more economical and expeditious. He went to a second-hand clothes dealer! But then it was fitting that a general of fortune should have a makeshift for a uniform.

Well, the general and his uniform combined went to the Hôtel de Ville. Now, it is the proper thing for processions to march at a slow pace, and this particular one did not depart from the usual custom. Étienne had time to go and deposit his despatch at the offices of the *National* and, by hurrying slightly, he was able to return to the Hôtel de Ville before General Dubourg had effected his entrance.

"Baude," he said, "do you know what is coming?"

"No."

"A general!"

"What general?"

"General Dubourg.... Do you know the person?"

"Not from Adam or Eve! Is he in uniform?"

"Yes."

"A uniform will go down well! Hurrah for General Dubourg! We will put him in a back room and show him off when occasion offers."

General Dubourg entered to the shouts of "Vive le general Dubourg!"

They took him to the back room Baude pointed out, and when he was there—

"What do you wish, General?" they asked him.

"A bit of bread and a chamber-pot," replied the general. "I am dying of hunger, and desire to make water!"

They gave him what he wanted. Whilst he devoured his piece of bread Baude brought him two proclamations to sign. He signed one without difficulty, but refused to sign the other. Baude took it and signed it with a shrug of his shoulders—"BAUDE, *Secretary to the Provisional Government.*"

Poor Provisional Government! It would have been curious to see what its behaviour would have been if Charles X. had returned to Paris.

Arago was on his way carrying these two proclamations, when he met a new troop near Saint-Eustache, proceeding to an attack on the Louvre. He could not refrain from joining it.

"Bah!" he said, "the proclamations will wait; let us go to the most pressing business first." And to the Louvre he went.

When the Louvre was taken, he took his proclamations to the *National* and there announced the people's victory. It was here that General La Fayette had seen him with a tricolour cockade and was made uneasy by his boldness.

When Étienne heard that the general was going to the Hôtel de Ville he did the same for him that he had done for General Dubourg: he ran to the Hôtel to announce to Baude the arrival of General La Fayette. In fairness to General Dubourg be it said that he did not even attempt to dispute the position of the new arrival, although he had come later than himself. He came forward to receive him on the steps and, bowing respectfully, said—

"*À tout seigneur, tout honneur!*"

For five hours, he had been master of Paris; and, for two of those five, his name had been on all lips. He was to reappear a second time to be hounded out of the Hôtel de Ville, and a third when he was very nearly assassinated. When he arrived, he sent for the tricolour tent and an upholsterer.

When the latter came—"Monsieur," the general said to him, "I want a flag."

"What colour?" the man asked.

"Black!" replied the general; "black shall be the colour of France until she shall have regained her liberty!"

And ten minutes afterwards a black flag floated over the Hôtel de Ville.

CHAPTER II

General La Fayette at the Hôtel de Ville—Charras and his men—"The Prunes of Monsieur"—The Municipal Commission—Its first Act—Casimir Périer's bank—General Gérard—The Duc de Choiseul—What happened at Saint-Cloud—The three negotiators—It is too late—M. d'Argout with Laffitte

As soon as General La Fayette was installed at the Hôtel de Ville, it immediately became as full of people as it had been deserted before his arrival. In the midst of all the shouts of joy, clamouring enthusiasm and yells of triumph, the poor general did not know to whom to listen. Men of the people, students, pupils from the École polytechnique, all came with their own particular tale. The general replied—

"Very good! very good!" and shook hands with the messenger, who rushed off down the stairs, delighted, shouting—

"General La Fayette shook hands with me! Hurrah for General La Fayette!"

Charras arrived, in due course, with his hundred or hundred and fifty men.

"Here I am, General," he said.

"Ah! You, my young friend!" said La Fayette. "You are welcome"; and he embraced him.

"Yes, General, I am here, but I am not alone."

"Who have you with you?"

"My hundred and fifty men."

"And what have they done?"

"They have acted like heroes, General! They took the prison Montaigu, the barrack de l'Estrapade and the one in the rue de Babylone."

"Bravo!"

"Yes, you may indeed say so! But now there is nothing left for them to take, what must I do with them?"

"Why, tell them to return quietly to their homes."

Charras laughed.

"Homes? You don't really mean that, General!"

"I do, really; they must be fatigued after the tasks they have performed."

"But, General, three-quarters of the brave fellows have no homes to go to, and the other quarter, if they went home, would not find either a morsel of bread or a halfpenny to buy any with."

"Ah! the deuce! that alters the case," said the general. "Then let them have a hundred sous per head."

Charras submitted the general's proposal to his men.

"Oh!... Come now!" they said, "does he think we are fighting for the sake of money?"

Baude ordered a distribution of bread and meat and, when it was done, Charras camped with his troop upon the square of the Hôtel de Ville.

Madame Guyet-Desfontaines' cup of chocolate and bottle of Bordeaux wine were now things of the past, and I felt as pressing a desire for a piece of bread to eat as had General Dubourg when he reached the Hôtel de Ville. I went to a wine merchant's at the corner of la place de Grève and the quai Pelletier and asked for some dinner. His house was riddled with bullets and he had become the possessor of a fine selection of grapeshot. He meant to set them up above his door as a future sign, with the following words inscribed above them:—

AUX PRUNES DE MONSIEUR

You know that the Comte d'Artois, as in the case of all the younger brothers of the kings of France, was styled "Monsieur" before he became Charles X. I approved the happy notion of the wine merchant, and flattered him so cleverly that I wheedled him out of a bottle of wine, a piece of bread and a sausage.

I was fully determined not to lose sight of the Hôtel de Ville and to take note of all that passed there. I found that Revolutions had an extremely amusing side. Pray excuse me, it was the first I had seen. Now that I have lived to see a third I do not find them quite so funny.

But, as we have many incidents to relate in these humble Memoirs which that arch-prude History leaves untold and as we have, therefore, no time to lose, let us say, on the one hand, what was happening at Saint-Cloud and, on the other, what was being plotted at M. Laffitte's, whilst I was drinking my bottle of wine and eating my bread and sausage at the sign of the *Prunes de Monsieur*, and whilst General La Fayette was busy installing himself in his dictatorial chair in the Hôtel de Ville, embracing Charras and sending his men to bed, since he thought they must badly need to rest.

Let us begin at the Hôtel Laffitte. La Fayette had scarcely left the salon to take up the dictatorship of Paris, when they began to be afraid of leaving the hero of the battle of the Federation twenty-four hours alone at the head of affairs, and set to work to discover some efficacious method of counterbalancing his power. They appointed General Gérard *Director of active operations* (an unknown office which they had invented for the occasion); and he was to be backed up by a Municipal Commission composed of MM. Casimir Périer, Laffitte, Odier, Lobau, Audry de Puyraveau and Mauguin. But, to form a part of a Municipal Commission was much too bold a step for M. Odier; and he refused. M. de Schonen was appointed in his stead. M. Laffitte's sprained foot was made the pretext for establishing the Commission at his house. Thus, everything was organised to combat General La Fayette's revolutionary sway. This was how the bourgeoisie began its reactionary work the very same day that popular enthusiasm and triumph was at its height.

Make friends again, rejoice, approach one another with shouts of joy, embrace, you men of the faubourgs, young people from the colleges, students, poets and artists! Raise your hands to heaven, thank God, and cry hosannahs! Your dead are not yet buried, your wounds not yet healed; your lips are yet black with powder, your hearts still beat joyfully at the thought of liberty, and already intriguing men, financial men and those in uniforms who went and hid trembling and praying whilst you were fighting, are shamelessly approaching to snatch victory and liberty out of your hands, to wrest the palms from the one, and to clip the wings of the other; to ravish your two chaste goddesses. Whilst you are shooting a man in the place du Louvre, for having stolen a silver-gilt vase, whilst you are shooting a man under the Pont d'Arcole for stealing some silver plate, you are insulted and slandered out there in that big fine mansion, which you will some day buy back by a national subscription (you short-memoried children with hearts of gold!), and give it back to its owner when he is ruined and has only an income left of four hundred thousand francs! *Audite et intelligite!* Listen and learn! Here is the first Act of that Municipal Commission which had just been self-elected:—

> "The deputies present in Paris have had to assemble in order to remedy the grave dangers which are threatening the security of persons and property. A Municipal Commission has been formed to watch over the interests of all in the absence of regular organisation.".

Royalists, beware! there is an edict of good King Saint-Louis giving power to pierce the tongue of blasphemers with a red-hot iron! This Commission had to have a secretary at the Hôtel de Ville and Odilon Barrot was appointed. It happened that, at the same time as the Commission was signing this insulting decree, they came and announced to it that half the combatants were dying of hunger in the public squares and were asking for bread. They turned towards M. Casimir Périer with one accord—the man who had offered the Duc de Raguse four millions the previous day.

"Well, messieurs," he replied, "I am truly sorry for the poor devils, but it is past four o'clock and my cash-room is closed."

And that was a man who had been a Minister and governed the French people—a man whose sons had been ambassadors to and representatives of the French nation!

At five o'clock, General Gérard condescended to show himself to the crowd. He still wore the white cockade in his hat, and it excited such comment that the general was forced to take it out; but no amount of persuasion could make him don the tricolour cockade in its place.

The Duc de Choiseul entered the Hôtel Laffitte as General Gérard was leaving it; the poor duke, whose complexion at ordinary times was quite yellow, now looked green. He had had enough to make him so! He had been taking part in the Provisional Government since the morning, signing proclamations and issuing decrees! Whilst fighting was going on in the streets, he had not dared to venture out of doors; he was too much in fear of being compromised and still more afraid of being killed. When the firing was stopped, M. de Choiseul had half opened his shutters, and he perceived that everybody was in the streets and that the city was in a state of rejoicing: he had descended his carpeted stairs step by step, had ventured one foot outside his Hôtel and had finally risked going as far as M. Laffitte's. What did he want to do there? By Jove! that is not a difficult question to answer: he came to protest against the abominable forger who had abused his name and who had held it in so little respect as to link it with that of M. Motié de La Fayette! True, M. de Choiseul; although descended from a good Auvergnese family, M. Motié de La Fayette did not spring from Raymond III., Count of Langres, and from Alix de Dreux, granddaughter of Louis le Gros; but I do not know that he could number among his ancestors any accused of poisoning a Dauphin of France, at the instigation of Austria. That fact should have been taken into consideration and should have made the duke more lenient to the poor gentleman and his family.

Now that we have seen what was passing at the Hôtel Laffitte, let us see what was happening at Saint-Cloud. They were furious against the Duc de Raguse; and they had not merely said that he had not defended Paris properly, but that he had betrayed them. Luckless fate pursued this man, accused by all sides, even by that to which he had devoted himself! The dauphin was substituted to take command in his place. All knew what a grand general the dauphin was! Did he not conquer Spain and drive out that lucky, foolhardy fellow of a Napoleon? His repartees, too, were they not most felicitously turned? He came to the bois de Boulogne to receive the troops and went up to a captain, asking—

"How many men have you lost, Captain? How many men have you lost?"

The dauphin had a habit of saying his sentences twice over.

"Many, monseigneur!" the officer replied sorrowfully.

"But you have plenty left still—plenty left?" His Highness said, with the tactful manner that was natural to him!

The troops continued their retreat and reached Saint-Cloud depressed with fatigue, broken down with heat and dying with hunger. They were not expected and nothing was prepared for them. The Duc de Bordeaux dined, and M. de Damas ordered the dishes that came from the prince's table to be sent out to the soldiers. The child took the dishes and himself handed them to the servants-in-waiting upon him. The hour predicted by Barras had come, but the poor royal child had been taught no other trade than that of being a prince—a bad trade in our days: ask His Majesty Napoleon II. and His Highness the Duc de Bordeaux, or Monseigneur le Comte de Paris.

However, Doctor Thibaut's negotiation had produced its effects and, whilst General Gérard was sticking to his white cockade at half-past five on the afternoon of 29 July, M. de Mortemart was reaching Saint-Cloud at seven that same evening. Charles X. did not give him a warm welcome; he did not like him and, indeed, M. de Mortemart was one of those doubtful Royalists, attainted with Republicanism, like the La Fayettes and Lameths and Broglies. M. de Mortemart tried to force the king into making concessions; but the king had replied with a determination that twenty-four hours later he was to belie—

"I will give no concessions, monsieur! I witnessed the events of 1789 and have not forgotten them. I do not wish to ride in a cart, like my brother; I choose to ride on horseback."[1]

Unfortunately for this fine resolution, the affairs of Paris changed their appearance the next morning. It was then Charles X. who urged M. de Mortemart to accept the Ministry, and M. de Mortemart who, in his turn, declined. He saw that the hour had gone by for a mixed Ministry to be effective, and made an intermittent fever, caught on the shores of the Danube, the excuse for refusing. But Charles X. had reached the point when kings no longer try to hide their fears, but openly utter cries of distress.

"Ah! Monsieur le Duc," the aged monarch exclaimed, "you refuse, then, to save my life and that of my Ministers? That is not the part of a faithful subject, monsieur!"

The duke bowed.

"Sire," he said, "if that is what you demand of me, I will accept!"

"Good—I thank you," replied the king.

Then, in a whisper—

"But it remains to be seen if the people will be satisfied with you...."

The violent measures imposed upon the old king were so bitter to him, that, even before the man who had been willing to sacrifice himself for his sake, he could not restrain his anger.

Three political personages were waiting in an adjacent room—thus, in our polite tongue, we speak of peers, deputies, senators, magistrates and councillors who take the oath of allegiance to monarchies, and who defend them so well, that, in forty years, they have allowed four to slip through their fingers! These political personages were M. de Vitrolles,—whom Doctor Thibaut had gone to look for on the evening of 27 July, to lay before him the Coalition,—Mortemart and Gérard; M. de Sémonville, the man of apocryphal flags, of whom M. de Talleyrand said, when he saw him falling away, "What interest can he take in that?" M. d'Argout who, in 1848, became so ardent a Republican that he dismissed from his offices my beloved and close friend Lassagne, who had obtained with him a small post at three to four thousand francs salary, because he recognised him as having been secretary to King Louis-Philippe.

"O holy discretion!" as said Brutus.

While they were waiting, M. de Polignac entered. The prince soon guessed what the three negotiators had come about; two of them were personal friends of his. They had come to ask for his dethronement. There was a greatness about the Prince de Polignac; a smaller-minded man would have attempted to prevent them gaining access to the king; but he at once introduced them into Charles X.'s cabinet. Perhaps he also reckoned upon the king's well-known aversion towards M. d'Argout. The king had just agreed to the Ministry of Mortemart. He received these gentlemen, who laid their mission before him. Charles X. did not even let them get to the end but, with a gesture at once full of bitterness and of nobility, he said—

"Gentlemen, go to the Parisians and tell them that the king revokes the Ordinances."

These gentlemen gave vent to the expression of their joy in murmurs of satisfaction. But the king went on to say—

"Allow me, at the same time, to tell you that I believe this revocation to be fatal to the interests of the Monarchy and of France!"

The interests of Monarchy and of France! Why on earth did Charles X, talk of these to such men? What did they care for beyond their own private interests? They departed in a carriage at full gallop. Upon the road they met all Paris in arms pouring out of the houses into the streets and from out the suburbs. M. de Sémonville shouted to that crowd of bare-armed men with bloodstained shirts—

"My friends, the king has revoked the Ordinances; the Ministers have been chucked out."

He thought he was speaking in the language of the people, but he was really only uttering the jargon of the lowest rabble. M. de Vitrolles was shaking hands freely all round. If the men who pressed his hands had known his name, they would have throttled him instead!

When the negotiators reached the quays they were obliged to abandon their carriages, as the barricades were beginning and, with them, no favouritism: locomotion was the same for all. When they reached the Hôtel de Ville and were climbing the flight of steps they met Marrast, and, recognising the three negotiators, he stopped to look at them. M. de Sémonville did not know Marrast, but, seeing a young man elegantly attired, in the midst of that ragged crowd, he addressed him.

"Young man," he said, "can we speak with General La Fayette?"

He dared not say *monsieur*, and did not wish to address him as *citoyen* (citizen).

Marrast directed him; and these gentlemen were introduced into the midst of the Municipal Commission. They were going to begin to declare their mission without its being thought necessary to inform General La Fayette, whom they had come to seek. It would, perhaps, have suited some members of the Municipal Commission for La Fayette not to be there; but M. de Schonen and Audry de Puyraveau, the most enthusiastic, and deeply implicated of the Commission, sent for him. They proclaimed the Ministry of Mortemart and Gérard.

"But, gentlemen," Mauguin interrupted, "two Ministers do not form a Government."

"The king," said M. de Sémonville, "willingly consents to the addition of M. Casimir Périer."

And he turned with a gracious smile towards the banker, who went terribly pale.

In the same moment, Casimir Périer received a letter which he read. All eyes were fixed upon him.... He made a gesture expressive of refusal. There was a brief moment of silence and hesitation, each trying to avoid being the first to answer, feeling the importance of his reply. Then M. de Schonen rose and broke the silence, and in firm tones uttered these terrible words:—-

"It is too late.... The throne of Charles X. has foundered in blood ...!"

Eighteen years later, these same words, repeated in the Tribune by M. de Lamartine and addressed in their turn to the envoys of King Louis-Philippe, were to hurl down the throne occupied by the Younger Branch, as they had done that of the Elder.

The negotiators wanted to press matters forward.

"Come! come!" said Audry de Puyraveau, "let us have no more of this, gentlemen, or I will call up the people, and we shall soon see what their wishes are!"

The deputies withdrew; but M. Casimir Périer went out by another door, and joined them on the staircase.

"Go and find M. Laffitte," he said to them as he passed; "perhaps something might be done from that quarter."

And he disappeared. Did he wish to transfer the negotiations to the Duc d'Orléans, or was he unwilling to detach himself entirely from King Charles X.?

M. de Sémonville shook his head and withdrew.

To go and find M. Laffitte, who was nothing but a financier, bah! La Fayette might perhaps be tolerated. He was certainly a Revolutionary, but one of a good family, who, when a boy, had worn powder and red heels, and had kissed the queen's hand at l'Œil-de-bœuf.

It was on the awful morning of 6 October that he had been granted this last grace. M. Laffitte was only a meritorious member of the proletariat, whose nobility of character and good works had made him powerful; they could not negotiate the interests of a descendant of Saint-Louis with an upstart like that! MM. de Vitrolles and d'Argout were not so proud as M. de Sémonville. Casmir Périer gave them a passport to enable them to enter Laffitte's mansion without difficulties. M. d'Argout, who was only unpopular, kept to his own name, but M. de Vitrolles, who was execrated, had his name given out as M. Arnoult. At the door the courage of M. de Vitrolles failed him: he pushed M. d'Argout inside the salon and remained behind in a kind of vestibule. M. Laffitte was expecting Oudard, who had been gone since five o'clock, but had not yet returned. At the sound of an opening door he raised his eyes. It was not Oudard, but M. d'Argout. On his entrance his manner, whether real or affected, was characterised by the assurance of a man who believes himself to be bringing news conciliatory to all the interests concerned.

"Well! my dear colleague," he said, "I have come to tell you some excellent news."

"Humph!" Laffitte responded, with that half—scornful manner peculiar to him, together with some of those mental endowments which he appeared to have borrowed from his friend Béranger. "Humph I what is it?"

"The Ordinances are withdrawn," said M. d'Argout.

"Ah!" remarked Laffitte with indifference.

"And we have fresh Ministers."

"Ah!" the banker again remarked, without even inquiring their names.

"Is that how you receive such news?" M. d'Argout said, with some show of disappointment.

"Surely."

"But why are you so cool over it?"

"Because it is of no importance now."

"No importance! Now!" repeated M. d'Argout.

"Yes," said Laffitte; "you are twenty-four hours too late with it, my good friend."

"But it seems to me that the interest remains the same."

"Quite possibly. Only the situation has changed in the last twenty-four hours!"

The salon door again opened at that moment. It was not, however, a negotiator this time, but a man of the people. He was in his working blouse; his beard was long and his head bound up in a bloodstained handkerchief; he held a rifle in his hand.

"Pardon, Monsieur Laffitte," he said, as he clashed his gun on the parquetry floor, "there is a rumour that they are negotiating through you with Charles X."

"Yes," said Laffitte, "and you do not want any negotiations, is that it, my friend?"

"We want no more Bourbons and no more Jesuits!" was the cry being shouted in the antechambers.

This cry was taken up even in the street outside.

"You see and hear for yourself?" said M. Laffitte.

"Then you will listen to nothing?"

"Is your business official?"

M. d'Argout hesitated.

"I must confess," he replied, "that it is not."

"Then you will plainly see that I cannot answer you, since any reply I made would lead to nothing!"

"But, if I returned with an official authorisation," urged M. d'Argout, anxious to sound the situation from every side.

"Ah!" said M. Laffitte, "we will cross that bridge when we come to it!"

M. d'Argout shook his head and withdrew.

"Well?" M. de Vitrolles asked him.

"All is lost, my dear Baron!" the future Director of the Bank replied, with a sigh.

"But suppose a final effort were made to force M. de Mortemart upon Paris?"

"Why, in desperate cases any means are worth trying."

"To Saint-Cloud, then!"

"To Saint-Cloud!"

"That devil of an Oudard is a long time bringing me the duke's answer," Laffitte murmured impatiently.

"Perhaps," replied Béranger, "the duke is somewhat long in giving it him...."

[1] See *l'Histoire de dix ans*, by Louis Blanc.

CHAPTER III

Alexandre de la Borde—Odilon Barrot—Colonel Dumoulin—Hippolyte Bonnelier—My study—A note in Oudard's handwriting—The Duc de Chartres is arrested at Montrouge—The danger he incurred and how he was saved—I propose to go to Soissons to fetch gunpowder—I procure my commission from General Gérard—La Fayette draws up a proclamation for me—The painter bard—M. Thiers to the fore once more

The foregoing incidents were all taking place at the time I was finishing my repast at the inn of the *Prunes de Monsieur*. I crossed through all the crowds encamped in the place de l'Hôtel de Ville, resting so quietly and cheerfully, in ignorance that the political Cyclops had set to work again and was busy forging a fresh chain out of the old broken one—an eloquent metaphor M. Odilon Barrot might have made use of in speaking at the Tribunal, had there been a Tribunal left.

Alexandre de la Borde was entering the great hall of the Hôtel de Ville at the same time that I was. Some men of the type that are for ever shouting out something, cried—

"*Vive le préfet de la Seine!*"

Odilon Barrot, whose name I have just jotted down in reference to Parliamentary eloquence, was writing at a table, dressed in the uniform of a National Guardsman. He raised his head in surprise that the former préfet of the Seine, M. de Chabrol de Volvic, could excite so much enthusiasm. He recognised Alexandre de la Borde and made a gesture of astonishment.

"Well, yes, it is I," the author of *l'Itinéraire en Espagne* said, with that bright, almost childish naïveté which was one of the chief characteristics of his personality; "they have just nominated me préfet of the Seine."

"You?"

"Yes, me."

"Who has done that?"

"How should I know?... Some monsieur with a plumed hat, a large sabre and a long scarf."

This "*monsieur*" was Colonel Dumoulin, who reappeared at every Revolution in exactly the same plumed hat, sabre and scarf, till one began to think he was the cause of all the misfortune.

Odilon Barrot shrugged his shoulders.

"You," he said, "you will belong to the Commune of Paris with us...."

And in a whisper he added—

"And yet!"

Only one who, like myself, was leaning over the back of his arm-chair, could have caught these last two words.

I could see from my position another secretary, who had just come and taken his place opposite, as a rival power. It was M. Hippolyte Bonnelier, La Fayette's secretary; he was, indeed, the counterpart to Odilon Barrot, secretary of the Municipal Commission. I shall never forget how peculiarly M. Hippolyte Bonnelier was accoutred. He wore his powder-horn slung round him on a red ribbon. In his belt he had stuck a tiny poniard of four inches in length. Did he load his poniard with the powder-horn or did he fill his powder-flask with his poniard? It was a problem I was never able to solve.

"I have felled eighteen trees along the boulevards!" he said to Étienne Arago.

"With your poniard?" Étienne laughingly asked.

"No," Bonnelier replied, laughing in his turn; "I meant to say that I marked them out with my poniard and that the people felled them."

And, meanwhile, he was secretary to La Fayette. It was from him that I learned what had passed between MM. de Vitrolles, Sémonville, and Argout and the Municipal Commission.

The situation was becoming more and more interesting. I felt certain that Oudard had gone to Neuilly; and I believed the answer would soon be given, so I made up my mind to spend the night at the Hôtel de Ville. I put myself under Bonnelier's protection and he took me to a kind of private office where was a mahogany desk and arm-chairs upholstered in green velvet. Upon the mantelpiece were five-branched candelabras but without candles in them. I should say that M. de Chabrol was a great and practical economist seeing he had five millions in his safe and no candles in his candlesticks.

I began my operations by putting the key of the cabinet in my pocket, then I went down and bought five candles, went up again, took pencil and paper from Bonnelier's desk and begged him, if any news came from Neuilly, to communicate it to me, which he promised to do. I returned to my room, put in my candles, of which I lighted two, and began to make notes of all I had seen during the day. I had not written more than four lines before I felt my eyes closing in spite of myself. As there was no reason for struggling to resist sleep and I was just dropping with fatigue, I arranged two arm-chairs like a camp bedstead and slept, in spite of the horrible tumult going all round, under and above me. I woke in broad daylight. Except for two or three alarms and the firing of a few shots, the night had been perfectly quiet. I looked into a glass and saw the need there was for me to return home. I had not changed my linen for three days, or shaved for two; my face was covered with freckles and half my drill-waistcoat buttons had been torn off by the weight of the bullets that had drawn it to one side; lastly, one of my gaiters and one of my shoes were covered with the blood of the poor fellow I had helped to lift to the Institut fountain. I left my cabinet and found Bonnelier at his post. He signed to me that he wanted to show me something. I went to him and he slipped a paper into my hands.

"Take a copy of that, if you care to," he said; "but whatever you do, don't lose my copy!"

"What is it?"

"Neuilly, 3.15 a.m.... Oudard, messenger.... Rubrique Laffitte."

"Good!"

I took a pen and copied the following note, word for word. By itself that note would be a curiosity, but, put into juxtaposition with the letter that will be given later, it rises to the dignity of a historic document, like those articles of furniture which are recognised as genuine and pass from an old curiosity shop to a museum. Here is the note:—

> "The Duc d'Orléans is at Neuilly with all his family. The royal troops are near him at Puteaux. It only needs an order emanating from the Court to remove him from the nation which may find in him a powerful security for its future safety. It is proposed to approach him in the name of constituted authorities, suitably accompanied, and to offer him the crown. If he raises scruples of delicacy of feeling with regard to his family connection, he will be informed that his residence in Paris is essential to the tranquillity of the capital of France and that he must be put in safety. The absolute certainty of this measure can be relied upon, and there is, moreover, no doubt that the Duc d'Orléans will not lose any time in associating himself heart and soul with the wishes of the nation."

The original note was in Oudard's handwriting.

Strange coincidence! whilst the father was founding a throne the son was incurring the danger of death.

Now we will see what happened.

Bohain and Nestor Roqueplan expected Étienne Arago to breakfast at Gobillard's, in the place de la Bourse. As Arago left the *National* on his way to the café he met Bohain's, servant looking for his master.

"Ah! monsieur," said the worthy fellow, when he caught sight of Étienne, "do you know where my master is?"

"He should be at Gobillard's," replied Étienne. "What do you want him for?"

"I am sent by his brother-in-law, M. Lhuillier, to tell him I that the Duc de Chartres has been arrested at Montrouge."

"Who had him arrested?"

"M. Lhuillier—he is the mayor of the village. He wants to know what he should do with the prince."

"Humph!" said a man sitting on the pavement, with a rifle between his legs, munching a piece of bread; "what he should do with him? We'll tell him what to do with him!..." Then, rising—"Here, friends!" he cried out loudly, "the Duc de Chartres has been arrested at Montrouge. Those who would like to taste a bite of prince's flesh come with me!"

"What did you say, my fine fellow?" exclaimed Étienne, laying a hand on the man's shoulder.

"I said that they killed my brother and that I will myself go and kill the Duc de Chartres this very day!"

There was no time to be lost. Étienne flew into the café.

"Look here!" he said to Bohain, "your servant has made a fine mess of it!"

"What has he done?"

"He went and spread the news that the Duc de Chartres was a prisoner in the hands of your brother-in-law, and a score of rascals have started off to kill the prince."

"The devil!" Nestor and Bohain exclaimed in a breath; "that must not be allowed."

"What shall we do?"

"Take upon yourself to lead them, put yourself at their head; keep them back as long as ever you can, and one of us will go and give General La Fayette warning of the danger the prince is in.... A man shall be sent off post-haste to M. Lhuillier, and the Duc de Chartres set at liberty before you and your men reach Montrouge."

"Good!" said Étienne; "but do not lose any time!"

Then, throwing himself at the head of a group of thirty men—

"To Montrouge!" cried Étienne Arago; "to Montrouge, my friends!"

Each one took up the cry, "To Montrouge!" and they started for the Maine barrière, whilst Nestor Roqueplan—as far I can recollect it was Nestor—ran to the place de Grève.

The Vaudeville lay on the route to the Maine barrière; they went across the Palais-Royal gardens, then crossed the square and threaded their way along the rue de Chartres. A scene-shifter was standing at the theatre door, Arago made a sign with his eyes for him to come up to him; the man understood and did so. Arago pretended to be receiving some confidence from the man.

"Good! my friends," he said; "here is a fresh business. You don't know what I have just heard! He says there is a Royalist conspiracy to come and burn down the Vaudeville, and, as you are aware, the insurrection started from the Vaudeville: had we not better begin by searching the theatre first?"

No objections were raised. Besides, many of those honest fellows were not at all displeased at the thought of seeing the inside of a theatre; only the man who had proposed the journey to Montrouge, who was a cooper from the quartier du Roule, tried to raise objections; but nobody listened to him. So they stopped at the Vaudeville, and Arago, lantern in hand, conducted his men from the lowest pit to the galleries; he did not spare them a single post, or trap-door, or side-scene. A whole hour was wasted over this visit. They then continued their course towards the Maine barrière.

Meanwhile, General La Fayette had been warned and had sent off to Montrouge M. Comte, one of the most brilliant students of the École polytechnique, who has since written a capital work on Positive Philosophy. M. Comte was the bearer of a letter couched in the following terms:—

> "In a free country, every man should be allowed to circulate wherever he likes; permit M. le Duc de Chartres to return to Joigny, at the head of his Hussars, and await the orders of the Government. LA FAYETTE

> "HÔTEL DE VILLE, 30 *July* 1830"

When I learnt the danger the Duc de Chartres was incurring, I wanted at once to return home and have my horse saddled to gallop off to Montrouge; but it was pointed out to me that, before I could reach the rue de l'Université, M. Comte would be at Montrouge and that it would be much better to await news at the Hôtel de Ville, so I waited. The hours, I must, confess, passed very slowly, from eight in the morning till two in the afternoon. At two, Étienne returned, covered with sweat and dust. The Duc de Chartres was saved. Thanks to the delay at the Vaudeville, and to a second incident which we will relate in due course, the messenger arrived in time.

The Duc de Chartres had with him General Baudrand and M. de Boismilon. M. Lhuillier made the aide-de-camp and the secretary get into the prince's carriage, and asked them to drive off and wait for the Duc de Chartres at la Crois-de-Berny, whilst he himself undertook to bring the prince to the same place safe and sound. Whilst General Baudrand and M. de Boismilon left in a barouche by the front entrance and took the main high road, M. le Duc de Chartres and M. Lhuillier went out by a back door, and left in a cab by a cross-country road, rejoining the road to Joigny, a quarter of a league below the place where M. Baudrand and M. de Boismilon were waiting for the prince.

One circumstance in particular had helped to expedite the flight and Arago's good intentions on the prince's behalf. When they reached the Maine barrière the men were stopped; no armed troops whatever were to be allowed to leave Paris. Their first instinct was towards forcing the obstacle in their way, but they consented to parley with the sentries on duty, and finally ended by fraternising with them. Some of the men even went inside the guard-house itself, while the rest sat down in the ditches hollowed out between the trees to catch rain-water. Arago ordered bread and some bottles of wine for them and I himself undertook to go in search of information. An hour later, he reached Montrouge. M. le Duc de Chartres had just left. He took a copy of General La Fayette's letter to justify the prince's release and carried it back to his men. They took the news in very ill humour, and Étienne could only manage to calm them down by promising that he would take them back to the Hôtel de Ville and give them powder to their hearts' content. Étienne had thus come back with this twofold object in view, of reporting the news of the flight of the Duc de Chartres to General La Fayette, and of giving his men their promised powder. But he had some difficulty in keeping his promise; there had been such a waste of powder that no one knew where to obtain any.

"I give you my word of honour," La Fayette, who could not believe in such a lack of ammunition, said to Étienne, "that if Charles X. were to return to Paris, we should not have four thousand rounds to fire with!"

I heard this answer, and did not let it fall to the ground.

When Arago had gone away, I went up to La Fayette.

"General," I said to him, "did I not hear you tell Arago just now that you were short of powder?"

"Quite true," the general said; "but perhaps I was wrong in mentioning it."

"Will you let me go and fetch some?"

"You?"

"I, myself, certainly."

"Wherefrom?"

"Wherever there may chance to be any, either at Soissons or at la Fère."

"They will not give you any."

"Then I will take it."

"What! you? You will take it?"

"Yes."

"By force?"

"Why not? The Louvre has been taken by force, surely!"

"You are certainly mad, my friend," the general replied.

"Not so, I swear it; I am sane enough!"

"Come, come, go home; you are tired out, past talking almost. They tell me you spent the night here."

"General, give me an order to get powder."

"Nothing of the kind."

"Do you really mean you do not wish me to go?"

"I do not wish to have you shot."

"Thank you; but pray be good enough to give me a free pass to General Gérard's presence."

"Why, yes, I will do that willingly. Monsieur Bonnelier, draw up a passport for M. Dumas."

"Bonnelier is busy, general; I will do it myself, and you can sign it immediately.... You are quite right, I must go home, for I am quite done up!"

I went to a table and drew up the following passport:—

"30 *July* 1830, 1 o'clock

"Allow M. Alexandre Dumas access to General Gérard."

I presented the paper in one hand and a pen in the other to General La Fayette, and he signed it.

I had got my order.

"Thanks, general," I said.

And, as the passport was in my writing, I added after the two words "General Gérard" the phrase, "To whom we recommend the proposition he has just communicated to us."

Furnished with this pass, I at once went to Laffitte's hotel and gained access to the general. He had seen me at M. Collard's when I was a child, and recognised me when I gave him my name.

"Ah! so it is you, Monsieur Dumas!" he said. "Well, what is this proposition?"

"This is it, general.... M. de La Fayette said in my hearing a few minutes ago, at the Hôtel de Ville, that he was short of powder, and that, in the event of Charles X. returning to Paris, there would probably not be four thousand rounds of shot left."

"It is a fact, and, as you will recognise, a sufficiently disquieting one."

"Well, I offered General La Fayette to go and obtain some powder."

"Wherefrom?"

"Soissons."

"How are you going to get hold of it?"

"How? Why, there are not two ways of taking things, surely? I shall ask politely for it, to be sure."

"From whom?"

"The commanding officer, of course."

"And suppose he refuses?"

"I shall take it without his leave."

"I have been waiting for that.... Once more tell me how you are going to take it?"

"Oh! that is my affair!"

"Is that the proposition recommended to me by General La Fayette?"

"You see it for yourself, the sentence reads clearly enough: 'To General Gérard, to whom we recommend the proposition he has just communicated to us.'"

"Did he not think your suggestion a mad one?"

"I must say, to be quite truthful, that we had just a little discussion about it."

"Did he not tell you that there are twenty chances to one that you will be shot in such an undertaking?"

"I fancy he did express some such opinion."

"In spite of that, he still recommended your proposal to me."

I succeeded in convincing him.

"Why did he not himself issue the order you come to ask of me?"

"Because he maintained, general, that orders to be given to the military authorities are your business, and not his."

General Gérard bit his lips.

"Hum!" he exclaimed.

"Well, general?"

"Well, I say it is impossible!"

"Why so?"

"I cannot compromise myself so far as to issue such an order."

I looked him straight in the face.

"Why not, general?" I said. "I am willing enough to compromise myself to the extent of carrying it out!"

The general shuddered and stared at me in return.

"No, no!" he said, "I cannot.... Apply to the Provisional Government."

"Ah! yes, that Provisional Government of yours! it will be an easy matter if I can find it, but I have been looking all over for it. I have asked all sorts of people to point it out to me, and when I have gone where I was directed, I have only found a large empty hall with a table in the middle, on which stood empty bottles of wine and beer, and in one corner a desk and a sort of minute book on it.... Believe in me, general, since I believe in reality and not shadows, and sign the order I want."

"Do you really want it?" he said.

"I do indeed, general."

"And you are ready to bear the responsibility yourself of whatever harm may come of it?"

"Would you like me to give you a repudiation of all responsibility with respect to my person before I go?"

"You can write the order yourself."

"On condition, general, that you will copy it completely in your own handwriting after ... it will have more weight if it is autograph."

"Very well."

I took up a piece of paper and wrote this rough draft of an order:—

> "The military authorities of the town of Soissons are asked to hand over immediately to M. Alexandre Dumas all the powder that can be found either in the powder magazine or in the town.
>
> "PARIS, 30 *July* 1830"

I presented the paper to General Gérard, who took it, read it and re-read it. Then, as though he had forgotten that I had asked him for an autograph order, he took a pen and, saying, "Since you really wish it...." he signed my order.

I let him do it, for an idea came into my head.

"Thanks, general."

"Are you really satisfied?"

"Very well satisfied."

"Then you are not hard to please."

And he returned to the drawing-room. I still held the pen, and, above his name, I wrote "Minister for War."

The first interpolation had succeeded so well that I ventured on a second one. Thanks to my second interpolation the order read as follows:—

> "The military authorities of the town of Soissons are asked to hand over to M. Alexandre Dumas instantly all the powder that can be found either in the powder magazine or in the town.

Minister for War,
GÉRARD

"PARIS, 30 *July* 1830"

But my readers must not suppose this was all. I had an order for the military authorities signed *Gérard*, but I also wanted a similar invitation to the civil authorities signed *La Fayette*. I laid great store by General Gérard's military reputation, but I counted still more upon General La Fayette's popularity; besides, one of the signatures would supplement the other.

When I returned to the Hôtel de Ville I sent to ask to see La Fayette, and he came to me.

"Well," he said to me, "haven't you gone to bed yet?"

"No, general, I am just off."

"To what place?"

"Soissons."

"Without an order?"

"I have one from General Gérard."

"Did Gérard give you an order?"

"Enthusiastically, general."

"Oh! oh! I should much like to look at it."

"Here it is"; and he read it.

"'Minister for War'?" he said, after he had read it.

"He thought that would assist my purpose."

"Then he did well."

"Will not you also give me something?"

"What is it you want?"

"An invitation to the civil authorities to second the revolutionary movement which I am going to try and proclaim to the town. You know well enough that I could not hope to succeed unless through the instrumentality of some popular surprise."

"Granted.... It shall not be said that, since you risk your life in the undertaking, I, on my side, risk nothing."

And he took up a pen, and wrote the following proclamation entirely in his own fine handwriting:—

To the Citizens of the town of Soissons

"CITIZENS,—You are acquainted with the events that have been happening in Paris during the three ever-memorable days that have just gone by. The Bourbons have been driven out: the Louvre is taken, and the people are masters of the capital. But the three days' victors may be deprived of the victory they have so dearly bought, for want of ammunition. They, therefore, apply to you in the person of one of our combatants, M. Alexandre Dumas, who comes to make a fraternal appeal to your patriotism and devotion. All the powder that you can send to your brethren in Paris will be considered as an offering to your country.

"For the Provisional Government, the Commander-General of the National Guard,

LA FAYETTE

"HÔTEL DE VILLE DE PARIS, 30 *July* 1830"

It will be seen that, on the whole, this proclamation did not contain much besides an appeal to patriotism and devotion. Now this was not quite what I wanted; but, there it was, and I had to make the best of it. I embraced General La Fayette, and I descended the steps from the Hôtel de Ville as fast as I could. It was now three in the afternoon; the gates of Soissons, being a fortified town, were shut at eleven at night. I must, therefore, reach Soissons before eleven, and I had twenty-four leagues to go. I caught sight of a young painter called Bard, a friend of mine, in the square. He was a handsome young fellow of eighteen, with a face as calm and impassive as a fifteenth-century marble statue. He looked just like Donatello's Saint George. I was seized with a desire to have a travelling companion, if it should only be for the purpose of getting me properly buried in case the prophecies of the two generals, La Fayette and Gérard, should come true. I went up to him.

"Ah! Bard, old chum," I said, "what are you doing?"

"I?" he said.... "I am looking on.... It's a queer game, is it not?"

"It is something more than that," I said, "it is magnificent! What have you been doing in it all?"

"Nothing.... I have no arms, but an old halberd that lies in my studio."

"Would you like to make up for lost time, then, in one stroke?"

"There is nothing I should like better."

"Then come along with me."

"Where?"

"To get yourself shot."

"I should love it."

"Hurrah! Run off to my rooms and fetch my double-barrelled pistols; have my horse saddled, and come and rejoin me at Le Bourget."

I have forgotten to mention that, out of the first proceeds of *Christine*, I had bought a horse of that same Chopin who, on the morning of the 29th, had been taken for the emperor upon the place de l'Odéon.

"What is Le Bourget?" Bard asked.

"Le Bourget is the first relay posting-station on the road to Soissons."

"Why take your horse, then, if there is a relay post?"

"Ah! in case the post-master should have sent out all his horses; they may have been seized. That is the reason I cannot take my carriage, because of the barricades and because all the posting-masters have not post-carriages in their sheds in spite of the law which legally compels them to have them. Then you see, my dear fellow, if we find a carriage, we will take it; if we only find one horse, we will ride side by side at full speed; if we find neither one nor the other, we shall still have my horse, and you must ride behind me, and we will represent the finest half of the four sons of Aymon."

"I understand."

"Then fetch my horse and the pistols, and whichever reaches Le Bourget first, waits for the other."

"I will fly the whole way!" cried Bard, as he dashed off towards the quay Pelletier.

"And I also," I replied, as I ran off down the rue de la Vannerie, which led straight into the rue Saint-Martin, my most direct way for reaching La Villette.

One word about what was passing while Bart was running along the quay Pelletier and I was scampering down the rue Saint-Martin.

Étienne Arago returned to the *National* office when he had dispersed his men.

"Do you know the news?" Stapfer asked him.

"What news?"

"Thiers is found once more."

"Pooh! Where is he, then?"

"He is up there, and has begun searching for some subject to write a leader on."

"Well, then, I will take him one."

"You know nobody is allowed to enter his office when he is working?"

"Rubbish! Haven't we been into the king's study?"

"Well, then, go in. You can give him that reason as an excuse, and he will indeed be hard to please if he is not satisfied with it."

Arago entered.

Thiers turned round to see who had the impertinence to defy his orders.

He recognised Arago, who had played a very important rôle in the drama being enacted. The frowning face of the famous political writer softened when he saw who it was.

"Oh! it is you!" he said.

"Yes.... I have hunted you out to give you a subject for an article."

"What is it?"

Arago related the whole adventure of Montrouge and how M. le Duc de Chartres had managed to escape in time.

Thiers listened with the deepest attention.

"Dear, dear," he said when Arago had finished. "Who knows but that you have probably saved the life of a son of France...."

Arago stood with his mouth gaping and his eyes inordinately wide open.

And that was the way the wind was blowing on 30 July 1830, at 3.15 in the afternoon! The wind changed Thiers' plans, and, instead of writing his article, he got up and ran off to Laffitte's.

We shall see, on my return from Soissons, what he did there.

CHAPTER IV

Gee up, Polignac!—André Marchais—Post-master at
Bourget—I display the Tricolour on my carriage—Bard
joins me—M. Cunin-Gridaine—Old Levasseur—Struggle
with him—I blow out his brains!—Two old
acquaintances—The terror of Jean-Louis—Our halt at
Villers-Cotterets—Hutin—Supper with Paillet

By the time I reached Villette I could not put one leg before the other. But, by good luck, I caught sight of a trap.

"Driver," I said, "ten francs if you take me to Bourget!"

"Fifteen?"

"Ten!"

"Fifteen!"

"Nonsense!"

"Well, then, jump in, governor."

In I jumped, and we set off. The horse was a slow one, but the driver was a good patriot. When he knew how great a hurry I was in, and the object of my journey, he said—

"Oh! it's no wonder, then, that my horse will not trot any faster, for I christened him Polignac; he is an idle good-for-nothing that one can do nothing with.... But don't be anxious, we shall get there all right."

And he took hold of his whip by the lash end, struck the horse with the handle instead of the thong, and shouted, "Gee up, get along, Polignac!" By dint of shouting, swearing and lashing we reached Bourget in an hour's time. The wretched horse was at the last gasp, and I thought that, like his illustrious namesake, he had reached the end of his tether. I paid the ten francs agreed upon, and I nobly added two francs as a tip—then I went into the posting-house yard. The posting-master was just harnessing a horse to a trap. I went up to him, gave him my name, showed him the order from General Gérard and General La Fayette's proclamation, and asked him to provide me with the necessary means of fulfilling my mission.

"Monsieur Dumas," he said, "I was putting my horse in to go to Paris in search of information; but there will now be no need for me to go since you bring such excellent news. I will therefore put post-horses into the trap and take you as far as Mesnil; if you do not find a conveyance there, you can keep my trap, and on your return you will replace it in the coach-house."

No one could have spoken fairer. In the midst of our conversation, I heard myself called by name, and, as it was too soon for Bard to have arrived, I turned round to see who it was. It was André Marchais, one of our warmest and most disinterested patriots; he had posted from Brussels, where the news of the insurrection had only arrived the day before. He was miserable when he learned that it was all over. Selfish fellow! He hoped to get killed or wounded for the good cause.

We embraced heartily. I afterwards learnt that, when he reached Paris, he found a writ awaiting him, signed by the Duc de Raguse, in common with the same sent to General La Fayette, Laffitte and Audry de Puyraveau. While we were greeting one another, the horses were being put to my carriage and to Marchais's, and then Marchais' started for Paris.

"I am now at your service," said the posting-master, who seemed surprised I was not in a great hurry.

"Pardon," I replied. "I am waiting for a companion who is coming from Paris with my horse and pistols.... I am intending, if you will allow me, to leave my horse here in exchange for your trap."

"Leave whatever you like," was his reply.

We gazed down the road as far as we could see, but nothing was yet in sight.

"We shall have time," I said to the posting-master, "to rig up a tricolour flag."

"What for?" he asked.

"To put on your trap.... It will indicate our opinions, and will prevent our being arrested for fugitives."

"Oh! oh!" he said, laughing, "on the contrary, they are more likely to stop you, because ... you look like something quite different."

"Never mind, I shall be delighted to sail under the three colours."

"Ah! as far as that goes, that's easy enough!"

He crossed the street, went into a draper's shop, bought half a yard each of white, blue and red merino, got the people to sew the three half yards together, and nailed them to a broom handle. The flag was ready in ten minutes, and it cost twelve francs, broom stick included. We fastened it with two cords to the hood of the trap. As we were accomplishing this task we caught sight of Bard, who arrived on my horse at full gallop. I signed to him to hurry yet more if it were possible, but he could not go faster. At last he joined us.

"Ah!" he said, "I am glad to see that you have got a carriage, for I am dreadfully saddle sore!"

Then, as he stepped to the ground, he said, "There are your horse and pistols."

"You did not think to bring a shirt too?"

"Upon my word I didn't! I don't think you mentioned anything about a shirt."

"No, it is my own fault.... Hand the horse to the stable lad, take the pistols and be sharp and get in; it is five o'clock already!"

"A quarter to five," the post-master remarked, looking at his watch.

"Do you think we shall reach Soissons before eleven to-night?"

"It will be a difficult job—but there, so many miracles have happened the last three days that it would not be impossible for you to perform this one."

And he gave orders to the postillion to mount the horse.

"Are you on?" he asked.

"Yes."

"Then off you go; gallop the whole way, you understand?"

"I understand, governor," said the postillion.

And he set off at a furious pace.

"You know the pistols aren't loaded," Bard said.

"All right! we will load them at Villers-Cotterets."

By a quarter to six we were at Mesnil: we had covered nearly four leagues in the hour.

Luckily there were fresh horses at the post. Our postillion here got another postboy to take up the running, and, in order that we might make even better speed, they put in three horses this time instead of two. I wanted to pay for the stage we had just done, but the posting-master had given his orders and the postillion refused to take the money. I gave him ten francs for himself; he commended us to the fresh postboy and we set off at top speed. Fortunately, the trap was well-seasoned, and in an hour we were at Dammartin. Our tricolour flag produced the desired sensation. The people came out all along our route and made the liveliest signs of enthusiasm; and, by the time we reached our relay at Dammartin, half the town had collected round us.

"This is capital!" exclaimed Bard; "but to make things more lively still, we ought to shout something."

"Right you are, my friend, shout away; and, while you shout, I will take a little nap."

"What shall I shout?"

"Why, *Vive la République!* to be sure!"

We came out of Dammartin amidst shouts of "*Vive la République!*"

Between Dammartin and Nanteuil we saw a post-carriage, which, when it caught sight of our tricolour flag, stopped, and its occupants stepped down.

"What news?" a man of about fifty asked us.

"The Louvre is taken and the Bourbons have fled; there is a Provisional Government composed of La Fayette, Gérard, etc. *Vive la République!*"

The gentleman of fifty scratched his ear and got into his carriage again. It was M. Cunin-Gridaine. We resumed our journey, and by twenty to eight we were at Nanteuil. We had only three hours and twenty minutes left and still had twelve leagues to go. It was not likely we could manage it, but my principle always is not to despair so long as there is any vestige of hope left; even then!... At Nanteuil we again changed horses, and the tricoloured flag had its usual effect. Nothing was known of Paris doings, so we brought the first really definite news. They gave us an old postillion, to whom I shouted—

"Four leagues an hour, and three francs as tip."

"All right, all right," said the old fellow. "I know my business. I've driven *the general.*"

The general was my father; for, you see, I was in my native country here.

"All right; if you have driven my father, you know he liked fast driving. I take after him."

"Right, I know my business."

"Off, then."

"We're off!"

"Oh!" said the postillion I was leaving behind, "I pity you, M. Dumas. You have a bad customer to deal with."

"I will make him go, never fear."

"I hope so. *Bon voyage!* Come, off you go, Levasseur; put a little quicksilver in your boots!"

And the postillion departed.

"Levasseur," I shouted to him, "I told you three francs for yourself if we reach Levignan by half past eight."

"If we don't get there by half-past eight we shall by nine. I know my business."

"You understand," I repeated, "I will be at Levignan by half-past eight."

"Bah! only kings say I *will.*"

"There is no longer a king.... Come, come. Quicker, quicker!"

"Let us climb the rise first, and then we will see about that."

So we climbed the rise, and then old Levasseur put his horses to the trot.

"Oh! Levasseur, this won't do at all," I said.

"How, then, do you want me to go?"

"Faster."

"Faster? It is forbidden."

"Forbidden by whom?"

"By the rules, deuce take it! I know my business, you bet!" "Look here, Levasseur ..."

"What is it?"

"Let me get down."

"Ooh!... ooh!"

The carriage stopped; I got out, and I cut a branch from an elm by the roadside.

"Look here," he said, looking on with great uneasiness, "you are not cutting off that switch to whip my horses with, I hope?"

"Make yourself easy on that score, Levasseur," I said, as I got back into the carriage. "Go on!"

"It is all very well to say go on; but have you cut that stick to beat my horses with is what I want to know?"

"All right, we shall see about that."

"Oh! we shall see about that, shall we? I'm not afraid of you because you have a gun."

"Look here, Levasseur, you know your business as a postillion, don't you?"

"Rather."

"Well, then, I too know mine as a traveller.... Your notion, it would seem, is to go as slowly as possible, while mine is to go as fast as I can. We will see which of us is the stronger."

"We will see whatever you like, I don't care."

I drew out my watch. "You have two minutes in which to make up your mind."

"What to do?"

"To put your horses to the gallop."

"And if I won't?"

"If not, I shall do so myself."

"You mean it?"

"Certainly!"

"Well, I shall like to see the fun."

"You shall, Levasseur, take my word for it."

He began to strike up the lament of Saint Roch. While all this was taking place we had been going at a slow trot.

"Look here, Levasseur," I said, at the end of the first couplet, "I warn you that one minute has gone already."

Levasseur began intoning the second at the top of his voice; but just as he was going to begin the third I gave his horses a sound whack across their quarters with the stick. They made a leap forward and set off at full trot.

"Now, now, what are you doing?" asked the postillion.

Instead of replying, I redoubled my blows and thrashed the horses into a gallop.

"Oh! curse it, curse it, is that what you mean? Let me get down for a second and you shall see, indeed! Ah! you will have to settle with me. Wo! wo! Good heavens, will you stop it?"

"What! stop it, Levasseur?" I shouted, continuing to beat with all the strength in my arms, "when I tell you that I know my business better than you know yours!"

"Once more, will you have done?... No?... Wo! wo! wo!"

It was in vain he cried "Wo!" or reined in his horses; they reared, but galloped all the same. Unluckily, my elm branch broke and I was disarmed. But the horses were so well started that he did not manage to pull them up for a hundred yards.

"Ah! Good heavens! Confound it all!" he shouted. "When I have stopped my horses you shall answer for this, I can tell you!"

"Now, what do you intend to do, Levasseur?" I asked, laughing.

"To unharness them, and leave you and your trap in the middle of the road.... We shall see if it is allowable to put the poor beasts into such a state."

And by degrees he calmed his horses down.

"Hand me one of my pistols," I said to Bard.

"What for?"

"Pass it, quick."

"You aren't going to blow his brains out?"

"I am, indeed!"

"They are not loaded."

"I am going to load them."

Bard gazed at me in terror.

I put a percussion cap on each nipple and rammed a wad down the centre of each barrel. I had just finished the operation when the carriage pulled up, and the postillion got down, swearing, to unfasten the traces, as he had threatened, lifting up his legs one after the other heavily in their great boots. I waited for him, pistol in hand.

"Look here, Levasseur," I said, "if you touch those traces I shall smash your head for you."

He raised his eyes and saw the two muzzles of the pistol.

"Stuff!" he said, "you daren't kill people that fashion!" And he put his hands to the traces.

"Levasseur, take care what you are doing! Do you mean to take out the horses?"

"The horses are mine, and, when they are over-driven, I unharness them."

"Have you a wife and children?"

Again he looked up; the question struck him as an unusual one.

"Yes, I have a wife and four children—a boy and three girls."

"Well, then, Levasseur, let me warn you that, if you do not let the traces alone, the Republic will be obliged to grant a pension to your family."

He began to laugh and to grip the traces with both hands. I pressed the trigger, the cap exploded and the wad hit my man in the middle of his face. He believed he was killed and fell backwards, his face between his hands, half fainting. Before he had recovered from the shock and astonishment I had drawn off his boots, as Tom Thumb drew off the Ogre's, put them on my own legs, jumped astride the saddle-horse, and we set off at full gallop. Bard nearly fell into the floor of the carriage with laughing. When we had gone three or four hundred yards, I turned round, though I still kept on whipping the horses, and I saw old Levasseur had sat up and begun to collect his senses. A tiny hill we were ascending soon hid him from my sight. I had still nearly a league and a half to make, but I caught up the lost time and did it in seventeen minutes. I reached the post at Levignan with a grand flourish of whips, and, when I pulled the horses up, two persons appeared on the threshold. One was the posting-master, M. Labbé, himself; the other my old friend Cartier, the timber-merchant. Both recognised me at the same time.

"Why; you, my boy!" said Labbé. "Things have gone badly with you then if you have come down to being a postillion?"

Cartier gave me his hands.

"What the devil have you come in such an equipage as that for?"

I related the story of old Levasseur, then all that had happened in Paris.

It was now half-past eight; I had only two hours and a half in which to reach Soissons, and there were still nine long leagues to travel. The probability of succeeding was getting less and less, but I would not give in. I asked M. Labbé for horses; he brought me them immediately, and in five minutes time they were harnessed.

"My goodness," said Cartier to Labbé, "I mean to go along with them. I am curious to know how it will end." And he got in with us.

"Remember me to the postillion," I said to M. Labbé.

And he nodded his head.

"Jean-Louis," he said to the postillion.

"Yes, governor."

"You know old Levasseur?"

"By Jove, I should think I do!"

"You see that gentleman?" pointing to me.

"Yes, I see him."

"Well, he has just killed old Levasseur."

"How?" said the postillion, gaping at me.

"With a pistol shot."

"What for?"

"Because he wouldn't go full gallop.... So take heed, Jean-Louis."

"Is that true?" the man asked, turning pale.

"You can see for yourself, since monsieur has driven in himself and is using the whip and wearing boots of the deceased."

Jean-Louis threw one terrified glance at the whip and the boots and then he set off at a tearing gallop, without saying another word.

"Oh! my poor horses," Labbé shouted after us, "they are going to have a bad time of it."

We reached Villers-Cotterets under the hour, and here quite an ovation awaited me. I had hardly given my name to the first person I met whom I knew, than the news of my arrival by post-conveyance in a trap surmounted by a tricolour flag flew all over the town as rapidly as though it had been sent on telegraph wires. As the news spread, the houses turned out the living with as great unanimity as the tombs will discharge the dead at the sound of the Last Trump. All these living beings ran to the posting-house and reached it as soon as I did. Much explanation had to be given to make them understand my costume, my rifle, my sunburnt condition, the trap, the tricolour flag and why Bard and Cartier were with me. Everybody in that beloved countryside loved me well enough to have the right to put these questions to me. I answered them all, and when the explanations were given, they cried in unison—

"Don't go to Soissons! Soissons is a Royalist town!"

But it scarcely need be said that I had not come as far as Villers-Cotterets without intending to proceed to Soissons.

"I not only intend to go to Soissons," I replied, "but I shall do all in my power to reach it before eleven o'clock, even if I have to give twenty francs in tips to the postillions."

"If you offer them forty, you will not reach there in time," said a voice I knew; "but you will get there by midnight, and they will let you enter."

The voice belonged to one of my friends who lived at Soissons, the one who, fifteen years previously, when a child like myself, came, an hour before me, to make a suggestion to General Lallemand when a prisoner, similar to the one I put to him an hour later.

"Ah! is that you, Hutin?" I exclaimed. "What shall I do to get in?"

"You will get in because I shall go with you and insist on it.... I belong to Soissons and know the gatekeeper."

"Bravo! What time shall we have?"

"The whole night; but it would be best to arrive before one o'clock."

"Good! then we shall have time for supper?"

"Where are you going to have it?"

Ten voices shouted—

"With me! With me! With us!" and they began to drag me from front, from behind, by the lappets of my coat and the cord of my powder horn and the strap of my gun and the ends of my cravat.

"Excuse me," said another voice, "but he has been previously engaged."

"Ah! Paillet!..."

It was my old head-clerk. I turned towards my many hosts.

"It is quite true. I promised Paillet the last time he visited Paris to come and dine with him."

"So much the better," said Paillet, "since the dining-room is large and those who wish to come and take supper with us will find room enough.... Come, those who are his friends can follow me!"

A score of young fellows followed us—my old comrades, Saunier, Fontaine, Arpin, Labarre, Rajade and many more. We went along the rue de Soissons and stopped at Paillet's house. In a moment almost, thanks to old Cartier, who lived nearly opposite, an excellent supper was improvised. Cartier senior, Paillet, Hutin, and Bard sat down to table. The others sat round, and I had to relate the history of that marvellous epoch-making three days while I was eating, not a single detail of it having penetrated so far as Villers-Cotterets. There were many exclamations of admiration. I next passed to the story of my own mission. And here enthusiasm cooled down. When I announced that I counted on taking alone, by myself, all the powder in a military town of eight thousand inhabitants and eight hundred soldiers, my poor friends looked at one another and said, as General La Fayette had done—

"Why! you must be mad!"

But more serious still than this unanimous opinion of the inhabitants of Villers-Cotterets was that Hutin, a native of Soissons, agreed with their opinion.

"However," he added, "as I said I would attempt the thing with you, I will do so; only it is a hundred to one that before this time to-morrow we shall have been shot."

I turned towards Bard.

"What did I say to you when I proposed you should accompany me, Seigneur Raphaël?" I said.

"You said to me, 'Will you come and get yourself shot with me?'"

"And your reply?"

"I replied I should be only too happy."

"And now?"

"I am still of the same opinion."

"Bless me! my dear fellow, you can see, you can hear. Reflect in time."

"I have reflected."

"And you mean to come?"

"Certainly."

I turned to Hutin again,

"So you are coming?"

"Of course I am."

"Then that is all right," and I raised my glass.

"My friends! to-morrow evening, meet again here! Cartier, a dinner for twenty, on condition that it is eaten whether we are dead or alive. Here are two hundred francs for the dinner!"

"You shall pay for it to-morrow."

"What if I am shot?"

"Then I will pay for it myself."

"Hurrah for old Cartier!"

And I swallowed off the contents of my glass. They all took up the chorus, "Vive Cartier!" and as we had finished supper and it was eleven o'clock and the horses were in the trap, we got up to go.

"Ah! confound it, one moment," I said, reflecting; "we may have to deal with rougher adversaries to-morrow than old Levasseur, therefore let us really load our pistols this time. What gentlemen among you have bullets of the right calibre?"

My pistols took twenty-four size, and it would be a chance, indeed, to find bullets of that calibre.

"Wait a bit," said Cartier, "I can manage that. Have you any bullets in your pocket?"

"Yes, but only size twenty."

"Give me four of them, or rather eight; it is best to have a re-load...."

I gave him eight bullets. Five minutes later, he brought me them back, elongated into slug shot, so that they fitted into the pistols. They were cleaned out, loaded and primed with the greatest care; just as though preparations were being made for a duel. Then for the last time we drank to the success of the enterprise; embraced each other several times and got into the trap, Hutin, Bard and myself; the postillion mounted his horses, and we set off at full gallop along the road to Soissons in the midst of cries of farewell and cheers of encouragement from my dear good friends. Two hours after we had left Villers-Cotterets the gate of Soissons opened at the voice and name of Hutin, and the gatekeeper let us in to the town, little knowing he was giving entrance to the Revolution.

CHAPTER V

Arrival at Soissons—Strategic preparations—
Reconnaissance round the magazine—Hutin and Bard
plant the tricolour flag upon the cathedral—I climb the wall
of the powder magazine—Captain Mollard—Sergeant
Ragon—Lieutenant-Colonel d'Orcourt—Parleys with
them—They promise me neutrality

After twenty-two years have passed, we almost hesitate to write the ensuing narrative, which now seems incredible even to ourselves; but we would refer any who doubt the story to *le Moniteur* of 9 August, containing the official report which General La Fayette inserted, so that those who were interested might either protest or deny as occasion required. Nobody protested, nobody denied.

At midnight, we were knocking loudly at the door of Hutin's mother's house, who welcomed us with cries of delight, no more I suspicious than was the gatekeeper, concerning the contents of the trap *à la Congrève* that she ordered to be put up in her stable yard.

The following day was market day, and the next business was to concoct a huge tricoloured flag to take the place of the white flag which was floating from the cathedral. Madame Hutin, not thoroughly understanding what we were up to, nor the consequences it might lead to, put at our disposition the red curtains from the dining-room and the blue ones from the drawing-room. A sheet taken from the linen cupboard completed the National Standard. The question of the staff did not trouble us; we should use the one belonging to the white flag. Flag-staffs do not declare their opinions. Everybody in the house—Madame Hutin, her cook, Hutin, Bard and I—all set to the task of sewing, and by three o'clock in the morning, in the early hours of dawn, the last stitch was put in.

This was how we proposed to divide the task: I was to begin by seizing the powder magazine, while Bard and Hutin, under pretext of going to the top of the tower to see the sun rise, were to gain access to the cathedral, pull down the white flag and substitute the tricolour. If the sacristan offered resistance, we intended to fling him from the top of the belfry. Hutin had armed Bard with a carbine and provided himself with a double-barrelled gun. As soon as the flag was raised, the sacristan shut up in the tower and the key of it in Hutin's pocket, the latter was to send Bard to me at the magazine, which was situated among the ruins of the Church of Saint-Jean. Bard could be more useful to me in the powder magazine, as it was kept by three old soldiers whose long service had been recompensed by a position that was almost a sinecure, and whose wounds, covered up in the case of two of them by the ribbon of the Legion of Honour, received during the Empire, allowed no question to arise as to their valour. They were Lieutenant-Colonel d'Orcourt, Captain Mollard and Sergeant Ragon. It was, therefore, highly probable I should need reinforcement.

Whilst Bard was on his way to join me, Hutin, bearing General La Fayette's proclamation, was to go at once to Dr. Missa. Dr. Missa was the head of the Liberal opposition party and had repeated over and over again the statement that he was only waiting a suitable opportunity to move forward. The present opportunity was an excellent one, and we hoped he would not let it go by. Hutin believed he could count on two of his friends equally, one named Moreau and the other Quinette. Quinette, son of a member of the Convention, was the same who, later, became a deputy under Louis-Philippe, and ambassador at Brussels under the Republic. We shall see how each of them responded to the appeal made in the name of the Revolution.

When I left the magazine I was to go to the commander of the town, M. de Linières, and with General Gérard's order in my hands, obtain the order from him to carry off the powder either willingly or by force. I had been warned that M. de Linières was more than a Royalist! He was an ultra-Royalist.

At the first news of the insurrection of Paris he had declared that no matter how things turned in the capital, he would bury himself under the ruins of Soissons and that the white flag should float from the highest stone of the ruins. It was, accordingly, pretty certain from what quarter we had to expect serious opposition. But I did not trouble myself much about it; each event of the day had to take its chance.

At ten minutes past three in the morning we left Madame Hutin's house. She was a splendidly courageous woman, and urged her son on rather than held him back. We separated at the end of the street, Hutin and Bard to go to the cathedral, and I to the powder magazine. As it would have been a dangerous thing to enter the precincts of the ruins of Saint-Jean by the main door, which was easy to defend, we had agreed that it would be best for me to jump over the wall. Bard was, however, to present himself at the main door, which I was to open to him when I should hear three knocks with an equal space of time between each one. I was at the foot of the wall in less than five minutes' time; it was easy to climb as it was low, with plenty of cracks between its stones to form natural steps.

However, I waited, as I did not wish to begin my excursion until I saw the the tricolour flag floating over the cathedral in place of the white one. Nevertheless, in order to get my bearings, I raised myself up gently by my wrists to the level of the top of the wall in such a manner as to be able to see over. Two men with spades were each engaged in digging quietly, turning over the square plot of a small garden. I recognised them by the pattern of their trousers and by their moustaches to be two of the soldiers who lived in the rooms in front of the powder magazine. The powder was in one or other of the first two sheds, probably in both. The oak door, solid as a postern gate, strengthened by cross-bars and studded with nails, stood between the two sheds. It was shut. Having explored the battlefield at a glance, I let myself drop down to the base of the wall and turned my eyes in the direction of the cathedral. Very soon I saw the heads of three men appear above the gallery and then the white flag become agitated in an unusual manner, which could not be attributed to the wind, the absence of which was obvious; finally, the white flag was lowered and disappeared, and the tricolour standard was raised in its place. Hutin and Bard had accomplished their part of the business; it was now time for me to begin mine. It did not take me very long. I examined my gun to see if the primings were in place, slung it over my shoulders, and, by the help of my hands and feet, I quickly got to the top of the wall. The two soldiers had changed their position and were leaning on their spades, looking with marked surprise at the top of the tower where the tricolour flag was triumphantly floating. I leapt down into the magazine premises. At the noise I made as I touched the ground they both turned round simultaneously. The second apparition evidently seemed more extraordinary to them than the first. I had had time to pass my rifle into my left hand and to cock the two triggers. I walked towards them, they still looking at me, motionless with astonishment. I stopped within ten yards of them.

"Gentlemen," I said, "I ask your pardon for the manner of my introduction to your premises, but as you do not know me, you would have refused me entry by the door, which would have occasioned all kinds of delays, and I am in a hurry."

"But, monsieur," Captain Mollard asked, "who are you?"

"I am M. Alexandre Dumas, son of General Alexandre Dumas, whose name you will have known if you served under the Republic; and I have come in the name of General Gérard to ask the military authorities of the town of Soissons for all the powder they can find in the town. Here is my order: will one of you gentlemen come and look at it?"

With my gun in my left hand, I held out my right to them. The captain came up, took the order and read it. Whilst he was doing so, Sergeant Ragon took some steps towards the house.

"Pardon, monsieur," I said, "but since I do not know your purpose in going into your house, I will beg you to remain where you are."

The sergeant stopped short. Captain Mollard gave me back my order.

"That is all right, monsieur. What do you want further?"

"I want a simple enough thing, monsieur.... Do you see that tricolour flag?"

He nodded as an acknowledgment that he saw it perfectly well.

"Its substitution for the white flag," I continued, "will prove to you that I have friends in the town.... The town is going to rise."

"And then, monsieur?"

"Then, monsieur, I was told that I should find brave patriots in the three keepers of the magazine, who, instead of opposing General Gérard's orders, would assist me in my enterprise. I therefore introduce myself to you with confidence to ask your co-operation in this business."

"You must know, monsieur," the captain said, "that our co-operation is out of the question."

"Well, then, promise you will be neutral."

"What is all this about?" asked a third interlocutor, who appeared on the doorstep with a silk kerchief tied round his head, attired only in a shirt and cotton trousers.

"Colonel," the sergeant said, stepping nearer to his superior officer, "it is a messenger from General Gérard. It seems the Revolution in Paris is accomplished, and that General Gérard is now Minister for War."

I stopped the orator, who continued his advance towards the house.

"Monsieur," I said to him, "instead of going to the colonel, please ask him to come to us. I shall be most happy to pay my addresses to him and to show him General Gérard's order."

"Is it in the general's handwriting, monsieur?" the colonel asked.

"It is signed by himself, monsieur."

"I warn you that I have just been a member of the general's staff, and therefore know his signature."

"I am very pleased to hear it, colonel, as it will, I hope, make my negotiations with you all the easier."

The colonel came towards me, and I handed him the paper, taking advantage of the moment's time thus given me, while the other soldiers collected round him, to get between them and the door of the house. I was, it is true, alone, but the three men I had to deal with were unarmed.

"Well, colonel?" I asked in a minute or two.

"I can say nothing, monsieur, seeing the order is indeed signed by General Gérard."

"On the contrary, colonel," I observed, laughing, "that seems to me a reason why you should say something."

He exchanged a few words with the captain and sergeant.

"What was it you were asking from these gentlemen when I came out?"

"Your neutrality, colonel. I do not presume to use intimidation or to urge you against your conscience. If your opinions incline you towards the movement afoot, hold out your hand to me frankly and give me your word not to oppose my mission; if, on the contrary, you wish to oppose it, make up your minds at once and do what you like to get rid of me, for I mean to do all I can to rid myself of you."

"Monsieur," said the colonel, when he had again held converse with his two comrades, "we are old soldiers, and have faced fire too often to be afraid; we accept the part you offer us, for, unfortunately, or rather, perhaps, fortunately, what you say with regard to our patriotism is true, and if you laid your hand on our hearts, you would feel the effect the sight of the tricolour flag we have been longing for for the past fifteen years has produced upon us.... What, monsieur, is the agreement we are to enter into with you?"

"To go inside your house, and not to come out of it unless you learn that I have been killed or until I shall myself come and release you from your promise."

"I promise on my honour as a soldier for both myself and my comrades!"

I walked up to him and held out my hand. Three hands were held out instead of one; three hands pressed mine with cordiality.

"Come, this is not all," said the colonel. "When one undertakes a task like yours, it should succeed."

"Will you assist me, then, with your advice?"

He smiled.

"Where are you going now?"

"To the commander of the fort, M. de Linières."

"Do you know him?"

"Not in the least."

"Hum!"

"Well?"

"Be on your guard!"

"Still, if I have the order?"

"Well?"

"Then I may count on you?"

"Oh! naturally.... Neutrality has ceased, and we have become your allies."

At that moment three knocks with an equal interval of time between each were given on the door.

"What is that?" asked the colonel.

"One of my friends, colonel, who has come to render me assistance if I should need it." I called out loud—

"Wait a minute, Bard; I will come and open it. I am among friends."

Then, turning towards the soldiers, I said to them—

"Now, gentlemen, will you go into your house?"

"Certainly," they said.

"I may rely on your word?"

"Our word once given is never taken back."

They went in, and I opened the door for Bard.

CHAPTER VI

How matters had proceeded with the sacristan—The four-inch gun—Bard as gunner—The commander of the fort—Lieutenant Tinga—M. de Lenferna—M. Bonvilliers—Madame de Linières—The revolt of the negroes—The conditions upon which the commander of the fort signed the order—M. Moreau—M. Quinette—The Mayor of Soissons—Bard and the green plums

Bard was perfectly cool; anyone seeing him with his rifle over his shoulder would have taken him for a sportsman who had been getting his hand in by firing at the target.

"Well," he asked me, "how have things gone here?"

"Splendidly, my dear boy! All is settled."

"Good! then you have the powder?"

"Oh! not yet. Hang it, what a hurry you're in! How about your flag?"

He pointed to the tower.

"You see for yourself," he said. "Doesn't it make a fine picture in the landscape?"

"Yes. How did it all go off?"

"Oh! all went smoothly enough. The sacristan raised a few difficulties just at first, but he ended by giving in to the reasons M. Hutin laid before him."

"What were those?"

"I don't quite know; I was looking at the landscape.... Your valley of Aisne is really magnificent, you know, especially over by Vauxbuin."

"So you heard nothing of what Hutin said to your sacristan?"

"I think he told him he would be killed if he did not keep quiet."

"Where is he now?"

"Who? M. Hutin?"

"Yes."

"He should be where he promised to be, at the doctor's."

"That's capital! You stop here."

"Good! What shall I do?"

"Wait a moment."

Bard's eyes followed me as I made an expressive movement in a certain direction.

"Ah! that pretty little cannon over there!" he exclaimed.

And I walked towards a pretty little four-inch gun—I even think it was, possibly, of smaller bore—under what was, I believe, a model of it, placed beneath the shelter of a sort of shed.

"Isn't that a charming toy?"

"Charming!"

"Then come and help me, my dear fellow."

"How?"

"To put it in position. In case of siege, I must leave you some artillery."

So we harnessed ourselves to the cannon, and I placed it in position about thirty yards from the door. Then I slipped half the contents of my powder-horn into the gun and wadded it with my pocket-handkerchief; on the top of this first wadding I slipped in a score of bullets; then I rammed Bard's handkerchief on the top of these and the cannon was loaded. When loaded, I laid and primed it.

"There!" I said, panting; "now listen to what you must do."

"I await your instructions."

"How many cigarettes can you smoke on end?"

"Oh! as many as I have tobacco to turn them into or money to buy them!"

"Well, then, my friend, smoke without intermission, so that you always have a lighted cigarette on hand: if they try to get inside without your leave and force the gate open, ask them three times to withdraw and if, upon the third request, they still persist in entering, place yourself where the recoil of the cannon cannot break your legs and then pass your lighted cigarette diagonally across the priming, and you will see how the machine will work!"

"All right!" said Bard, not raising the slightest objection.

I believe, if, whilst he had been on the gallery of the tower, I had said to him, "Bard, jump over!" he would have done it.

"And see here!" I said: "now you have both a rifle and a cannon, my pistols are a superfluous luxury to you, so let me have them."

"Oh! true," he said, "here they are"; and he drew them out of his pocket and returned them to me.

I again examined them and found them in good trim. I slipped them into the two back pockets of my jacket and turned to go to the house of the commander of the fort. A sentinel stood in the street outside, and I asked him where M. de Linières' office was. He pointed it out; it was on the first floor, or entresol. I climbed the staircase, and left my gun outside the door of the office. The commander was alone with an officer whom I did not know. He had just got up on hearing the news that the tricolour flag was floating high over the cathedral. He was probably still unaware of my arrival; for, just as I came in, he was interrogating the officer upon the details of this extraordinary event.

"Pardon, Monsieur le Vicomte," I said to him, "but if all you require is the full details, I can supply you with them, and I may add no one could give you them so well."

"Well, but first of all who are you, monsieur?" the commander asked, looking at me in astonishment.

I have already described my get-up: my cravat was in ribbons, my shirt had been worn for four days, my jacket was bereft of half of its buttons. There was therefore nothing very surprising in the question put by the commander of the fort. I gave my surname, Christian name and profession. I briefly painted the situation in Paris, together with the object of my mission, and I tendered him General Gérard's order. The commander of the fort, or king's-lieutenant, as he was indifferently called in those days, read it attentively and, handing it back to me, said—

"Monsieur, you must know that I do not recognise the sovereignty of the Provisional Government in the slightest degree. Moreover, General Gérard's signature does not present any sort of authenticity: it is not legal, nor is the document even sealed."

"Monsieur," I replied, "of one thing I am certain: I can triumphantly convince you of its legality and genuineness. I give you my word of honour that the signature is really that of General Gérard."

A half-ironical smile crossed the commander's lips.

"I believe you, monsieur," he said; "but I can tell you news that will render all further discussion useless: there are not at the present moment more than two hundred cartridges of powder in the magazine."

But M. de Linières' smile had somewhat angered me.

"Monsieur," I replied, with equal politeness, "as you do not know exactly the number of cartridges that there are in the magazine, I will go and inquire of the three soldiers there who are my prisoners on parole."

"What! your prisoners on parole?"

"Yes, Monsieur le Vicomte: Lieutenant-Colonel d'Orcourt, Captain Mollard and Sergeant Ragon are my prisoners on parole.... So I am going, as I had the honour of mentioning to you just now, to find out for myself what quantity of powder there is in the magazine and then I will return and inform you."

I bowed and went out, looking at the sentry's shako as I did so, which bore the number 53. I was in luck; for, it will be observed, the garrison of Soissons was composed of the depot of the 53rd, and the 53rd, it will be recollected, had turned to the people's side at the very moment the Louvre was being taken. I met an officer in the street.

"Are you M. Dumas?" he said.

"Yes, monsieur."

"Is it you who have placed the tricolour flag on the cathedral?"

"Yes, monsieur."

"Then go forward and fear nothing from us: the soldiers were distributing tricolour cartridges among themselves yesterday."

"So I can count upon them?"

"You can rely upon their keeping in their barracks."

"Your name?"

"Lieutenant Tuya."

"Thanks!" And I entered his name in my pocket-book.

"What is that for?" he asked me.

"Who knows?" I replied. "When I return to the Hôtel de Ville I may find a second epaulette going begging.... You would not be angry with me for sending it you?"

He began to laugh, shook his head and made off rapidly. At the same moment, I saw the officer whom I had found closeted with the commander of the fort going faster still. There was no time to be lost; no doubt he was going with orders. I quickened my pace accordingly, and was at the magazine in a trice. I knocked at the door and called out my name.

"Is that you?" Bard asked.

"Yes."

"Good! I will open to you."

"Don't trouble. Ask the officers how much powder, for artillery purposes, there is in the magazine."

"All right!"

I waited, and through the keyhole I could see Bard hurrying to the house. He disappeared, then reappeared after a few minutes.

"Two hundred pounds!" he shouted to me.

"Prodigious! It is always the way.... Now throw me over the key of the door, or slip it under, so that I can come in without disturbing you."

"Here you are."

"Right! Whatever you do, don't quit your post."

"Make your mind easy!"

And upon this assurance I retraced my steps back to the house of the king's-lieutenant. I found the same sentinel at the street door, but there was now a second one at the door of the office. I expected to see him bar my passage, but I was mistaken. As upon the first occasion, I deposited my gun outside the door and then I went in. The company had been increased by two other persons, and, besides the commander of the fort and the unknown officer, there were now in that small office, as I re-entered it, M. le Marquis de Lenferna, Lieutenant of the Police, and M. Bonvilliers, Lieutenant-Colonel of the Engineers. These gentlemen were all arrayed in their respective uniforms, and, consequently, had sabres and swords by their sides. I entered and closed the door behind me. I had hardly come face to face with these four officers before I regretted I had left my rifle outside, for I realised that grave matters would be discussed between us. I felt the lapels of my waistcoat to see that my pistols were still in my pockets. They were there safe and sound.

"Monsieur," the commander said to me in a jeering tone, "I have sent for M. le Marquis de Lenferna and M. Bonvilliers, in your absence, who are my colleagues in the military command in this town, in order that you may lay before them the object of your mission here, as you did to me."

I saw I must assume the same tone of conversation as that used by M. de Linières, so I replied—

"Well, monsieur, the object of my mission is simple enough: it is merely a question of my taking the powder that I have found in the magazine and transporting it to Paris where they are short.... And, in respect of that same powder, allow me to inform you, Commander, that you were wrongly instructed: there are two hundred pounds of powder in the magazine—and not two hundred cartridges."

"Whether two hundred pounds or two hundred cartridges is not the question, monsieur: the question is that you have come to seize powder from a military town containing a garrison of eight hundred men."

"Monsieur does, indeed," I replied, "put the question on its true footing: I have come to take powder from a garrison town containing eight hundred men, and here is my order for so doing."

I presented General Gérard's order to the king's-lieutenant, who, no doubt because he knew it already, took hold of it with the tips of his fingers and handed it to his neighbour, who handed it back to M. de Linières after he had read it, with a slight inclination of the head.

"You are probably backed by an armed force to carry out the order, in case we refuse to comply with it?"

"No, monsieur; but I have a most determined intention of taking that powder, since I swore to General La Fayette I would either take it or be killed. That is why I asked your leave for the opening of the magazine doors, and I now renew my request."

"And you think that alone, Monsieur Dumas ... I think you told me your name was Dumas?"—

"Yes, monsieur, that is my name."

"—You can force me to sign such an authorisation? You have noticed probably that there are four of us?"

I had noticed still more—the commander's jeering tones and that, from the wording of his sentences, the situation was growing warm; I therefore edged myself gradually back until I was master of the door and, while doing so, I placed my hands inside my coat pockets and silently prepared the double locks of my pistols. I then suddenly drew them from my pockets and pointed the muzzles towards the group in front of me.

"True, there are four of you, messieurs,... but there are five of us!" And I took a step forward and said, "Messieurs, I give you my word of honour that if the order is not signed within the next five seconds I will blow out the brains of all four of you, and I will begin with you, Monsieur le Lieutenant de Roi—honour to whom honour is due!"

I had turned deadly pale, but in spite of my pallor my face expressed immovable determination. The double-barrelled pistol which I held in my right hand was only a foot and a half off M. de Linières' face.

"Beware, monsieur!" I said to him: "I am going to count the seconds"; and after a pause I began, "One, two, three!..."

At this moment a side door opened and a woman burst into the room in a paroxysm of terror.

"Oh! my love, yield! yield!" she cried; "it is a second revolt of the negroes!.."

And, saying this, she gazed at me with terrified eyes.

"Monsieur," began the commander of the fort, "out of regard for my wife...."

"Monsieur," I replied, "I have the profoundest respect for Madame, but I too have a mother and a sister and hope, therefore, you will have the goodness to send Madame away, so that we can thrash this matter out between men alone."

"My love!" Madame de Linières continued to implore, "yield! yield! I implore you! Remember my father and mother, both massacred at Saint-Domingo!"

I had not until then understood what she meant by her words, "It is a second revolt of negroes!"

She had taken me for a negro, from my fuzzy hair and complexion, burnt deep brown by three days' exposure to the sun and by my faintly Creole accent—if, indeed, I had any accent at all, from the hoarseness that had seized me. She was beside herself with terror, and her fright was easily understood; for I learnt, later, that she was a daughter of M. and Madame de Saint-Janvier, who had been mercilessly killed under her very eyes during a revolt. The situation was now too strained to be prolonged much further.

"But, monsieur," the commander exclaimed in despair, "how can I yield before one single man?"

"Would you like me, monsieur, to sign a paper attesting that you gave me the order with a pistol at your head?"

"Yes, yes! monsieur," shrieked Madame de Linières.

Then turning to her husband, whose knees she had been clasping, she reiterated, "My love! my love! give him the order! Give it him, I entreat you!"

"Or would you prefer," I continued, "that I went and hunted up two or three friends so that our numbers may be equal on both sides?"

"Indeed yes, monsieur, I should much prefer that course."

"Be on your guard, Monsieur le Vicomte! I go, relying on your word of honour; I go, because I have you at my mercy and could blow out the brains of every one of you.... I can promise you it would soon be done.... Shall I find you on my return where you are and as you are?"

"Yes, yes! monsieur," exclaimed Madame de Linières.

I bowed courteously but without ceding one jot.

"It is your husband's word of honour I require, madame."

"Well, then, monsieur," the king's-lieutenant said, "I will give you my word."

"I presume that it includes these gentlemen equally?"

The officers bowed in the affirmative. I uncocked my pistols and replaced them in my pockets. Then, addressing myself to Madame de Linières—

"Reassure yourself, madame," I said; "it is over. In five minutes, gentlemen, I shall be back here."

I went out, picking up my gun, which I found in its corner outside the door. I had gone beyond my resources, for I did not know where to look for Hutin; and Bard was guarding an important point. But chance served me; for, as I stepped into the street, I saw Hutin and one of his friends, who, faithful to their rendezvous, were waiting ten yards away from the house: the friend was a young man called Moreau, a warm patriot of Soissons. They both had double-barrelled guns. I beckoned to them to come into the courtyard. They came in, not knowing quite what was expected of them. I went upstairs; parole had been strictly maintained and none of the gentlemen had left his place. I went to the window and opened it.

"Messieurs," I said to Hutin and Moreau, "have the goodness to inform Monsieur the Commander that you are ready to fire upon him and upon the other persons I shall point out to you, if he does not instantly sign an authorisation for taking the powder."

For answer, Hutin and Moreau cocked their guns. Madame de Linières followed all my movements and those of her husband with haggard eyes.

"That will do, monsieur," the king's-lieutenant said; "I am ready to sign"; and, taking a piece of paper from his desk, he wrote—

"I authorise M. Alexandre Dumas to take away all the powder belonging to the artillery which is in the magazine Saint-Jean.—King's-lieutenant and Commander of the Fort,

VICOMTE DE LINIÈRES"

SOISSONS, 31 *July* 1830"

I took the paper which the count handed me, bowed to Madame de Linières, made my apologies to her for the unavoidable fright I had caused her and went out.[1]

We met M. Quinette, the second friend whom Hutin had mentioned to me, in the street. He had come to join us. It was rather late, as will be seen, especially since he was soon to leave us. His advice was that we ought to do things legally and that, to this end, I must be assisted by the mayor. I had no objection to this proposition, as I had possession of my order, so I went to find the mayor. I have forgotten the name of that worthy magistrate: I only remember that he made no difficulty about accompanying me. Accordingly, five minutes later, accompanied by the mayor, Hutin, Moreau and Quinette, I cautiously opened the gate of the Saint-Jean cloisters, first having notified to Bard that it was I who was opening it.

"Come in, come in!" he replied.

I entered and saw the cannon in position, but, to my great astonishment, Bard had disappeared. He was twenty yards from his cannon, perched up in a plum tree eating green plums!

---

[1] I believe I ought to take the precaution, at the conclusion of this story that I took at the beginning, namely, to refer my reader to the *Moniteur* of 9 August 1830, in case they think I have been romancing. See the notes at the end of this volume.

CHAPTER VII

The Mayor of Soissons—The excise-office powder—M. Jousselin—The hatchet belonging to the warehouse-keeper—M. Quinette—I break open the door of the powder magazine—Triumphant exit from Soissons—M. Mennesson attempts to have me arrested—The Guards of the Duc d'Orléans—M. Boyer—Return to Paris—"Those devils of Republicans!"

Now, thanks to M. Quinette's excellent advice, no one could have been acting more legally than we were, since we were proceeding (like Bilboquet) *with the mayors authorisation.* So Lieutenant-Colonel d'Orcourt hastened to open the artillery powder magazine to us. It was the shed on the right of the door as we entered. We hardly found two hundred pounds of powder in it, as a matter of fact. I was preparing to carry it off when the mayor laid claim to it for the defence of the town. The claim was fair enough, only, as I had decided to carry powder to Paris, no matter what the quantity might be, it seemed likely I should have to go through the same scenes with the mayor as I had with the commander of the fort, when Lieutenant-Colonel d'Orcourt approached me and said in a whisper—

"There is certainly only about two hundred pounds of powder in the artillery magazine, but in the shed opposite there are three thousand pounds belonging to the town."

I opened my eyes wide.

"Say that again," I said.

"Three thousand pounds of powder there"; and he pointed to the shed.

"Then let us open it and take the powder."

"Yes, but I haven't the key."

"Where is it?"

"M. Jousselin, the storehouse-keeper has it."

"Where does he live?"

"One of these gentlemen will show you."

"Very good!"

I turned towards the mayor.

"Monsieur, I can at present say neither yes nor no to your request: if I find more powder, I will leave you the two hundred pounds; if I do not find any, I shall take it from you. Now do not let us lose any more time, but each take our share. My dear Monsieur Moreau, you go and find a waggon and horses among the carters in the town; they shall be paid what is right, on condition they are here within an hour. As soon as the powder is in the cart we will start off.... Is that clear?"

"Yes."

"Off with you, then."

And M. Moreau set off at the swiftest rate of speed possible.

"Bard, my friend, you can see that the situation has grown more complicated, so take up your position close to the cannon, re-light your cigarette and keep away from the green plums."

"Make your mind easy on that score! I hardly ate three and they set my teeth horribly on edge!... I would not bite a fourth, no, not even for M. Jousselin and all his powder!"

"You, Hutin, go to M. Missa, to find out his intentions, and if he has not done anything get from him General La Fayette's proclamation; it should be useful to us in dealing with the civil authorities, who may possibly decline to believe in the validity of General Gérard's orders."

"I'll run off at once!"

"You, Monsieur Quinette, have the goodness to take me to M. Jousselin."

"It is a long way off."

"Bah! what matter? If we work in harmony, things will come out all right! In half or three-quarters of an hour at longest we shall all be back here again!"

Bard resumed his post, Hutin left to fulfil his commission and M. Quinette and I to fulfil ours. We reached M. Jousselin's door.

"Here we are," M. Quinette said, "but you will understand my feelings: I belong to the town and have to stop in it after you have gone, so I would rather you went alone to see M. Jousselin."

"If that is all, I don't mind!"

With that, I entered M. Jousselin's house. I must confess that, at the moment, neither my looks nor my dress were calculated to inspire confidence in the minds of others. I had lost my straw hat somewhere or other, my face was sunburnt and streaming with perspiration; my voice, at one moment, would sound loud like a trumpet, at the next, it was shrill almost to imperceptibility; my jacket, bulging with the pistols, was gradually losing what few buttons had adorned it and, finally, my gaiters and shoes were still soiled with blood which the dust of the road had not effaced. It was not, therefore, surprising that, when M. Jousselin saw me thus equipped and with my double-barrelled gun on my shoulder, he recoiled in his armchair as far as he could get.

"What is your business with me?" he asked.

I explained the object of my visit as succinctly as I could, for I was pressed for time; moreover, had I wanted to use lengthy phrases I could not have done so, as I could scarcely speak for hoarseness. M. Jousselin raised several objections, which I cleared away as fast as he put them; but I saw we might go on endlessly.

"Monsieur," I said, "let us stop. Will you or will you not give me the powder in your magazine for a thousand francs, which I have here with me?"

"Monsieur, it is impossible; there is twelve thousand francs' worth of powder."

"Then will you take my thousand francs on account and accept a draft for the remainder on the Provisional Government?"

"Monsieur, we are forbidden to sell on credit."

"Then will you give me the excise powder for nothing? It is Government powder, which is as much as to say it belongs to me, since I hold a Government order to take it and you hold none for keeping it."

"Monsieur, I would have you take notice.."

"Yes or no?"

"Monsieur, you are at liberty to take it, but I would have you know that you must be answerable for it to the Government."

"Oh, monsieur, why didn't you tell me that at first and so have ended our discussion long ago!"

I went up to the fireplace and took hold of an axe that lay there for chopping firewood, which I had had my eye on.

"But, monsieur," the astounded excise-keeper exclaimed, "what are you going to do now?"

"I am borrowing this axe from you to break open the door of the powder magazine.... You will find it all right at Saint-Jean, Monsieur Jousselin."

And I left him.

"But, monsieur," he shouted after me, "you are committing theft!"

"Yes, both theft and housebreaking, Monsieur Jousselin!"

"I warn you I shall write about this to the Minister of Finance!"

"Write to the devil, if you like, Monsieur Jousselin!"

Whilst we were talking we had reached the street door. M. Jousselin went on shouting and people began to collect in a crowd. I began to go back the way I came.

"Oh! do give us a bit of peace, monsieur!" I said, seizing hold of the axe by its handle.

"Murder! assassin!" he shouted at the top of his voice, and, shutting the door in my face, he bolted it inside.

I had not time to amuse myself by breaking open his door.

"Quick, quick!" I said to M. Quinette; "the enemy is in retreat; let us go on!"

I ran off axe in hand to the church of Saint-Jean. I had not gone a hundred yards before I again heard M. Jousselin's voice, whose maledictions reached me across that distance. He was at his window, endeavouring to rouse the population against me. M. Quinette had prudently disappeared.

I did not see him again until 1851, in Brussels. If, at Soissons, I found he left too soon, he made up for it afterwards at Brussels, where it seems to me he stayed too long; for, after the 2nd of December, he waited for them to send him his dismissal as ambassador to the Republic....

I did not worry about the excise-storekeeper or the hostile attitude of the populace, but continued on my way to the magazine. Bard was at his post this time.

"Well," Lieutenant-Colonel d'Orcourt asked me, "have you leave from M. Jousselin?"

"No," I replied, "but I have the key of the powder shed!"

I produced the axe, and at this juncture Hutin arrived.

"Well," I said, "what has your Dr. Missa done?"

"Just think of it!" Hutin replied; "that great patriot has not dared to put his nose outside his door! It was all I could do to get him to give me back General La Fayette's proclamation!"

"I hope you have brought it!"

"Rather! Look here! here it is!"

"Give it me.... Good! Now to business!"

"And what have you done?"

"I have acquired this hatchet from M. Jousselin's fireplace.... We are going to break open the door of the powder magazine, load it on to a waggon Moreau has gone to fetch and then we will depart."

"Can you rely on Moreau?"

"As I would on myself!... By the way, what has become of Quinette?"

"He has disappeared—vanished—flown! But we will not bother ourselves about him. Set to work!"

It was not such an easy task to accomplish. The lock that we had to burst was fixed into the wall itself and the wall was built of flint rubble, so every badly aimed blow which fell on the wall instead of the lock or woodwork produced millions of sparks. Lieutenant-Colonel d'Orcourt was a stout-hearted man, but, at the third blow which sent out a shower of sparks, he shook his head and turned to his companions.

"Don't let us stop here any longer," he said; "it is no use ... these gentlemen must be mad to undertake such a task"; and he departed as far as the walls of the enclosure would permit, the others following him.

After five minutes' work I had to pass on the axe to Hutin, who took his turn and set to work on the door. And, as things were not going as fast as I wished, I raised the largest piece of stone I could find, and, striking an attitude like Ajax, I shouted to Hutin to look out; then I hurled the stone and, at this final effort, being already shaken, it flew into splinters. At last we were in touch with the three thousand pounds of powder! I was so eager lest it should still slip away from our grasp, that I sat down on a barrel, after the fashion of Jean Bart, and begged Hutin to go and hurry up Moreau and his waggoners. Hutin went to do so. He was of an active disposition, all nerves; an indefatigable sportsman, a fine shot and a man of few words; but, to appreciate him properly, he should be seen working, no matter what the work might be. He returned with the waggon a quarter of an hour later, but without Moreau.

What had become of him?

He had collected a score of young townsfolk and a whole corps of firemen, and they were all waiting to escort me as far as Villers-Cotterets. Moreover, Moreau sent me his horse to ride during my exit. So we loaded the waggon with the powder and I paid the price arranged (four hundred francs, I think it was). We were then free to take our carriage and post-horses; the waggoner was to follow the coach, and was to manage as best he could in bringing it back again: he was to get four hundred francs for his pains.

When we had got the powder away, we halted at Madame Hutin's house; for it was four o'clock in the afternoon and none of us had broken his fast, with the exception of Bard, who had eaten three plums. He was dying with eagerness to carry away the four-inch gun and I was equally anxious to make him a present of it; but the worthy keepers of the magazine implored me so urgently to leave it them, that I had not the heart to rob them of it. A good dinner awaited us at Hutin's; but, hungry though we were, we ate it hurriedly while the post-horses were being harnessed to the trap. Finally, by five o'clock, we started; Hutin, Moreau and Bard behind the waggon in the trap and I on Moreau's horse, walking by the side of the wheels, one hand on my holster, ready to blow up the waggon, myself and half the town, if anybody attempted to stop our going away. But no one made any objections: we even heard some patriotic shouts behind us as we travelled on. We could not help being grateful to the people for expressing themselves thus, as in 1830 no one knew exactly the right cry to utter. The most dangerous spot we had to pass was the gate of the town; for as soon as we had reached the gateway the portcullis might be dropped in front of us, and they would attack us from the two guard-houses. But we passed these Thermopylae without harm and found ourselves on the outside of the walls and in the open country. Our men awaited us fifty yards beyond the gate: then, and not until then, I confess, I dared to breathe freely.

"By Jove! my friend," I said to Hutin, "do go back into the town and send us out twenty bottles of wine to drink the health of General La Fayette.... We have well earned them!"

A quarter of an hour later, we were raising our glasses and drinking to the general's health—a toast which the inhabitants of the town received with acclamation, many having climbed up on the walls to witness our departure. When we had emptied the twenty bottles, we resumed our journey. At Verte-Feuille, half-way between Soissons and Villers-Cotterets, I left Moreau's horse with the posting-master: I could not have sat in the saddle ten minutes longer, for I was dropping with fatigue. Whilst they were putting four post-horses to the waggon (for I began to perceive that we should never get to our destination with the Soissons horses) I lay down on the edge of a ditch and fell into such a deep sleep that they had the greatest difficulty in the world to wake me at the time of starting. Moreau then rode his horse, for he wished to accompany us as far as Villers-Cotterets. I took his seat in the trap and was hardly in it before I fell asleep again. I had probably been sleeping for an hour when I felt myself being shaken vigorously. I opened my eyes and saw it was Hutin.

"Oh! do wake up!" he said.

"What for?" I asked, yawning. I was sound asleep.

"Why, because it appears that your former lawyer, M. Mennesson, has roused the town into a state of revolution, telling them you are carrying out the orders of the Duc d'Orléans, and they do not mean to let us go through."

"I carry out orders for the Duc d'Orléans? My goodness! the man must be either mad or drunk!"

"Mad he may be, but, meanwhile, he means to have the matter out with you."

"Have it out! and by means of whom?"

"By means of the foresters, in the first place."

"The foresters? Let me think. How can we have it out with the foresters who belong to the Duc d'Orléans, if I am doing the business of the duke?"

"Oh! I don't understand it at all—I only warn you. Now you know, let us proceed."

I managed to rouse myself from sleep. We were at the foot of the mountain of Dampleux and one of my Villers-Cotterets friends had run out to warn us of the plot afoot against us. I called Moreau, who alone comprised all the cavalry we could muster.

"Moreau," I said to him, "do me the favour of finishing off your horse by putting him to a gallop and going to inquire either at Cartier's or Paillet's house what amount of truth there is in the news they have just brought us. If you meet M. Mennesson, threaten him that I have two bullets in my rifle and that if he does not want to become acquainted with them, he must keep himself out of range."

Moreau set off at a gallop: I placed myself and Hutin with six or eight men who seemed to me equal to any emergency, in the van, leaving Bard and twenty-five to thirty others as escort to the waggon; and then we continued on our journey. In ten minutes' time we saw Moreau on his way back. There was really an assembly of people before M. Mennesson's door and he was holding forth to them; but, when Moreau went up to him and whispered in his ear, he disappeared. There still remained the Guards, who, it was said, were commanded by an old officer called M. Boyer. This resistance of the Guards under M. Boyer was the more surprising to me, since the Guards, as I have mentioned, were attached to the House of Orléans, in league with which I was accused of raising a disturbance in the province; also M. Boyer, who had formerly been an officer but was deprived of his post by the Restoration, owed everything to the Duc d'Orléans. Well! we reached Paillet's door, where we were expected, as on our first entrance to the town; supper was ready and we consumed it rapidly. All our men were at supper in Cartier's back courtyard. We expected to be attacked at any moment, and we all ate with our guns held between our legs. Supper, however, passed off without hindrance. While we were at table, the horses of both the trap and the waggon were changed and, towards ten at night, we resumed our journey; this time, we were escorted by the whole of the National Guard of Villers-Cotterets.

We parted with our escort from Soissons with many embracings and hand-shakes; they had covered six leagues in less than four hours. When we reached the summit of the Vauciennes hill, and while my whole being was basking in sweet sleep—as sound as that from which Saverny sadly reproached his executioner for rousing him—I was a second time shaken by Hutin.

"Wake up! Wake up!" he said.

"What is it?"

"M. Boyer is asking for you; he wants to fight you."

"All right! Where is he?"

"Here I am!" said a voice.

I rubbed my eyes and saw a man of between thirty-five and forty years of age, upon a horse lathered with sweat and foam. I got down from the trap.

"Pardon, monsieur," I asked, "but I understand you wished a word with me."

"Monsieur," the cavalier began in great excitement, "you have insulted me!"

"I?"

"Yes, you, monsieur! And you will, I hope, give me satisfaction!"

"What for?"

"For saying I was either mad or drunk!"

"Stop a minute, please; I said so of someone, it is true, but of whom, then, did I say it?"

"What the deuce!" exclaimed Hutin. "You said it of M. Mennesson!"

"You see, monsieur, I did not whisper it to M. Hutin.... Had you any other reason for picking a quarrel with me?"

"None whatever, monsieur."

"In that case, it was hardly worth while waking me."

"Monsieur, I thought—"

"Do you still think so?"

"No, as I am told it was not true."

"Well, then?"

"I wish you a good journey, monsieur."

"Thanks!"

M. Boyer turned his horse about and galloped back to Villers-Cotterets. We have often met since and laughed over this misunderstanding.

But I had other things to do than to laugh at that moment. I left Bard to guard the powder and got into the carriage again; I deputed Hutin to pay for the relays of horses, went off to sleep again and did not wake up until we reached the yard of the post-house at Bourget. It was then nearly three in the morning. I could not see General La Fayette before eight or nine o'clock. We therefore accepted the post-house master's offer of a cup of coffee and a bed. But, as I was not sure of myself and afraid of sleeping twenty-four hours, I begged I might be waked at seven—a promise that was given and kept religiously. At nine o'clock in the morning we entered the Hôtel de Ville. I found the general at his post in his usual blue uniform, with white waistcoat and cravat, but it was slightly more dishevelled, his waistcoat rather more open and his tie more soiled than when I left him. Poor general! he was not so fortunate as I, who was still able to speak, while he could not utter a word. He held out his arms and embraced me—that was the utmost he could do. Happily, in subsidiary matters, Carbonnel could take his place, so, when a deputation from a commune arrived, while the general greeted the mayor and his associates, Carbonnel attended to the reception of the ordinary municipal councillors. But the general made a special effort for me: he not merely held out his arms and embraced me, but he tried to congratulate me on my success and to express his satisfaction at seeing me back safe and sound; however, unluckily for my *amour-propre*, his voice gave out and the sound stuck half-way in his throat. The same thing occurred, if Virgil is to be believed, three thousand years before, to Turnus. Bonnelier, who was still able to speak, took me by the arm and exclaimed, lifting his eyes to heaven—

"Oh! my friend! what a bad time of it your devils of Republicans gave us yesterday! Happily, however, it is all over now!"

This was Hebrew to me, but the phrase, *Happily it is all over now!* troubled me much, I, who was myself a Republican; it was clear some battle must have been lost. And, indeed, events had marched on violently during the forty-four hours of my absence! Let us see what had happened and bring things up to their present juncture.

CHAPTER VIII

I Think I ended one of my preceding chapters, saying, "This story changed the plans of M. Thiers, who, instead of writing his article, got up and ran off to Laffitte's house!"

M. Thiers was an Orléanist, like M. Mignet: a dinner at M. de Talleyrand's, at which *Dorothée* had been charming, had led these two public men astray; Carrel, alone, had separated from them and remained Republican.[1] So, on the morning of the 30th, M. Thiers and M. Mignet had issued a proclamation couched in the following terms:—

> "Since Charles X. has shed the blood of the people he can no longer re-enter Paris. But a Republic would expose us to frightful divisions and embroil us with Europe. The Duc d'Orléans is a prince who is devoted to the Revolutionary cause. The Duc d'Orléans has never fought against us. The Duc d'Orléans was at Jemmapes. The Duc d'Orléans is a citizen king. The Due d'Orléans has carried the tricolour standard into battle and he, alone, can still uphold it: we want no other colours. The Duc d'Orléans does not proclaim himself, but waits for our devotion. Let us give it and he will accept the Charter as we have always intended and wished him to do. He will have his crown from the French people themselves!"

This proclamation was evidently the answer to the written note in Oudard's hands sent from Neuilly to Paris at a quarter-past three o'clock in the morning. Unfortunately, the proclamation had been hooted in the place de la Bourse and torn down from the walls upon which it had been pasted. The Revolutionary spirit was still abroad in the streets. Thiers had gone back to the *National* offices when he saw the effect produced by his proclamation. The news of the escape of the Duc de Chartres made an excuse to go to Neuilly: all gates open to a messenger who comes to announce to a father and mother the safety of their child. When he reached Laffitte, he learnt that negotiations were going on with Neuilly. The Duc d'Orléans was in direct correspondence with M. Laffitte by means of Oudard and Tallencourt. In all probability, the duchess herself did not know to what length negotiations had been carried. Madame Adélaïde was, no doubt, better acquainted with the secrets of her brother than was the wife with her husband's: the Duc d'Orléans had great belief in the almost masculine intelligence of his sister. Laffitte no longer presided over his salon; but Bérard was its head. What was the reason of Laffitte's absence? The answer given to inquirers was that he was suffering too much pain from his sprain. The fact was that Laffitte, urged to it by Béranger, was busy making a king. M. Thiers complained loudly that he would be forgotten. Béranger laughed in his face, with that smile peculiar to the author of *Dieu des bonnes gens*.

"Why the devil shouldn't the absent be forgotten?" he said to him.

And, indeed, M. Thiers had been absent for four hours from Laffitte's salon; four hours during a Revolution is equivalent to four years! In four hours a world may disappear or be completely changed.

M. Thiers went to find M. Sébastiani, and got a programme from him. Everybody wanted to add his own little brick to the building of the new kingdom. Scheffer, the painter, an artist of immense distinction and a man of great consequence, a friend of the Duc d'Orléans, and almost an official of his household, was preparing to set out for Neuilly as the Embassy of the Municipal Commission. M. Thiers attached himself to Scheffer and accompanied him. But the road to Neuilly was cut off by a regiment of the Guards.

"The devil!" exclaimed Thiers, "suppose they arrest us and discover the programme!..."

"Give it to me," said Scheffer.

He took it from the hands of Thiers, reduced it as small as possible, slipped it in the hollow of his left hand through the opening of his glove, and they reached Neuilly without accident. But the Duc d'Orléans had found he was too near the royal troops at Neuilly and had retired to Raincy, after dictating the famous note to Oudard; it was, therefore, with Raincy that Laffitte corresponded during the 30th. The two emissaries only found the duchess and Madame Adélaïde at Neuilly. Louis Blanc's information on this subject is very full and he has related the scene most accurately; we therefore refer those of our readers who desire to know every detail to his account. We will confine ourselves to saying that the queen[2] indignantly repulsed the offer of the throne, but that Madame Adélaïde, less scornful and indignant, repulsed nothing, promising nearly everything in her brother's name. M. de Montesquieu was immediately sent to Raincy.

The movement the race of Orléans had been waiting for, since it had existed in close proximity to royalty, had come at last. The object of that ambition, awakened in the mind of the duke since 1790, and nourished with the greatest care during the fifteen years of the reign of Louis XVIII. and Charles X., could now be attained; there was nothing to do but to stretch out his arm and give the word. But, at that decisive hour, courage nearly failed the Duc d'Orléans. He had decided to set off behind M. de Montesquieu, he sent him on to announce his arrival and did in fact really start; but he returned after going only a quarter of a league. What made Louis-Philippe king of the French was by no means his ambition, which had collapsed on the Raincy road; it was the fear of losing an income of six million francs that really decided him to become king of the French.

Meanwhile, at the same time that the Duc d'Orléans was returning to Raincy as fast as his horses could gallop, the Chamber opened and M. Laffitte was enthusiastically nominated its President: this was the first flattering sign of coming power—M. Laffitte, so to say, laid the foundation-stones of the kingdom of July.

Whilst M. Thiers was returning from Neuilly, and relating to those who were disposed to listen the charming reception bestowed upon him by the princesses; whilst the Duc d'Orléans was nearly forfeiting his destiny, by turning his back on the power he had greatly coveted; whilst M. Laffitte was pursuing his dream of ten years and serving that weakening ambition, which, in process of realisation, blew upon his fortune and popularity and extinguished, instead of reanimating both, let us say in few words what the Royalists were doing on one side and the Republicans on the other.

When Charles X. had given in to M. de Vitrolles', M. de Sémonville's and M. d'Argout's desires; when he let them extort a promise from him that MM. de Mortemart, Gérard and Casimir Périer should be the three chief members of a new Ministry; when he had persuaded M. de Mortemart to be the chief of this new Cabinet, he thought he had done all that was needful, and began playing whist with M. de Duras, M. de Luxembourg and Madame la Duchesse de Berry. Whilst Charles X. was playing, M. Mortemart was waiting for the king to give him orders for Paris; the dauphin, fearing the king would give these orders, after having positively forbidden the sentinels at the bois de Boulogne to allow anyone whatsoever to pass through Saint-Cloud to Paris, stood mechanically gazing at a geographical map. When the game was finished, the king announced that he was going to bed. Then M. de Mortemart, who could not understand why the king should have been eager for him to accept office, and then, since he had accepted it, to become inert after doing so, approached and asked—

"Does your Majesty command me to go?"

The king, who had just been eating burnt almonds, replied, while he chewed a toothpick—

"Not yet, Monsieur le Duc, not yet.... I am waiting for news from Paris."

And he went to his bedroom.

M. de Mortemart felt ready to leave Saint-Cloud, but a final sentiment of devotion towards the royal fortune, which was near foundering, kept him at the palace. So he went back into the apartments that had been assigned to him, but did not go to bed.

We have seen how MM. de Vitrolles, de Sémonville and Argout had been received both by the Municipal Commission and by M. Laffitte. MM. de Vitrolles and d'Argout returned to Saint-Cloud in order to relate the result of their mission; they lost sight of M. de Sémonville on the way. M. de Sémonville's conscience was quite satisfied by his first visit to Saint-Cloud and he now thought he had a right to do something to secure his position as grand referee. So he remained in Paris. In the opinion of MM. de Vitrolles and d'Argout, there was not a moment to be lost, though, even in not losing a moment, still, in all probability, nothing more could have been done to save the Monarchy. They found M. de Mortemart up and in a state of despair.

All that night, whilst the king was tranquilly playing whist and the dauphin was mechanically consulting his geographical charts, he had stood on the balcony looking towards the capital, bursting with impatience and trembling at every noise that came from the direction of Paris, as a filial son might tremble at each crack of the paternal foundations that are about to fall. He related to MM. de Vitrolles and d'Argout the various alarms and agonies of disappointment he had suffered. His hearers wanted to carry him back to Paris with them.

"What shall I do there?" replied M. de Mortemart. "I have no official character. Can I go and say like a mere adventurer, 'The Ordinances are revoked and I am Minister'? Who would believe me? An order, or signature or some means of recognition and I would join you at once."

It had been decided, then and there, to draw up the fresh Ordinances and to revoke those of the 25th, and that, when they were drawn up, the king should sign them. They were actually drawn up then and there, but the hitch came when the signing by the king was needful. Etiquette was rigid: only those in high quarters who had the right of entrée were privileged to have direct access to the king's private rooms and none of these three gentlemen possessed that right. So the Life Guards refused them an entry. They tried to win over the valet de chambre. He, too, refused to let them pass.

Why not? Did not the valet de chambre refuse M. de La Fayette's entrance to Louis XVI.'s cabinet on 6 October 1789, when he came to save the lives of Louis XVI. and his family from the universal slaughter going on—because he had not the right of entrée?

Alas! King Charles X. had not even a Madame Élisabeth by him to exclaim to the stupid valet de chambre—

"No, monsieur, he has not the right of entrée, but the king grants it him."

No, they had to resort to threats and to tell the man they should hold him responsible for the misfortunes that would attend his refusal. The valet de chambre was terrified and gave way under the heavy weight of such a responsibility. The king was asleep: they had to wake him and tell him that Paris was in a state of revolution, preparing to create a Republic; that it was up in arms and threateningly dangerous, but might yet be overcome; to-morrow Paris would be inexorable: all these arguments had to be used before the king made up his mind. The struggle continued from midnight until two in the morning and, at a few minutes after two, the king signed.

"Ah!" he murmured, as he laid the pen down, "King John or François I. would have yielded only on the field of battle!"

M. de Mortemart overheard this aside and was for returning and throwing the Ordinances upon the ungrateful monarch's bed, but MM. d'Argout and de Vitrolles led him away.

"Oh!" he muttered, "if it were not a question of saving the head of a king!..."

They entered a coach and set off, but were stopped when they reached the bois de Boulogne. The dauphin, as we said, had given strict orders to the sentinels not to let anyone coming from Saint-Cloud pass on to Paris. He had foreseen what would happen. M. de Mortemart was obliged to go round the bois de Boulogne on foot, to make a detour of three leagues and to enter Paris by means of a breach in a wall made for contraband purposes. When he entered Paris, he saw the Orléanist proclamations posted up on its walls. The Republicans had also seen them. Pierre Leroux was among the first to reach one that had only just been stuck to the wall; he pulled it down and carried it off to Joubert, in the passage Dauphine.

"If that is true," they exclaimed unanimously, "we must begin all over again; stir up the hotbeds afresh and start making new bullets."

Messengers were instantly sent off to rally the scattered Republicans and, within an hour, a meeting was held at Lointier's house. I took no part in that meeting. I was running from the Hôtel de Ville to Laffitte's at the time, trying to find that mysterious Provisional Government which everybody had heard of but no one had seen. I had just left the Hôtel de Ville as a Republican deputation arrived; it, too, had drawn up a proclamation. M. Hubert, a former lawyer and one of the most honourable men I ever met, who has recently died, leaving the whole of his fortune to hospitals and philanthropic institutions and to citizens persecuted for their democratic opinions, was deputed to present the following address to General La Fayette:—

> "The people yesterday won back their sacred rights at the price of the shedding of their own blood; the most precious of these rights is that of a free choice of its own government; any-proclamation must be withheld that designates a head before a form of government has been determined upon. There already exists a provisional representation appointed by the nation, let this be maintained until the wishes of the majority of the French people be known."

It will be seen that everybody believed in the truth of the mythical and invisible trilogy consisting of La Fayette, Gérard and Choiseul. The members of this deputation were Charles Teste, Trélat, Hingray, Bastide, Guinard and Poubelle. Hubert, the head of it, walked in advance, carrying the note they were going to read, at the point of his bayonet. The deputation was at once admitted: nobody was kept waiting in antechambers by General La Fayette. There was a lively discussion; La Fayette knew nothing of all the Orléanist plots and protested with the candour of ignorance. The Republicans on their side affirmed it with instinctive vigour.

"General," said Hubert, "we adjure you by the bullet holes on the ceiling over your head to take the dictatorship!"

They had got to this point and the general was, perhaps, on the verge of yielding, when he was told that M. de Sussy wished to speak to him. The Republicans stood there uneasy, gloomy, full of doubt, with looks turned as though interrogating the general and summoning him to repeat aloud the communication that was being whispered to him. The general well knew there must not be any hedging at such a crisis; moreover, his upright mind and loyal heart detested all dissimulation.

"Show M. de Sussy in," he said aloud.

"But, General, M. de Sussy desires to speak with you privately."

"Tell M. de Sussy to come in," repeated the general; "I am in the midst of friends."

M. de Sussy entered and was obliged to divulge the business that had brought him there. His news was well-timed: he came to announce to General La Fayette the revocation of the Ordinances, the appointment of the Mortemart, Gérard and Casimir Périer coalition, the arrival of M. de Mortemart at Paris and, finally, the refusal of the Chamber, which favoured the Duc d'Orléans, to receive the new Ordinances signed by Charles X. at three in the morning— just at the very time when the Duc d'Orléans was dictating the famous note which had put MM. Thiers and Mignet in such a state of commotion.

Matters having thus come to light, the hands of each party were exposed to view on the same table at once: the hand played by Charles X. in making the Mortemart, Gérard and Casimir Périer Ministry; M. Laffitte's hand in proposing the Duc d'Orléans to the suffrage of the nation; and, finally, the hand of the Republicans, urging La Fayette to accept the dictatorship.

Had the thing been done on purpose and at a pre-arranged hour it could not have succeeded better.

So there was trouble which was nearly fatal to M. de Sussy, from the clash of powerful interests in that room. Bastide had taken him by the collar and was just about to fling him out of the window when Trélat restrained him. I shall have occasion to refer to Bastide more than once, and I can speak for his honesty and courage, then and now. Like all extreme excitement, this one was followed by a reaction. In this case, reaction resulted in letting M. de Sussy go quietly under the escort of General Lobau, who had opened the door and run in at the infernal din he heard proceeding from La Fayette's cabinet.

The Republicans were now alone again with the general. They renewed their entreaties to him until someone came and warned them that M. de Sussy had inveigled himself into the Municipal Commission and was laying before it Charles X.'s fresh proposals, to which the Commission appeared anything but hostile. This was not the moment to argue with La Fayette over the relative theories of constitutional government in France and Republican government in the United States, whilst questions of life or death were being debated by the Municipal Commission. They must fly to that Commission: this was done, but the door was shut. They knocked, but no one answered. A few blows with the butt-end of their rifles and the door gave way to violence, exposing M. de Sussy expounding his reasons to the members of the Municipal Commission, who appeared to be listening to them with the greatest favour. This apparition of six or eight armed men, who were well known for strength of character, flung terror into the midst of the meeting; the members rose and dispersed, trying to look as though nothing important was going on. Whilst this was happening, Hubert felt a paper being slipped into his hand; he turned round and recognised M. Audry de Puyraveau, the only true patriot on the Commission.

"Take this proclamation," he said excitedly; "it was very near to being signed an hour back by the Municipal Commission, but M. de Sussy's arrival deferred all questions; climb up a post and read the proclamation, spread it abroad, impose it upon the people.... They will sign it if you make them afraid."

Well and good! This style of action just suited the politics of the victors of the Louvre. All rushed down the steps of the Hôtel de Ville; Hubert climbed up on a post, called the people round him and, surrounded by his companions, read the following proclamation as though issued by the Municipal Commission. Pay special attention to it, for it was the only serious Republican manifesto which was produced in 1830. Pay special attention to it, as it will show how far the most advanced minds had reached at that time. Pay good heed, for it will teach you what were the desires of the men who had been under persecution for eighteen years because they were supposed to wish to overturn society. When you have read that proclamation (it would be advisable to compare it with those of MM. Thiers and Mignet), recall the Rights of Man of 1789, and you will see that the Republicans of 1830 were behind that Declaration.

> "France is a free country. She must have a Constitution. She has only accorded the Provisional Government the right to consult her. Meanwhile, until she has expressed her wishes by means of fresh elections, let her respect the following principles:—Let there be no more kingships, but a Government controlled solely by representatives that shall be elected by the nation—Executive power to be entrusted to a temporary President—The mediate and immediate concurrence of all citizens in the election of deputies— Religious liberty—No more State religion—A guarantee of the use of the land and sea forces against all arbitrary dismissals—The establishment of National Guards in every district of France, entrusting them with the defence of the Constitution. These principles, for which we have recently risked our lives, we will uphold, if need be, by means of legitimate insurrection."

Whilst Hubert was reading this proclamation in the place de l'Hôtel de Ville, M. de Sussy entered La Fayette's cabinet and, in spite of all entreaties and bringing to bear the claims of relationship which bound the La Fayettes with Mortemart, he could only extract the following letter from the general:—

"MONSIEUR LE DUC,—I have received the letter with which you have honoured me, with the habitual sentiments which your personal character has always inspired. M. de Sussy will give you an account of the visit he has been good enough to pay me. I fulfilled your wishes by reading the contents you addressed to me to the many persons who surrounded me; I invited M. de Sussy to proceed to a small gathering of the Commission then sitting at the Hôtel de Ville; finally, I will remit the papers to General Gérard which he entrusted to me; but the duties that detain me here render it impossible for me to come and see you. If you will come to the Hôtel de Ville, I shall be happy to receive you; but it will be useless with respect to the subject of our correspondence, since my colleagues have been informed of your communications."

From that side, at any rate, M. de Mortemart could see that there was no hope to be entertained. Meanwhile, Saint-Quentin, rising in revolt simultaneously with Paris, had sent a deputation to General La Fayette to ask for two students from the École polytechnique to command its National Guard. The deputation added that they would only need to risk one attempt upon La Fère and that, doubtless, they would be able to drive away the 4th Regiment of artillery garrisoned in that town under the command of Colonel Husson. Students of the École were often about the Hôtel de Ville and were all so brave that there was no need to pick out any of them specially. General La Fayette sent Odilon Barrot for the first two he should happen to come across. He brought back Charras and Lothon. Charras still had his hundred and fifty to two hundred men encamped in a corner of the Hôtel de Ville, which formed a corps of its own. The two young men were introduced to General La Fayette's presence, who explained to them what was wanted and gave them the opportunity of going to ask for the necessary authority from the Provisional Government. Charras and Lothon then began to search for that notorious Provisional Government for which I had hunted in vain, and no doubt they were put on the same track as I was, for they reached the same large hall adorned with the same great table covered with the same bottles of wine and beer (empty ones, of course) and occupied by the same quill-driver who was still writing with fierce assiduity.... What—nobody could ever discover. But nothing at all was to be seen of any Provisional Government. Odilon Barrot himself went in search, but it remained as unknown as the passage to the North Pole. They made Mauguin join them, but he was not able to discover it either. The most curious thing of all was, that those who had the greatest knowledge of affairs believed in the existence of this fantastic Provisional Government. Tired of their fruitless search, the two students, still accompanied by Odilon Barrot and Mauguin, returned to the hall and its large tables, its empty bottles and its clerk. They looked each other full in the face.

"I cannot go and carry off a regiment without at least a letter to show the officers," said Charras.

"I will write you one," Mauguin replied manfully.

"I thank you with all my heart," said Charras, "but, in the soldiers' eyes, in spite of your courage and deserts, you will only be lawyer Mauguin.... I would prefer a letter from General La Fayette."

"All right," replied Mauguin, "I will go and draw up your letter and you can get him to sign it for you."

"Very well."

Mauguin took the pen from the solitary scribe, who, being interrupted from his everlasting scribbling for a moment, got up and went to investigate, one after another, the thirty bottles that littered the table. His exploration was all in vain! He might as well have been looking for the Provisional Government. Meanwhile Mauguin wrote, while Charras read over his shoulder, shaking his head as he did so.

"What is wrong?" inquired Odilon Barrot.

"Oh!" said Charras, low enough so as not to be overheard by Mauguin, "that isn't the way to write to military men ... dear, dear!"

Mauguin had come to the same conclusion himself, for he suddenly flung down his pen and exclaimed—

"Devil take me, I don't know what to say to them!"

"Oh, hang it all," said Odilon Barrot, "let the gentlemen write their own letter—and let us be content with getting it signed—they will understand it better than we do."

And the pen was passed to Charras.

In a moment the proclamation was drawn up. Charras was writing the last line when General Lobau came in; he, too, no doubt, was looking for the Provisional Government.

"Hullo!" exclaimed Charras, "this exactly suits our book! Here we have a real general under our thumb, and he shall sign our proclamation."

They addressed themselves to General Lobau, explained the situation, and read him the letter, but the general turned his head away.

"Oh! dear me no! I am not such a fool as to sign that." And he went away.

"Eh?" said Charras.

"I'm not surprised," said Mauguin. "A little while ago they refused to put their signatures to an order to go and fetch powder from Soissons."

"That was my order."

"Then, he shrinks back?"

"No doubt of it."

"But, my goodness, in a revolution the man who does that is a traitor.... I will go and have him shot down," cried Charras.

Odilon Barrot and Mauguin leapt to their feet.

"Have him shot! What are you thinking of?" ... Have General Lobau, a member of the Provisional Government, shot! Who will you get to do the job?"

"Oh! you need not be anxious on that score!" said Charras.

And, drawing Mauguin away towards the window, he said, pointing out to his hundred and fifty men, "Do you see those fine fellows down there round a tricolour standard? Well, they have taken the barracks of Babylon under me; they recognise and obey me only, and if the Eternal Father Himself were to betray the cause of liberty—which He is quite incapable of doing—and I were to tell them to go and shoot Him, they would do it!"

Mauguin bent his head down. He was terrified at what such men as these might do. It was these men, these Republicans, as he called them, who had done such injury to poor Hippolyte Bonnelier.

An hour later, Charras and Lothon departed for La Fère provided with a letter signed by Mauguin and a proclamation by La Fayette. It differed but little from mine, which, as we have seen, had been of little use to me, as it had been in the hands of M. Missa[3] the whole time of my stay in Soissons.

[1] I have been told I was mistaken in this information. But I appeal to M. Thiers himself and to his *Souvenirs of 1829.* M. Thiers will not have forgotten the reply made him at a masked ball, by a domino who gave his arm to M. de Blancmesnil, a reply that obliged him to quit the ball instantly. Perhaps, by the domino's permission, I shall be able to relate the scene later.

[2] Translator's note.—Dumas probably means the duchess.

[3] See notes at end of volume.

CHAPTER IX

Philippe VII.—How Béranger justified himself for having helped to make a King—The Duc d'Orléans during the three days—His arrival in Paris on the evening of the 30th—He sends for M. de Mortemart—Unpublished letter by him to Charles X.—Benjamin Constant and Laffite—Deputation of the Chamber to the Palais-Royal—M. Sébastiani—M. de Talleyrand—The Duc d'Orléans accepts the Lieutenant-Generalship of the Kingdom—Curious papers found at the Tuileries

My first care after my warm reception by General La Fayette was, it will be readily understood, to go and have a bath and change all my clothes. The bath was not a difficult matter to obtain, as the Deligny swimming bath was nearly opposite my rooms. When I entered, I must say I frightened everybody, down even to old Jean. I consigned my gun, pistols, powder and bullets to the page boy, with the remainder of my three thousand francs. After which, whilst someone went to find Joseph to tell him to bring me fresh linen and clothes, I took the most delicious plunge I ever had in my life. An hour later I was quite in a condition to present myself even before the Provisional Government, if anybody could have told me where they were sitting. I sent home my recently worn fighting outfit, and took my way in the direction of the Hôtel Laffitte. I was eager for news. I had the very greatest difficulty in gaining access to the famous banker. Nobody would recognise me now; I was too well dressed. Discussion of the nature of noisy talking was going on in the Salon. M. Sébastiani was said to have come back from Prince Talleyrand bringing important news. What was that news? Suddenly the door opened and M. Sébastiani, with a radiant face, flung the substance of the following words to the three to four hundred persons who crowded the dining-room, ante-chambers and passages.

"Messieurs, you may announce to everybody that from to-day the name of the King of France will be Philippe VII."

Although I was expecting something of the kind, the shock was a violent one. King for king, I liked King Charles X. almost as much as King Philippe VII. Béranger went by at the moment, and I knew he must have had a great deal to do in that nomination. I flung myself on his neck, partly to embrace him, partly to provoke him to a quarrel, and, laughing and scolding both together, I said:

"Ah! by Jove! you have just served us a fine trick, father."

I called Béranger "father," and he was so gracious as to call me his "son."

"What is it I have done, my son?" he replied.

"What have you done? Well, you have made a king."

His face assumed its usual expression of gentle seriousness.

"Pay deep attention to that which I am going to say to you, my child," he resumed. "I have not exactly made a king ... No...."

"What have you done, then?"

"What the little Savoyards do in a storm.... I have put a plank across the stream."

How many times since have I pondered on that sad and philosophical illustration! It modified some of my ideas; it directed my historical studies in 1831 and 1832; and, in 1833, it inspired me with the epilogue to *Gaule et France*. Béranger moved away. I remained in meditation. What would have happened, supposing I could have foreseen that the most prosaic of any throne upon earth should be raised by a poet in 1830, and overthrown by another poet in 1848? What a strange setting Béranger and Lamartine were to those eighteen years of reign! I was only distracted from my reveries by the murmurs which went on around me. A violent scene was being enacted close by.

A former secretary of Ouvrard, named Poisson, had just opened the door of M. Laffitte's salon, and was declaring, with oaths that were enough to shake the house, that he would have no king. And this opinion was shared, too, by all those who were there.

No, I repeat it, that election was not popular at first, and, from the Hôtel Laffitte to the Palais-Royal, where I next went in pursuance of the flight of the news, I heard more imprecations than applause. I went to No. 216 for fuller details. The Duc d'Orléans was at the Palais-Royal. But if Oudard were within he kept himself invisible. There were porters and clerks, however, all extremely visible and well-informed, because everything was talked of in their presence, they being regarded as of no importance; they are a garrulous lot when they condescend to step down from their self-imputed importance. And I should add that, besides the porters and clerks, there were two or three people who were also perfectly well-informed of the news.

Now, I will guarantee the accuracy of what had occurred and I challenge anybody to dispute the fact. The Duc d'Orléans returned to the Palais-Royal at eleven on the night of the 30th. Let us follow his movements curiously during the three days. The news of the Ordinances and the noise of firing reached the duke at Neuilly, where he spent his summers. From the few words we have already spoken, by the silence and delays with which Laffitte's suggestions were first received, it could be seen that his Highness was extremely anxious. As long as the kingdom hung before his eyes, like a motionless phantom on the horizon, the duke approached it obliquely, timidly and by tortuous ways; yet none the less did he aim for it. But when that phantom took definite shape and drew nearer to him, he grew alarmed. The phantom could no longer label itself a kingdom, but usurpation; it no longer wore the crown of Saint Louis, but the red cap of Danton and Cellot-d'Herbois. The Duc d'Orléans was courageous, but not to the point of audacity. We repeat—and we look upon it as a virtue in him—that he was afraid. During the 28th and 29th he remained hidden in one of the small huts in his park at Neuilly, which bore the name of the Laiterie (the Dairy). On the morning of the 29th they brought him a bullet that had fallen in the park. And on that same day, after he had received from Laffitte the message "A crown or a passport," his uneasiness increased to such an extent that, thinking he was not thoroughly concealed in the hut, he started with Oudard for Raincy. He wore a maroon-coloured coat, blue trousers and a grey hat in which blossomed a tricolour cockade that Madame Adélaide had made him. Before he started, he left behind a note, dated 3.15 in the morning, to make people believe he was at Neuilly. On the 30th, as we have told, after the visit of MM. Thiers and Scheffer, they despatched M. de Montesquieu to him. We have related how he left Raincy and then returned to it. During the whole of the 30th he remained at Raincy without showing any signs of his existence. But all the time messages were piling up, and one of them having announced that a deputation from the Chamber had come to offer him the crown, he then decided to return to Neuilly, which he reached towards nine in the evening. Madame Adélaide had taken possession of a copy of the declaration from the Chamber, perhaps even the actual declaration itself. It was read aloud in the park by torchlight, in the presence of the whole family. He could no longer hold back, but had to choose between the throne—that is to say, the everlasting ambition of his race—or exile, which was the perpetual terror of his life. He embraced his wife and children and set out for Paris only accompanied by three persons: M. Berthois, M. Heymes and Oudard. It was ten at night when they left the carriage at the barrier; they entered Paris, climbed over the barricades and reached 216 rue Saint-Honoré. The duke re-entered the Palais-Royal by the side entrance used by the employés, and not by the main court and staircase of honour. He went upstairs to Oudard's office, which was, it will be remembered, next to my old office. There, exhausted with fatigue, running with sweat, and shivering convulsively, he flung off his coat, waistcoat and shirt, even to his flannel vest, changed clothes, sent for a mattress and threw himself upon it. He knew of M. de Mortemart's arrival in Paris, and with what honourable object the duke had come; he sent for him to beg him at once to come to the Palais-Royal. A quarter of an hour later M. de Mortemart was announced. The Duc d'Orléans raised himself on one elbow.

"Oh! come here, come here, monsieur le duc!" he exclaimed in a short, feverish voice when he saw him; "I hasten to tell you, so that you may transmit my words to King Charles, how very grieved I am at all that has happened."

M. de Mortemart bowed.

"You are returning to Saint-Cloud, are you not? You will go and see the king?"

"Yes, monseigneur."

"Well, then," the duke continued in agitation, "tell the king they have brought me to Paris by force. I was at Raincy yesterday, when a crowd of men invaded the Château of Neuilly.... They asked to see me in the name of the re-union of the Chamber, but I was absent. They threatened the duchess, telling her she would be taken to Paris a prisoner with her children until I reappeared, and she was afraid ... that is surely easily conceivable in a wife?... She wrote me a note urging me to return ... you know how fond I am of my wife and children;... that consideration weighed with me before all others, and I returned. They were waiting for me at Neuilly, seized me and brought me here ... that is how I am situated."

Just at that moment, cries of "Vive le Duc d'Orléans!" resounded in the street and penetrated right into the Palais-Royal courtyard. M. de Mortemart shuddered.

"You hear, monseigneur?" he said.

"Yes, yes, I hear ... but I count for nothing in those shoutings, and you can tell the king I would rather die than accept the crown."

"Should you have any objections, monseigneur, to assure the king of these honourable intentions in writing?"

"None at all, monsieur, none at all.... Oudard, bring me a pen, paper and ink."

Whilst Oudard was looking for them, the duke tore a blank sheet from a sort of register which lay within his reach: it was a register in connection with the Chevaliers de l'Ordre. Then, according to his habit, to economise paper, he made the rough draft of his letter upon the sheet he tore out of the register. It was, no doubt, owing to this economy of his that we are able to give the public a copy of that highly important, extremely curious and authentic letter. When the Duc d'Orléans had written his letter, he crumpled up the rough copy in his hands, threw it away behind him, and it rolled into a corner by the fireplace, where it was picked up the next day. By whom, I cannot say. I can only state that I copied the letter you are about to read from that very rough draft itself. As for the fate of the final letter, M. de Mortemart folded it, placed it inside his white cravat, and went away to carry it to the king. It was this letter that Charles X. re-read with much bitterness, when he learnt that Louis-Philippe had accepted the crown. Here is the rough draft with his autograph and erasures; we have not altered one single letter from the original, but left it exactly as His Royal Highness wrote it.

> "M. de —— will tell Your Majesty how they brought me here by force. I do not know to what point these people may go in the employment of force towards me; but (*if it should happen*) if in this fearful state of disorder it should happen that they were to impose upon me a title to which I have never aspired, Your Majesty may be (*convinced*) very well assured that I will receive no kind of power except temporarily, and in the sole interest of Our House.
>
> "I hereby formally swear this to Your Majesty.
>
> "My family share my feelings in this matter.
>
> "(Your faithful subject)."
>
> PALAIS-ROYAL,
>
> *July* 31, 1830.

We will now invite our readers, those especially who like to form an exact impression of the character of the men who are chosen for leaders of humanity; we will, we say, invite them to compare this copy of the letter with the note sent from Neuilly during the night of the 29th of July.

Louis-Philippe as a private individual, Louis-Philippe as politician and Louis-Philippe as king, are all faithfully depicted by his own hand in that note and that rough draft of a letter. But the date of 31 July puzzles us, especially after the lapse of twenty-two years. Is it an error of the duke's, or was the note not signed until after midnight?—this would make the date of the 31st correct; or, again, as is just conceivably possible, was it signed only on the evening of the 31st? Our own opinion is that it was signed on the morning of the 31st, between one and two o'clock, after midnight. And we base our opinion on the fact that, at one o'clock in the morning M. Laffitte had not yet been informed of the arrival of the Duc d'Orléans. Besides, the salons of the illustrious banker, deserted little by little by those whom the silence and absence of the Duc d'Orléans rendered anxious, kept on thinning in a manner far from re-assuring. At two o'clock in the morning, indeed, no one was left in the salon but Laffitte and Benjamin Constant. Béranger had just retired, worn out with fatigue.

"Well!" Laffitte remarked with his accustomed imperturbability, "what do you think of the situation, Constant?"

"I?" the author of *Adolphe* laughingly replied "Well, my dear Laffitte, it is a hundred chances to one that by to-morrow at this hour we shall be hung."

Laffitte made a gesture.

"Ah! I quite understand that. You are not madly in love with hanging; it would spoil your pretty pink face and your well-groomed hair and your perfectly adjusted cravat; while I, with my long yellow face, look as though I had been hanged already, and the cord would add little to my physiognomy."

With this compliment, the two men separated at half-past two in the morning. It was only at five that they waked M. Laffitte to warn him of the arrival of the Duc d'Orléans in Paris.

"Oh!" said he, "Benjamin Constant is distinctly wrong, and we shall not be hanged."

Now, at eight o'clock in the morning the deputation from the Chamber, which had presented itself at Neuilly the previous day, appeared at the Palais-Royal, headed by General Sébastiani. He was the very same general who, on 29 July, said, "Beware lest you go too far, gentlemen ... we are merely negotiating, and our part is that of mediators, we are not even deputies!"—the same who, on the 30th, said, "The only national thing in France is the white flag!"—again, on the 31st, "Go, Monsieur Thiers, and try to persuade the Duc d'Orléans to accept the crown!" and, again, on I August, "Gentlemen, tell the whole world that the name of the King of France is now Philippe VII.!" In a word, he who later was to say, "Order reigns at Warsaw!"

Nor let us forget that it was this same General Sébastiani who, on my first visit to Paris, received me with four secretaries, each stationed in the four corners of his room ready to offer him snuff out of a gold snuff-box.

A regular character to be studied during a revolution, and one whose memory I should like to preserve to posterity! Why have not such men the power of imprinting their images (like that of the Christ) on the handkerchiefs with which they mop their ambitious brows?

The Duc d'Orléans put in an appearance this time; he promised nothing definite, but he pledged himself to give his answer in an hour. He, too, like Brutus, had a Delphic Oracle to consult. His special Oracle lived at the corner of the rue de Rivoli and the rue Saint Florentin.

Louis Blanc relates how, on 29 July 1830, at five minutes past noon, a window was timidly opened at the corner of the rue Saint Florentin, but, timidly as it opened, a shrill cracked voice cried out—

"Monsieur Keiser, Monsieur Keiser, what are you doing?"

"I am looking into the street, prince."

"Monsieur Keiser, you will be the cause of my house being broken into."

"No chance of that, prince: the troops are beating a retreat and the people are busily engaged in pursuing them."

"Oh! really, Monsieur Keiser?"

Then the person addressed by the title of prince rose, limped towards the clock, and in a reassured and almost solemn tone of voice, he said—

"Monsieur Keiser, make a note in your diary that on 29 July, at five minutes past noon, the Elder Branch of the House of Bourbon ceased reigning over France."

That lame old man, who in prophetic utterance had announced the downfall of Charles, was Charles Maurice de Talleyrand Périgord, Prince of Benevento, once Bishop of Autun, who was the first to suggest the sale of the benefices of the clergy in 1789; who said mass upon the altar of patriotism on 14 July 1790, the day of the fête of the Federation; who was sent, in 1792, to London by Louis XVI. to assist the Ambassador M. de Chauvelin; who was Foreign Minister in 1796, under the Directory; created Grand-Chamberlain on the accession of the Emperor in 1804; created Prince of Benevento in 1806; and received the title of Vice-Grand Elector, with a salary of five hundred thousand francs, in 1807; who was made a member of the Provisional Government in 1814; and Minister for Foreign Affairs and envoy extraordinary to Vienna, by Louis XVIII. in the same year; who was appointed Ambassador to London by Louis-Philippe in 1830; and who, finally, died, more or less of a Christian, on 18 May 1838.

Now, I have frequently heard men who were most conversant with contemporary politics and with the corruption of the times wonder how M. de Talleyrand had managed to get pardoned by Louis XVIII. for having been a member of the Constituent Assembly, sworn Bishop, officiating Minister at the Champs de Mars, Minister of the Directory, plenipotentiary of Bonaparte, Grand-Chamberlain to the Emperor, etc. etc.

I am going to tell you a thing of which future history would otherwise be unaware, a fact that will probably not come out until true Memoirs of the Prince are published.

M. de Talleyrand was warned of the First Consul's intention to arrest and shoot the Duc d'Enghien eight or ten days in advance. He summoned a courier upon whom he knew he could rely, and sent a letter by him to the duke, telling him to sew it into his coat collar, to set off at top speed and only to give the letter to the Duc d'Enghien himself. The letter urged the prince to leave Ettenheim instantly, and warned him of his threatened danger. The courier left in the night of 7 and 8 August 1804. It is known that the order to arrest the prince was not issued till the 10th. The courier started as we have described, but, going down the hill of Saverne at a gallop, his horse fell, and broke its rider's leg. Unfortunately, he could not intrust his mission to the first-comer, and he dared not take any such responsibility, so he wrote to ask M. de Talleyrand what he was to do. By the time M. de Talleyrand had received the letter it was already too late to take any step; the order for the arrest had already gone forth. But Prince Condé and Louis XVIII. and Charles X. knew the story, and hence arose the pardon granted to a Republican and Bonapartist, for misdeeds of the former Bishop of Autun. Now it was Talleyrand that his future majesty of the Palais-Royal wished to consult before venturing to pick up the crown which had rolled from the head of Charles X. in the blood of the barricades. It was General Sébastiani whom the Duc d'Orléans commissioned to interrogate the oracle. The said oracle was extremely vexed that everything had been done without him until then, that M. Laffitte had looked upon him as of little account, and he only condescended to reply in these words: "Let him accept."

After this reply, the prince accepted at the end of the promised hour, and the following proclamation was affixed to all the walls of the capital announcing this acceptance to the Parisians:—

"INHABITANTS OF PARIS,

"The deputies of France, at this time assembled in Paris, have expressed the desire that I should come to the capital in order to discharge the duties of Lieutenant-General of the kingdom. *I have not for one moment wavered in coming to share your dangers*, by placing myself in the centre of the heroic population, and I will use all my endeavours to preserve you from civil war and anarchy. In returning to the City of Paris, I wore with pride those glorious colours which you have regained and which I for a long time have worn. The Chambers are about to re-assemble; *they will confer concerning the best means of bringing about the reign of law and the maintenance of order. A* Charter will henceforth be a fact.

"L. P. D'ORLÉANS"

There were three noticeable points in this proclamation:

The duke, first of all, declares that he *did not waver for one moment in coming to share the dangers* of the Parisian people. A lie, since, on the contrary, he hid himself both at Neuilly and at Raincy during the time of danger, and only reached Paris when the danger was over on the night of the 30th. Next, he announces that the Chambers were about to assemble to *confer concerning the best methods of bringing about the reign of law and the maintenance of order*, which statement was a calumny against the people; for, if ever people respected law and maintained order it was the people of July 1830. Finally, M. le Duc d'Orléans said that *a* Charter would henceforth be a genuine fact. He should have said that, from the very next day, not *a* Charter but *the* Charter, a change imperceptible to the eye and almost to the ear, which brought with it, however, the grave consequence that France, instead of having a new charter, was simply to have the Charter of Louis XVIII., and this meant that the king of the barricades, by appropriating that old charter, not only did not take the trouble to draw up another, but, with a new form of government, only promised to give the people the same amount of liberty as that promised by the fallen Government. This was, indeed, a bold start on a career of kingship. Lying, calumny and chicanery: Louis XI. himself could not have gone farther.

I said that, at the close of this chapter, I would give some idea of the stinginess of the Duc d'Orléans. Perhaps this is not exactly the place for the fragments we are about to introduce to our readers' notice; but those who think they interrupt the course of the narrative, can carry their imaginations elsewhere.

Let us first of all explain how these fragments of information fell into our hands. To do this in one step we must skip over a period of eighteen years; and, instead of the young man who took active part in all we have just read, substitute the mature man who stood aside, and sadly watched the passing of the events of that long reign; we must suppose the Lieutenant-general, to whose proclamation we have just listened, to be a king, also grown old and unpopular and driven away in his turn; we must imagine ourselves to have left behind Sunday morning, August 1830, for three o'clock in the afternoon of 24 February 1848. Then, the king gone and the Tuileries seized and the Republic proclaimed, I returned alone, sad and anxious, more of a Republican than ever, but of the opinion that the Republic was ill-constituted, ill-matured and ill-promulgated; I returned, my heart depressed by the spectacle of a wife cruelly repulsed, two children separated from their mother, two princes put to flight, one hunted through the rostral columns of the Place de la Concorde, the other along the circular staircases of the Palace of the Deputies; I returned, wondering if all I had seen and heard could actually be true, or whether I was not rather under the influence of a strange nightmare, a mysterious vision; I returned and, metaphorically speaking, felt myself to see if I could really be alive—for it is sometimes as easy for us to doubt our own existence as to doubt the weirdly strange events that we see passing under our very eyes;—I returned, I say, by the Tuileries, with its windows all open and its doors broken in, as on that famous 29 July which I have described at, perhaps, too great length; but how could I help myself? There are some memories which fill such a space in our lives that we feel compelled to impress them upon the lives of others. I was possessed with the idea of looking over the château that I had entered once before and to begin in the same way, at the apartments of King Louis-Philippe, on 24 February 1848, as I had through the rooms that belonged to King Charles and on 29 July 1830.

The account of what I saw will be given elsewhere. I have only one thing to relate, and here it is. As I went through the king's cabinet, where all kinds of papers lay scattered over the floor, all soiled with mud, in the midst of these forgotten, useless papers, condemned to the fire and oblivion, I detected some pages covered with characters which made me tremble. It was the king's writing; that very writing which, twenty-five years before, had often passed under my eyes. A patriot of 1848, as ragged as a former patriot of 1830, kept guard over the king's broken-open desk.

"Comrade," I said to the man, "may I have some of these papers that litter the floor?"

"You can take them," he replied; "they are probably left because they are of no value."

So I took them.

At the first Revolution I had come into possession of a copy of *Christine* inscribed with the arms of the Duchesse de Berry. At the second, I obtained some old yellow papers that lay on the floor, which I was allowed to take because the sentinel thought they were valueless. It will be noticed that I am not one of the persons who grow rich out of revolutions. True, I do not come under the category of those who are submerged by them. I sail above them, like birds and clouds; then, when the revolutions are over, I direct my flight, not to the side where lie power and fortune, but to the 1 side of justice and faithfulness, even though I should have to follow justice into exile and loyalty through proscription.

But here is a copy of the papers: they themselves will speak better than any notes or commentaries could.

THE CHILDREN'S BREAKFASTS

Fr. C.

The young princes and their {Six portions, at 90 c.   5.40

  tutors   {Seven loaves, at 20 c.   1.40

Princesses Louise and Marie {One soup, at at   1.50

  and Madame de Mallet.   {Two portions   1.80

                {Two loaves   0.40

Princesse Clémentine and   {One soup, at   1.50

  Madame Angelet   {One portion, at   0.90

                {Two loaves   0.40

THE CHILDREN'S BREAKFASTS--(*continued*)

Fr. C.

Duc de Nemours and M.   {Cold meat   1.50

Larnac, who take them to   {Entremet   1.50

the college   {Two portions   0.80

               {Two loaves   0.40

_____

[Extra sugar paid for separately]

Total by day, without coffee paid separately   18.50

Extra, 10 c. per portion   1.10

_____

19.60

25 c. Soup and entremet   1.20

11 S., 13 loaves, 4 portions

_____

20.80

New Tariff of Expenses--Housekeeping Establishment

For my table, the same except the suppression of the two fixed price meals of 6 fr. and 12 fr. (18 fr. altogether), the two monthly settlements of 1000 fr. and 150 fr. and a discharge to the contractor, of the payment of 1010 fr. per annum for the water-carrier.

FOR MY CHILDREN'S TABLE, INCLUDING THEIR TEACHERS

Breakfast--(A special tariff kept up during my absence as well as presence).

Fr. C.

Saucers of fruits or sweetmeats	1.0
Soup	1.80
Chicken or cold meat	1.80
Entremet of vegetables, etc	1.80
Each loaf	0.20
French rolls à la Reine	0.10
Cup of coffee, simple	0.50
Id. with cream	0.75
Tea and bread and butter	1.50

Dinner and Supper, charged at half mine when it is served at same time, but at the same tariff as mine when I am absent and when it is omitted. The demi tariff is accordingly as follows:--

	Fr. C.
Soup	2.50
Entrees	4.50
Roast or flank	6.0
Entremets	2.50
Plate of dessert	1.50
Bread, coffee, tea, etc., the same as at breakfast	
Sugar basins table	Nothing
Id. in the rooms	2.0

Extra 2 francs per head and per day in case of absence or omission of the superior meals, for those fed in the pantry and the kitchen.

Another Tariff of Household Expenses

For the Princes' table, the same.

FOR THE CHILDREN'S

Breakfasts

		Instead of
	Fr.C.	Fr.C.
Portions	0.90	1.0
Soups	1.25	1.80
Chicken and cold meat	1.25	do.
Entremet or vegetable, etc.	1.25	do.
French rolls	0.10	
Bread, per person	0.20	

Cup of coffee, simple	0.50
Id. with cream	0.75
Tea, complete	1.50

Less per day

Regular meals	18.0
Per month	37.80 60/61
Children's	48.0

———

Per day	103-80
Id.	104+46

———

Extra	66c.

———

Dinner or Supper

	Fr.C.
Soups.	2.50
Entrees.	4.50
Roast or flank	6.0
Entremets.	2.50
Dishes of dessert	1.50

[Bread, coffee and tea as before]

Except when there is only the Children's table to serve, in which case it is tariffed the same as the Princes' table.

Extra per day

Children's breakfast (without coffee)   20.80

Dinner   43.0

Supper   38.90

Water-carrier   2.76 60/61

                                    ———

Extra per day   105.46

                                    ———

In addition to this, in case of omission of these two tables,
the contractor receives 2 fr. per day per head both, for each
person maintained in the kitchen and in the office.

By means of this fresh tariff he is discharged from having
to pay the water-carrier; but he does not receive the fixed 12 fr.
per dinner and 6 fr. per breakfast for the Princes' table, nor the
1150 fr. per month for wood, coal and washing.

After this tariff the Children's breakfast--

                          Fr. C. Fr. C.

                          17.30+ 3.50

          Fr. C.   20.80

Less   18{   12 Their dinner   42.0 } Coffee not

           {   6 Their supper   38.90} included

    And price per day

of 13,800 fr. per year,   Total   98.20

        37.80   Formerly   48.20

        ———   ———

        55.80   Difference extra   50.20

Extra 56.46   Plus water-carrier   2.76

Bonus 0.66   Extra per day   52.96

_____

ACCOUNTS

13,800 {365   Extra on breakfast

_____   tariff

{37.80 60/61

Portions, 1 fr. each:

2,850   Soup, cold meat, and

2,950   entremet

300   Each   1.80 3.50

_____ 1.010

365   Makes   56.46 per day extra

_____

2800 {_____

{2.76 52/61

2,450

260.52

_____   98.20

2.76

565.61   _____

_____   100.96

_____

CHAPTER X

The Duc d'Orléans goes to the Hôtel de Ville—M. Laffitte in his sedan-chair—The king *sans culotte*—Tardy manifestation of the Provisional Government—Odilon Barrot sleeps on a milestone—Another Balthasar Gérard—The Duc d'Orléans is received by La Fayette—A superb voice—Fresh appearance of General Dubourg—The balcony of the Hôtel de Ville—The road to Joigny

We have not yet finished the account of the events that transpired during my absence. Let me therefore be permitted to recall them: every minute, unknown detail gives us the key to an uprising and helps to explain the 5th of June, the 14th of April, or the 12th of May. Then, too, it is well to know that there were men who never did accept that government, but who resisted it for eighteen years, and succeeded in the end in overthrowing it. These men ought to be paid the justice that was their due: in spite of the calumnies, insults and trials to which they were, and are still, subjected, their contemporaries ought, indeed, to learn of their valour, courage, devotion, persistence and loyalty. True, perhaps their contemporaries will not believe me. Never mind! I shall have said it; others will believe me. Truth is one of those stars which may remain buried in the depths of the heavens for months, years, or even centuries, but which in the end, are invariably discovered some day or other. And I would rather be the madman who devotes his life to the discovery of those stars, than the wise man who hails and worships one after the other all those suns that we have seen rise, which were said to be fixed and immovable, but which proved to be nothing but transitory meteors, of some brilliancy, more or less deceptive, but always fatal in their influences!

The Duc d'Orléans, as we have seen, had already advanced a good way: he had won over the Chamber of Peers—(we have not even alluded to that conquest of his: except for the presence of Chateaubriand and Fitz-James, it was not worth the trouble of registering it, and, as is known, Chateaubriand and Fitz-James resigned);—he had won over the Chamber of Deputies; at least, ninety-one signatures attested it.

It now only remained for him to conquer the Hôtel de Ville. Oh! but that was quite another matter! The Hôtel de Ville was not the palace, spoilt by the orgies of the Directory or the proscriptions of 1815; it was not a factory where ambition and cupidity were forged, under the disguise of devotion to the various powers which succeeded one another for half a century. No, indeed; the Hôtel de Ville was the stronghold of shelter for that great popular goddess termed Revolution, during each fresh insurrection. And the spirit of

Revolution again held sway there. Power had come to the Duc d'Orléans; but, before that power could be established, the duke had to come to the Revolution. Her representative was an old man, true-hearted and clean-souled, but enfeebled with age. Forty years before, when in the full tide of youth, he had been found wanting at a time of Revolution: would they find what they had vainly looked for at thirty, now he was seventy years of age?

Yes, perhaps, had he stood alone and free to exercise his own convictions; for, since the former devotion to the cause of royalty, he had thought and suffered much; he had known imprisonment and exile; his name had been uttered in every Republican conspiracy, at Béfort and Saumur; and we will describe later under what singular circumstances he escaped proscription with Dermoncourt and execution with Berton. But he was no longer a free agent. One party, the Orléanists, had circumvented him; it was, in fact, quite a siege, cleverly conceived by Laffitte and carried out by Carbonnel.

From hence arose that pregnant saying of Bonnelier: "Vos diables de républicains nous ont donné bien du mal!" ("Your republican devils have done us no end of harm!")

Indeed, it was only with difficulty that republicans gained access to the good old general. They could easily be known, since their number, at the period of which I am speaking, was small, and hardly had one or other of these men come to see him before some one would come in and, under various pretexts, either cut the conversation short or act as a spy.

This was the man with whom the Duc d'Orléans had to deal, and an easy task it was to the prince, who, when he liked, could be most seductively fascinating. Still, the future king wished to be accompanied by a deputation from the Chamber. The Chamber would sooner have sent two deputations than one, and, had the duke expressed the wish, it would have brought up the rear of the procession in a body.

M. Laffitte took the deputation to the Palais-Royal at the appointed hour. They started; but the situation was more serious even than was apparent; it was true that, under pretext of various missions, they had sent the most zealous republicans away from Paris; but there were still a good number left, and these proclaimed loudly that the newly-elected monarch should not reach the Hôtel de Ville. The Duc d'Orléans was on horseback, feeling, no doubt, uneasy at the bottom of his heart, but looking calm outwardly. It was one of the prince's finest qualities: fearful and irresolute while he could not fathom or see the danger; when he was face to face with it, he met it bravely. He could not have said with Cæsar: "Danger and I are two lions born at the same time, I being the elder!" but he could have said he was the younger. M.

Laffitte followed in a sedan-chair carried by Savoyards; his foot caused him horrible suffering; he was shod in slippers. Except for the bandages which swathed it, one leg was bare. So, after he had offered the crown to the prince, as president of the Chamber, he leant to him and whispered low in his ear—

"Two slippers and only one stocking. This time, at any rate, if *la Quotidienne* saw us it would say we were creating a king *sans culotte.*"

All went well from the Palais-Royal to the quay. They were still in the bourgeoisie quarter, and they had come to make a king in their own image, as God made man after His own image. The bourgeoisie saw in the king its own reflection, and gazed with complacency at its own image, up to the moment when it discovered how ugly it was, and then it broke the glass. So the bourgeoisie hailed his election. But, when on the quay, and across the Pont Neuf, and the Place du Châtelet reached, not only did the cheers cease altogether, but the faces of the crowd looked dark, and tremors of anger could be felt in the air. Surely the spirits of the dead were protesting against this new type of Bourbon. At the Hôtel de Ville itself there was a great agitation going on. At last the famous Provisional Government, hitherto invisible, materialised itself: Mauguin, de Schonen, Audry de Puyraveau, Lobau, were all anti-Orléanists: Lobau especially, who had refused to put his signature to an order the previous day, was furious.

"I don't want this one any more than the rest!" he exclaimed; "he is still a Bourbon!"

M. Barthe, the former Carbonaro, was present. The question of drawing up a Republican proclamation arose, and he offered to undertake it, picked up a pen and began to write. While he wrote, General Lobau grew more and more exasperated and went up to M. de Schonen.

"We are risking our heads," he said to him; "but, what matters! Here are two pistols, one for you, one for me ... it is all that is left to two men who have no fear of death!"

These proceedings were not exactly re-assuring. Odilon Barrot could be relied upon; he it was who had uttered those famous words at the municipal commission the day before that are attributed to La Fayette, as Harel's and Montrond's were attributed to M. de Talleyrand: "The Duc d'Orléans is the finest Republic." Odilon Barrot was deputed to go to the Palais-Royal to give the contrary order. Odilon Barrot, in common with most people, had had little sleep for three days and he was worn out with fatigue; he went down and found such a dense crowd and the heat so intolerable that he called for a horse. Some one hastened to fetch him one. While waiting, he leant against a milestone and fell asleep. They were an hour before they could find him again, and, just when they had succeeded and he had mounted the horse, the head of the procession appeared in the Place de Grève.

Now I saw a great deal of Odilon Barrot at the Hôtel de Ville and watched him very attentively, and I declare that no one could possibly be more coolly courageous than he.

So the Duc d'Orléans had arrived; he had reached the Place de Grève, and was, therefore, entering into the very centre of the Revolutionary party. His horse's breast separated the crowd in front of it as a ship's prow separates the waves. A frigid silence was maintained all round him as he passed on. He was deadly pale. A young man, who was even paler still, awaited him on the steps of the Hôtel de Ville with arms crossed, hiding a pistol in his breast. He had conceived the terrible resolution of firing at the prince point-blank.

"Ah! so you are playing the part of William the Silent," he said; "you shall end as he did!"

One of his friends was standing by his side.

Just when the Duc d'Orléans stepped down from his horse and began to ascend the Hôtel de Ville steps, this would-be Balthasar Gérard took a step forward, but his companion stopped him.

"Do not compromise yourself uselessly," he said to him, "your pistol is unloaded."

"Who unloaded it?"

"I did."

He led his friend away.

This was not the truth: the pistol was really loaded, but the lie probably prevented the Duc d'Orléans from being shot down on the steps of the Hôtel de Ville.

What reward did the man receive who saved the life of the future king of the French? I will tell you: he was killed at Saint-Mery and died cursing himself!

The Duc d'Orléans mounted the Hôtel de Ville steps with a firm tread; he passed close to Death, unwitting that Death, who so nearly touched him, had folded up his wings again. The gloomy vault of the old municipal palace, like the huge throat of a stone gargoyle, swallowed up the prince and his cortège. General La Fayette awaited him at the head of the staircase of the Hôtel de Ville. The situation was so great that men themselves appeared dwarfed. And, indeed, what did it mean: that the prince of the Younger Branch of the Bourbons was paying a visit to the hero of 1789? It meant that a democratic monarchy was to break off for ever from an aristocratic monarchy; it was the fulfilment of fifteen years of conspiracy; and the consecration of revolt by the pope of liberty.

We ought, perhaps, to stop here at this great moment, since all other details will seem paltry beside it.

The Duc d'Orléans, La Fayette and several of his friends formed the central point of interest of a vast crowd of men holding very different opinions. Some cheered, others protested. Four or five students from the École Polytechnique were there bareheaded, but with swords bare also. Some working men passed by, through the clearer spaces, shouting with sunburnt, lowering faces, some of them bloodstained, and they were gently pushed back so that the prince should not be offended by such a sight. It was, indeed, remorse that was being driven back, with the respect which is its due.

The matter in hand was the reading of the proclamation of the Chamber. M. Laffitte had spoken at such great length, as had everybody else, that he could not talk any longer. He held his proclamation in his hand, and goodness alone knows what effect a proclamation read in the grotesque tones of hoarseness would have produced!

"Give it me, give it me, my dear friend," shrieked M. Viennet, seizing the proclamation out of the hands of the famous banker, "I have a splendid voice!"

And it was, indeed, in superb tones that he read the proclamation of the Chamber. When the reader reached the words, "The Committee for judging delinquencies of the Press," the man who was to make the Laws of September, leant over to La Fayette and, shrugging his shoulders, asked—

"Will there be any more Press misdemeanours, now?"

When the reading was done he put his hand on his heart, a gesture much affected by all newly crowned kings, which, however, always produces the same successful effect.

"As a Frenchman," he said, "I deplore the harm done to the country and the blood that has been shed; as a prince I am happy to contribute to the welfare of the nation."

Suddenly a man advanced to the middle of the circle. It was General Dubourg, the man of the black flag, the phantom of 29 July. He had disappeared, and now reappeared only to disappear again once more.

"Take heed, monsieur," he said to the Duc d'Orléans; "you are aware of our rights, the sacred rights of the people; if you forget them, we will remind you of them!"

The duke stepped back, not because of this threat, but to take hold of La Fayette by the arm, and leaning upon it, he replied—

"Monsieur, what you have just said proves that you do not know me. I am an honest man, and when I have a duty to perform I do not let myself be won over by entreaties, nor intimidated by threats."

Nevertheless the scene had made a vivid impression, an impression that required to be combated.

La Fayette led the Duc d'Orléans out upon the balcony of the Hôtel de Ville. And for the second time he staked his popularity on a throw of the dice. The first time was on 6 October 1789, when he kissed the hand of the queen upon the balcony of the Palais de Versailles. The second time was on 31 July 1830, when he appeared upon the balcony of the Hôtel de Ville, holding the Duc d'Orléans by the arm.

For a moment one might have supposed that this dramatic effect had fallen flat; the square was lined with heads, with flashing eyes, with gaping mouths,—all dumb. Georges La Fayette handed a tricolour flag to his father. The folds floated round the general and the duke, and brushed against their faces; both seemed to the people not resplendent with self-emanating light, but illuminated by some celestial glory, and the people burst into applause.

The game was won.

Oh! political players, how strong you are when a new man is to be raised! How weak when it comes to the supporting of a power grown old!

The return of the Duc d'Orléans to the Palais-Royal was a triumph. He had nothing left to desire: he had the triple recognition of the Chamber of Peers, of the Chamber of Deputies and of the Hôtel de Ville. He was the chosen-elect of M. de Lémonville, of M. Laffitte and La Fayette.

That very same night one of the carriages called *Carolines* fetched the wife, sister and children of the Lieutenant-General of the realm from Neuilly to the Palais-Royal. The Duc de Chartres was alone missing from that reunion. He had, as we know, been sent away to Joigny. On the road to Joigny his carriage had passed another carriage. It contained Madame la Duchesse d'Angoulême, returning from her watering-place, where she had been informed by telegraph of the grave troubles that were agitating Paris. The two carriages pulled up, as the prince and princess had recognised one another.

"What is the latest news, Monsieur de Chartres?" asked the Duchesse d'Angoulême.

"Bad! madame, very bad!" replied the prince; "the Louvre is taken!"

Indeed, it was bad news for you, for your brothers, for your father and for the whole family. And it is you, poor prince, who in the eyes of posterity will be right!

BOOK IV

CHAPTER I

M. Thiers' way of writing history—Republicans at the
Palais-Royal—Louis-Philippe's first ministry—Casimir
Périer's cunning—My finest drama—Lothon and
Charras—A Sword-thrust—The Posting-Master of
Bourget once more—La Fère—Lieutenant-Colonel
Duriveau—Lothon and General La Fayette.

Whilst the Duc d'Orléans was making his triumphal and happy entry into the
Palais-Royal, six or eight young men were gathered together above the offices
of the *National* in the set of rooms shared by Paulin and Gauja. They were
looking at one another in silence—a silence all the more threatening since
they were still armed as on the day of battle. These young men were Thomas,
Bastide, Chevalon, Grouvelle, Bonvilliers, Godefroy Cavaignac, Étienne
Arago, Guinard, and, possibly, a few others whose names have escaped me.
According to the measure of their impatience, they were either seated or
standing. Thomas was seated in the embrasure of a window, with his fowling-
piece between his legs. He was at that period a fine, handsome fellow,
brimming over with loyalty, courage and ingenuousness, with a cool head
and a warm heart. So there they all were relating the episode of the Odyssey
of the Hôtel de Ville, and M. Thiers came in while they were discussing the
situation.

That morning an article had appeared in the *National* on the arrest of the Duc
de Chartres at Montrouge. This article put the whole thing in a perfectly new
light. The Duc de Chartres had visited Paris to lay his sword at the disposition
of the Provisional Government, and M. Lhuillier had offered him hospitality.
The duke had left Montrouge filled with enthusiasm with regard to the events
happening in Paris, and had promised to return with his own regiment.

A few days later, M. Lhuillier was decorated in recognition of this article. It
was really written by M. Thiers. The appearance, therefore, of the future
minister in the midst of this handful of Republicans was not very auspicious.
He had completely revealed his tactics since the previous morning, and was
now an Orléaniste. In this new character he was uneasy at the meeting going
on above his head, and decided to take the bull by the horns; so he ascended
to the first floor and entered, as we have seen, unannounced. A significant
murmur greeted his coming, but M. Thiers met it with audacity.

"Messieurs," he said, "the Lieutenant-General wishes to have an interview
with you."

"For what purpose?" asked Cavaignac.

"What have we and he in common?" asked Bastide.

"Listen, though, gentlemen," said Thomas.

M. Thiers thereupon fancied he had found a supporter, advanced to Thomas and laid a hand on his shoulder.

"Here we have a first-rate colonel," he said.

"Oh! indeed!" replied Thomas, gently shaking his shoulder; "so you are by way of mistaking me for a turncoat?"

M. Thiers withdrew his hand.

"Proceed," said Thomas; "we will listen to you."

M. Thiers then explained the object of the interview.

The Duc d'Orléans wished to further his future political influence, by taking counsel with these brave young fellows whose heroic insurrection had brought about the Revolution of July. According to the statement made by M. Thiers, he should expect them between eight and nine that night at the Palais-Royal. The Republicans shook their heads. To place foot inside the Palais-Royal seemed to them equivalent to entering into compact with the new powers, which was contrary both to their conscience and to their inclinations. But Thomas again came to the aid of the negotiator.

"Look here," he said, rising, "let us prove to them we are all right."

And, laying his gun in the chimney-corner, he said—

"At nine o'clock to-night, monsieur ... you can tell the Lieutenant-General of the kingdom that we will appear in answer to his invitation."

Thereupon M. Thiers went away.

There had been no such thing as an invitation from the Lieutenant-General of the kingdom; that gentleman had not the least desire to see MM. Thomas, Bastide, Chevalon, Grouvelle, Bonvilliers, Cavaignac, Arago and Guinard. M. Thiers had evolved the idea entirely out of his own head, hoping that an interview might conciliate their opinions. It will have been observed, from what he had said to Thomas, that by opinions he meant ambitions.

The Republicans were punctual to their engagement that night. The Duchesse d'Orléans, Madame Adélaide and the young princes and princesses had just arrived, when the Duc d'Orléans was informed that a deputation awaited him in the large Council Chamber. Deputations had succeeded one another all day long, and the salons were still not empty.

So another deputation was no surprise to the prince; though he was surprised by the personnel of this particular one.

M. Thiers was there. As he accompanied His Highness from the salon to the chamber where the gentlemen were awaiting him, he endeavoured to put him into possession of the situation, taking half of the responsibility upon himself, and crediting the Republicans with the remainder. This had occupied nearly a quarter of an hour, during which time the deputation was kept waiting, and it began to find the wait rather long. Then the door suddenly opened, and the duke entered with a smile upon his lips; but it had not time to mount as far as his eyes; his mouth smiled, but his expression was questioning.

"Gentlemen," said the prince, "do not doubt my pleasure in receiving this visit from you—only ..."

Bastide guessed the truth, and looked at M. Thiers.

"You do not understand why we came? Ask M. Thiers to give you the true explanation, and I am sure he will be pleased to make it, if only to save the honour and dignity of the cause we represent."

M. Thiers made some equivocal explanation or other, much embarrassed, which the Duc d'Orléans cut short by saying—

"That will do, monsieur, that will do. I thank you for procuring me the visit of these, our brave defenders."

Then, turning to them, he waited for one of them to begin. Bonvilliers was the first to speak.

"Prince," he said, "to-morrow you will be king."

The Duc d'Orléans made a movement.

"To-morrow, monsieur?" he said.

"Well, if not to-morrow, it will be either in three days' time or a week ... the actual day is of little consequence."

"King!" repeated the Duc d'Orléans after him; "who told you that, monsieur?"

"The steps your partisans are taking; the coercion they are exercising upon affairs, not daring to exercise it openly upon men; the placards with which they have covered the walls; the money they are distributing in the streets."

"I do not know what my partisans may be doing," the duke replied; "but I know I have never aspired to the crown, and even now, although I am being urged by many to accept it, I do not desire it."

"Nevertheless, monseigneur, let us suppose that they will urge you to such an extent that you will not be able to refuse, may we, in that case, ask your views on the treaties of 1815? Pay particular attention to the fact that it is not merely a Liberal revolution that has just taken place, but a national one; it has been the sight of the tricolour flag which has roused the people; we have been firing off the last mine of Waterloo, and it will be easier to drive the people across the Rhine than to Saint-Cloud."[1]

"Gentlemen," replied the duke, "I am too loyal a Frenchman and patriot to be a partisan to the treaties of 1815; but I believe France is tired of warfare; the rupture of treaties means a European war.... Believe me, it is most important to be very circumspect with regard to foreign powers, and there are certain sentiments which should not be expressed too openly."

"Let us then pass on to the aristocracy."

"Very well."

The duke bit his lips like one accustomed to question, who is compelled in his turn to submit to a cross-examination.

"The aristocracy, you will be compelled to agree," continued Bonvilliers, "has no longer any hold on society. The Code, in abolishing the right of primogeniture, of trusts and of entailed estates and by dividing inheritances to perpetuity has nipped aristocracy in the bud, and hereditary nobility has had its day. Perhaps, gentlemen, you are mistaken in this question of heredity, which is, according to my opinion, the sole source of independence underlying political institutions.... A man who is sure of coming in to his father's inheritance need not be afraid of having an opinion of his own, whereas the man to be elected will hold whatever opinions are imposed on him. But it is a question worth consideration, and, if hereditary nobility really crumbles away, *I shall not be the one to build it up again at my own expense.*"

"Prince," Bastide then replied, "I believe in the interest of the crown offered you; it will be as well to call together the Primary Assemblies."

"The Primary Assemblies?" said the duke, shuddering. "Now, indeed, I know that I am conversing with Republicans."

The young men bowed; they had come less in the spirit of allies than of enmity: they accepted instead of rejecting the qualification. Their intention was to define the situation between themselves and the ruling power as clearly as possible.

"Frankly, gentlemen," said the duke, "do you believe a Republic is possible in a country like ours?"

"We think that there is no country where the good cannot be substituted for the bad."

The duke shook his head.

"I thought that 1793 had given France a lesson from which she might have profited."

"Monsieur," said Cavaignac, "you know just as well as we do that 1793 was a Revolution and not a Republic. Besides," he continued, in strong tones and with a clear utterance which did not allow a single syllable of what he said to be lost, "so far as I can recollect, the events which transpired between 1789 and 1793 obtained your entire adhesion.... You belonged to the Society of the Jacobins?"

There was no room for him to shrink back; the veil over the past was rudely torn down, and the future King of France appeared between Robespierre and Collot-d'Herbois.

"Yes, true," said the duke, "I did belong to the Society of the Jacobins; but, happily, I was not a member of the Convention."

"Both your father and mine were, though, monsieur," said Cavaignac, "and both of them voted for the death of the king."

"It is exactly on that account, Monsieur Cavaignac," replied the duke, "that I do not hesitate to say what I have said.... I think that the son of Philippe-Égalité should be permitted to express his opinion upon the regicides. Besides, my father has been grossly calumniated; he was one of the men most worthy of respect that I have ever known!"

"Monseigneur," replied Bonvilliers, who realised that if he did not interrupt the conversation, it would degenerate into mere personalities, "we have still another fear...."

"What is it, gentlemen?" asked the prince. "Oh! say it out whilst you are about it."

"Well, we are afraid (and we have reason for so being), we are afraid, I say, of seeing the Royalists and the priests block the avenues to the new régime."

"Oh! as to those people," exclaimed the prince, with an almost menacing gesture, "set your minds at rest; they have given too many hard knocks to our House for me to forget them! Half the calumnies to which I have referred came from them; an eternal barrier separates us.... It was a good thing for the Elder Branch!"

The Republicans looked at one another in astonishment at the strong feeling, almost amounting to hatred, with which the prince uttered the words, "It was a good thing for the Elder Branch!"

"Well, gentlemen," the prince continued, "have I perchance advanced a truth which was unknown to you, in proclaiming thus openly the difference of principles and interests which have always divided the Younger Branch from the Elder, the House of Orléans from the reigning House? Oh! our hatred does not date from yesterday, gentlemen; it goes back as far as Philippe, the brother of Louis XIV.! It is like the case of my grandfather, the Regent; who was it that slandered him? The priests and the Royalists; for some day, gentlemen, when you have studied historical questions more profoundly, and dug to the roots of the tree you want to cut down, you will realise what the Regent was, and the services he rendered France by decentralising Versailles, and by making money circulate all over the country, to the extreme arteries of social life, as he did by his system of finance. Ah! I only ask one thing: if God calls upon me to reign over France, as you said just now, I hope He will grant me a portion of the Regent's genius!"

He then held forth at length upon the ameliorations to which the Regent's scheme of politics had led in the diplomatic relations of France with Europe; in connection with England, he spoke a few words showing that he should look for the same support from her as his grandfather had received.

"Pardon me, monsieur," Cavaignac said, "but I think a King of France should find his real support in his own country."

The Duc d'Orléans did not evade giving an explanation, but, with his customary facility of elocution, to do him justice, he revealed the system which afterwards gained great celebrity under the name of *Juste milieu.*

Cavaignac, to whom he addressed his remarks more particularly, since he had raised the question, listened to the prince's lengthy political propositions with the utmost impassiveness. Then, when he had finished, he said—

"All right, we need not be uneasy; with such a system as that, you will not reign longer than four years!"

The duke smiled dubiously. The Republicans, who had now learnt all they wanted to know, bowed to indicate their wish to withdraw. And the prince, noticing this, returned their bow; but, not wishing to leave them the last word, he said—

"Well, gentlemen, you will come to my way of thinking.... See if you do not!"

"Never!" Cavaignac pronounced sharply.

"Never is too positive a word, and we have an old French proverb which asserts that we must not say it: Fontaine...."

But before he could finish his sentence, the deputation had already reached the door. The duke watched their retreat with a gloomy expression of countenance., This was the first cloud to darken his sun, and it contained all the constituents of the storms that were to overthrow him.

Now that we have seen both men and principles face to face, my readers will, I hope, be better able to follow the events of 5 and 6 June, 13 and 14 April, 12 May and 24 February.

Ten minutes after the withdrawal of the Republicans, they brought word to the Lieutenant-General of the Kingdom of the resignation of the members of the Municipal Commission. Underlying this resignation the Duc d'Orléans discovered the presence of a complete ministry all ready made. It was composed of the following: Dupont (of l'Eure), Minister of Justice; Baron Louis, of Finance; General Gérard, of War; Casimir Périer, Home Minister; de Rigny, of Marine; Bignon, for Foreign Affairs; Guizot, for Public Instruction. But, even before this list had reached the Palais-Royal, one of the newly appointed ministers had already sent in his resignation—namely, Casimir Périer. Casting a glance in the direction of Versailles, he had seen that Charles X., who had only just left Saint-Cloud, had not yet reached Rambouillet. It was a very bold act to show one's colours to a new Government when the old régime was still close to the new. Ambition had led him to accept his post, but fear made him decline it. M. Casimir Périer rushed off to Bonnelier and begged him to strike out his name from the list. But it was too late; the list had gone, and Bonnelier could not do anything beyond suggesting an erratum in the *Moniteur*, which Périer accepted as better than nothing. M. de Broglie's name was inserted in the place made vacant by Casimir Périer's resignation.

Was it not a strange thing that men who were to occupy high positions in the future reign dared not risk their names, when so many others who would gain nothing by the great change had been willing to risk their heads in the cause? True, those who had risked their heads had done so for France and not for Louis-Philippe.

The next morning, when I went to call on the new lieutenant-general, he was talking with Vatout and Casimir Delavigne, whom he left to come across to me. Already acquainted with my expedition to Soissons, he held out his hand and said—

"Monsieur Dumas, you have just enacted your very finest drama!"

At that moment, General La Fayette was suffering one of the most terrible assaults at the Hôtel de Ville that had hitherto been directed against him.

Now let me relate what had become of Charras and Lothon: I take some pride, as will be understood, in dwelling at greater length upon the men whose names were not to melt away with the smoke of the battlefield. We saw them leaving the Hôtel de Ville, bearers of an order from Mauguin and a proclamation from La Fayette. We forgot to tell how Lothon, whom we left on the 29th, stretched on the pavement at the Palais-Royal, happened to be at the Hôtel de Ville with Charras on the 30th. Lothon (alas! he is now dead!) was one of those rare men whose heart was as good as his head, whom powder intoxicates, who are excited by noise, and who probably love danger for its own sake more than for the honour it may bring. When Lothon had lain on the pavement for nearly an hour, he was picked up for dead; a bullet had pierced his forehead and seven others had riddled his hat, which had fallen beside him. The hat might have been taken as a target. Whilst he was being carried away to be buried along with others at the Louvre, he moved his head slightly; and this protest, feeble though it was, against being treated as was evidently intended by his bearers, proved incontestable. A soldier of the National Guard took him in, dressed his wounds, put him to bed, and then left him to go in search of news, never supposing that a man who had had his head broken by a bullet would dream of getting up to return to the firing, should there by chance be fighting still going on in any corner of Paris. However, that was Lothon's first idea. Scarcely had he recovered consciousness than he re-dressed himself, buckled on his sword again (that sword which he had seized from the properties of the théâtre de l'Odéon, as was evident from its cross handle and sheath, which had lost its leathern end), and, in spite of the outcries made by the wife of his host, he set off, stumbling like a drunken man. Charras found him that evening on returning home. Lothon could not recollect half what he had done, or anything at all of where he had been. But next day he felt well enough to rejoin Charras at the Hôtel de Ville. We have seen how they were deputed to go and fetch the 4th Regiment of artillery, in garrison at la Fère. For three days Charras had been penniless. When the insurrection had broken out he possessed fifteen francs and a bill of exchange for a hundred crowns, sent him by his father, a Paris banker; but since the 26th every bank had been closed, and if his bill had not been accepted by Laffitte, he would certainly not have obtained from the boldest bill-broker of Paris fifty francs out of his hundred crowns. Fifteen francs went on the 26th and 27th; on the 28th he got food where he could; on the 29th he dined at the Hôtel de Ville, with the rest of Paris; finally, on the morning of the 30th, Lionel de l'Aubespin, grandson of La Fayette, shared his purse with Charras. When he and Lothon started for la Fère, they found themselves the possessors of twenty francs! They could not afford to take post on that small amount; so the two heroes asked for a letter to the new director of posts, M. Chardel, who had been appointed, the day before, by Baude and Arago. By virtue of this letter, M. Chardel gave them an order to the various posting-masters along the route, putting horses at their service, and he himself gave them the two best cobs out of his stable. Charras and Lothon set off at as fast a gallop as the barricades would allow; two or three shots were fired at them because they were taken for officers of the Royal Guard attempting flight; but they reached Bourget, and drew up at the livery stables of the same posting-master who had given me horses and a carriage an hour previously.

The roads to Soissons and to la Fère both start together, and only divide at the Gonesse and at a spot called the *Patte-d'oie*; here the bifurcation on the right leads to Dammartin, Villers-Cotterets and Soissons, and the other to Senlis, Compiègne, Noyon and la Fère. The worthy patriot of whom the two young men inquired for saddle-horses perceived at once that they (Lothon especially) could not manage half that distance at full speed; he brought out a second trap, which he horsed, and he despatched them in it, wishing them God-speed. This wish, like that of "Good hunting!" no doubt brought them misfortune. Lothon was the first to get into the trap, and, to make room for Charras, he had to raise his sword. Night began to fall, and Charras, not noticing the sword, the point of which, as we have mentioned, was poking out at the end of its sheath, suddenly felt the icy cold of steel through his armpit, and tried to fling himself forward; but Lothon took him by the shoulders, thinking he had lost his footing, and tried to draw him in farther towards his side. Charras in vain shrieked, "You are killing me, I say!" but Lothon could hear nothing because of the bandage round his head, which stopped up his ear, and continued to draw him closer on the sword-point. Luckily, Charras was able to make a violent effort, tore himself out of his companion's hands and fell into the arms of the post-master, who, seeing that something extraordinary was happening inside the trap, seconded Charras's efforts by drawing him backwards. They went back into the house, and Charras took off his coat, waistcoat and shirt. The steel had penetrated an inch and a half or so under the armpit, and blood was flowing freely. They scraped some tinder and plugged the wound with a wet handkerchief, and, thanks to this apparatus, kept in its place by the wounded man's arm, the bleeding was stopped. Lothon was in a state of desperation, but, as his despair led to nothing, Charras encouraged him to give it up. As they re-entered the carriage, the post-master asked them—

"Have you any arms besides your swords?"

"Upon my word, we haven't!" they replied.

Then the post-master went to a cupboard and brought out a couple of pistols, which he loaded and pushed into the tails of Charras's coat. I should like to mention this excellent fellow's name, but who knows whether his patriotism of 1830 might not get him into trouble in 1853? The two wounded men fell asleep, ordering the postillions to put the horses between the shafts. Generally, postillions proved true patriots, and, although Charras could not give them large tips out of his twenty francs, they acquitted themselves conscientiously, by driving fast and changing horses quickly. Moreover, the post-master of Bourget had advised the two young men to send a second postillion on ahead of them; since M. Chardel's order proscribed no limits, it cost them no more to do this. All went well as far as Ribécourt. Here they woke Charras.

"What is the matter?" asked the sleeper, rubbing his eyes.

"The post-master will not give us any horses," said the head-postillion, who had been obliged to stop there because of this refusal.

"What! the post-master won't give us horses!"

"No; he says he does not know anything about the Provisional Government."

Charras, who had been hunting for it long and vainly, very nearly said he did not know anything about it either; but this was not the moment for joking; time was flying. He left Lothon still asleep, who had not heard him when he cried out, "You are killing me!" and had therefore no right to hear anything else. Leaping from the trap, he ran to the post-master, who was furious at being waked at two in the morning, and stood on his doorstep with the evident intention of contesting the point.

"So you do not intend to give me horses?" asked Charras.

"That is so."

"In spite of the order from the Director of Posts?"

"I don't know this man Chardel!"

"Ah! So you do not know Chardel?"

"No."

Charras drew the proclamation from his pocket.

"Do you know that signature?"

"La Fayette? Not any more than the other!"

"No?"

"No!"

Charras next drew his pistols from his pocket, cocking them at the same moment as he placed them against the postmaster's breast—

"Ah!... Very well, do you recognise these?" he said.

"But, monsieur," exclaimed the man, "what are you going to do?"

"Going to do? By Jove! To kill you, if you don't give me horses!"

"But, monsieur, devil take it! men do not kill people like that ... they explain things."

"Yes, when they have time, which I have not."

The postillions, ranged behind the post-master, were grinning in the shadow, rubbing their hands and making signs to Charras to stick to it. They need not have been anxious on this score.

"Well, then, monsieur, if you take up such an attitude as that, I must give you horses; but be very sure it is only because you compel me by force to do so."

"What does that matter to me so long as you give them me!"

"Horses for these gentlemen!" said the post-master, returning to his room and yielding the battlefield to Charras.

"And good ones, look you, postillions."

"Oh! don't be uneasy, young gentleman; we will see to that," replied the postillion. "Get back into your carriage and continue your nap.... You are going to Noyon?"

"To la Fère."

"It's all the same."

Charras returned to the carriage, and so great was his fatigue that he fell asleep again before the horses were harnessed. Probably the postillion kept his word, for when Charras woke again, they had passed Noyon and day had begun to appear. Annoyed at witnessing the dawn alone, he poked Lothon till he too awoke. The sky was superb, "and jocund day,"[2] to quote Shakespeare, stood "tiptoe on the misty mountain tops," ready to descend into the plain like a luminous cloud; the leaves on the trees whispered together; the golden corn swayed gracefully; and from the midst of the fast-ripening ears the lark, daughter of day, flew up with quick-beating wing, making the air resound with her clear, joyous song. The peasants opened their doors to inhale the morning breeze, and made ready to go to work or to market, to the fields or to the town.

"Diable!" exclaimed Charras. "Look at this countryside: it has not the least appearance of being in a state of revolution."

"No, indeed it has not!" replied Lothon.

"Do you suppose these folk know about Chardel, Mauguin and La Fayette?"

"I would rather not say."

"Hum!" said Charras, who fell into a train of reflection that was not exactly rose-coloured.

Lothon took advantage of Charras's ponderings to resume his slumbers. They reached Chauny. The town was just as peaceful as the villages, the streets were as quiet as the fields! As a diver can feel the temperature of the water grow colder the deeper he plunges, so the farther they advanced into the provinces did they feel an ever-increasing frigidness take the place of the feverishness of Paris. Exactly the same experience happened to Charras as did to me: he reached the gates of la Fère determined to carry out his project, but filled with doubt as to how things would turn out.

He woke Lothon, who still slept, as they came nearer to the town. Soon they would find themselves confronted by the 4th Regiment of artillery, and the situation was sufficiently serious for them to face it with an attention fully wide awake. The gate was open, and the two young fellows went straight to the guard-house overlooking the gate. Lothon, with his black bandage over his eye and his hat placed over one ear on account of his wound, looked ten years older than he really was; moreover, his sword of the time of François I. aged him by another three centuries. Charras, who had been discharged from the École polytechnique four months previously, had allowed his moustache to grow since (this would not have been allowed at the École); with his borrowed coat too long and too large for him, his policeman's sword hung round him by a shoulder-belt instead of a proper sword-belt, his trousers all covered with the blood of a Swiss soldier—who, badly injured, had thrown himself into Charras's arms to prevent being despatched completely—Charras looked far more like a bandit than an honest man. But indeed to practised eyes neither of them looked like a student of the École polytechnique. However, all went well so long as they remained in the carriage. They had lowered the hood, and the soldiers on guard could see Lothon's tricoloured cockade, and the bunch of three-coloured ribbons which Charras had exchanged for the sleeves of the Swiss, a decoration all very well in Paris, but too eccentric for the provinces. The magic colours produced their usual effect: the sentinel presented arms, and the quarter-master who answered the summons addressed Lothon as *mon officier.*

"Well!" said Charras to Lothon, "so far things don't seem to be going badly."

"Yes," said Lothon, "but it is with the colonel we shall have to deal...."

"Ah! by Jove! then we shall see," said Charras.

"You are going to try and be very eloquent, I hope?"

"Rather! Hurrah for Marengo, Austerlitz, Jena, the Grand Army and the devil and his horns! I cannot help touching him, unless his heart be encircled with three layers of steel, as Horace says."

"And suppose it is?"

"In that case.... Ah! I don't know! But then ... Oh, hang it all, man, you worry me with all your 'ifs'!"

"Never mind. Just answer that question: suppose he isn't touched?"

"Well! Shan't we still have the Bourget post-master's spring crucifixes to fall back on? We will play on them. Upon my word and honour, anybody would think you did not know the air!"

"Of course, I do!"

"If so, why are you quibbling?"

"I wished to know if you had really decided on anything."

"Oh! I say, what humbug!"

This dialogue, as will be easily understood, took place in an undertone, whilst the quarter-master, who was to conduct the young men to the colonel's house, was preparing his military toilet. He returned and got into the carriage, which set off at full trot till it reached the colonel's house. At the gate, Charras, like the conscientious man he was, handed one of the pistols to Lothon.

"Good!" said Lothon, "thanks.... Give me the other one too now."

"What for?"

"To see if they are in good order and have not lost their primings.... Anyhow, come, give it me."

"Here it is."

"Now get out.... You can see the quarter-master is waiting for you."

Charras leapt down from the carriage, and they went upstairs to the first floor. At the door Charras turned round towards Lothon.

"What about the pistol?"

Lothon had stuffed it into his pocket.

"It is all right where it is: go on."

"What do you mean by 'it is all right where it is'?"

"Never mind: go on."

He pushed Charras into the anteroom. Lothon, just by chance, more prudent then than his comrade, had uncocked it. But they had chosen an unfortunate place to quarrel in, especially a quarrel of that nature. The two young men went on conversing mutely with their eyes, and a few seconds later found themselves inside the colonel's drawing-room. Colonel Husson was a man of forty, with strongly marked features and a resolute and proud expression, a real soldier type. He was chatting with one of the majors of his regiment. He received our two messengers politely but with reserve.

"What can we do for you, gentlemen?" he asked, after the preliminary interchange of compliments.

Charras in a few words related the story of the three days: the taking of the Louvre, the flight of the king and the nomination of the Provisional Government—the whole history of the Revolution, in short.

The two officers listened to the recital more and more coldly as he reached the end.

Charras deemed this was the right moment for producing the two papers from his pocket. He handed them both to the colonel. The one was in an envelope and sealed—that was Mauguin's letter; the other was simply folded in four—this was La Fayette's proclamation. By chance, the colonel began by breaking open first the sealed envelope containing Mauguin's letter. He read the first lines, then looked at the signature.

"Magin ... Maguin.... Who is this person?"

"Mauguin," replied Charras, "why, M. Mauguin, a member of the Provisional Government!"

"Mauguin?" the colonel repeated, looking at the major.

"Yes, a lawyer," the latter replied.

"A lawyer!" said the colonel, in tones that sent a shudder through Charras.

"Ah!" he said in a whisper to Lothon, "I believe we are done for!"

"I myself am sure of it!" said Lothon.

"Then now for our pistols!"

"Wait a bit ... there is time enough yet."

The colonel was reading the second despatch, and General La Fayette's name seemed to be correcting the bad impression made by the name of Mauguin. Had they but possessed a third letter signed by a second general they would have been saved. But, unluckily, they had no third letter.

"Well, gentlemen?" asked the colonel, when he had read the second letter.

"Well, colonel," Charras replied plainly, "the Provisional Government thought it was sending us to patriots; it seems that it was mistaken, that is all."

"Do you know, messieurs, to what this error of yours exposes you?"

"Why, yes!" said Charras; "to be shot."

"I am obliged to leave you, messieurs; give me your word of honour that you will not attempt to leave this room."

"Our parole?... Come now!... Have us shot, if you will,—you must answer for the responsibility of the execution to the Provisional Government,—but we will not give you our parole."

"At all events, give up your swords, then."

"No, no, no!"

The colonel bit his lips and said something in a low voice to the major and prepared to go out. Charras made a backward movement in order to touch Lothon, then said in a whisper—

"The pistol, for goodness' sake give me the pistol! You can see that this rascal means to have us shot!"

"Bah!" was Lothon's reply, "*à la guerre comme à la guerre.*"

"You seem to take things very easy, you donkey; you are half dead as it is, and won't take much finishing off.... But, except for the hole you were imbecile enough to make in me, I am hale enough, and I have no desire to be killed like a chicken!"

"Oh! set your mind at rest!... They do not shoot people down like this without warning, you bet!"

Meanwhile, the colonel went away, and the two messengers were left with the major. The major seemed a better sort than the colonel; he had evidently remained, by his chiefs order, to make the young men talk and to find out whether all they had stated was really the truth. As their story was correct, there was no danger of their contradicting each other. Moreover, Lothon left the whole brunt of the conversation to Charras; for, as he was lounging on a sort of sofa, he fell asleep in five minutes' time. In the midst of the interview an officer appeared on the scene.

"Comrade," he said, addressing Charras, "I have come from the colonel, to whom you would not give your parole.... My instructions are not to let you out of my sight;... but as I am not a policeman—why there!..."

He unbuckled his sword and flung it into an arm-chair.

"You can do what you like!"

"Monsieur," said Charras, "our intention is not to quit la Fère, and in proof thereof look...."

And he pointed out to the officer Lothon sound asleep.

The colonel returned in an hour's time. He appeared very much excited and very irresolute. Suddenly he stopped in front of Charras.

"I will wager you are hungry?" he said.

Charras merely shrugged his shoulders and answered—

"That is a singular question to put to me, surely?"

"Ah!" said the colonel, "we must not let anyone die of hunger, not even prisoners."

"Yes, it is better to fatten them up before you shoot them, is it not?" remarked Charras.

"Who is talking of shooting you? Come," exclaimed the colonel, opening a door, "breakfast."

A table was brought in, fully laid as on the stage. The colonel departed from his usual custom and breakfasted in his drawing-room instead of his dining-room—or, rather, he did not breakfast, for he did not sit down to the table. Charras roused Lothon, who was in a bad temper at being waked, specially since he did not know for what purpose he had been awakened. When he knew that it was for breakfast, he softened. They had just finished the cutlets when the door opened quickly and a man of about fifty dressed in uniform appeared.

"Pardon, colonel," he said, "but I am Lieutenant-Colonel Duriveau of the Engineers and second in command at the École polytechnique under the Empire.... I have been told that you are keeping two of my old boys prisoners, and have come to see if it is so."

Then, addressing himself to Charras and Lothon, he said—

"Good-day, messieurs; I bid you welcome."

"Welcome?" repeated the colonel.

"Yes, yes, that is what I said.... And to you, colonel, I say that you have no right to detain these gentlemen. I am told they have been sent on a mission from the Provisional Government.... They are officers with a flag of truce, and it is the universal custom not to arrest those intrusted with missions of that nature."

So saying, he shook Charras's hand with such heartiness as to make him cry out, for it caused his wound to re-open.

"What is the matter?" asked Lieutenant-Colonel Duriveau.

"Nothing, nothing at all, merely that I have a wound under my arm."

"Indeed, and it looks as though your friend had one in his head, too.... We must have all these wounds dressed before anything else, colonel."

"I have thought of that, monsieur," replied the colonel, "and I do not know why the surgeon-major has not yet come."

At that moment he came in.

"Here, monsieur," the colonel said to him, "these are the young men I spoke of.... See if they require your services."

Charras wanted to refuse, but Lieutenant-Colonel Duriveau signed to him to allow it, and took the colonel and major away into an adjoining room. The surgeon-major first dressed Lothon's head; the bullet had penetrated to the bone, which it had twisted and left bare. He must have been bewitched to be out of his bed after receiving such an injury. The surgeon wanted to bleed the wounded man, but to this he positively objected.

"I may at any moment require the use of both my arms," he said, "so leave them intact.... My head is quite bad enough without other hurt!"

Then came Charras.

"Good gracious, monsieur," said the surgeon-major, "you had a lucky escape! An inch or two more to the left and you would have had the artery severed."

"And to think," Charras said, pointing to Lothon, "that it was that brute who did it for me with his François sword!"

"Come," said Lothon, "there you go, crying out about your blessed artery which is not even scratched!... I did not know you were as soft as that!"

Charras began laughing, when Lieutenant Colonel Duriveau entered.

"All is going right," he whispered to Charras. "I will not leave you for a minute until you are outside the town."

There had just been a meeting of officers, who had decided that, whether with or without the colonel's participation, they would range themselves on the side of the Provisional Government. The colonel returned in half an hour's time.

"Messieurs," he said, "you must give me your word of honour to leave la Fère instantly, and then you shall be free."

"I will give you nothing of the kind," said Charras.

"You will not!"

"No."

"You will, at any rate, engage not to cause any disturbance in my regiment?"

"I will not.... I like your suggestions, indeed! We come in the name of the constituted Government, and it is we who possess authority, you who are rebels; we could do you a bad turn for having us arrested, and you ask us for our word of honour to quit la Fère, and not to try to influence your regiment.... Come now! Either shoot us or let us go free!"

"Well, then," said the colonel, "go to the devil with you!" and he held out his hand to them, laughing.

They both pressed his hand and went out, accompanied by Lieutenant-Colonel Duriveau, who, according to his promise, kept as close to them as a shadow.

It may be gathered that the town was in a state of excitement. The officer who had been set to mount guard over them left the house with them, and, after shaking hands at the door, set off at a run to rejoin his comrades. The carriage had returned to the posting-house, to which they wended their way. At every step of the road the young men received manifest tokens of sympathy. When they reached the post, they were rejoined by the major.

"Messieurs," he said to them, "the colonel begs you as a favour to go away; he gives you his word of honour that he and his regiment will yield allegiance to the Provisional Government.... But, at the least, you might allow him the credit for this adherence."

"Oh! if that is all," Charras and Lothon both exclaimed together, "by all means let us start!"

"One moment," said Lieutenant-Colonel Duriveau, "how are you off for money?"

Charras turned out his pockets; he had hardly five francs left out of Aubespin's twenty francs.

"How much would you like?" said the lieutenant-colonel, pulling out several bags of five-franc pieces from his trouser-pockets.

"A hundred francs," said Charras.

"Will that be enough?"

"Surely! we came with but twenty."

"Then we'll say a hundred."

And he handed a rouleau to Charras, who broke it in two as though it had been a stick of chocolate, and gave half or thereabouts to Lothon.

"Now for the carriage and horses!" shouted the two young men.

"Oh! the posting stage between here and Chauny is my affair. I am going to drive you," said a jovial-faced, sturdy-looking butcher, who had stationed himself in front of the post-house with his little spring cart, inside which five or six trusses of straw composed the seats, and he rolled up his sleeves; "and I guess," he added, "you will never have been driven so fast."

"Very well, thanks, comrade!" said Charras, he and Lothon seating themselves beside him.

"Here! postillion, follow us with the carriage!" they shouted. "Adieu, colonel!"

"Adieu, my lads!"

"Off we go!" cried the butcher, cracking his whip, "and *Vive la Charte! Vive La Fayette! Vive le Gouvernement Provisoire!* Down with Charles X., the dauphin, Polignac and the whole lot of them! Houp!..."

And, as the butcher had promised, the cart whirled away as fast as a waterspout. At Chauny, they parted from the butcher and re-mounted their carriage. Next day, at ten in the morning, an hour after me, Charras and Lothon reached the Hôtel de Ville just at the moment when General La Fayette, who was always gallant, was kissing the hand of Mademoiselle

Mante, who, accompanied by M. Samson and a third member, had come to lay the Comédie-Française under the protection of the nation. This deputation kept the two young men waiting for half an hour, during which time they acquainted themselves with what had happened since their departure: how the Duc d'Orléans was made lieutenant-general, and how Louis-Philippe was going to be made king.

"Ah! that is how matters stand," Lothon exclaimed to Charras; "well, you shall hear what I have to say to it all to old La Fayette!"

It was now Charras's turn to try and calm Lothon. But Lothon would not be quieted: his wound, the heat, the excitement, the little wine he had drunk, his refusal to be bled, all combined to send him into a state of delirium. Brain fever had set in. He entered the room where La Fayette was, hustling everybody who tried to prevent him; for, as I have mentioned, La Fayette was very carefully guarded. Charras followed Lothon. Then, crossing his arms over his breast, his hat that had been riddled into holes by the seven bullets thrown on the ground, his forehead bound up in the black bandage, his eyes flashing with fever, his cheeks purple with anger, the young fellow called the old man to account in terms which ought to have been taken down in shorthand to be properly reproduced, with respect to the liberty which had been bought at the price of much bloodshed, which the People had confided to him and which he had allowed himself to be robbed of by the chicanery and ambition of courtiers. He was so fine, so great, so eloquent, so full of untold poetic feeling, to the point even of frenzy, that no one dared interrupt him.

"General," Charras whispered to La Fayette, "forgive him.... You see he is delirious."

"Yes, yes," said La Fayette.

Then to Lothon—

"My friend—my young friend—there, there ... calm yourself!"

Then, turning round—

"Is there no doctor at hand to bleed this young man?" he asked.

Lothon heard the suggestion.

"To bleed me?" he exclaimed. "Oh! no, no! Since we have again lost liberty, my blood shall not flow by the lance of a doctor ... but by the bayonets of the Royal Guard, under the bullets of the Swiss.... Leave me the blood in my veins, general; so long as the Bourbons remain in France, both Older and Younger Branches, I shall have need of it! Come, Charras. Come!"

He rushed from the room, leaving La Fayette thoughtful and troubled. Perhaps the words that had just fallen on the general's ear corresponded to the voice of his conscience; perhaps he had already reproached himself in the same way that Lothon had just done.

"I should like to be alone," he said.

And, before the door was closed, they could see him bury that fine and noble head between his hands, that head upon which the children of the Republic had just invoked the anathemas of posterity.

[1] As none of the above conversation has yet been reported entirely, I appeal to history and to the memories of persons who were present at the interview. As to the words spoken by Godefroy Cavaignac and the king's reply, I can certify their authenticity, as I wrote them down at the time, from Godefroy's own dictation, and he was quite incapable of untruthfulness.

[2] *Romeo and Juliet.*

CHAPTER II

Letter of Charles X. to the Duc d'Orléans—A conjuring trick—Return of the Duc de Chartres to the Palais-Royal—Bourbons and Valois—Abdication of Charles X.—Preparations for the expedition of Rambouillet—An idea of Harel—The scene-shifters of the Odéon—Nineteen persons in one fiacre—Distribution of arms at the Palais-Royal—Colonel Jacqueminot

---

Meanwhile the Duc d'Orléans hid his grave preoccupation of mind beneath his affable manner that morning when he came up to me and told me I had produced my best drama. He had just received the answer to the letter which he had sent to Charles X. by the Duc de Mortemart.

My readers will recollect that letter, wherein he says to the old king, that *he had been brought to Paris by force; that he did not know what they wanted him to do, but that if he accepted power it would only be in the best interests of* THE HOUSE. Only he did not specify *what House.* Did he mean in the interest of the *House of Orléans* or of the *House of Bourbon?* Re-read the sentence and you will see he reserves his choice.

Charles X. replied to this letter by a declaration couched as follows:—

> "The king, desirous of putting a stop to the troubles that exist in the capital and in another part of France, *relying especially on the sincere attachment of his cousin the Duc d'Orléans,* appoints him Lieutenant-General of the Kingdom. The king, having seen fit to withdraw the Ordinances of 25 July, approves the assembling of the Chambers on 3 August, and he hopes they will be able to re-establish tranquillity in France. The king will await at Rambouillet the return of the person charged to bear this declaration to Paris. If any attempt is made upon the lives of the king and his family or upon his liberty, he will defend himself to the last.
>
> "Drawn up at Rambouillet, I August 1830.
>
> "*(Signed)* CHARLES"

The courier left Rambouillet at six in the morning, and reached Paris at half-past eight. The Duc d'Orléans received the despatch at a quarter to nine. M. Dupin was already with him. It is well known how early M. Dupin could be the day, or day but one, after revolutions had taken place; moreover, thanks to the *Caricature*, the impressions of the shoes of this famous lawyer, printed along the route to Neuilly, both going and returning, and *vice versâ*, acquired a celebrity that afterwards became proverbial. M. Dupin, then, was with the Duc d'Orléans when he received the letter from Charles X. The Duc d'Orléans read it and passed it on to him. M. Dupin, remember, was head of the prince's Privy Council. M. Dupin read the proclamation in his turn, and advised that they should break openly and even brutally with the Older Branch.

"Diable!" said the prince, "such a letter as you suggest my writing will be anything but easy to draw up!"

"Shall I draw it up, your Highness?" asked M. Dupin.

"Yes, certainly. Try ... we will see."

M. Dupin wrote a letter as rough as himself. The Duc d'Orléans read it, approved, re-copied, signed, put it in an envelope and was going to seal it when, all at once, he said—

"Good gracious! I was going to send off a letter of such importance as this without showing it to the duchess.... Wait a moment, Monsieur Dupin, I will soon come back."

The letter must have been brutal indeed, for M. Dupin has himself confessed that it was; he was by nature rough and the plane of education had not effaced this roughness. He continued to argue with King Louis-Philippe in just the same fashion as he had done when he was Prince of Orléans. Once, during a political discussion, he forgot himself so far as to say to the king—

"Look here, sir, we shall never agree!"

"I was thinking the same thing, Monsieur Dupin," replied Louis-Philippe, "only I dared not tell you so."

I know few sayings more insolently aristocratic than this. King Louis-Philippe was diabolically witty. In proof whereof, he returned holding the same envelope and a letter that was to all appearances the same.

"Poor duchess!" he said, "it made her very sad; but, by Jove, it can't be helped!"

Then he slipped the letter into the envelope, held the wax to a candle, sealed the despatch with his seal and gave it to a messenger. But the letter he sent to Charles X. was not by any means the one M. Dupin had drawn up: it was one of his own composing, in which he renewed his assurances of devotion and respect towards the old king. This little game of sleight-of-hand was hardly finished before the outcries of the people gathered in the courtyard of the Palais-Royal summoned him out on the balcony. Louis-Philippe was obliged to show himself on this balcony twenty times a day for a week. Very soon this was not enough to satisfy the crowd, for the moment he appeared, the crowd struck up the *Marseillaise*; then, he himself must needs join in too, in a voice which, as I have remarked, was as out of tune as that of King Louis XV. Soon, this did not suffice them; when the lieutenant-general had shown himself and joined in singing the *Marseillaise*, he had to go down into the courtyard and shake hands with the rag-and-bone men and porters and pat them on the back. I have seen him go down two or three times in an hour and return with his wig awry, mopping his forehead, washing his hands and cursing vigorously the part he was compelled to play.

Ah! monseigneur, did you not know that in order to become king, after being prince, you would have frequently to mop your forehead and wash your hands?

The Duc de Chartres next arrived at the head of his regiment, and entered the Palais-Royal just as his father was courting popularity in the manner above described. I shall never forget the way he straightened himself in his saddle, and the look he cast on the scene. The arrival of her eldest son was a great delight to the poor duchess; he was the only one of her children that had been missing. She was well aware of the danger he had incurred and he was all the dearer to her on that account. As he entered his father's apartments I was leaving them, and I was only to return there once more at the summons of the king himself. This spectacle of a prince begging for a crown stirred me to the heart. The young duke held out his hand to me: I took it and pressed it with tears in my eyes. It was to be four years before I touched that loyal, open hand again, though, at that moment, I thought I should be parted from him for ever, and was therefore touching it for the last time. In due course I will relate the circumstances under which I was again to meet him.

As I left the Palais-Royal I came across a placard which openly asserted that the Orléans princes were not *Bourbons*, but of the house of *Valois*. I could hardly believe my eyes and stood for a quarter of an hour reading and re-reading it. Ten yards away I met Oudard, took him by the arm and led him in front of the placard.

"Oh!" I said, "it seems it was not enough for Philippe-Égalité to disown his father, but that the son must disown even his very race?"

I returned home, I must confess, completely cast down. I do not know which day this was, but I think it must have been the 2nd of August.

The powder had arrived with Bard that morning; I had handed it over to two students of the École polytechnique, who gave me a receipt for it and took it to la Salpétrière. It must have been on the 2nd, for I saw M. de Latour-Foissac, whom I knew by sight, driving to the Palais-Royal; I had met him at the house of Madame de Sériane, sister of General Coëtlosquet.

M. de Latour-Foissac was taking the answer to the lieu-tenant-general's letter of the previous day, the letter substituted, as we know, for the one written by M. Dupin. This answer was the abdication of Charles X. and that of the Duc d'Angoulême; it gave permission to the Duc d'Orléans to proclaim the Duc de Bordeaux under the title of Henri V. The lieutenant-general declined to receive the messenger, but he took the message.

Now, what was to be done? M. Sébastiani was consulted, and advised a Regency. Béranger was for a Monarchy. The Duc d'Orléans cut the difficult knot by saying—

"Be Regent? I would rather be nothing at all than Regent.... At the very first stomach-ache Henri V. might have, it would be proclaimed upon the housetops that I had poisoned him."

And from that moment there was no longer any doubt in anyone's mind that Louis-Philippe would become king.

The abdication was dated from Rambouillet, as the letter had been. Rambouillet was only thirty-six miles from Paris; Charles X. had still fourteen thousand men round him, with thirty-eight pieces of cannon. He had something even better than those—he had the two letters of the Duc d'Orléans. Charles X. could not remain at Rambouillet; by some combination or other he must be forced to leave Rambouillet, and, more than that, France itself. It did not prove a difficult matter to manage to bring this to pass—the means were probably already prepared. Meantime, on 2 August, General Hulot was sent to Cherbourg to take up the command of the four departments which separate Paris from the Channel; the same day also M. Dumont-d'Urville received orders to start for Havre with all haste, and there to freight two transport ships. The day before, they risked inserting in the *Courrier français* the protest of the Duc d'Orléans against the birth of the Duc de Bordeaux. The reader knows how this proclamation, which in 1820 had caused the exile of the Duc d'Orléans, suggested a doubt as to the legitimacy of the young prince. Well, on 1 August the *Courrier français* was asked to give it a place in one of its next issues. It did not keep the future king waiting long in impatience! Next morning, 2 August, the *Courrier* contained the protest. Very likely it was set up by the very same compositors who had printed the placard stating that the Orléans princes were Valois by descent, and not Bourbons.

So all these things happened on 2 August, for on the 3rd I was awakened by the call to arms, which was being beaten furiously in the street, and by

Delanoue, who burst into my room, a double-barrelled gun in his hand. A gun was such an unusual toilet accessory in the case of Delanoue that I was more struck by it than by all the rest of the commotion.

"What the dickens is happening?" I asked him.

"Charles X. is marching on Paris with twenty thousand men and fifty pieces of cannon, my dear boy, and all Paris on its part has risen to march against him. Will you come too?"

"By Jove! of course I will!" I cried, leaping out of bed. "I should rather think I would!"

I called Joseph, whose terrified face I had not seen behind Delanoue.

"Here I am, monsieur!" he said, "here I am!"

"Give me my shooting clothes, and take my rifle to the nearest gun-maker's to be cleaned."

"Don't let him take your gun to a shop," said Delanoue; "they will take it from him on the way."

"What!" I said, "they would seize it?"

"Without a doubt.... Things are worse than during the Three Days!"

"Then, my dear Joseph, clean it yourself!"

"Good heavens! good heavens!" said Joseph, "is monsieur going to return to Soissons?"

"No, Joseph; I am going, on the contrary, in exactly the opposite direction."

"Thank goodness!"

Harel came in whilst I was dressing.

"Good—morning, Harel.... What is the news, my friend?"

"The news is," said Harel, drawing his snuff-box from his pocket and plunging in his finger and thumb up to the first joint, "the news is that I have a cunning idea in my head." He breathed up his pinch of snuff with sensuous enjoyment, and, as is usual with great connoisseurs, scattered three-quarters of his snuff over the floor and into the air. "An excellent idea!" he went on.

"Well, my friend, you shall communicate it to me on my return."

"Where are you going?"

"To Rambouillet, of course!"

"Excellent! That's the finishing stroke! You ran the risk of being shot three days ago at Soissons, and now you want to go and get some limb or other broken at Rambouillet!"

"But don't you realise that Charles X. is marching on Paris with twenty thousand men and fifty pieces of cannon?"

"I know that is the report; but let fools believe such news as that. Poor Charles X.! I will wager, if he marches to any town whatsoever, it will be towards Havre or Cherbourg."

"Never mind, my dear friend! Delanoue has come to fetch me, and if it is nothing more than to hunt big game in the park at Rambouillet, I do not wish to miss the opportunity... So once more you must put off telling me your piece of news till my return, if I do return."

"Give me a part in your piece," Delanoue said in a whisper.

"Certainly, I promise."

I turned round to Harel.

"How did you come here?" I asked him.

"Why, in a cab, of course."

"Good! we will take it."

"What for?"

"To drive to Rambouillet."

"You must take me as far as the Odéon, then!"

"Agreed!"

"Besides," said Delanoue, "it is on the place de l'Odéon people are collecting."

"Ah! you will lend us your tricolour flag, Harel, won't you?"

"What tricolour flag do you mean?"

"The one under which they have been singing the *Marseillaise* at your theatre for the last three days."

"What am I to do, then?"

"You will make an announcement to the public, telling them that I carried it away to Rambouillet.... The public is good-natured enough, and will do without the flag for a day or two."

"Come along and get it ... you know very well the whole theatre is at your service."

Whenever Harel wanted to get a play out of me, he always made this remark. My gun had been washed and rubbed and dried in the sun; I took it, we got into the cab and set off for the Odéon. There were two or three thousand persons in the square and its vicinity. I had scarcely put my foot to the ground, leaving Delanoue inside the cab, before I was surrounded by a score of men, calling me by my name and asking me to put myself at their head. They were the scene-shifters belonging to the Odéon, who still had in warm remembrance the tips I had given them when *Christine* was being performed. I told one of them to go and find the flag, and whilst we left the cab under the protection of others (to whom I sent out seven or eight bottles of wine to keep up their patience) we went and had breakfast at Risbeck's. By the time we came out of the restaurant our troop was further augmented by a drummer. I have remarked before with what rapidity drummers multiply during times of revolution. We got into our cab, naturally taking the seat of honour; then everybody else crushed inside with us, or outside on the box with the driver, some behind, some on the shafts, and some on the imperial. The unlucky horses started, dragging nineteen people! Most of my men were only armed with pikes. At the corner of the rue du Bac and the quay, a man who seemed to be posted there on duty for this purpose shouted after us—

"Have you any arms?"

"No!" replied most of my men.

"Well! arms are being distributed at the Palais-Royal."

"To the Palais-Royal!" cried the men. "To the Palais-Royal."

The cab crossed the place du Carrousel and made its way towards the Palais-Royal. Traffic was becoming possible once more, little by little the barricades had disappeared and the paving stones had somehow or other been laid down again. We reached the Palais-Royal.

"One moment," I said; "order, if you please! I am known here, and, if there is any chance of obtaining anything, I shall have it."

We went into a low room, which was packed with people. As I went in, I knocked against a student of the École who was going out.

"Is that you, Charles?"

"Yes.... Have you come to get arms?"

"Of course."

"In that case, you had better hurry up. I have only been able to get a pistol."

He had a pistol stuck into his coat, the butt end projecting between two buttons.

"You are going there too?"

"Why, of course!"

"Then we shall meet again?"

"Probably."

"Good-day!"

"Adieu!"

We managed with the greatest difficulty to push our way to the distributor of arms. Fortunately, a valet in the livery of the Duc d'Orléans recognised me, and made room for us.

"Monsieur de Rumigny," he said, "here is M. Dumas."

"Very well, let him come to me."

The distributor was M. de Rumigny himself: he was then about thirty-five, and was a splendid figure in his uniform. He had a big case full of swords and pistols in front of him; the rifles had all gone. They had come from Lepage.

Swords and pistols were given to my men, and then, when all had been equipped, M. de Rumigny asked—

"Are your men thirsty?"

"Rather," I said, "they are scene-shifters from the théâtre de l'Odéon!"

"Give them a glass of wine each, then."

They went to a table full of bottles and glasses, and were served by His Royal Highness's own lackeys.

"Well?" I asked, when they had drunk.

"The livery is fine enough," they replied, "but the wine is poor."

"What do you mean?"

"It is not equal to that you sent us out on the place de l'Odéon.... We bet this wine here is not worth twelve sous a bottle."

"If you have any more like it again to-night, upon my word I shall think you very lucky."

"Messieurs," said a lackey, "please make room now for others."

"Quite right": so we went out.

Paris presented quite a new aspect—it seemed incredible after the many different spectacles it had been exhibiting. Whether the cabs were chartered by the Government, or whether their drivers shared the general enthusiasm, they placed themselves at the disposal of the combatants. At the corner of the rue Saint-Roch I caught sight of Charles Ledru running at full speed. I called out to him—

"Hi! come with us."

"Have you room for me?"

"We are only nine inside, and if we squeeze up a little more we can get you in."

"Thanks, I have a horse ready for me at Kausmann's."

"Stop," I said, "that reminds me I have one too.... I always forget it." I had only had it a short time.

I pulled up before my friend Hiraux's café, porte Saint-Honoré, and he regaled all my men with a *petit verre* of eau-de-vie. The bottle was emptied in the process. But, as the flag waved, my men sang the *Marseillaise* and the drum beat a roll. We had taken nearly three-quarters of an hour in coming from the Palais-Royal to the porte Saint-Honoré, the street was so crowded and the carriages walked in files as at Longchamp.

We now made a fresh start, some taking the road by the water and others the grand avenue of the Champs-Élysées. At the place Louis XV. "Make way!" was being shouted by General Pajol, who had just received the command of the Expeditionary Army, and who came along full gallop to take the head of the column. He had with him Charras, Charles Ledru and two or three others. We drew up, and he passed and went along by the water's edge. We kept to the grand allée. At the circus of the Champs-Élysées we turned to the left, to regain the quai de Billy by the avenue Montaigne. In the middle of this avenue stood a group of horsemen with Colonel Jacqueminot in the centre. He was in the dress of a deputy and still wore the silver fleur-de-lis on his collar. General Pajol had doubtless been sending to look for him, for he was talking eagerly with Charras. Étienne Arago passed at that moment with a band of about a hundred men. Every time we met they shouted "*Vive la Charte!*" and we shouted back the same! This seemed to annoy Colonel Jacqueminot, and with good cause, I think: it was not amusing at all to live in the din of those everlasting shoutings.

"Yes! yes! shout *Vive la Charte!* It will make you as fat as eating bits of wafer!"

The phrase was so original that I have not forgotten a word of it in all these twenty-two years. We only shouted the louder, then went on our way in the direction of Versailles.

CHAPTER III

May I now be permitted to lose my own poor little individuality in the vortex of the general movement that was urging thirty to forty thousand human beings with one common impulse towards Rambouillet.

Ever since the previous day, when, as we have stated, the lieutenant-general had received official information of the abdication of Charles X., he had tried to think of the best means of ridding himself as quickly as possible of that inconvenient neighbour. Now this is what he did. He decided that, in order to protect Charles X. from the outburst of public anger that would break out next day, he would send him four commissioners. These four were: Marshall Maison, Colonel Jacqueminot, M. de Schonen, whom they desired to win over, and Odilon Barrot, who needed no persuading, as he had been one of the most powerful upholders of the new power that had just arisen. There was a certain amount of interest attaching to Marshall Maison, because it was he who had been to Calais to meet Louis XVIII., and now he was getting ready to escort Charles X. back to Cherbourg. Moreover, by presenting themselves at Rambouillet, the four commissioners believed they were being summoned there by Charles X. They set off on 2 August at four o'clock in the afternoon; by nine o'clock they had reached the outposts. They passed through the Royal Army by the light of bivouac fires, and reached Rambouillet, but not without, however, catching sight of some eager glances and half-drawn swords. Luckily, the Duc d'Orléans conceived the idea of adding to their number M. de Coigny, whose name was connected with the ancient monarchy by traditions of glory, by the devotion of his father and his ancestors. The name of M. de Coigny protected them and procured their admission to the palace. Charles X. did not understand their presence at such an unusual hour and, to their request for an audience, sent word that the time for audiences was past, but that he offered them hospitality at the château de Rambouillet. Charles X. was, however, waiting for the answer of the Duc d'Orléans to the letter he had sent him that morning by M. de Latour-Foissac which the duke had taken from the hands of M. de Mortemart, although he would not consent to receive the messenger who had brought it. The hospitality of the château de Rambouillet! that was not what the four commissioners had come for; so they at once got back into their carriage and immediately returned to Paris. They returned more quickly than they had come, and re-entered the Palais-Royal at half-past twelve midnight. The future king was not as punctilious as the retiring one: he would receive at any hour, especially when the news was worth his while. The news the four commissioners brought compelled him to take a resolution there and then, without loss of time: Charles X. must be compelled to leave Rambouillet the very next day. To this end a great patriotic demonstration was essential, and Colonel Jacqueminot was commissioned to stir up such a demonstration. At daybreak, two or three hundred policemen were let loose in every quarter of Paris with orders to cry out—

"Charles X. is marching upon Paris!... To Rambouillet! To Rambouillet!"

They were also deputed to send forth all the drummers they knew of and to let these beat the *rappel*. And this was the cause of the infernal racket that had waked Paris.

The Government possessed one man at this crisis on whose courage they could rely: this was General Pajol. He was the true type of a soldier; courageous, honourable, open and loyal, quick in making decisions, persistent in determination. At some battle or other, when he was either colonel or major of a regiment, just in sight of the emperor, a shell pierced his horse's stomach and burst inside it. Pajol was sent flying fifteen feet into the air. Napoleon saw the strange ascension.

"By Jove!" he said, "if that beggar comes down, he must have a tough life!"

A fortnight afterwards, a superior officer came and presented himself before the emperor, limping slightly.

"Who are you?" asked Napoleon.

"I am the tough-lived beggar," replied Pajol.

And to this incident was due his rapid advance in an admirable military career, only interrupted by Waterloo.

Pajol belonged to the Opposition and was almost Republican in his views.

Three days before this, when the Chamber was laying the preliminary foundations of a new monarchy, Pajol, who saw the turn things were taking, was walking sadly along the rue de Chabrol, in company with Degousée, who himself deplored the direction in which the Revolution was turning, when, suddenly, Pajol stopped.

"You told me, a minute ago, that you led a company of devoted men in the attack on the Louvre?" he asked.

"No doubt of it."

"Well, could you still rely on those men?"

"I believe so."

"To the pitch of executing to the letter, and without any discussion, any order you might give them?"

"What sort of order?"

"Suppose it were to arrest the deputies?"

"Oh! I would not answer for them in that respect!"

"In that case, the Revolution has miscarried!..."

He went to his home, in the rue de la Ferme des Mathurins, to await the turn of events.

Events soon happened: they made him commander of the insurrection on the 3rd and they counted upon him to lead the democratic army, which he did. It was all one to him, so long as he was serving France. Charras had heard it cried in the streets that General Pajol was to be commander-in-chief of the expedition and he rushed off to the general's house. Let us begin by saying that he had been beforehand to the stables of Kausmann and had taken his best horse, over which he had had a dispute with a man who was a great judge of horses and had chosen it himself. The horse-fancier was Charles Ledru, who had left me in the rue Saint-Honoré, refusing the seat I offered him in my cab, to go and bestride the horse waiting for him at Kausmann's. Just as he entered the stables, Charras was leaving them at full gallop on the very horse he, Charles Ledru, had selected. He chose another, however, and rode after the first. Luckily, he found the second a good one, and accordingly, when he overtook Charras, he merely shook him by the hand. Charras, without any previous introduction, presented himself to General Pajol. That general, accustomed to taking all sorts of precautions during military expeditions, was having two enormous saddlebags taken down: one was full of hams, legs of mutton and fowls, and the other was filled with bread. At the fourth word Charras addressed to him, and at the first look he cast at him he said—

"Look here, I like you!"

"So much the better," said Charras.

"You appear to be a nice young dog!"

"Dogs are not allowed to take a share in things."

"Will you be my aide-de-camp?"

"Yes, indeed; that was what I came for!"

"Then it is settled"; and he held out his hand to the young man.

"Now," he replied, "will you have a bit of food?"

"I shall be delighted!... I am dying of hunger."

"Go into the dining-room, then.... Madame Pajol! Madame Pajol!"

The general's wife entered.

"Give this young fellow a good breakfast ... he has come to offer me his services as aide-de-camp; he little knows what work I shall cut out for him."

Charras sat down at the table, devoured his food by huge mouthfuls, drank like a fish and was ready to start in ten minutes' time.

"Come along now, *en route!*" said the general.

They went down into the courtyard, where three or four persons were waiting for them, leapt into their saddles and the general set off at a gallop, turning short round the corner of the stable-yard gate and making his horse change feet, like the perfect horseman he was. Charras was an excellent horseman himself and stood this first test victoriously. But the horse that was being ridden by another student of the École was pushed on to the footpath and fell down on the left hand. This happened outside a chemist's shop and both student and horse disappeared into the shop—breaking in the front as they fell. The accident was not thought worth wasting time over and the others went on their way without even turning their heads to look. When they reached the barrier at Passy, the general took command of the column. Our cab was one of the first, after the general's staff, which consisted of Jacqueminot, Charras, Charles Ledru, d'Higonnet, M. de Lagrange, Vernon and Bernadou. Vernon and Bernadou wore the uniform of students at the École. Charles Ledru was in the old uniform of the National Horse Guards, and wore a helmet; Higonnet wore the uniform of a pupil of the School of Cavalry at Saumur; and M. de Lagrange that of the Light Cavalry. General Exelmans appeared farther on, beyond the quai de Billy.

"Here I am, Pajol!" he said, breaking through the ranks to get to him.

"You are somewhat late ... but never mind," Pajol replied; "you can command the rearguard."

"Good!" was Exelmans' reply.

And he passed along to the rearguard, where he found the Rouennais, who had but just arrived.

Pajol pulled up his horse at Point-du-Jour.

"By Jove!" he exclaimed, "I bet...."

"What?" they inquired.

"That nobody here has a map of the department of Seine-et-Oise... Eh? Has anyone got a map of the department of Seine-et-Oise?"

Nobody replied.

"Shall I go and find one?" asked Charras.

"Where?"

"I don't know! Wherever I can!"

"But if you don't know where to look?"

"Oh! if one hunts, one always finds what one wants."

Charras started off at a gallop—he had a notion where to look. He went to the manufactory of Sèvres: it would surely be impossible not to find a map of Seine-et-Oise there. Nor was he mistaken: they had two. They were put at his disposal by my namesake, M. Dumas, the chemist, erewhile minister and present senator. Pajol received the two maps a quarter of a league outside Sèvres.

"Now, then, Jacqueminot," he said, "we must have bread, and plenty of it, too.... Go to Versailles and order ten thousand rations."

Jacqueminot started off.

"And we must also have spies," said Pajol. "Who will undertake to find me spies?"

"I will," said Charras.

"Ah! do you mean to undertake to find everything?"

"Why not?" said Charras. "I must make myself useful."

"Where will you find me these?"

"At Versailles."

"Do you know anybody there?"

"Not a soul ... but don't trouble on that account."

"I will go with you," said Bernadou.

"Come, then."

The two young men set off as fast as their horses could go. They reached the Hôtel de Ville of Versailles consumed with thirst. Somebody had conceived the notion of breaking open a dozen barrels of beer in the courtyard, in the full sunshine: they attempted to drink it, but found it like poison. A man in civilian dress was there, representing the mayor, sweating like an ox: for that matter, everybody, mayor, deputies, municipal councillors, were all melting with the heat.

"Look quick!" said Charras; "come, we want spies, horses and a carriage!"

"Excuse me?" asked the perspiring citizen.

"Are you deaf? I ask you for spies, horses and a carriage!"

"Where do you suppose I can find them?" replied the citizen, perspiring more and more.

"That is no concern of mine.... Find them—I must have them. That is all I have to say to you."

"But, all the same, monsieur, who may you be?"

"I am M. Charras, first aide-de-camp to General Pajol, who is commander-in-chief of the Expeditionary Army of the West."

Charras had invented this phrase on the spur of the moment, and, thinking it sufficiently high-sounding, had adopted it to impress the country town's folk.

"All I can do," he said, "is to give you the names of carriage proprietors."

"Give them me.... We shall discover the other things, for you do not seem to me to be very much up to matters yourself."

The man gave the addresses of two or three cab proprietors. They left the mansion-house, which was on the left as you enter the town, about three hundred yards before you come to the château, and they returned in the direction of Paris. A magnificent signboard was grilling in the noonday sun: it represented a coach drawn by four horses, with two saddle-horses held by grooms. This set Charras's mouth watering.

"Hullo there! Where is the proprietor?" he shouted.

"Here I am!" said an individual in a somewhat bad-tempered tone.

"I want a carriage with a couple of horses immediately."

"What for?"

"For the persons whom I shall put inside it."

"Who are they?"

"I don't know yet."

"I haven't any carriages."

"What! no carriages?"

"No."

"What about those in the yard?"

"They are engaged."

"Ah! very well."

Charras looked about him: there were over a hundred people already gathered round, and amongst these spectators were a dozen or so soldiers of the National Guard together with a sergeant.

"Sergeant," said Charras, "do me the kindness to lay hold of that gentleman."

Now a Frenchman is by nature prone to laying hands on people, especially if he wears the uniform of the National Guard. Sergeant Mercier, who refused to seize Manuel, was an exception to this rule and that was why such honours were paid him. The sergeant moved towards the carriage proprietor and seized him by the collar.

"Good!" said Charras; "presently we will see what is to be done with him."

"Really, monsieur," said the proprietor, "who are you?"

"I am M. Charras, first aide-de-camp to General Pajol, who is commander-in-chief of the Expeditionary Army of the West." "Why did you not say so before, monsieur? That quite alters matters."

"Shall I liberate him?" asked the sergeant.

"Not until he has given me a carriage and two horses.... Bernadou, go and choose a couple of good horses and a good carriage."

"All right!"

Bernadou, the sergeant and the proprietor disappeared beneath the large gateway and were lost to sight in the dim distance of the stableyard and the darkness of the stables themselves.

"And now," said Charras, "for two volunteers!"

"What for?" asked a score of voices.

"To go and examine the position of the royal army and to return and give us full particulars."

"Where?"

"Wherever we ... the staff ... and General Pajol may be; there will be no difficulty in discovering that."

"We will go," said two men.

Charras looked at them.

"I do not know who you are," he said; "who will be responsible for your good faith?"

"I," said a gentleman, who was equally unknown to him.

"Very good," continued Charras; "but you must know, messieurs, that you are patriots for us, but spies in regard to the royal army."

"Well?"

"And suppose you are caught...?"

"They will shoot us.... And then...?"

"Good! if you had begun by telling me that I should not have asked for a surety."

The carriage and horses were now brought out. Charras did not leave until he had seen the carriage and the two men safely started upon the road to Rambouillet. The head of the column now came in sight on the Paris road. In a few seconds Charras was beside Pajol.

"It is done, General," he said.

"What?"

"I have found spies."

"Where are they?"

"Gone."

"Really, my dear lad, you are worth your weight in gold!... Now you must go to the village of Cognières; we shall probably halt there."

"Where is it?"

"Here ... see...!"

The general showed the position of the village on the map, four leagues from Rambouillet.

"Good! What am I to do at Cognières?"

"You must tell the mayor I shall want ten thousand feeds of hay by this evening."

"Ten thousand feeds of hay? He will never be able to get so much!"

"What do you think we are to do, then? We have two or three thousand fiacres, twelve or fifteen hundred cabriolets, and tilburys and waggons and the devil knows what beside!"

"All right! don't despair: if we can't get hay, we will get something else...."

"What?" the general interrupted impatiently.

"Why, we will take the standing crops of oats!"

"Excellent!" exclaimed Pajol; "upon my word, you understand the art of war! What is your name?"

"Charras."

"I shall not forget it, be sure! Go! I shall feel as confident of my ten thousand feeds as though I had them here already."

"Oh! you may rely on them."

And again Charras set off. Meanwhile, we had arrived and were dispersing ourselves over Versailles. I, for my part, ran to the barracks of the Guards; I had an intimate friend there, in Grammont's company, a man of irreproachable bravery and, what I appreciated still more, he was marvellously clever. He was called d'Arpentigny. Young though he was, he had been a soldier under the Empire, and he wrote one of the most amazing books imaginable upon his captivity in Russia.

There was not a single Guard at the palace; everyone had followed the king to Rambouillet; they accompanied him as far as Cherbourg, as is known.

After a halt of half an hour, the order was given to resume our march. Just at starting, General Pajol learnt that there were two regiments stationed in Versailles. Would it be wise of him to leave them behind? Three parlementaires were sent and the two regiments gave themselves up without resistance; their arms were distributed among the men of the expedition and my seventeen soldiers got hold of three rifles. On arrival at Saint-Cyr, Degousée proposed seizing the artillery belonging to the École; he asked for volunteers and we offered ourselves, two hundred of us setting out to seize eight pieces of cannon. We harnessed ourselves to them to drag them out as far as the road, and messengers, sent out in all directions, brought back horses and traces.

The Expeditionary Army of the West now had artillery, but it lacked cartridges and bullets. At this moment, we were joined by Georges La Fayette and, as the command of the artillery was vacant, Pajol gave it to him. I never heard whether they succeeded in obtaining bullets and cartridges. When the Expeditionary Army reached the top of the hill of Saint-Cyr, they began to find the high road strewn with sabres, rifles, cartridge boxes and soldiers' caps. So demoralised was the retreat that the men had actually flung away their arms all along the route. Five more of my men thus found arms for themselves, thanks to these spars of the royal wreckage. We reached Cognières at about seven in the evening, harassed with fatigue and dying with hunger. We had, indeed, managed to pick up some scraps of bread and a few glasses of wine, at Versailles; but, as my scene-shifter said, there was only enough to stop a hollow tooth with. By the time we reached Cognières, there were a terrible number of hollow teeth: the horses had found their ten thousand rations of hay and oats, but the men had found nothing at all to eat. Yet Jacqueminot had scrupulously fulfilled his mission: they had promised him that, as soon as the new prefect arrived (and he was expected any moment), the bread should be hurried up. Every man among us set to work like the lion of Scripture, seeking whom he might devour. I had pitched our camp round a great stack of straw that stood on the right of the road and our flag was planted on the top of the stack by one of the scene-shifters, to serve as a guide-post. I had been singularly unlucky in my search, until, happily, I spied out the curé's house. I went inside and laid my wants and those of my troop before the worthy man. He gave me a fine loaf of bread, which must have weighed three or four pounds, and, as he had no bottles in the house, he filled with wine a bottle intended to hold milk. Whilst I was on my foraging expedition, two things were being attended to elsewhere: thirty of the peasants of Cognières, armed with swords and rifles picked up on the road, were placed as an advance-post, a quarter of a league from the village; and, with the three or four thousand fiacres, fifteen to eighteen hundred cabriolets, tilburys and waggons, etc., they built up a big line of barricades across the road stretching across the plain to left and right, covering the whole of the front of the camp and bending back on two sides upon the flanks. On my way, I had been buttonholed by a gentleman in black coat and trousers with a white waistcoat—the whole forming a pearl-grey picture. He had met the procession, was carried away by the whirlpool, had climbed up the back of a fiacre and been thus transported. He had no weapons of any sort, not even a penknife. I could see he was a very green hand at this sort of business. He had not had a bite to eat since the previous day and was clamouring for some sort of food. By trade, he was a broker and his name was Detours. I pointed our flag out to him and encouraged him to continue his hitherto unfruitful hunt a little longer, and then to join us at our stack, whether his hands were full or empty.

After a quarter of an hour's time, I saw him coming along with a piece of bread and half a leg of mutton. He had met Charras, who had taken pity on him and had put General Pajol's canteen at his disposal. He apologised for not bringing more. My men had, however, gone abroad among the neighbouring farms and had annexed a few fowls and eggs. We put all the provender together and supped as well as possible. But only we four or five hundred, perhaps, who had arrived first, got supper: the groans of hunger of those who came after us were audible all around. When the repast was done, I dug out a sort of vault under the stack, into which Delanoue and I got with sybaritic appreciation. The rest of our men strewed straw on the ground and camped in the open air. As for M. Detours, I do not know whether he lives in Paris or in the provinces, whether he be dead or alive, Bonapartist or Republican, for I have never seen him again. It is by a miracle that I happen to have remembered his name.

CHAPTER IV

Boyer the Cruel—The ten thousand rations of bread—
General Exelmans and Charras—The concierge at the
prefecture of Versailles—M. Aubernon—Colonel Poque—
Interview of Charles X. with MM. de Schonen, Odilon
Barrot and Marshal Maison—The Royal Family leave
Rambouillet—Panic—The crown jewels—Return to Paris

Whilst Delanoue and I slept the sleep of the just; whilst the men in the second
line had not half appeased their appetites and were taking in their belts; whilst
the men of the third line, who hadn't eaten anything at all, were roaring like
a herd of lions in the desert; whilst the drivers were snoring inside their
carriages, and the horses were eating their hay and oats; whilst the camp-fires
were going out and throwing their uncertain light over an area of three
leagues of trampled-down harvest-fields, over sleeping men and wandering
phantoms, let us describe what was going on at headquarters.

The advance-guards had hardly established themselves on the road between
Cognières and Rambouillet before they brought to the post-hostelry, on the
left of the road, a general who had forcibly tried to break through the line of
sentinels. He still wore the white cockade: it was old General Boyer, whom
we all knew, he who afterwards had a command in Africa, and who won for
himself out there, whether justly or not, the nickname of Boyer the Cruel.
General Pajol had not yet arrived. Inside the inn parlour were seated, eating,
at a round table, M. de Schonen, M. Odilon Barrot and M. le Maréchal
Maison; they were on their road to Rambouillet for the second time. Charras
was in command, in the absence of General Pajol. They brought General
Boyer to him, who frankly gave his name and admitted that he had come to
offer his sword in the service of Charles X. This was, indeed, an embarrassing
prisoner for Charras to deal with. The young aide-de-camp went into the
room where the three commissioners were dining and, addressing Marshal
Maison, he said—

"Monsieur le Maréchal, they have just arrested General Boyer."

"Well," asked the marshal, "what do you want me to do in the matter?"

"Will you make him give his parole? I will set him free."

"No, good gracious! no," exclaimed the marshal. "Keep an eye on him, and,
when Pajol comes, he can do what he likes with him."

They brought General Boyer into a room adjoining the one in which the
commissioners were dining.

Charras had not eaten anything since the morning he had breakfasted with General Pajol, and the commissioners could easily detect that their dinner was attracting his attention. They therefore offered him a share, which he accepted. Marshal Maison never drank any wine but champagne; he poured out three or four glasses successively (they drank out of a sort of tumbler) for General Pajol's aide-de-camp, who, upon an empty stomach, with nerves excited by his campaign to la Fère and forehead burning from six days' consecutive sun, found himself overcome by quite a fresh kind of excitement. So, accordingly, when General Pajol rejoined them, finding that the bread had not yet arrived, and asking for a volunteer to go to Versailles, Charras, who, reckoning for ins and outs, had already done some twenty leagues during the day,—Charras, I say, seeing that nobody offered, himself volunteered.

"But," said Pajol, "are you made of iron?"

"Iron or no," said Charras, "you can see very well that if I do not go, no one else means to go."

"Off with you, then!... But, of course, if you meet the bread on the road, you will return back with it."

"You bet!"

Charras ran to the stables, saddled his horse and set off at a quick trot. When he had got as far as Trappes he was stopped by an outpost of the rearguard, who blocked the road.

"*Qui vive?*" cried the sentinel.

"Friend."

"That isn't enough!"

"Why isn't it enough?"

"It isn't! Who are you?"

"Charras, first aide-de-camp to General Pajol, commander-in-chief of the Expeditionary Army of the West."

"Advance one and give the countersign."

Things were all conducted in proper military order, as will be seen.

"Who is in command here?" asked Charras.

"General Exelmans."

"I congratulate him: take me to him."

They gratified his wish, which seemed quite reasonable. The general was asleep under a plum tree, wrapped in his cloak, to the left of the roadside. His son was asleep near him. Charras laid bare the object of his coming.

"Do you know," Exelmans replied, "that we too are all famishing of hunger?"

"General, it is through no fault of General Pajol's; he sent Colonel Jacqueminot to Versailles to order ten thousand rations of bread at eleven o'clock this morning."

"To whom?"

"To the prefect."

"And hasn't the brute sent it?"

"You can see for yourself he has not, since I am on my way to look for it."

"You are quite sure it was ordered?"

"Colonel Jacqueminot started in my presence."

"In that case, monsieur, I, General Exelmans, command you to have the prefect shot."

Charras drew a note-book and pencil from his pocket.

"One word in writing, General, and it shall be accomplished within an hour."

"But, monsieur...."

"In pencil will be all I want."

"But, monsieur...."

"Come," said Charras, "I see the Prefect of Versailles won't be shot to-night."

"But, monsieur, think what it is you are asking me to do!"

"I am only asking you to let me pass through your lines, General."

"Allow this gentleman to pass through," said General Exelmans.

He lay down to sleep again under his plum tree, and Charras continued his journey. He reached the barrier of Versailles, made himself known, took four National Guards with him and made his way to the Prefecture. It was one o'clock in the morning and everyone was asleep. He had to knock a quarter of an hour before extracting the least sign of life from the house. Charras and the Guards went at it tooth and nail, some knocking with the butt-end of their pistols and others with that of their rifles. At last, a voice called out from the courtyard—

"What do you want?"

"I want a word with the prefect."

"What! with the prefect?"

"Yes."

"At this time of night?"

"Certainly."

"He is asleep."

Well, I will wake him up, then. Come, come, open the door, and quickly too, or I shall break it in!"

"You would break open the prefect's door!" exclaimed the stupefied concierge.

"Yes," said Charras. "By Jove! what a gift of the gab the fellow has!"

The concierge opened to them: he was only half awake, half brushed up and half dressed.

"Come now, take me to the prefect."

"But I tell you he is asleep."

"And I tell you to proceed to his room, you rogue!"

He gave the concierge a kick that made him climb the stairs in double quick time and, opening the prefect's room, the concierge placed his tallow candle on the night-table, revealing to Charras a man who was rubbing his eyes; then the concierge went out, saying—

"There is M. le Préfet, settle what you like with him."

The prefect raised himself on his elbow.

"What!" he said,—"what do they want with me?"

"I want to inform you, Monsieur le Préfet," said Charras, "that, whilst you are sleeping tranquilly, there are ten thousand men round Rambouillet who are mad with hunger through your fault."

"How through my fault, pray?"

"No doubt of it.... Did you not receive an order to send off ten thousand rations of bread to Cognières?"

"Well, monsieur?"

"Well, monsieur, those ten thousand rations are still in Versailles, that is all I can say."

"Heavens! What do you want me to do?"

"Want you to do? Oh! that is plain enough.... I want you to get up and come with me to the military bakehouse to have the bread loaded in carriages; I want you to give the order for them to start on their journey at once."

"But, monsieur, you speak in such a tone...."

"I speak as I ought."

"Do you know who I am?"

"What does it matter to me who you are?"

"Monsieur, I am M. Aubernon, Prefect of Seine-et-Oise."

"And I, monsieur, am M. Charras, first aide-de-camp to General Pajol, commander-in-chief of the Expeditionary Army of the West, and I have orders to shoot you if you do not instantly send off the bread."

"To shoot *me?*" cried the prefect, leaping up in his bed.

"Neither more nor less than that.... Will you run the risk?"

"Monsieur, I will get up and go with you to the bakehouse."

"So, well and good!"

The prefect rose and went with Charras to the bakehouse, where the carts were loaded with the bread.

"I will leave you here, monsieur," said Charras; "for you know it is to your best interest to send the carriages off quickly."

And back the indefatigable messenger went, along the road to Cognières.

Meanwhile, the three commissioners had reached Rambouillet, where they arrived about nine o'clock at night. Everything was in the greatest confusion. An event, which was not wanting in a certain degree of solemnity, had clouded people's spirits with trouble. That morning, the identical Colonel Poque by whom La Fayette had sent word to Étienne Arago to discontinue wearing his cockade had arrived with an early troop of insurgents. He may, perhaps, have had some special commission for General Vincent, under whom he had served in 1814. However this may be, when he reached the outposts, he left his little troop behind him and approached within earshot, handkerchief in hand. He was accompanied by a cuirassier, who had passed with the people and who followed Colonel Poque as his orderly. General

Vincent was with the Royalist outposts and shouted to the colonel to stop. The colonel stopped, but, waving his handkerchief, he announced that he did not mean to withdraw until he had spoken to the soldiers. General Vincent declared, on his part, that if Poque did not retire he would fire upon him. Poque folded his arms and waited. The general challenged him three times to withdraw and, seeing he remained immovable at the third time, gave the order to fire upon him. All in the front rank obeyed. The cuirassier's horse was struck down under him by three bullets. Colonel Poque had his ankle broken by another bullet and lay down on his horse's back in agony, but still he did not budge. They went to him, took him off and carried him into the out-buildings of the château. This example showed the soldiers the temper of the men with whom they had to deal.

Charles X. was in despair over the incident: he inquired who Colonel Poque was and sent word by Madame de Gontaut to ask if there was anything he wanted.

Poque, whose mother was in the Pyrenees, desired that she should be told of the accident but not how serious the wound was. Charles X. sent his own doctor to the colonel and the doctor saw that there was nothing for it but to cut off his leg! Madame de Gontaut herself wrote to the mother of the injured man.

At five o'clock they learnt of the approach of the Parisian army; at seven they announced its arrival. Materially, so to speak, this army was not at all terrible; but, morally, it meant the spirit of Revolution advancing against Royalty.

In the midst of these troubles and various counsels and differing decisions they debated what should be done. Some wanted to hold out to the last, proposing a retreat on the Loire, a second Vendée and a Chouans war. Others took a more desponding view of the fortunes of the Monarchy and advised a prompt flight. The dauphin, who had tried to snatch Marshal Marmont's sword from him, had cut his fingers and was sulking like a child. The marshal considered he had been insulted and shut himself up in his room, without a word. At eight o'clock, Rambouillet was already half deserted: the courtiers (those who had dined that very day at the king's table) had disappeared, some of them in such haste that, they had not even stopped to pick up their hats. The soldiers alone remained at their posts although they were moody, sullen and depressed.

It was through this funereal atmosphere, then, that MM. de Schonen, Odilon Barrot and Marshal Maison had to pass to reach Charles X. The old king received them with frowning face and a curtness of manner most unusual to him.

"What more do you want of me, messieurs?" he asked.

"Sire, we have come on behalf of the lieutenant-general."

"Well, but I have come to an agreement with him and everything is settled between us."

The commissioners kept silence.

"Did he not receive the letter I sent him by M. de Latour-Foissac, which contained my abdication and that of the dauphin?"

"Yes, sire; but has he replied to it?"

"No, true, he has not. But what need had he to reply, as he answered my two earlier letters, in each of which he assured me of his devotion?"

The commissioners again remained silent.

"Come, gentlemen, speak," said Charles X.

"Sire, we have come from the Lieutenant-General of the Kingdom, to warn your Majesty that the people of Paris are marching upon Rambouillet."

"But my grandson?... Henri V.?" exclaimed Charles X.

For the third time, the commissioners made no reply.

"His rights cannot be challenged, surely," Charles X. resumed with vehemence; "his rights are reserved by my act of abdication; I have fifteen thousand men round me ready to die to preserve his rights!... Answer me, gentlemen! By all that France holds dear, I adjure you to answer me!"

Marshal Maison made a backward movement, in distress at the sight of the overwhelming grief that revealed itself on the old man's countenance.

"Sire," said Odilon Barrot, "you must not found the throne of your grandson on bloodshed."

"And," added Marshal Maison, "may the king ponder on the fact of sixty thousand men marching towards Rambouillet!"

The king stopped short in front of Marshal Maison and, after a moment's silence, he said—

"Two words aside with you, Monsieur le Maréchal."

The other commissioners drew back.

"I am at the king's commands," said the marshal.

The king signed to the marshal to come to him, and the marshal obeyed.

"Upon your word of honour, monsieur," the king said, looking the marshal straight in the face, "does the Parisian army really number as many as sixty thousand men, as you have assured me?"

The marshal no doubt thought it would be a pious fraud to save the country from civil war. And, perhaps, he may at the same time have believed he was telling the truth: the plain, the road, the whole country between Versailles and Rambouillet was covered with men.

"On my word of honour, it is so, sire!" he said.

"That is all," said Charles X.; "you may withdraw.... I shall take the advice of the dauphin and of the Duc de Raguse."

The commissioners went away; but the dauphin declined to offer advice.

"Sire," the Duc de Raguse replied, "I offer my king a final proof of fidelity by counselling him to retreat."

"Good, Monsieur le Maréchal," said Charles X. "Let everything be ready for our departure to-morrow at seven in the morning."

Alas! thus it was that, compelled, driven into a corner by circumstances, this last of our knightly kings yielded up his sword, not, however, like King John or François I., who did not consider that it could be surrendered except on the field of battle.

But the royal cause now suffered a more disastrous defeat than those at Poitiers or Pavia.

Whilst all these grave concerns were being debated between the powerful or, rather, between the weak ones of the earth (for were not these kings who had to go away, each in his turn, and die in exile at Goritz or at Claremont among the weakest of men?), I, who had had nearly as much difficulty to conquer my straw stack as Louis-Philippe had to conquer his throne, certainly slept better under my straw roof than the king under his velvet canopy. Towards four or five o'clock in the morning, I was awakened by a well-sustained fusillade; the bullets whizzed past one another and the fiacres which were meant to serve us as barricades against the attack of the Swiss and Royal Guards, ran away in all directions across the plain as fast as their horses could gallop. It proved a false alarm! Good Heavens! what would have happened had the alarm been real? This was what had taken place. Some men had let off their guns as they ran away from Rambouillet, and the camp thought the fight had begun: it rose half asleep and fired haphazard; the first instinct of any man who has a gun in his hands is to use it, and hence the firing and cross-firing which awaked me. Finally, it was all explained and cleared up, and nothing worse resulted than one man killed and two or three wounded; the army thundered out a tremendous *Marseillaise* and went on its way back to Paris. But Delanoue and I made the journey on foot: our fiacre had been one of the first among the deserters and it was impossible for us to lay hands on it. I remember we returned as far as Versailles across the fields with my dear good friends Alfred and Tony Johannot, who both died before their time, brothers in death as well as in life! At Versailles, we took a carriage back to Paris.

But we must relate what became of the general and staff of the *Expeditionary Army of the West*. Pajol mounted his horse at the first sound of firing and rode through the midst, trying vainly to make his voice heard above the hubbub. Bullets were raining round him, but he did not trouble himself about them any more than he would have done had they been hailstones. I once recalled this incident to him and complimented him upon his courage and *sang-froid*.

"Bah!" he said, "it would have been a fine thing indeed if an old soldier who had been through all the upheavals of the Empire had taken any notice of a little wall-peppering like that!"

The storm calmed down round him as it did round us, but everyone was not as disposed to retreat as we were: one portion of the Expeditionary Army did not see the fun of having come to Cognières for nothing, and decided to push on to Rambouillet. Pajol looked after these fanatics with a certain feeling of terror and sent Charras and Degousée at their head; but those two leaders soon saw the hopelessness of holding this human flood in bounds and allowed themselves to be borne along with it. They advanced as far as the courtyard of the château de Rambouillet, where the mayor of the town pointed out below his breath, in secrecy, an ammunition waggon, the keys of which he had handed to Marshal Maison. This waggon contained the crown jewels, valued at eighty millions.

"Good!" said Charras: "they must be confided to the care of the people; it is the only way to prevent them coming to harm."

They concocted a little tricoloured flag upon which they inscribed in black letters "*The Crown Jewels*": this flag they planted on the waggon and there the matter ended. Then they proclaimed that any who wished to return in company of, and to guard, the crown jewels could travel in the king's coaches. This device of Degousée's was to prevent them setting fire to these carriages. But part of the volunteers preferred to give themselves the pleasure of shooting, and went off into the royal park in pursuit of deer, does and hinds. Others established themselves in the château, made vast orgies of the scraps found about the kitchens of the ex-king and drank the best wines in the cellars. At last, the most reasonable or, perhaps, the vainest among them, climbed into the royal carriages and drove them back to Paris, with the waggon containing the crown jewels in the middle, treated with as much respect as the Israelites showed to the sacred Ark. The comparison is all the more complete as any imprudent man who had dared to lay a finger tip on this modern ark would, assuredly, have been killed and by a very different method of death from that of which the sacrilegious person died who touched the ancient Ark. The whole procession was extraordinary by the contrasts it afforded between lackeys in grand liveries, magnificent harness, and gilded coaches and men in rags riding in carriages. When it had passed at a solemn slow pace along the quai de Passy, the quai de Billy, the quai de la Conférence and the quai des Tuileries, it crossed the Carrousel and stopped in the courtyard of the Palais-Royal. I need hardly say that every one of these unlucky men who accompanied, escorted and mounted guard over eighty millions' worth of jewels were dying of hunger, not having had anything that day but one portion of bread which had been sent the night before by the Prefect of Seine-et-Oise. And as these bread carts had been pillaged, some had only had a half ration and others, again, only a quarter; some, none at all. The lieutenant-general came down and thanked them, smiled upon them and went up again.

"By Jove!" Charras exclaimed to Charles Ledru, "he might have invited us to dinner with him. I am simply starving!"

"Well," said Ledru, "let us go and dine at Véfour's."

"You are most beguiling! But I haven't a sou.... Have you any money at all?"

"I have fifteen francs."

"Oh! then *Vive la Charte!*"

They went along joyfully together to dine at Véfour's with their arms round one another.

General Pajol, the commander-in-chief of the Expeditionary Army of the West, returned merrily to Paris in a coach which he had picked up at Cognières. Before his departure, the cash-box of the Expeditionary Army had been opened and M. Armand Cassan, the improvised cashier, had paid out to the uttermost farthing for corn that had been cut down, fowls plucked, eggs taken from nests, fruit gathered and wine drunk.

A hundred to one, the peasantry round Cognières did not make a bad thing out of the expedition to Rambouillet.

CHAPTER V

Harel's idea—It is suggested I should compose *La Parisienne*—Auguste Barbier—My state of morals after the Three Days—I turn solicitor—Breakfast with General La Fayette—My interview with him—An indiscreet question—The Marquis de Favras—A letter from Monsieur—My commission

I must confess that on this occasion I returned home dead beat, and if the most fascinating expedition imaginable had been suggested to me it would not have dragged me from my bed next day. So I was in bed when Harel called upon me. The idea he brought me for a new play, which he thought would be all the rage in Paris, was one on *Napoléon*. Let us render justice where it is due. Harel was the first of any of the theatrical directors who conceived the idea of making something out of the great man who had made us all pay dear—Harel or, rather, Mademoiselle Georges. For, indeed, Mademoiselle Georges owed him much! Unfortunately, although the notion struck me as a splendid business speculation, it did not take my fancy from the point of view of art. The injuries Bonaparte had done my family inclined me to be unjust towards Napoleon; moreover, I did not think it possible to write such a drama without rousing evil passions. I therefore refused to undertake the task. Harel burst out laughing.

"You will think better of it," he said.

And he left me, as Louis-Philippe had left the Republicans, humming—

"Il ne faut pas dire: 'Fontaine....'"

I must also say it struck me as curious, at such a time, that anyone could dream of taking pen in hand and writing on paper to make a book, or compose a drama.

Zimmermann also approached me to write a cantata to be set to music.

"My friend," I said to him, "ask a man to do that for you who has not been fighting, who has not seen anything of recent events, a poet who has a property in the country, and who, perchance, has remained on his property during the Three Days and he will do it for you to perfection! But I, who have seen and taken an active part, could not do anything good: it would fall below the realities I have witnessed."

He hunted up Casimir Delavigne, who wrote *La Parisienne*.

But, suddenly, in the face of *La Parisienne*, and as if to emphasise the hollowness of this imperial poetry, arose *La Curée*, a torch brandished by an unknown poet. This wonderful masterpiece, this iambic poem, burning with the fever of battle and hot sunshine, where Liberty went by with firm step, walking with great strides, with fiery glance and naked breast, was signed Auguste Barbier. We all hailed it with delight. Here was another great poet in our midst; a reinforcement that came to us, as it were, through a trap-door in the midst of the flames, like one of the spirits that take part in the transformation scene of a pantomime. But, whilst the verses of Barbier and even of Hugo roused my enthusiasm, they did not spur me to emulation: I felt so completely indifferent to both prose and poetry, that I realised I must let all this political turmoil have time to subside in me. I should have liked to have rendered France some service: I could not feel that the crisis was past, I felt there was still something to do, in some corner of our great kingdom, and that a fierce storm could not possibly have calmed down suddenly. Finally, I felt disgusted, I might say almost ashamed, of the muddle Paris had made of things. I tried for two or three days to throw myself into something outside my usual life. Apart from my past or my future, I might have obtained another post at the Palais-Royal, and asked for some mission or other, to be sent to Prussia or Russia or Spain; but I would not. I had taken an oath not to re-enter the palace, at least of my own accord. So I turned my thoughts towards la Vendée. There might, perhaps, be work to do there.

Charles X. had been seized with momentary hesitation at Saint-Cloud; M. de Vitrolles had talked to him of la Vendée, and he was within an ace of embarking in the venture. At Trianon, M. de Guernon-Ranville was of opinion that there was only one course left to the king, that of retreating to Tours and convoking both Chambers and all the generals and high public functionaries and great dignitaries of the kingdom. Charles had, doubtless, brushed the suggestion aside; no doubt, he was making for Cherbourg and going to embark for England crushed and dazed; but if the ghosts of the victims of Quiberon rose up and forbade him to go to la Vendée, that province was not averse to receiving other members of his family.

I therefore considered that it would be prudent and politic and humane to influence la Vendée in an opposite direction. Possibly, also, I looked at it in this light because I wanted to travel in The Vendée. So I went and found General La Fayette. I had not seen him since my expedition to Soissons: he knew I had also taken part in that to Rambouillet. He held out his arms when he caught sight of me.

"Ah!" he said "here you are at last! How is it that having seen you during the struggle, I have not seen you since the victory?"

"General," I said, "I have waited till the most pressing matters were over; but now here I am and in the capacity of a beggar."

"Come, now!" he said, laughing, "is it a prefecture you are wanting, by the way?"

"God forbid, no!... I want to go to la Vendée."

"What for?"

"To see if there is any means of organising a National Guard."

"Do you know the country?"

"No, but I can learn all about it."

"There is something in your idea," said the general. "Come and breakfast with me some morning and we will discuss it."

"Here, General?"

"Certainly."

"Thanks, General.... And, at the same time, may I ask you to tell me something?"

"What?"

"Tell me ... I am going to ask you an odd question, I know, but the fall of the Bourbons deprives it of half its gravity ... tell me how it has come about that, after being mixed up—as I know through Dermoncourt you have been—in all the conspiracies of Béfort, Saumur and la Rochelle, you have never yet been arrested."

La Fayette began to laugh.

"You put me a question that has already been asked more than once, and to which I have replied that I attribute my impunity to good luck; that has been my answer to the question hitherto; but now, thank God! I can give another reason.... Your wish, however, changes the place of our breakfast together, and, instead of coming here, come to my house.... You know my address?"

"Do you not recollect that I was there a week ago?"

"I beg your pardon, so you were."

"When shall the breakfast be, General?"

"Let me see ... to-day is the 5th ... what about to-morrow? or if not then, it must not be until the 10th or the 11th."

"I would prefer to-morrow, General; I am eager to start. So it shall be to-morrow in the rue d'Anjou-Saint-Honoré?"

"Yes."

"At what time?"

"Nine o'clock.... It is early, I know, but I should like to be here at eleven."

"Don't be afraid, General, I will not keep you waiting."

"We shall be by ourselves, for I wish to talk at length and undisturbed with you."

"You are conferring a twofold favour on me, General."

Some deputation or other was announced at this juncture and I withdrew.

Next day, at ten minutes to nine, I presented myself at No. 6 Rue d'Anjou-Saint-Honoré. The general was waiting for me in his study.

"We will have breakfast in here, if you don't mind. We shall then have certain things to hand necessary for our conversation."

I smiled.

He stopped me short, seeing that I was going to renew my question of the previous day.

"Let us first talk of your plan for la Vendée."

"Willingly, General."

"Have you thought more about it?"

"As much as I am capable of reflecting on any subject: I am a man of impulses and not given to reflection."

"Well, then, tell me all about your proposition."

"My proposal is that you send me to la Vendée to see if it be possible to organise a National Guard there to protect that part of the country itself; and to oppose any Royalist plots, should such arise."

"How do you think it possible to preserve a Royalist country from Royalist attempts?"

"General," I said, "there I may be at fault, but first listen to me, for I do not think what I am going to lay before you is entirely devoid of reason; and what appears to you at the first glance impracticable is, nevertheless, I am of opinion, at least possible, though, perhaps, not easy of accomplishment."

"Proceed: I am listening."

"La Vendée of 1830 is a different matter from la Vendée of 1792: the population was formerly exclusively composed of nobles and farmers; it has been increased since then by a new social class, which has inserted itself between the two others, namely, that of the proprietors of national estates. Now, this great work of territorial division, whether it was the real intention, or whether it was the result of measures brought about by the Convention, as you please, has had considerable trouble in becoming established in the country in question, in consequence of the twofold influence of the priests and of the nobility, and especially by reason of that terrible disintegrating factor, civil war, and there were few big landholders who did not leave some remnants of their inheritance in the hands of the Revolution.

"Well, then, General, these remnants have gone to form a secondary class of landholders who are possessed with a spirit of progress and liberty, because progress and liberty alone can secure to them the tranquil possession of their estates, the right to which any reactionary Revolution might call in question. Have you not thought of this yourself at times, General? It is just that secondary class which has sent us since 1815 patriotic deputies; and it rejoiced in the Revolution of 1830, because it looked upon itself as an offspring of the Revolution of 1792, although but a maimed representative. This class it is which, seeing in the Revolution a fresh consecration of the sale of national property, must, consequently, uphold it by every means in its power. Now, I ask you, General, by what better means could it possibly support it than by the organisation of a National Guard, commissioned to watch over the tranquillity of the country, which, composed of a class sufficiently numerous to obtain a majority at elections, will naturally also be sufficiently powerful to impose peace on the country through armed force? You see, General, that my plan is like a solution in Algebra, as substantial as every problem based on figures is, logical in idea and, therefore, possible of execution."

"Ha, ha! my dear poet," said La Fayette; "so we also dabble in politics, do we?"

"General," I replied, "I believe we have reached a crisis of social genesis, to which every man is called upon to contribute, either his physical or mental powers, either materially or intellectually: the poet with his pen, the painter with his brush, the mathematician with his compass, the workman with his rule, the soldier with his gun, the officer with his sword, the peasant with his vote. Very well, then, I bring my contribution as poet: my part is the desire to do good, scornful of danger, hopeful of success. Frankly speaking, I do not esteem myself greater than I really am. Do not value me at my own estimation, but at yours."

"Good!... after breakfast you shall have your letter."

We sat down to table. General La Fayette had a delightful mind, fair and sensible: he erred on the side of goodness, but not from want of ability; he had seen much, and this made up for his lack of book-knowledge. Think what it was for a young man like me, to talk face to face with the history of half a century as it were; with the man who had known Richelieu, shaken hands with Major André, argued with Franklin, been the friend of Washington, the ally of the native tribes of Canada, the brother of Bailly, one of the denouncers of Marat, the man who saved the queen's life, the antagonist of Mirabeau, the prisoner of Olmütz, the representative abroad of French chivalry, the upholder of liberty in France, the person who became a hero by proclaiming the rights of man in the Revolution of 1789, and again made himself a prominent figure by the part he took in the programme of affairs at the Hôtel de Ville in the Revolution of 1830! Alas! I was terribly ignorant of history at that time, and my admiration of the general was so much that of an amateur as hardly to be flattering to him. This world-wide conversation brought us by degrees to dessert and naturally led us back to the topic suggested by my question.

"Now, General," I asked him, "will it be impertinent of me to repeat what I said yesterday? How has it come about that, after having taken part in all the conspiracies of Béfort, Saumur and la Rochelle, you were never put to inconvenience?"

The general got up, went to a secretaire, opened it, pulled from it a locked portfolio and took out a paper which he kept in the palm of his left hand; with this he returned and sat down at the table again.

"Have you ever heard of a man called Thomas de Mahi, Marquis de Favras?" he asked me.

"Was he not the leader of a plot who was executed in 1790 or 1791?"

"Precisely the same.... He was the first and last nobleman who was hanged. He plotted on behalf of Monsieur the king's brother, and tried to carry off poor Louis XVI. from the Tuileries, whether voluntarily or by force, and to transport him to some strongly fortified place or other, in order to get Monsieur appointed regent."

"Monsieur, who afterwards became Louis XVIII.?"

"The same.... Well, on the evening of Christmas Day 1789, M. de Favras was arrested; all the papers he had upon him were seized and, as I was commander-in-chief of the National Guard, they brought them to me. Among those papers was this letter. Read it."

I unfolded the paper which I supposed, after what the general had told me, had been taken from the pocket of a man who had been tried, condemned to death, executed and been dust for forty years past, with a shudder of aversion. I might have spared my feelings, for the paper was only a copy, not the original. This was the contents:—

"1 *November* 1790

"I do not know, monsieur, to what purpose you will employ the time and money I am sending you. The evil gets worse and worse; the Assembly keeps on taking away something or other from the royal power—what will be left if you put it off? I have told you often, and in writing, too, that it is not by means of lampoons, paid tribunes and by bribing a few wretched political parties that you will succeed in getting Bailly and La Fayette out of the way; they have incited the people to insurrection; it wants another insurrection to correct them and to prevent them from relapsing. This plan has, moreover, the advantage of intimidating the new Court and of causing the removal of a king of straw; when he is at Metz or at Péronne, he must abdicate. All these things that we desire are for his welfare; since he loves the nation, he will be delighted to see it properly governed. Send a receipt at the foot of this letter for two hundred thousand francs.

"LOUIS-STANISLAS XAVIER"

"Ah! indeed," I said. "I begin to understand. But why have you only the copy and not the original?"

"Because the original, to the possession of which I attribute my impunity, is in London in the hands of one of my friends, a great collector of autographs, who looks upon it as extremely precious, and who, I am very sure, will not lose it; whilst in France," the general added, smiling, "you understand ... it might be lost."

I understood perfectly. I was burning with the desire to ask leave to take a copy of the duplicate. But I did not dare to.

In due course I will relate how it is I am now able to give the reader a copy.

The general folded up the letter again, put it back in the portfolio and consigned both to his desk. Then he took a pen and paper and wrote:—

"M. Alexandre Dumas is authorised to travel through the departments of la Vendée, the Loire-Inférieure, Morbihan and Maine-et-Loire, as Special Commissioner, to confer with the local authorities of these various departments on the question of the formation of a National Guard.

"We commend M. Alexandre Dumas, an excellent patriot from Paris, to our brother-patriots in the West.—All good wishes.

LA FAYETTE

"6 *August* 1830"

He handed me the paper which constituted my commission.

"Do you authorise me to wear some sort of uniform, General?" I asked after I had read it.

"Of course," he replied; "have something made resembling an aide-de-camp's uniform."

"Very well."

"Only, I must warn you that a uniform is the most unsafe dress you could adopt in travelling through la Vendée; there are many hedges and not a few deep lanes, especially in le Bocage, and a rifle-shot is soon despatched!"

"Bah! General, we will see about that when we are there."

"All right! it is settled, then, and you mean to go?"

"Directly the uniform is made, General."

"And you will correspond with me direct?"

"Of course!"

"Then go, and *bon voyage!* I must now attend the Chamber."

He embraced me, and I took leave.

I have often seen the noble, dignified, excellent old man since. The reader will meet him again at my house at an evening's entertainment I gave, an artists' fancy dress ball, himself in costume, playing écarté with Beauchesne, dressed as Charette, playing his stakes with louis bearing the effigy of Henry V., like the true Vendean he was.

I was astonished to come across the matter of the original letter of Favras, as far as I can remember, word for word, in that excellent and conscientious work by Louis Blanc upon the Revolution. It is from that work I borrow my copy, and I refer my readers to it if they would like more details about the unfortunate Favras, who denied Monsieur to La Fayette whilst the latter had the prince's letter in his pocket and only had to draw it forth to prove his dishonourableness.

CHAPTER VI

Léon Pillet—His uniform—Soissonnais susceptibility—
Harel returns to the charge with his play—I set out for la
Vendée—The quarry—I obtain pardon for a coiner
condemned to the galleys—My stay at Meurs—
Commandant Bourgeois—Disastrous effect of the
tricolours in le Bocage—Fresh proofs that a kindness done
is never lost

As I crossed the place du Carrousel on my way to see Madame Guyet-
Desfontaines, whom I had not yet thanked for her hospitality during the
perilous days of the Revolution, I saw coming towards me a man I
recognised, and I ran to meet my good friend Léon Pillet. Léon Pillet was
one of my best friends, and, although his father, who was proprietor of the
Journal de Paris, had given me rather a dressing down about *Henri III.*, it was
done so deftly and in such good taste that, instead of bearing a grudge against
the old Classicist, I had thanked him. But as I ran towards him I was more
taken up with the brilliant costume Léon Pillet was attired in than anything
else: he had a shako with flowing tricoloured plumes, silver epaulettes, a silver
belt and a royal-blue coat with trousers to match. Here was the very uniform
for a man in search of one for his travels in la Vendée. My first word to Léon
Pillet, after inquiring about his health, was to ask him in what corps he was
an officer, and what was the charming uniform he wore. Léon Pillet was not
an officer in any corps; the uniform was that of an ordinary soldier in the
mounted National Guard, a uniform which, I suspected, he had just invented
and was advertising to the world on his own person. The advertisement
certainly produced its effect on me, for I was much taken with it: I asked for
his tailor's address, and he gave it me. The tailor's name was Chevreuil; he
was one of the best in Paris, and then lived in the place de la Bourse. I rushed
off to Chevreuil immediately, and he measured me, undertaking to provide
me with shako, epaulettes, sword and belt, and to send them all home by the
9th or 10th. I returned by the Pont des Arts. It was the first time I had passed
by the Institut since I had been stationed there; its façade was riddled with
the marks of bullets and shot, like the face of a man pitted with smallpox.
On coming in, I found two young men awaiting me: from the gravity of their
greeting I guessed they had some serious motive in their visit. They gave their
names: one was M. Lenoir-Morand, captain of the military firemen, from
Veilly; the other was M. Gilles, of Soissons.

I do not know what paper it was that related my expedition to Soissons in a
way that insulted the town; I think it was, perhaps, *le Courrier français*; the

feelings of the two Soissonnais had been hurt, and they had come to demand an explanation.

"Messieurs," I said to them, "I can easily explain the matter to you."

They bowed.

"This is what I would suggest to you. In order not to draw public attention to my very inferior personality in the midst of important events that were in process of accomplishment, I only gave a verbal report to General La Fayette upon my expedition to Soissons. I am going to draw up a written report, which is intended to go into the *Moniteur*; if that report contains the exact truth *according to your thinking*, you shall sign it. It shall be inserted in the official journal with the confirmation of your two signatures, and the matter will be at an end. If, on the contrary, the report does not seem to you suitable, and it is only true *according to my version of the facts*, you will refuse to sign it—though I give you notice that that will not prevent my putting it in the *Moniteur*; but the same day it appears I will be at your service, and I will fight a duel with whichever of you two lot may decide.... Will that satisfy you?"

MM. Lenoir-Morand and Gilles accepted my proposition.

I sat down there and then at a sort of desk which was almost useless to me to work at, as I had the habit of working only in bed, and, as fast as my pen would go, I drew up a report containing the account of the events I have herein related. When I had done it, I read it out to the two Soissonnais, who considered it to be so exact that they both signed it without making a single objection. This report, signed first by myself and Bard and Hutin, and then by MM. Lenoir-Morand and Gilles, can be read in the *Moniteur* for 9 August 1830.[1]

This point cleared up, I paid a long visit to my good mother, whom I had neglected somewhat in the midst of all these events; but I first made an appointment for the Soissonnais and Parisians all to dine together at the *Frères provençaux*. My poor mother had learnt that something had been happening in Paris, and was eagerly awaiting my coming to tell me that M. le Duc d'Orléans had a chance of succeeding to the throne and to congratulate me upon the advantages which the new king's accession would bring me. It was my sister, who had just arrived from the provinces to petition me on behalf of her husband, who had told her this. Poor mother! I took good care not to let her know that, far indeed from being able to do anything to further my brother-in-law's administrative career, my own was quite done for in the Palais-Royal quarter.

A messenger came from Harel whilst I was with my mother. That stubborn manager urged me by every means in his power, as did also Mademoiselle Georges, to write a *Napoleon* play. He was expecting me to discuss conditions, which should be of my own fixing, he said. I sent word to Harel that I was starting for la Vendée the next day or day after; that I would reflect upon the subject deeply, and, if I saw the makings of a drama in it, I would write it and send it him. This was not at all what Harel wanted, but he had to be content with the promise, vague as it was. Besides, he had a play by Fontan to put on, called *Jeanne la Folle*. Fontan was liberated from prison, as a matter of course, after the Days of July, without which he would have been shut up at Poissy for ten years, and he was hurrying on his rehearsals.

I paid farewell visits to M. Lethière, and to M. de Leuven and to Oudard. Oudard wanted to retain me forcibly in Paris, or, rather, to despatch me to St. Petersburg with M. Athalin, who was going as Envoy Extraordinary to the Emperor Nicholas, he said. Here was the very opportunity for me to obtain the cross of the *Légion d'honneur* which I had missed at the last promotion, in spite of the letter M. le Duc d'Orléans had written to Sosthènes. I thanked Oudard and begged him to look upon me in future as in no way connected with the royal duke's administration. Oudard persisted strenuously in trying to make me renounce my resolution, and I left him genuinely grieved at my departure, which he knew very well meant a complete rupture. Finally, on 10 August, the day after the proclamation of the July Monarchy, I entered the diligence, very unhappy that I could not make up an equivalent for Paris of the farewell that Voltaire had made for Holland.[2]

Thus I started on the evening of 10 August in the grand uniform of a mounted National Guard. My first stop was at Blois; I wished to visit its bloodstained château, and I climbed the ladder-like streets which lead up to it. I hunted in vain for the equestrian statue of Louis XII. over the gateway, before which Madame de Nemours had stood weeping, craving vengeance for the murder of her two grandsons; I went into the courtyard, and admired that quadrangular enclosure built under four different reigns, each side showing a distinctly different style of architecture: the wing built by Louis XII., beautiful in its severe simplicity; that of François I., with its colonnades overloaded with ornamentation; Henri III.'s staircase, with carved open work; then, as a protest against the Gothic and Renaissance styles—against imagination and art, that is to say—the cold, tasteless building by Mansard, which the concierge kept pointing out to me persistently, amazed that anybody could admire anything but it in that marvellous courtyard! The rapidity with which I examined it, the kind of grimace that expressed itself involuntarily on my face by the unwonted curl of my lower lip, brought a smile of contempt to the honest fellow's lips, which I was not slow in justifying entirely, by refusing to believe his obstinate asseverations that a special spot was where the Duc de Guise was said to have been assassinated.

True, I discovered, beyond reach of any doubt, at the other end of the apartment, which had been a dining hall, a secret staircase, by which the Duc de Guise had left the state room; the corridor which led to the king's private oratory; and everything, even to the very place where the duke must have fallen when Henri III., pale and imploring, lifted the tapestry curtain and asked in a whisper, "Messieurs, is it all over?" for it could only have been at that moment that the king caught sight of the blood flowing across the passage and saw that the soles of his slippers were soaked in it; then he came forward and gave the face of the poor dead body a kick with his heel,—just as the Duc de Guise in his turn had kicked the admiral on St. Bartholomew's Day,—then, drawing backward, as though alarmed at his courage, he said, "Good Lord! how tall he is! He looks taller lying down than upright, dead than alive!"[3]

Meantime, while I was remembering these things, the concierge was tenaciously endeavouring to bring me round to his way of thinking.

"But, monsieur, only you, and a big fair gentleman named M. Vitet, have ever disbelieved what I state," he said.

Then he went on to show me the fireplace where the bodies of the duke and cardinal had been cut in pieces and burnt; the window out of which the ashes of the two bodies had been scattered to the winds; the oubliettes made by Catherine de Médici, eighty feet deep, with their steel blades as sharp as razors, their cramp-irons as pointed as lances, so numerous and so artistically arranged in spirals that a man who fell from above would be a creature in God's image the moment before falling, but, losing a piece of flesh or some member of his body at each impact, would be nothing but a shapeless, hacked-up mass by the time he reached the bottom, upon which quicklime was thrown the next day in order to consume the remains. And the whole of this castle, the royal palace of the Valois, with its memories of assassination and its marvellous art treasures, was now the barracks of the cuirassiers, who reeled about drinking and singing; who, in their transports of love or patriotism, scraped with the point of their long swords some charming bit of carving by Jean Goujon in order to write on the wood thus planed down, "I love Sophie!" or "Long live Louis-Philippe!"[4]

When I left the château I took the mail-coach, and reached Tours that same night. People there could talk of nothing but the arrests of MM. de Peyronnet, of Chantelauze and of Guernon-Ranville; a host of details concerning these arrests were related to me with exultant volubility, which details shall be given in their due time and place. I continued my journey by steamer, and when I arrived at Ponts-de-Cé I landed in order to go to Angers. Here I had a friend named Victor Pavie, an excellent young fellow, warm-hearted and true. What has become of him now? I don't in the least know; I have hardly ever seen him since then. When I arrived at his house I learnt that he was at a sitting of the Assizes. They were trying a poor devil of a Vendean, from Beauprèau, who had silvered Republican sous with quicksilver, and tried to pass them off for thirty-sous pieces. The poor wretch's object in coining false money was to buy food for his starving children. A great interest was felt in the prisoner throughout the whole town; but at that date the penalty for false coining was terribly severe: it was not merely a matter of warning that I bank-notes bore an inscription threatening sentence of death on any who tried to forge them. In spite of the simplicity of his confession, and the tears of his wife and children, and the pleading of his counsel, the accused was sentenced to between twenty and thirty years' penal servitude. I was present when the sentence was passed, and, like everyone else, I received my share of the blow which smote the poor wretch. While I listened to that sentence, which, although severe, was not illegal, the idea came to me that Providence had sent me there on purpose to save the man. I returned to Pavie's house, and, without saying a word to anyone, I wrote two letters: one to Oudard, the other to Appert. I believe I have already mentioned Appert and have said that he was almoner of the private charities of the Duchesse d'Orléans. I laid the case before them and begged them to ask for the pardon of the condemned man: the one of the king, the other of the queen. I laid great stress upon the good effect, politically, an act of clemency towards a Vendean would produce, at a time when there was reason to fear trouble from that quarter of the country. I made known to both of them that I looked upon my petition as so just that I should remain at Angers until I obtained a favourable reply. Whilst waiting, I explored all the town and neighbourhood under Pavie's guidance. Excellent fellow, Pavie! He pointed out to me, with an indignation most characteristic of his national love of art, some workmen, who, by order of the préfet, under the direction of a local architect, were busy converting the grotesque figures on the cathedral into brackets! So what you now see, to your great satisfaction, if you do not appreciate the wonderful grimacing faces which the Middle Ages fixed to its cathedrals, is a Roman entablature upheld by Grecian brackets after the model of those on the Bourse, another modern marvel, a mixture of Greek and Roman styles, with nothing French about it but its stove-pipes. Furthermore, they were scraping the cathedral remorselessly without any respect for the brown colouring that eight centuries had spread over its surface; and this scraping gave it a sickly paleness which they called "rejuvenating it"! Alas! it takes twenty-five years to complete a man: a good Swiss royalist may fire upon him, and then he is killed! It takes six or eight centuries to colour a building, and then an architect with good taste arrives, and scrapes it!... Why does not the Swiss kill the architect? or why doesn't the architect scrape the Swiss? We went down to the promenade, and I walked past the tenth-century ancient castle, which is encircled by a moat and flanked by a dozen massive towers—the labour of a people, the asylum for an army. "Ah!" my poor Pavie said, sighing, "they are going to pull it down.... It spoils the view!"

On that day I received a letter from Oudard telling me the pardon was granted, and that only the formalities to be gone through with the Minister of Justice would retard the liberation of the prisoner; so I hastened to share the letter with the person most directly interested in its contents, and, nothing further detaining me at Angers, I jumped into a passing carriage, so great was my wish to quit a town of Vandal destroyers, and I was driven to Ponts-de-Cé.

To save Angers still further maledictions, let it be mentioned that it was the birthplace of Béclard and of David. Upon the journey we passed through a long village, called, I believe, la Mercerie; they were inaugurating a new mayor. Two worn old pieces of cannon, which exploded by the vent, saluted as we entered. Every house displayed its flag, and we passed under a tricolour canopy. The mayor and all his family were on the balcony, and the youthful mayoress, who, in her affection for his people, had stepped close to the edge of the terrace, looked to be the possessor of a very fine pair of legs; I cannot speak for her face, as the perpendicular position she occupied with regard to me prevented me from catching a sight of it.

The spot that I had picked out for my centre of operations was a small farmhouse belonging to M. Villenave. I have mentioned this farm before; it lay between Clisson and Torfou, and was called la Jarrie. Madame Waldor had been living there the last three or four months with her mother and daughter. My plan was to reach my objective by describing a large circle and touching Chemillé, Chollet and Beaupréau on my way. By this means, when I should finally reach la Jarrie, I should already have gained some idea of the temper of the country, and should know how to go to work upon individuals and also upon the people collectively. I intended to go short stages at a time, to stop just where fancy took me, to leave at the hours that should suit my own convenience and to stay when it pleased me to remain. There was, therefore, no other means of transport to adopt than to buy or hire a horse; for it was out of the question for me, wearing the uniform of the mounted National Guard, to go afoot. This uniform and a second, which was a shooting suit, was all the wardrobe I had thought it convenient to bring away with me. I hired a horse at Meurs. I stopped one day there to pay a visit to the battlefield of Ponts-de-Cé. There, in 1438, the Angevins defeated the English; and in 1620 Maréchal de Créquy defeated the troops of Marie de Médici; finally, in 1793, the Republicans were defeated here by the Vendeans—defeated, though with difficulty, since they were Republicans. That defeat of 26 July 1793 was a great one, a defeat equal to one of those that made Leonidas immortal, and yet nobody knows who was Commander

Bourgeois. When it is my good fortune to come across one of these forgotten names upon my journey, names buried in the dust of the past, I take it up and breathe upon it till it shines out conspicuously before my contemporaries. It is both my right and my duty, the more so as Bourgeois is one of those brave heroes of '93 who are slandered when not forgotten.

After the rout of Vihiers, whilst our army was trying to reorganise itself again at Chinon, Bourgeois, who was in command of the 8th Parisian battalion, the one that was called the Lombard battalion, received orders to leave Ponts-de-Cé and to occupy the rock of Meurs. It was an odious position: to the north, the perpendicular rock, commanding one arm of the Louet, a little river which runs into the Loire; to the west, a small plain of undulating ground; to the south, a ravine, at the bottom of which the Aubance flows; on the other side were the heights of Mozé, of Soulaines and of Derrée. When camped on that unlucky plain, there is no possible way of retreat if one is attacked in front and on the flank. But the command was given, and he had to obey it. Bourgeois and his four hundred men were encamped on the rock of Meurs.

"What a queer name, la roche de Meurs, commandant!" one of the soldiers remarked.

"My good fellow, it is the imperative of the verb *mourir* (to die)," answered Bourgeois.

"What in the world is an imperative?"

"I will show you when the time comes."

The Vendeans debouched from the Brissac road. There were twelve thousand of them, commanded by Bonchamp and supported by d'Autichamp and Scépeaux. The Lombard battalion, as we have said, only numbered four hundred men. The fight lasted five hours. When the redoubts of the camp had been carried and the camp stormed, d'Autichamp shouted, "Stop killing!" but there were priests in the Vendean ranks who cried, "Give no quarter!" Three hundred and ninety-six men perished in the massacre! Bourgeois flung himself into the river with his three remaining men, two of these men were killed in the river by his side and he and his companion were both wounded. But, wounded though he was, Bourgeois made his way along the Angers road and caught up at *l'Image de Morus* the 6th battalion of Paris which was also fleeing. He rallied the fugitives and stopped them. Just at that moment the Jemmapes battalion was marching out of Angers, and Bourgeois found himself at the head of a battalion and a half. He retraced his steps, in his turn attacked the Chouans and forced them to entrench themselves in the château and island. An eye-witness told me that, for more than a league, red serpents could be seen on the foam of the waves of the Loire! Whole squads were being carried by the river to the ocean.[5]

I left Meurs, as I have said, after a day's sojourn there.

On this journey through la Vendée, the same phenomenon occurred to me a second time as that during my Soissons excursion—namely, the farther the distance increased between me and Paris, the nearer did I seem to advance towards the North Pole. My uniform excited enthusiasm in the neighbourhood of Paris and at Blois I still found admirers; at Angers, this was reduced to mere curiosity; but at Meurs and Beaulieu and Beaumont I fell into frigid regions and felt that, as La Fayette had forewarned me, if it went on much longer there would be some danger in passing along within range of hedges and thickets. At Chemillé my uniform nearly caused a riot. As I have mentioned, I had with me a change of dress; it was a new shooting costume. After the three days and the journey to Soissons and the expedition to Rambouillet, the old one was not fit to wear again. Well, this costume was in a kind of long portmanteau, one compartment of which contained my rifle, which was taken to pieces. All I should have to do, then, would be to divest myself of my National Guard uniform, fold it up neatly and pack it into my portmanteau, in the place of my shooting suit, put that on my back and continue my journey, and, evidently, three-fourths of the dangers I might be running would disappear; but it seemed to me that to do such a thing would be an act of cowardice unworthy of one who had taken part in the fighting of July. So I stuck to my uniform and contented myself instead with airing my gun. Next day I ordered my horse for eight in the morning. I ostentatiously loaded my gun with two balls (which was a fresh imprudence), I slung it across my back, and I passed through half the town in the midst of what I felt was a distinctly menacing silence.

I did not mean to sleep at Chollet (it was hardly six leagues from Chemillé to Chollet), but to arrive at two in the afternoon and stop there until the following morning.

At eleven o'clock I had passed Saint-Georges-du-Puy, and Trémentines by noon; finally, about one o'clock, I approached a place which looked dangerous (should there be danger abroad at all), because the road I had to traverse ran between the wood of Saint-Léger and the forest of Breil-Lambert. I was debating in my mind whether it would be better to pass this *malo sitio*, as they say in Spain, at a foot pace or at a gallop, when I thought I heard my name pronounced behind me in a panting voice. Directly I heard my name called I felt no fear of the person who was uttering it. It was scarcely probable, however, that I had heard correctly. But I now heard it repeated a second time and more distinctly than the first. Who on earth could know me in the department of Maine-et-Loire, between Chemillé and Chollet? I turned my horse's head in the direction whence the voice came and soon saw a man running with breathless haste from the corner of the road to Nuaillé, signing to me with his hat that it was he was calling me to stop. There was no longer any doubt that the man wished to catch me up and that he was calling to me; but what could he possibly want? As he came nearer, I could distinguish his costume, which was that of a peasant. I waited, more puzzled than ever. The man ran as fast as his legs would carry him, and, as his voice failed him for want of breath, he put more and more expression into his gestures. At last he joined me, and flinging himself on my boot, began to kiss my knees.

Speech was altogether out of the question; I believe if he had had only fifty yards more to run he would have fallen dead on his arrival, like the Greek of Marathon. Finally, he got his breath again.

"You do not know me," he said, "but I, I know you: you are M. Alexandre Dumas, who saved me from the galleys!"

Whereupon he fell on his knees and thanked me in the name of his wife and children.

I jumped down, took him in my arms and embraced him. After a few moments he calmed down.

"Ah! monsieur," he said, "what recklessness! and what good luck that I was set at liberty in time!"

"What do you mean?"

"Whoever advised you to travel in la Vendée in such a uniform as that?"

"Nobody.... I acted according to my own wishes."

"But it is a miracle you have not been killed before this!"

"Ah, indeed! then are your Angevins as bad as that?"

"It is not that they are wicked, monsieur, but it is believed everywhere that you want to set this country at defiance.... I was set free last night at four, monsieur; I tried to gain information as to where I could find you to thank you, and I was told you had taken the road to Chollet. At Ponts-de-Cé I asked for news of you, and was told you had stopped a day at Meurs: there is no doubt about it, you are easily recognised, and you are called *le monsieur tricolore*. At Meurs I was told you had hired a horse, and that you left there yesterday morning. I only stopped at Beaumont. At break of day I started off again: by ten I reached Chemillé, and you had left the market-town at eight.... I learnt, moreover, that your visit had produced an extremely bad effect there; then I set off running till I was out of breath, and I have run like that since ten this morning.... Just as you were turning the corner at Nuaillé I caught sight of you and recognised you; that was why I called you.... I hoped to catch you up before the forest of Breil-Lambert, and, thank God, I succeeded! But now here you are, my dear monsieur.... In the name of our Lord Jesus Christ, do not expose yourself any longer!"

"To what, my friend?"

"To the danger of assassination."

"Bah!"

"But I tell you they believe you have come to upset the countryside."

"Well, then, they have been badly brought up! And so much the worse for them!"

"Let me precede you or go with you, monsieur; and when they know that you have saved a Bocage man from the galleys, you can go wherever you desire, dressed just as you like. I will answer for it, on the faith of a Chouan, that no harm will come to you ... none whatever.... They will not touch a single hair of your head. Will you leave it to me?"

All things considered, I thought it was the best thing to do.

"Arrange things as you think proper," I said.

"Ah! that's right! Where are you going at this moment?"

"To la Jarrie, between Clisson and Torfou."

"You are not on the right road."

"I know it all right, but came a long way round on purpose."

"Are you going to friends?"

"Yes."

"Well, then, let me take you to your friends.... We can easily reach there the day after to-morrow. Stay a week with them; during that time, I will make such good use of my feet and hands that you can resume your journey.... Do you agree?"

"Upon my word, yes.... I will give myself entirely into your care.... You know the country; you are a native! Now, if any accident happens to me it will be on your shoulders."

"Yes, monsieur, and from this moment I will answer for you to your guardian angel."

Two days later I reached la Jarrie, not only without accident, but, moreover, loaded with all kinds of good wishes received all along my route, freed from all danger, thanks to the story my man related a score of times, who went before me like a herald, telling everybody who would listen to his story, and even those who did not care to listen, the service I had done him. I confess with deep regret, bordering on remorse, that I, who can remember the name of M. Detours well enough, have completely forgotten the name of my Vendean.

---

[1] See first note at end of volume.

[2] See note at end of volume.

[3] I must say, in justice to myself, that recent archæological researches have proved the correctness of my opinion as against that of the concierge of the château de Blois.

[4] Owing to the efforts of King Louis-Philippe the cuirassiers have been moved elsewhere since my visit, and the château has been beautifully restored.

[5] I refer readers for fuller details to that curious work by M. Fr. Grille, *La Vendée en 1793.*

CHAPTER VII

A warning to Parisian sportsmen—Clisson—The château
of M. Lemot—My guide—The Vendean column—The
battle of Torfou—Two omitted names—Piffanges—
Tibulle and the Loire—Gilles de Laval—His edifying
death—Means taken to engrave a remembrance on the
minds of children

The day after my arrival at la Jarrie I dressed in my shooting outfit, and, with
gun on shoulder and game bag on back, I set off for Clisson. Two hours later
I arrived there with my thighs torn by furze, my hands bleeding from briars,
without having killed even a single lark.

Here a word of warning, in passing, to Parisians who should imagine that la
Vendée is still a country abounding in game, and who should make the
journey of a hundred and twenty leagues under that belief: I have shot there
for a month, and have not raised fifteen partridges! On the other hand, vipers
swarm there; one comes across them at every step, and every sportsman
ought to carry a flask of alkali in his pocket.

To return to Clisson, which I was in so great a hurry to see that I left my
excellent hosts to visit it the day after my arrival. Well, Clisson, which people
had praised so highly to me, would have been an extremely pretty town in
Greece or Italy, but in France and in la Vendée it was not: there is something
incompatible between the misty skies of the west and the flat roofs of the
east, between the pretty Italian factories and our dirty French countrysides.
The château de Clisson itself, thanks to the care of M. Lemot, the celebrated
sculptor, is so well preserved that one is tempted to be angry with its owner
for not having allowed a single spider's web to crawl over its walls. It
reminded one of an old man made up on shaving days, with false teeth and
false hair and rouged. M. Lemot spent enormous sums to produce a
picturesque effect, and only made an anomaly; and this anomaly was
illustrated all the more forcibly by the presence of the tricolour flag floating
over the eleventh-century ruin: the mayor would not allow it to be placed on
the clock tower. The park is like every other park in existence—like
Ermenonville or Mortefontaine: a river, rocks, grottoes, statues and temples
to the Muses, to Apollo and to Diana. Instead of all these, imagine on both
sides of the valley cottages grouped where the temples stand, some seeming
to be climbing up the hillside and others descending it, dotted here and there
according to the fancy or convenience of their owners; the river flowing at
the bottom of the ravine, and, on the top of the hill, the castle: an old ruin
rent by cracks, surrounded by stones which time has caused to roll down like

dead leaves round the trunk of an oak tree. Add to this its old memories of Olivier de Clisson and its modern memories of the Chouans and the Blues; the vault which was used as a dungeon by the Barons, and the well that forms a tomb for four hundred Vendeans—and, if you possess a romantic turn of mind, you will have food for centuries of contemplation.

M. Lemot had done all he could to try and organise a National Guard at Clisson; he had already found ten volunteers, who were drilled in secret by the quarter-master and the gendarmerie. This quarter-master was an excellent fellow; though, for all that, he was extremely anxious to arrest me: telling the Liberals that I looked like a Chouan, and the Chouans that I looked like a Liberal; the consequence thereof being that the town would have been very pleased to see me marched off to gaol. I had my choice of a safeguard in my passport, which was perfectly correct, and in the letter from General La Fayette. I decided upon the passport, and I believe I was rightly inspired in my decision. I returned that same night to la Jarrie, although they did not expect me till next day and reproached me terribly for my imprudence; they could not get over their surprise that I had not rested during the journey. It was settled in council that I was to risk no more excursions without my guide, who had asked for a few days to go and visit his children and to spread abroad in the neighbouring villages the story of his adventure, which was to serve as a safeguard for me. He reappeared at the time arranged and put himself at my disposal, making himself answerable for everything. We took the road to Torfou. My man had made himself smart when he was to be condemned to penal servitude; for the type of his face and the style of his dress were those of a town dweller, which had not struck me before; but he adopted the costume of the countryside while acting as my guide. I now for the first time examined him with some attention. He had preserved the primitive type of the peasantry of the second race: from his narrow forehead, his serious face and his hair cut round, he looked like a peasant of the time of Charles le Gros. He scarcely opened his mouth, except it was to point out some topographical point on the right or left hand—

"It was here that the Blues were defeated!"

I don't think he had undertaken too much in promising me his protection, for, although he had been pardoned by King Louis-Philippe, the good man was a Chouan to the finger-tips. Moreover, in his eyes, it was I who had pardoned him and not the king at all.

A quarter of a league from Torfou, in the middle of a space made by four cross-roads, rose a stone column, twenty feet in height, almost after the pattern of that in the place Vendôme. M. de la Bretèche had it erected at his own expense at the time of the Restoration. Four names in bronze letters, enclosed in a crown of the same metal, were inscribed on it, each name facing one of the four roads, of which this pillar forms the meeting-place: the names are those of Charette, d'Elbée, Bonchamp and Lescure. I asked my guide for an explanation.

"Ah!" he said, in his own language, interspersed with old words which seemed to have come back to him as he stepped on the ground immortalised by these old memories, "because it was here that Kléber and his *thirty-five thousand Mayençais* were beaten by the Chouans."[1]

Then he burst out laughing, and, putting both hands close together, imitated the cry of the screech-owl.

I stood on the very spot where the famous battle of Torfou had taken place.

Then memories as befitted the son of a Republican came crowding upon me, and it was now my turn to relate and the peasant's to listen.

"Oh! yes!" I said to myself, looking at the inscription carved on the column, "'19 September 1793.' Yes, that's it."

Then I turned my eyes on the surrounding villages of Torfou, Buffière, Tiffanges and Roussay.

"Yes," I went on, "all that was in flames and formed a ring of fire on the horizon when Kléber arrived with the vanguard of the army of Mayence, and shouted to his three thousand men the command, 'Halt! To battle!' For, besides the noise of the conflagration, another loud sound like the trampling down of leaves and breaking of branches was heard ever coming nearer without anything being seen on the roads which converged to the centre of the forest. By this forest, which the Vendeans knew well, they drew slowly nearer and nearer; sometimes they were obliged to crawl, sometimes to cut a passage through with their swords, yet their line pressed closer and closer together and each minute lessened the distance which separated them from their enemies. Finally, they reached so near the outskirts of the wood that they could see the army, restless but resolute, within gunshot and could each pick out his own man before firing.... Suddenly, musketry-firing soared aloud in a radius of three quarters of a league, died down, then rose again, before anyone could tell either against whom, or how, they could best defend themselves. The Vendeans seized the opportunity this moment of disorder gave and rushed down the roads to charge the Blues. Three thousand men were attacked from four different sides by more than thirty thousand, who knew the geography of the country and were fighting for their hearths and their faith! Each one of the leaders whose name is inscribed on that column made his appearance by the road towards which his name now points. Directly our soldiers could distinguish the enemy, their courage returned. 'Come on, my brave fellows!' Kléber shouted, flinging himself at their head; 'let us give these beggars some lead and steel to digest!' He charged haphazard down one of these four roads, met Lescure's army corps, broke it up like glass and, whilst the latter was trying on foot, gun in hand, to rally the inhabitants of Aubiers, Courlé and Échauboignes, he rushed to his rearguard, which had followed up his action, and which was surrounded by the three corps led by Ellbeé, Bonchamp and Charette. The artillery had just arrived: fifteen pieces in position made holes at the rate of six rounds a minute in the masses, which soon closed up again; three charges of Vendean cavalry hurled themselves one after the other upon the brazen muzzles and disappeared. This lasted two hours, Kléber pushing Lescure before him, who always rallied his men again. Kléber himself, pressed hard by the three other Vendean leaders, valiantly carried on his retreat, until a fifth army of ten thousand men, led by Donniss and la Rochejaquelein, came and threw themselves on his flanks, firing point-blank, killing at every blow, and at last dealt confusion in the Republican ranks. The head of the army, still commanded by Kléber, reached la Sèvre; the heroic general captured the bridge, crossed it and, calling a quarter-master named Schewardin, cried out, 'Stop here and be killed with two hundred men.' 'Yes, general!' was Schewardin's reply. He picked his men, kept his word and saved the army!"

"Oh! yes, that was how it happened," my Chouan answered, "for I was there.... I was not quite fifteen then.... Look, monsieur," he went on, taking off his hat and lifting his hair to show me a scar that furrowed his forehead, "I got that here"—he struck the ground with his foot.—"Here!... It was one of the general's aides-de-camp who struck me, quite a young fellow, almost as young as I was; but, before falling, I had time to thrust my bayonet in his body and to fire at the same moment.... When I came to my senses he was dead ... we had fallen on top of one another ... and all round us, for a radius of a league, lay Blues and Vendeans, so that you did not know where to place your foot for fear of stepping on them. They were buried where they had fallen, and that is why the trees here are so vigorous and the grass so green."

I turned towards the column: nothing on it made mention of Kléber's courage and Schewardin's devotion, nothing but just those four Vendean names. I forgot where I was, for this one-sidedness made the blood rise to my face.

"I do not know what it is prevents me from putting a bullet into the middle of that column, and signing it Schewardin and Kléber!" I said aloud, talking to myself without imparting to my man the reflections that led to this monologue.

I felt my guide put a trembling hand on my shoulder, and I turned round; he was very pale.

"For the Lord's sake, monsieur," he said, "don't do that; I have vowed to bring you through safe and sound, and if you were to commit any folly like that, I could no longer answer for you.... Do you know that those four men are our gods, and every Vendean peasant says his prayers here, as at the stations of the Virgin which you see at the entrance of our villages? Do not do that; or beware of the hedgerows!"

We reached Tiffanges without saying another word.

Tiffanges is an ancient Roman station. During Cæsar's wars with the Gauls, he sent Crassus, his lieutenant, there with the Seventh Legion; from thence Crassus proceeded to Theowald, the Doué of our day, where he pitched his camp. *Crassus adolescens cum legione septimâ, proximus mare Oceanum in Andibus hiemârat.*[2] This region of the Gauls was never wholly subdued by the Romans; the Pict kings always fought for their liberty there. Augustus had hardly ascended the throne before le Bocage uttered a fresh war-cry. Agrippa went there immediately, believed he had subjugated the inhabitants and returned to Rome. Again they rose in revolt. Messala succeeded him, and took Tibullus with him, who in his capacity of poet claims for himself a portion of the honours of the campaign—

> "Non sine me est tibi partus honos: Tarbella Pyrene Testis,
> et Oceani littora Santonici; Testis Arar, Rhodanusque celer,
> magnusque Garumna, Carnuti et flavi, coerula lympha,
> Liger!"

—as much as to say, "You did not win this honour without me. Witness Tarbella the Pyrenean, and the coasts of the Santonic Ocean (Saintonge); remember also the Arar (the Saône) and the rapid Rhône and wide Garonne, and the Loire, the blue waters of the fair Carnute."

Possibly, too, Tibullus followed Messala in the same way that Boileau followed Louis XIV.; as to the Loire, if it was blue in the time of Augustus, it has changed its colour singularly since that day! Tiffanges is, indeed, a place full of memories of Cæsar, Adrian, Clovis and the Visigoths; near the Roman tomb springs the Frankish cradle, as can be clearly traced through the history of twenty long centuries. The château, the ruins of which we visited, seems to be an eleventh-century erection continued during the twelfth, and only finished at the end of the thirteenth century. The famous Gilles de Laval, Marshal of Raiz, who was known in the country under the name of *Barbe-Bleue*, inhabited this castle, and by his way of living gave rise to a multitude of popular traditions that are still quite fresh in the neighbouring villages. In short, as there is justice in heaven, and a man who pillaged twenty churches, ravished fifty maidens and gained riches must always end badly, to acquit Providence you ought to know that this Gilles de Laval was burnt in the meadow of Bièce, first being beheaded at the solicitation of his family, which had great influence with the sire de l'Hospital, who granted him this favour; but, previously, the condemned man made a speech, at the conclusion of which, says history, nothing could be heard but the sobbing of women. History also tells (but as it is history, you need not pin faith to it) that the fathers and mothers of high rank who heard Gilles de Laval's last words fasted three days to win Divine forgiveness for him, which, doubtless, he obtained, since his confessor was one of the cleverest of the time. That done, these same parents inflicted a whipping on their children, on the place of execution, to fix in their memories the recollection of the punishment that overtook the great criminal! History omits to tell us if the children of the sixteenth century were as fond of executions as those of the nineteenth.

---

[1] The army corp which had evacuated Mayence and which was ordered to la Vendée was really only composed of ten thousand four hundred men.

[2] Cæsar's *Commentaries*, I. iii. § 7.

CHAPTER VIII

Le Bocage—Its deep lanes and hedges—The Chouan
tactics—Vendean horses and riders—Vendean politics—
The Marquis de la Bretèche and his farmers—The means I
suggested to prevent a fresh Chouannerie—The tottering
stone—I leave la Jarrie—Adieux to my guide

I have of course put on one side as well as I could, until now, particulars
relating to statistics and the topography of the country; but one must come
to it eventually. On the outskirts of Tiffanges, la Vendée is first seen with its
undulating country, which proved so disastrous to us in the Chouan War.

Let me be permitted to reproduce here a part of the report which I submitted
to General La Fayette on my return to Paris, which report, as will be seen
later, was also submitted to the inspection of King Louis-Philippe:—

"... In the first place, the word *Vendée*, politically speaking,
comprises a much larger area of ground than it does
topographically. And this was because the name of a single
department christened a war which was really spread over
four departments. So, under the collective name of Vendée
the departments of Maine-et-Loire, Morbihan, Deux-Sèvres
and la Vendée were all included. No other part of France at
all resembles la Vendée; it is a country quite unique. But few
main roads pass through it. I will speak further of them in
due course. The other means of communication—and,
consequently, those of commerce—consist of lanes of
between four and five feet in width, edged on either side by
steep banks, crowned by a quickset hedge trimmed to the
height of a man, and at every twenty yards stand oak trees
whose interlacing branches form an arbour over the road.
Hedges bounding private fields intersect them at right
angles here and there, thus forming enclosed spaces which
hardly ever consist of more than one or two acres, always
of an oblong shape. Each of these hedges has only one
opening, called *échalier*, which is sometimes a kind of gate
like those which enclose sheep-folds; more frequently it is
made out of wood from the hedges themselves, and, set in
the hedge, it does not look any different from the hedges
themselves to the eye of a stranger, especially in winter. The
native of the country will make straight for this hurdle,
which he knows, but other persons have generally to go

along all four sides of the fields before they can discover the way out. These hedges thoroughly explain the tactics employed in the Vendean War: to shoot accurately without being seen; to fly when the shot has been fired through the opening without the risk of being hit. Besides, with the exception of la Rochejaquelein's fine harangue: 'If I advance, follow; if I retreat, kill me; if I die, avenge me!' the leaders hardly ever uttered any other words before battle than the simpler and indeed clearer ones to the peasantry: 'Egayez-vous, mes gars!' which meant, 'Make yourselves scarce, my lads!' Then each copse would conceal a man with his gun—before, behind, on each side of the advancing army; the hedges would blaze forth, bullets whistle past one another and soldiers fall before they had time to discover from what side the storm of fire was coming! Finally, tired of seeing their dead lying in heaps at the bottom of these defiles, the Blues would rush off in each direction, climb the bank, scale the hedges and, losing half of their men in the process, would arrive at the top, only to see a sudden cessation of the firing: everything had disappeared as by magic, and nothing could be seen, far or near, but a country as prettily mapped out as an English garden, and here and there a sharp-pointed slate-roofed tower, piercing the misty western skies, or the red roof of a farmhouse standing out against a green background of oaks, beeches and walnut trees. These lanes or, properly speaking, defiles, which at first sight appear only to have been hollowed out by the hoofs of oxen, are natural staircases formed by the inequalities of the ground, over which only the little horses of the country can walk surefooted. We must say a little about these horses and the manner of driving them. In summer the lanes are picturesque enough, but in winter they are impracticable, as the slightest rainfall turns each of them into the bed of a torrent, and then, for nearly four months of the year, communication is established by foot and across country. But let us return to the horses. The cleverest riding-master in Franconi's would find himself at a disadvantage, I believe, if he were perched up on one of the huge Breton saddles, which rise out of the middle of the animal's back like a dromedary's hump. And as to the animal himself, the rider might imagine he could guide him by the help of bridle and knees; but he would very quickly find out that the legs of the Vendean rider are only used for preserving his balance, and that the bridle is of no use except to pull his mount up short by reining him in hard with both hands. After a little practice, however, he would learn to assist himself with the cudgel, and this it is which takes the place in Breton horsemanship of the use of one's knees and the bridle. In order to turn the horse to the right you must hit him over the left ear with the cudgel, and *vice versâ*; and in this manner, which simplifies the art of the Larives and the Pelliers enormously, one guides the animal by roads that would turn a Basque dizzy!

"This picture, however, of the lanes and riders who frequent them, is beginning to change in the departments of la Vendée and of the Loire-Inférieure, where Bonaparte had roads cut; but it is still correct as regards the department of Deux-Sèvres and especially the southern half of the department of Maine-et-Loire.

"It is in these latter portions of the country, therefore, that the Vendean politicians took shelter. There, the opposition to any form of Liberal government is energetic and flagrant. Happily, as if in defiance, civilisation has surrounded them with a girdle of Liberal townships, which starts from Bourbon Vendée, crosses Chollet, Saumur and Angers, reappears at Nantes and even runs over into la Vendée itself, at Clisson, which is a sort of forlorn outpost from whence alarm could be given in case of a rising. A single road passes through this country at one corner, in the shape of a Y; the tail standing for the route from Chollet to Trémentines, and the two forks, those from Trémentines to Angers and Saumur—this latter road is not even a posting route. La Vendée, then, consists nowadays of a single department, without exit for attack or flight.

"Four very distinct classes of individuals are active in the midst of this political furnace: the nobles or *gros*, the clergy, the bourgeoisie and the peasantry or leasehold farmers.

"The nobility is entirely opposed to any form of constitutional system; its influence is practically evil with the bourgeoisie, but it has immense influence over the tenant farmers who are nearly all in its pay. For instance, here is a case in point: the Marquis of la Bretèche alone possesses one hundred and four farmsteads; suppose each farm contains merely three men capable of handling a gun, one word from him will bring into action three hundred and twelve armed peasants!

"The clergy share the opinions of the nobles and have a greater influence still through their pulpits and the confessional.

"The bourgeoisie are, therefore, the interior of the triangle formed by the nobility, which lays down its laws, the clergy who preach them and the people who accept them.

"So the proportion of Liberals in this department (I am referring to the interior) is scarcely one to fifteen: the tricolour flag is nowhere to be seen, in spite of the formal order of the prefect; and the priests will not chant the *Domine salvum* except under special command of the bishop.

"The pole to which the white flag was affixed still exists, and by its very nakedness acts as a protest against the tricolour flag; but the priests recommend from their pulpits that Louis-Philippe should be prayed for, *as he must inevitably be assassinated.* So the agitation goes on incessantly. It is upheld by meetings of from forty to fifty nobles, which take place once or twice a week, either at Lavoirs, or at Herbiers, or at Combouros. The means they make use of for exciting the people is the withholding of newspapers, which are only brought by specially appointed agents, the post only passing through Beaupréau, Chemillé and Chollet. Among the towns and villages which make no kind of secret of their hopes of another insurrection must be reckoned, first and foremost, those of Beaupréau, Montfaucon, Chemillé, Saint-Macaire, le May and Trémentines. The heart of the Royalist revolution is centred at Montfaucon; were it extinguished throughout the whole of France, the pulse of civil war would still beat here. A revolution would infallibly break out if the dauphin or Madame appeared among the people, or even on a day when war should be declared between France and any foreign power, specially if that power were to be England, and if, for the third time, it were to pour men and arms along the coast, which is only from ten to eleven leagues' distance from the department of Maine-et-Loire, where it is an easy matter to smuggle men and weapons in through the opening between Clisson and Chollet.

"The following seem to us to be the best means of preventing an insurrection:—

"I. To make roads. Generally people only see in a road formed right across an impracticable country facility offered for the extension of commerce. The Government, if of liberal views, sees it as a political means to its own end; civilisation follows commerce, and liberty civilisation. Relations with other departments will deprive the one to be feared of its primitive wildness; reliable information will quickly spread and false reports be as quickly disproved; post-offices will be opened in all the chief towns of the district; the gendarmerie will be established in regular and active service; then, finally, troops will, in case of need, be marched all over the district in an impressive manner. The roads to be made in the department of Maine-et-Loire should run from Palet to Montfaucon, passing through Saint-Crespin. At Montfaucon the road should branch off into two, one going to Beaupréau by la Renaudiére, Villedieu and la Chapelle-au-Genêt; the other should proceed as far as Romagne, where it should rejoin the one from Chollet via la Jarrie and Roussay. The commerce that would spring up along these roads would be in Anjou wines, Bretagne cattle and the linens of Chollet. At the present time it can only be carried on by means of ox waggons which do not overturn, but which, by reason of the bad roads, have to be drawn by a team of eight or ten beasts for a single carriage very slightly loaded; or else goods are carried on the backs of men. These roads should be made by the workmen of the country itself, so as to distribute money among the poor classes; for the peasants know the places where the best road metal can be obtained; also because the nobles, whose positive intention it is to oppose the opening of such roads, would easily rouse the peasantry againt strange workmen, who would draw pay that the natives would regard as their own legitimate due; because, finally, the peasants chosen to make these roads would themselves oppose any attempts on the part of the nobility to prevent their execution.

"2. To transfer into villages across the Loire ten or twelve priests, raising their stipends some hundred francs or so to prevent them posing as martyrs—especially those from Tiffanges, Montauban, Torfou and Saint-Crespin. To send into the parishes in their place priests whom the Government can safely trust. These priests would have nothing to fear; their sacred office would protect them from the peasants, who might detest them as men, but would respect their cassocks.

"3. A large proportion of the nobles who meet together to discuss the means for renewing civil war enjoy very considerable pensions, which the Government continues paying them; nothing would be easier than to catch them in the very act, and then the Government could justifiably cease paying these pensions, and divide the money in equal proportions between the old Vendean and Republican soldiers, whose mutual hatred would gradually die down as quarter days succeeded one another.

"In this way, there would in the future be no possibility of fresh Vendean risings, since on the slightest outbreak the Government would only have to stretch out its arm and to scatter troops along the main roads to separate gatherings.

"If people think that these men, enlightened in their views since 1792, have reached the point of never rising again under the influence of fanaticism and superstition, they are strangely mistaken; even those that Bonaparte's conscription drew from their homes and took away out into the world have gradually lost their temporary enlightenment since they returned to their hearths again and resumed their primitive ignorance. I will cite one instance of this. I went shooting with a fine old soldier who had served a dozen years under Napoleon. On the slope of a hill near la Jarrie a stone was standing a dozen feet high that was in the shape of an inverted cone, touching the mountain by one of its upper edges and at its base, which was as narrow as the crown of a hat, resting on a large boulder of rock; although this stone weighed from seven and a half to ten tons, it was so perfectly balanced that a man could easily shake it with his hand. I thought it was a Druidical monument, but, not trusting to the false teaching of educated men, which so often is upset by the rude simplicity of peasants, I called to my companion and asked him what this stone was and who had put it there.

"'The devil!' he replied, with a conviction which did not seem to fear the faintest denial on my side.

"'The devil, did you say?' I repeated, in astonishment.

"'Yes,' he replied.

"'But what did he do it for?'

"'You see from here the stream of la Maine ... over there down in the bottom of the valley?'

"'Perfectly.'

"'Well, then, you can make out a spot where one could cross it on stepping-stones which rise to the surface of the water were it not that just in the middle of these stones there is a gap.'

"'Yes.'

"'Well! that gap ought to be refilled by the rock we are now leaning against.'

"'It is certainly hewn in such a way as to fit in exactly and to dissipate the effect of want of continuity caused by its absence.'

"'I do not follow what you mean,' replied the peasant; 'but this is how it came about. The devil was building a bridge on which to cross over the river in order to steal the farmers' cows; he had finished it all but this one stone, which he was carrying on his shoulder, forgetting that the day he was going to finish his work was a Sunday, when, all of a sudden, he caught sight of the procession from Roussay, which also saw him. Whereat the priest made the sign of the cross, and very soon Satan's strength began to go from him; he was obliged to put the stone down here and for ever, just where we are, as he never will be able to raise it again. That is why the bridge is broken and why this stone shakes.'

"As this explanation was as good as any other, I was obliged to be contented with it, since had I given him my own version, it would probably have sounded as absurd to him as his did to me."

At the end of six weeks, thanks to my guide, who accompanied me all over, I knew the country as well as, and perhaps even a good deal better than, one of its own inhabitants, both la Vendée of the past and la Vendée of the future. I said good-bye to Madame Villenave and her daughter, kissed little Élisa on her forehead and set off to Nantes. The company of my Vendean was unnecessary farther than Clisson, and I parted with him after trying to make him accept some reward for the services he had rendered me; but he obstinately refused, saying that, no matter what he had done or might still be able to do for me, he should be eternally my debtor. We embraced and I took my departure, but he stood where I left him, waving to me whenever I turned round. I lost sight of him round a corner, and all was ended between us. I do not know whether he is alive or dead, whether he has forgotten me or still keeps at the bottom of his heart that precious stone called gratitude, or whether he has cast it so far away from him that he will never be able to find it again. I reached Nantes an hour and a half after I left him.

CHAPTER IX

The Nantes Revolution—Régnier—Paimbœuf—
Landlords and travellers—Jacomety—The native of la
Guadeloupe and his wife—Gull shooting—Axiom for sea-
bird shooting—The captain of *la Pauline*—Woman and
swallow—Lovers' superstition—Getting under sail

Nantes, like Paris, had had its revolution; its Raguse, who had given orders
to fire upon the people; and its people, who had crushed Raguse. They
pointed out houses to me that were almost as much marked as the Louvre
or the Institut; the firing was so well maintained by the Royal troops that a
young man named Petit had from a single discharge received three bullets in
his arm, one in his chest and a gunshot wound right down his face; the latter
had been fired from a window by a compatriot of his. The wounded man
was recovering well; but one of his friends who had only received a charge
of buckshot was at the point of death. If he died, he would make the eleventh
who had lost his life in that secondary affray.

Régnier—who was at that time a charming comedian and who later became
one of the main pillars of the Comédie-Française—happened to be at Nantes
at the time, giving a series of representations, that were much run after.

I spent two or three days in the midst of old recollections of the Revolution,
renewed for me by M. Villenave, who, as we know, nearly played the part of
victim in the great drama composed by the Convention, which was put into
action by Carrier. If there is a name on earth execrated by the public, it is that
of Carrier!

I left Nantes for Paimbœuf. I had only seen the sea at Havre, where I was
told it scarcely deserved the name; so I was curious to behold a real sea, a
stormy sea, one which even sailors call *la mer sauvage*. I do not know anything
more melancholy on earth than that band of houses, called Paimbœuf, which
fringes the Loire for five or six hundred yards! One seems to be a thousand
miles from Paris, and outside the pale of civilisation, confronted with these
brave fellows who live by a river as wide as a sea almost, and who seem
occupied with nothing outside the mending of their nets and going fishing. I
wondered how the revolutions of the Parisian crater could possibly matter
to them, seeing that its lava could not reach them, nor could they ever see
even its flame or smoke.

But that did not matter to them, for at Paimbœuf they were boldly talking of
another Vendean insurrection. Furthermore, the distance that separates
Paimbœuf from Paris makes the very essentials of life of such a price as is

beyond the conception of people in the central provinces of France to realise. The traveller who has heard of the cheapness of its fish; of lobsters being sold at six to eight sous, turbots at two francs, and skates—which no one will eat—and shrimps being flung at your feet, is labouring under a mythical delusion: for him, the prices at inns are very nearly the same all over; north, south, east and west, landlords adopt an even tariff which never lets the traveller come off too well in the matter of expenses.

We dined at the *Philippe* of the place, which was called Jacomety; our table d'hôte dinner cost us fifty sous—only between ten to twenty sous difference between other table-d'hôte tariffs all over the kingdom. At this meal, near me, a young, sad-looking woman was dining; or, rather, was not dining, for she ate nothing. Her husband, on her right hand, was attending to her with the solicitude of a lover, and yet, every few minutes, the breast of the lovely one in distress would heave with sobs, tears would come to her eyelids and, in spite of her efforts to restrain them, they rolled down her cheeks. I could not refrain from listening to the conversation of my two neighbours; I soon learnt that the young man was a native of Guadeloupe, and had just married this charming young woman from the neighbourhood of Tours, whom he was transplanting from the garden of France to that of the Antilles. The poor child, apart from the confidence which she had just placed in that blind side of life which we call the future, knew nothing of the country to which she was going, and, until she could have children who would suck her milk and dry her tears, she mourned for the friends and relatives she was leaving behind in the old land of Europe and, probably, for the old continent itself too. At the same table was dining the captain of the vessel which was to take the young married pair over seas; and it was from him that I learnt most of these details. They were to set sail the next day. I asked his leave to go on board and to stay till his ship sailed, which he readily granted me. The boat was at anchor between Paimbœuf and Saint-Nazaire, and was called *la Pauline*. She was a pretty three-masted trader with very graceful lines, and of five or six hundred tons.

I did not say anything of my plan to my two neighbours, certain that, indifferent to them as I was, the next day at the moment of leaving I should become even more to them than a fellow-countryman—namely, a friend! I spent the rest of that day by the river banks shooting at ordinary gulls and blackheaded gulls, amazed that they did not fall. A native sportsman, amused at my disappointment, whom I approached to question as to whether the Loire, like the Styx, had the property of rendering invulnerable the men and animals which bathed in its waters, informed me, to my great surprise, that, for want of the knowledge of measuring maritime distances, I was firing from double the ordinary length of range. He laid down the following rules as essential:—

Never fire at a sea-bird unless you can distinctly see its eye; when you see its eye, its body is within range of your lead.

I instantly applied this maxim to practice. I waited patiently; I let a gull come near enough for me to see its eye distinctly like a little black speck, then I fired, and; the bird fell. The purveyor of these counsels bowed and continued his shooting, pleased with himself for having taught something to a Parisian.

I reproduce the lesson just as it was given me; one cannot spread abroad a truth too widely, no matter whether small or great.

I forget which philosopher it was who said that, if he had his hands full of truths, he would have them surrounded by a circle of fire for fear he should open them absent-mindedly and let the truths escape. I should open both my hands and blow the truths abroad with all my might. Nothing flies so slowly and haltingly as the real truth! But, as a truth always costs something to somebody, the one I have just divulged cost the life of three or four great gulls.

Upon my return to the hotel I did not see our bride and bridegroom; they had retired into their own room.

After eight o'clock in the evening, at the end of September, there are not many diversions in Paimbœuf, so I followed the example of the young couple and retired to my room, giving orders that I was to be waked in time to take advantage of the first ship's boat that was going out to *la Pauline*. The captain himself knocked at my door. I think the worthy man had, during the night, under the sweet and deceiving dew of sleep, let the hope spring up in his heart of taking me on the voyage with him. He extolled the delights of a long voyage on board a good vessel, spoke of his cook, whom he rated far higher than Jacomety's, and praised his table, which was unrivalled by any other than that of the *Rocher de Cancale* in Paris. The captain had dined once at the *Rocher de Cancale*, and he never missed a chance of putting in a good word as to the excellence of Borel's cuisine.

It was still lovely late summer weather, and, as I simply meant to pay a short call on *la Pauline*, I was clad only in nankeen trousers, a white piqué waistcoat and a velvet jacket. These details, as will soon be seen, are not without their importance to those who have learnt to their cost what it is to suffer from cold. This was the first time I had seen at such close quarters a ship that was on the point of sailing. I had indeed been over one or two steamers at Havre that were bound for Boston or New Orleans; but the elegance of these boats, which are fitted up for carrying passengers, makes them seem more like hotels, like furnished apartments and like the corridors of theatres, than like ships. But the *Pauline*, on the contrary, was a thoroughbred three-master. I examined every little thing about her with a curiosity that enabled me to hope that some day, if occasion offered itself, I might be able to write novels connected with the sea, like Cooper's, or, at any rate, like those of Eugène Sue. I was in the full flush of my examination when the boat came alongside for the second time, bringing the young couple and their luggage. The young wife made no attempt to restrain her tears, but wept abundantly and openly. So she did not see me come towards the starboard companion, and when I gave her my hand to help her from the ladder to the bridge she uttered a little cry of surprise.

"Ah! monsieur!" she said, "are you also going to Guadeloupe?"

"Alas! no, madame," I said; "greatly to my regret I am not; but it is precisely because I am remaining behind that you find me here."

"I do not understand you, monsieur."

"I noticed your sadness, and know that you are leaving those who are very dear to you. Therefore, as I am a fellow-countryman of yours, I thought I would take your last messages to your friends."

"Oh, monsieur," she said, "how good of you!"

And she looked at her husband as if to ask him how far she might enter into a conversation of this nature with a stranger.

He smiled, and held out his hand, and with one quick glance gave his wife leave to do what she liked.

"Yes," he said, "be so good as to take my dear Pauline's last farewell messages to her family; and tell her mother especially, if you see her, that in less than three years' time we will come back and pay her a visit."

"Three years!" murmured the young wife dubiously.

"And tell this foolish child, monsieur," he went on, kissing his wife's forehead, "that it is easier to get to and from Guadeloupe now than it was in old days to get to Saint-Cloud.... I am not yet thirty, and I have already made a dozen voyages between Pointe-à-Pître and Nantes."

"Yes, my dear! You tell me that now, but eighteen hundred leagues is a long way!"

"Six weeks' voyage ... that isn't much surely?"

I pointed out to the young wife a swallow which was skimming about the masts.

"That bird takes just such a voyage twice a year, madame," I said to her, "guided by its instinct alone."

"Yes, but it is a bird," she said, sighing.

I tried to give a fresh turn to the conversation.

"Monsieur," I said to the husband, "I heard you addressing madame as Pauline... *La Pauline* is the name of the boat on which we are standing; is it a mere coincidence or by your own selection that the names are the same?"

"It was my own choice, monsieur; there were three or four ships in the river, and I decided on this one.... I thought that besides her saintly patron I would give her one in addition.... Are you amused at my superstition?"

"Not at all, monsieur, quite the reverse. I appreciate all superstitions— particularly those which have love as their basis. It has always seemed to me impossible to love sincerely without feeling vague terrors on behalf of the beloved object, that make even the stoutest hearted a prey to superstitious feelings."

The young wife listened to me for a little while.

"Oh, monsieur," she then began, holding out her hand, "what a kind idea it was of yours to see us off!"

"I hope then, madame, that you will depute me to carry any last messages to your family."

"I wrote to my mother this morning, monsieur, but if you happen to be stopping at Tours, and have a little time to spare, be so good as to inquire for the house of Madame M——, and tell her you met us and saw us on the ship, and that you were witness" (she smiled rather doubtfully) "that Léopold promised to bring me back to France in three years' time."

"I will tell her, madame; and I will undertake to be surety for your husband's word."

Meantime, operations were taking place on board preparatory to sailing. The wind was east-south-east, just right for sailing out of the river; they had only been waiting for the tide to turn before making a quick start with the combined assistance of both wind and tide. Thus, all of a sudden, the captain's voice made us start. The pilot had just arrived from Saint-Nazaire, and the captain was issuing his first order: "Heave short at the anchor!" At this unexpected order, the poor traveller seemed as though she realised for the first time that she must actually leave France. She uttered a little cry, and threw herself on her husband's breast and burst into sobs. I took advantage of this renewed outflow of tears to quit the newly-married pair, and to tell the captain I was ready to return to shore at his convenience.

"Eh!" he said, "are you in such a hurry to leave us? I had counted on keeping you to luncheon and to dinner—or at any rate to luncheon; for," he added, looking at the sky, "I doubt there won't be many passengers dining to-day."

"Good!" I replied; "but, when at sea, how did you propose to get rid of me?"

"The easiest way imaginable: you would have returned to land with the coasting pilot."

"Stop! Is that really possible?"

"Everything is possible that one wants very much."

"Well then, I will have luncheon with you."

"Then you will not leave us until we get to Piliers; you will return with the pilot, to whom you can give a crown-piece, and you will pass for an Englishman who wanted a taste of sea-sickness."

"Done! Arrange matters with him for me."

He called to the pilot, spoke a few words to him in a whisper, pointed me out with a glance, and the pilot nodded in sign of acquiescence.

"There," said the captain, "that matter is fixed up all right!"

Then, addressing the sailors who had been heaving the anchor apeak, he said—

"Up aloft with you and let go the top-sails and the courses, the jibs and the spanker!"

"Ah, captain," I said, "do not go and serve me the trick that Bougainville did to his friend the curé of Boulogne!"

"Oh, no fear of that! Besides, I am not going all round the world!"[1]

Lastly, turning to his men, he shouted—

"Get ready to hoist and haul in the top-sails!"

The story of Bougainville and the curé of Boulogne is a popular one in the French navy, and, as you see, the captain answered me just as a communicant answers a question on the Catechism. Now, as it is quite possible that my reader may not be a sailor, and that ladies, in particular, may be quite unacquainted with the legend to which I have just referred, I will tell in as few words as possible the story of Bougainville and the curé of Boulogne. Then we will return to our two Paulines.

[1] See *le curé de Boulogne*, p. 59 of vol. ii. of *Bric-à-Brac*.

CHAPTER X

Story of Bougainville and his friend the curé of Boulogne

On 14 November of the year 1766, an open carriage, drawn by post-horses, containing three naval officers, one seated on the front seat and the other two on the back one,—which signified a decided difference in their rank,— was driving along the *Bois de Boulogne*, coming from the *barrière de l'Étoile>* and going towards the *Avenue de Saint-Cloud*. By the *Château de la Muette* it passed a priest who was walking slowly along in one of the side-walks reading his breviary.

"Hi! postillion!" shouted the officer sitting at the back of the carriage; "stop a moment, please."

The postillion stopped. This request, given in a loud voice, and the noise the postillion made pulling up his horses, naturally led to the priest raising his head and fixing his eyes on the carriage and its three occupants.

"Pardieu! I am not mistaken," said the officer sitting behind; "it is really you, my dear Rémy!"

The priest gazed in astonishment. However, his face gradually cleared as light dawned on him, and his lips turned from amazement to smiles.

"Ah!" he said at length, "it is you!"

"Why *you (vous)*?"

"It is thou *(toi)* then, Antoine."

"Yes, it is I, Antoine de Bougainville."

"Mon Dieu! What have you been doing with yourself during the twenty-five years since we parted?"

"What have I been doing with myself, dear friend?" repeated Bougainville. "Come and sit down by me a few minutes and I will tell you."

"But ..." The priest looked round him uneasily, as though he were afraid to go far away from his home, Bougainville understood his fear.

"Do not be anxious; we will go at a walking pace," he replied.

A valet got down from the seat behind and lowered the step.

"It is a quarter past eleven," said the priest, "and Marianne expects me for dinner at twelve."

"In the first place—where do you live? But sit down, though!"

He lightly drew the priest by his gown, and the priest sat down.

"Where do I live?" asked the latter.

"Yes."

"At Boulogne.... I am curé of Boulogne, friend."

"Ah! ah! I offer you my congratulations; you always had the vocation."

"So, you see, I entered Orders."

"Are you satisfied?"

"Enchanted, my friend! The curé of Boulogne is not one of the best: it only has an income of eight hundred livres; but my tastes are modest, and there still remain four hundred livres over to give away to the poor."

"Good Rémy!... You can go at a slow trot, so that we lose as little time as possible."

The postillion set the horses to the required pace, which, moderate though it was, none the less brought a cloud of distress on the curé's countenance.

"Set your mind at rest," said Bougainville, "seeing we are going in the direction of Boulogne."

"Friend," the Abbé Rémy said, laughing, "I have been curé of Boulogne for twenty years; Marianne has been fifteen years with me, and never, except when detained by the side of a dying parishioner, have I been five minutes later than twelve; punctually at twelve the soup is on the table, and ... you understand?"

"Yes; don't be afraid, I do not want to upset Marianne.... You shall be home exactly by twelve."

"Now my mind is easy.... But talk about yourself a little: are you not wearing the uniform of the Navy?"

"Yes; I am captain of a ship."

"How comes that about? I thought you were a barrister—Really?—when you left college did you not begin to study law?"

"What is to be done, my dear Rémy? You, God's anointed, ought to know better than anyone the proverb:

"'Man proposes and God disposes.' It is true I was entered as a barrister in 1752 at the High Judicial Court of Paris."

"Ah! I knew it!" said the good priest, withdrawing the finger from his breviary, which marked the place where he had left off reading. "So you did become a barrister?"

"Yes; but at the same time that I was called to the Bar," continued Bougainville, "I enlisted in the Musketeers."

"Oh, indeed! You always had a taste for arms and a special talent for mathematics."

"You remember that?"

"Why, of course! Was I not your best friend at College?" "Ah, that is very true!"

"Is it you or your brother Louis who belongs to the Academy?"

Bougainville smiled.

"It is my brother," he said; "or rather, it was, for you must know that I had the misfortune to lose him three years ago."

"Ah! poor Louis.... But what can you expect. We are all mortal, and it is well to look upon this life as a voyage which leads us to port.... Pardon, friend, it seems to me we are passing Boulogne."

Bougainville looked at his watch.

"Bah!" said he, "what does it matter! It is only half-past eleven, and consequently you have still a good twenty minutes before you.—Faster, postillion!"

"Why faster?"

"Because you are in a hurry, my friend."

"Bougainville!..."

"What! does not the wish to know what I have been doing outweigh your fear of upsetting Marianne by being five minutes late?... That is a queer sort of friendship, to be sure!"

"You are right, upon my word; five minutes more or less.... Tell me about yourself, my dear Antoine. Besides, when I tell Marianne that it was for you and through you I am late, she will stop scolding."

"Marianne knows me, then?"

"Knows you? Of course she does! I have spoken to her of you a score of times.... But be quick and finish telling me how it is that, having been called to the Bar, and after enlisting in the Musketeers, I find you a naval officer."

"It is very simple, and I can explain it all to you in a word. In 1753 I became assistant-major in the provincial battalion of Picardie; the following year I was appointed aide de camp to Chevert, whom I left to become Secretary to the Embassy in London, and to be made a member of the Royal Society; in 1756 I went as captain of dragoons with the Marquis of Montcalm, charged with the defence of Canada.."

"Capital! capital!" interrupted the Abbé Rémy. "I can see you doing it! Go on, my friend, I am listening."

The abbé, completely fascinated by Bougainville's narrative, had not noticed that the horses had quietly passed from a slow to a quick trot. Bougainville continued his story.

"When in Canada, I was pretty much master of my future; I had but to conduct myself well to attain to anything. I was put in charge of several expeditions by the Marquis de Montcalm, which I brought to a successful issue. Thus, for instance, after a march of sixty leagues through forests which were believed to be impenetrable, sometimes over tracks of country covered with snow, sometimes on the ice of the river Richelieu, I advanced as far as the end of the lake of Saint-Sacrement, where I burned an English flotilla under the very fort which protected it."

"What!" said the abbé, "was it you who did that? Why, I read the account of that event; but I did not know you were the hero...."

"Did you not recognise my name?"

"I knew the name but not the man.... How could you expect I should recognise in a member of the Basoche, whom I left studying law, and aspiring to become a barrister, a dashing fellow who burns fleets in the far-away depths of Canada?... You can surely see that it was impossible!"

At this moment the carriage stopped before a posting-house.

"Oh!" said the Abbé Rémy, "where are we, Antoine?"

"We are at Sèvres, my friend."

"At Sèvres! What time is it?"

Bougainville looked at his watch.

"It is ten minutes to twelve."

"Oh! Mon Dieu!" exclaimed the abbé, "but I shall never be at Boulogne by noon."

"That is more than probable."

"A league to go!"

"A league and a half."

"If only I could find a posting-carriage...."

He rose to his feet in the carriage and cast a look round him as far as his sight could reach, but there was no sign of even the smallest sort of vehicle.

"Never mind," he said, "I will walk."

"You shall not walk!" said Bougainville.

"What! you will not let me walk?"

"No, it shall not be said that you caught pleurisy because you took a drive with a friend."

"I will go quietly."

"Oh, I know you! You would be afraid of being scolded by Mademoiselle Marianne, you would hurry your pace, arrive in a state of perspiration, drink cold water and give yourself inflammation of the lungs.... Some idiot of a doctor would purge you instead of bleeding, or bleed you instead of purging; and, three days later, Good-bye, there would be the end to the Abbé Rémy!"

"All the same I must return to Boulogne.... Hi! postillion! postillion! Stop!...."

The carriage, with its fresh horses, set off at a quick trot.

"Listen," says Bougainville, "this is the best thing to do."

"The best thing to do, my good friend, my dear Antoine, is to stop the horses, so that I can get down and make my way back to Boulogne."

"No," says Bougainville; "the best thing to be done is for you to come with me as far as Versailles."

"As far as Versailles?..."

"Yes; as you have missed Mademoiselle Marianne's dinner you must dine with me at Versailles. Whilst I am receiving final commands from His Majesty, one of these gentlemen will undertake to find a travelling carriage to convey you back to Boulogne."

"Of course that would be a great pleasure, my friend, but...."

"But what?"

The Abbé Rémy felt about in his waistcoat pockets, plunging both hands in up to his armpits.

"But," he Continued, "Marianne has not put any money in my pockets."

"Never mind about that, my dear Rémy! At Versailles I will ask the king for a hundred crowns for the poor of Boulogne; the king will grant them me, and I will give them to you. You can borrow a few crowns from them until you return in the travelling carriage to Boulogne, and the thing is settled."

"What! You think the king would give you a hundred crowns for my poor?"

"I am sure of it."

"On your word of honour?"

"On my faith as a gentleman!"

"My friend, that decides me then."

"Thanks! You would not come for my sake, but you will for your poor. It seems to be better worth being one of your poor parishioners than your friend!"

"I do not say so, my dear Antoine; but you know a curé who deserts his post must have a good excuse."

"An excuse?... Oh! if you slept away, I do not say...."

"What! if I slept away!" exclaims the Abbé Rémy, terrified. "Do you mean, then, to make me stop away the night?... Postillion! hi! postillion!"

"No, do not be afraid.... At the rate we are going we shall reach Versailles in an hour; we shall dine by two, and you can leave at three."

"Why at three, and not at two?"

"Because I must have time to see the king and ask him for the hundred crowns."

"Ah! that is true."

"Three hours for you to return by carriage from Versailles to Boulogne; you will be home at six o'clock."

"What will Marianne say?"

"Bah! when she sees you return with a hundred crowns direct from the king, Marianne will be happy and proud of your influence,"

"Upon my faith you are right.... You must tell me all the king says to you; this adventure will give her enough to talk of to her neighbours for a week to come."

"So it is settled, we are to dine at Versailles?"

"Agreed as to Versailles! But now tell me the end of your story."

"Ah! true.... We had got to my expedition on the Saint-Sacrement. It earned me the rank of quarter-master of one of the Army Corps, and the commission to go to Versailles to explain the precarious situation of the Governor of Canada, to ask for reinforcements for him. I stayed two years and a half in France without obtaining anything that I asked. True, I got what I did not ask for, that is to say, the Cross of Saint-Louis and the rank of colonel in the staff of the regiment of Rovergne. I arrived in Canada just in time to receive from the Marquis of Montcalm the command of the Grenadiers and Volunteers, at the famous retreat from Quebec, which I was ordered to effect. When Montcalm arrived beneath the walls of the town, he thought he might risk a battle. The two generals were killed: Montcalm in our ranks; Wolfe in those of the English. Montcalm dead, our army defeated, there were no means of defending Canada. I returned to France, and went through the campaign of 1761 in England, as aide-de-camp to M. de Choiseul-Stainville."

"Then it was you to whom the king made the present of two guns?" interrupted the curé de Boulogne.

"Who told you that?"

"I read about it, my friend, in the *Gazette de la Cour*.... How could I have dreamt this Bougainville was my friend Antoine?"

"What did you think of the present?"

"Bah! I thought it well deserved ... but, all the same, I thought the king ought to have given this M. Bougainville, whom I was far from suspecting to be you, something more easily carried about than two cannons; for, of course, though a great honour, one cannot carry them about wherever one goes."

"There is truth in what you say," Bougainville resumed, laughing; "but, as at the same time the king made me captain of a ship, and entrusted me with the founding of a settlement for myself and the inhabitants of St. Malo, in the isles of Malouines, I thought my two cannon might be of use there."

"Ah! quite right," said the Abbé Rémy; "but, excuse my ignorance of geography, my dear Antoine, where are the Malouines Isles?"

"I beg your pardon, my friend," said Bougainville, "I should have called them the Falkland Isles, for it was I who gave them their name of Malouines Isles in honour of the town of St. Malo."

"Very good!" said the Abbé Rémy, smiling; "I recognise them under that name! The Falkland Isles belong to the archipelago of the Atlantic Ocean; I know where they are, near the southern extremity of South America, to the east of Magellan Straits."

"Upon my word," said Bougainville, "Strong, who christened them, could not have determined their bearing more accurately himself. You study geography, then, in your curé of Boulogne?"

"Oh, my friend, when I was young I always longed to be a missionary to the Indies.... I was born with the love of travel, and I would have given anything to go round the world ... in those days, but not now."

"Yes, I understand," says Bougainville, exchanging a glance with his two companions, "to-day it would put you out of your regular habits.... So you have travelled?"

"My friend, I have never been further than Versailles."

"Then you have not been to the sea."

"No."

"You have never seen a ship?"

"I have seen sails at Auxerre."

"That is something, but it can only give you a very imperfect idea of a frigate of sixty guns."

"I should think so," added the Abbé Rémy innocently. "So you say you went to the Malouines Isles, where the Government had authorised you to found a settlement. I have no doubt that you did so?"

"Unluckily the Spaniards, after the peace of Paris, laid claim to these islands; their claim was considered just by the Court of France, which gave them up on condition they indemnified me for the money I had laid out."

"But did they do so?"

"Yes, my dear friend, they gave me a million francs!"

"A million francs? *Peste!* what a pretty sum."

It will be observed that the good abbé nearly swore.

"Now," continued he, "where are you going?..."

"I am going to Havre."

"What to do? Forgive me, friend, perhaps I am inquisitive."

"Inquisitive? Oh, certainly not!... I am going to Havre to see a frigate of which the king has made me captain."

"What is its name?..."

"*La Boudeuse.*"

"Is it a very fine ship?"

"Superb!"

The Abbé Rémy heaved a sigh. It was evident the poor priest thought what pleasure it would have given him in times past, when he had been free, to have seen the sea and to go over a frigate.

This sigh led to a fresh interchange of looks and smiles between Bougainville and the two officers. Both smiles and glances passed unnoticed by the worthy Abbé Rémy, who had fallen into so profound a reverie that he did not return to himself until the carriage stopped before a large hotel.

"Ah ! so we have arrived," he says. "I am very hungry!"

"Very well. We will not wait as the dinner was ordered beforehand."

"What a delightful life a sea captain's must be!" says the abbé. "He gets millions from the Spaniards; he travels post in a good carriage; and, when he arrives, he finds a dinner all ready for him! Poor Marianne! she has dined without me!"

"Bah!" says Bougainville, "once does not mean always. ... We will dine without her, and I hope her absence will not take away your appetite."

"Oh, don't be anxious ... I am really very hungry."

"Well then, to table! to table!"

"To table!" merrily repeated the Abbé Rémy.

It was a good dinner; Bougainville was a gourmet; he drank no other wine than champagne; the fashion of icing it had just been invented.

All priests, whether they be curés of a small town or hamlet, or officiating priests of a chapel without a congregation, are inclined to be a little greedy; the Abbé Remy, modest though he was, had the sensual side with which nature has endowed the palate of the ecclesiastic. At first he would not drink more than a few drops of wine in his water; then he mixed wine and water in equal parts; then, finally, he decided to drink his wine pure. When Bougainville saw he had arrived at this point, he rose, and announced that it was time for him to present himself before the king, to whom he was going to address the request relative to the poor of Boulogne. In the meantime the two officers were to keep the Abbé Remy company. As Bougainville had said, he was absent an hour. In spite of the efforts of the officers the worthy priest's hopes see-sawed up and down in a way which did credit to his kindliness of heart.

"Well!" he said, when he caught sight of Bougainville, "what about my poor people?"

"It is not three hundred livres that the king has given me for them," said Bougainville, drawing a roll from his pocket, "but fifty louis!"

"What! Fifty louis?" exclaimed the Abbé Rémy, quite overcome by this regal bounty; "twelve hundred livres!"

"Twelve hundred livres."

"Impossible!"

"Here they are."

The Abbé Rémy held out his hand.

"But the king has given them to me on one condition."

"What?"

"That you drink to his health."

"Oh, if that is all!"

He held out his glass, into which Bougainville tipped the neck of the bottle.

"Stop! stop!" said the abbé.

"Come, now!" Bougainville insisted, "half a glass? Well! the king would not be pleased to see only half a glass drunk to his health."

"Really," the Abbé Rémy said jovially, "twelve hundred livres deserve a whole glass. Fill it quite full, Antoine; and here's to the king's health!"

"To the king!" repeated Bougainville.

"Ah!" said the Abbé Rémy, putting his glass on the table, "that is what one might call a real orgy!... True, it is the first I have taken part in, and I shall not have the opportunity of a second for a very long time."

"I tell you what it is...." said Bougainville, resting his elbows on the table.

"Well?" replied the Abbé Rémy, whose eyes were shining like carbuncles.

"Something you ought to do."

"What is it?"

"You tell me you have never seen the sea."

"Never."

"Well! you ought to come to Havre with me."

"I ... come to Havre with you?... But you are not dreaming of such a thing as that, Antoine?"

"On the contrary, it is just what I am doing. Have a glass of champagne?"

"Thanks, I have already drunk too much!"

"Ah! to the health of your poor people ... that is a toast you cannot resist."

"Yes, but only a drop."

"A drop! When you drank the glass full to the king? Ah! that is not scriptural, my dear Remy. Our Saviour said: 'The first shall be last ...' A full glass for the poor of Boulogne or none at all."

"Here goes, then, for a full glass; but it is the last."

The abbé, good Catholic as he was, emptied his toast to the poor as gaily as that to the king.

"There!" said Bougainville. "Now it is agreed we set off for Havre."

"Antoine, you must be mad!"

"You shall see the sea, my friend ... and such a sea! Not a lake like the poor Mediterranean; but the ocean, which rolls round the world!"

"Do not tempt me, you wretched fellow!"

"The ocean, which you yourself admit it has been the desire of your life to see!"

"*Vade retro, Satanas!*"

"It is only a matter of a week."

"But do you not know, then, that if I absent myself for a week without leave I shall lose my curé?"

"I have foreseen that, and as monseigneur, the Bishop of Versailles, was with the king, I made him sign you a permit, telling him you were coming with me."

"You told him that?"

"Yes."

"And he signed me a permit?"

"Here it is."

"Dear me, it is indeed his signature! Good! I would swear to it!"

"My friend, you are a sailor at heart."

"Give me my fifty louis and let me go."

"Here they are, but you shall not go."

"Why not?"

"Because I am authorised by the king to hand you fifty more at Havre, and you will not be so mean a Christian as to deprive your poor people—your children, the flock over which the Saviour has given you charge—of fifty beautiful golden louis!"

"Very well!" cried the Abbé Rémy, "then I will go to Havre! But it is only for their sakes I consent."

Then, stopping suddenly—

"No," he said violently, "it is impossible!"

"Why impossible?"

"Marianne!..."

"You shall write to her to relieve her anxiety."

"What shall I tell her, my friend?"

"Tell her that you have met the Bishop of Versailles, and that he has given you leave to go to Havre."

"That would be lying!"

"To lie for a good motive is not a sin, but a virtue."

"She will not believe me."

"You can show her the permit signed by the bishop."

"Stay, that is true.... Ah! you barristers, you soldiers and sailors, you do not stick at anything."

"See, you want pen and ink and paper?"

The Abbé Rémy reflected for a minute, and no doubt he said to himself that a written lie was a bigger sin than a spoken one, for suddenly he said—

"No, I would rather tell her on my return.... But she will think me dead."

"She will be all the more pleased when she sees you back alive!"

"Then, my friend, do not leave me time to reflect, but carry me off now!"

"Nothing easier."

So, turning to the two officers—

"The horses are in, are they not?"

"Yes, captain."

"Well then, let us go!"

"*En voiture!*" repeated the Abbé Rémy in the tones of a man who flings himself head-first into some unknown peril.

"*En voiture!*" repeated the two officers gaily.

They got into the carriage, travelled very fast all night, and by five next morning they were at Havre. Bougainville himself chose the room to be occupied by his friend, who, tired with the journey, and still a little heavy from the previous day's dinner, slept and did not wake till noon. Just as he was waking, Bougainville came into his room and opened the windows. The abbé uttered a cry of surprise and admiration: the windows looked out on the sea. A quarter of a league away *la Boudeuse* was riding gracefully in the roadstead, moored with two anchors down.

"Oh!" asked the Abbé Rémy, "what is that magnificent vessel?"

"My friend," said Bougainville, "that is *la Boudeuse*, where we are expected to dinner."

"What! Do you mean me to go on board?"

"Surely! You would not come all the way to Havre and return without having seen over a ship! Why, my dear friend, it is just as though you went to Rome without seeing the pope."

"True enough," said the Abbé Remy; "but when shall we return?"

"When you like.... after dinner—it is for you to decide.... You shall give your orders and be captain on my vessel."

"Very good! Let us go soon rather than late.... We have taken fourteen hours to come, but I shall take quite five or six days to return."

"What does it matter, as you have leave for a week?"

"I know that quite well, but, you see, there is Marianne...."

"You are picturing to yourself the cries of joy she will utter when she sees you again?"

"Do you think they will be cries of joy?"

"Zounds! I hope so indeed!"

"I, too, hope so," said the Abbé in tones expressive of more doubt than hope.

Then, like a man who has flung his cap over the windmill—"Come, come," he said, "to the frigate!"

Bougainville appeared to be waited on by genii, who also did the bidding of the Abbé Rémy, and to such good purpose that, when the latter exclaimed "To Havre!" he found the carriage all ready; and in the same way, when he exclaimed, "To the frigate!" he found the captain's gig in waiting. He got into the boat and sat down by Bougainville, who took the helm. A dozen sailors waited with raised oars.

Bougainville made a sign; the twelve oars fell and hit the water with so regular a movement that they seemed to strike it as one man. The gig flew over the sea like those long-legged water-spiders which glide over water. In less than ten minutes they were alongside. It hardly need be said that the maritime wonder called a frigate roused the enthusiasm of the good Abbé Rémy to the highest pitch; he asked Bougainville the name of each mast, of each yard and of each rope. No sails were set, but they were hanging in brails. In the middle of the naming of the different parts of the ship, a messenger came to tell the captain that dinner was served. The abbé and he went down into the captain's cabin. This cabin might have vied with any drawing-room belonging to one of the richest châteaux round Paris in comfort and elegance. The abbé's surprise increased more and more. Fortunately, although it was 15 November, the sea was all ablaze; it was one of those beautiful autumn days, which seem like a farewell sent to the earth by the summer sun before its disappearance for six months.

The Abbé Rémy was not in the least seasick, upon which fact the superior officers admitted to the captain's table, and the captain himself, offered their congratulations. However, towards the middle of dinner it seemed to him as though the motion of the frigate was increasing; Bougainville replied that it was the ebb tide, and delivered a learned lecture on tides. The Abbé Rémy listened to his friend's scientific dissertation with the greatest animation and attention; and, as he was not unacquainted with physical science, he made observations in his turn which seemed to call forth the delighted admiration of the officers.

The dinner was protracted longer than the diners themselves realised; nothing is so deceptive as to the passing of time as interesting conversation, enlivened with good wine. Then came coffee, that sweet nectar for which the abbé confessed a weakness. Captain Bougainville's coffee was such a cunning and happy mixture of Mocha and Martinique, that, when he was imbibing it, in small sips, the abbé declared he had never tasted its equal. Then, after the coffee, came liqueurs, those famous liqueurs de Madame Anfoux which were the delight of the gourmets of the latter part of the last century. Finally, when the liqueurs had been enjoyed, and the Abbé Rémy proposed to go back to the deck, Bougainville raised no opposition to this desire; but he was obliged to give his arm to his friend up the companion, the abbé naïvely attributing his instability of balance to the champagne, Mocha coffee and liqueurs de Madame Anfoux which he had drunk.

The frigate was on the larboard tack, with her head to the north-east, and the wind blowing free; all sail was set, including lower and top-gallant studding sails. Only the stay-sails were stowed. They must have been going at eleven knots an hour!

The good abbé's first feeling was that of whole-hearted admiration for this masterpiece of naval architecture in full sail. Then he noticed that the frigate was moving. Next he looked around him,—and, finally, he uttered a cry of terror. The land of France looked no more than a cloud upon the horizon.... He regarded Bougainville with an expression in which was concentrated all the reproaches of a betrayed confidence.

"My dear fellow," said Bougainville, "it gave me so much pleasure to see you, my oldest and dearest comrade, that I resolved we would remain together as long as possible. ... I wanted a chaplain on board my frigate; I asked His Majesty to let you fill this post, and he graciously granted it, together with a stipend of a thousand crowns.... Here is your commission."

The Abbé Rémy flung a frightened glance at his appointment.

"But," he said, "where are we going?"

"Round the world, my dear man!"

"How long does it take to go round the world?"

"Oh, from three to three years and a half, more or less.... But reckon three and a half years rather than three."

The abbé fell back, overcome, against the raised stand of the officers' watch.

"Oh!" he murmured, "I shall never dare to appear before Marianne again!..."

"I promise to take you to the presbytery and to make your peace with her," said Bougainville.

On 15 May 1770, the frigate *Boudeuse* re-entered the port of Saint-Malo. It was exactly three years and a half since she had left Havre; Bougainville was not a day out in his calculation. In that time she had been all round the world.

Heaven alone knows what passed at the first interview which took place between the Abbé Rémy and Marianne.

CHAPTER XI

Breakfast on deck—Saint-Nazaire—A thing husbands never think of—Noirmontiers—Belle-Ile—I leave the two Paulines—The rope-ladder—The ship's boat—A total immersion—The inn at Saint-Nazaire—I throw money through the window—A batch of clothes—Return to Paris

While these manœuvres were being put into execution, I rejoined our young married couple.

"Well, monsieur," said the bride to me, "the moment has come for you to return to land and to leave us."

"Not yet, madame," I said.

She fixed her gaze on me.

"Not yet?" she repeated.

"No, madame; I have obtained permission from the captain not to leave you till the very last minute.... I am to lunch with you, and we shall still have several long hours to spend talking of France."

"Thank you, monsieur," the husband replied.

But now everybody who had come on board, either for business matters or for affairs of the heart, bade their adieux, got down into the boats, and went away from the ship. The anchor was drawn out of the water and catted, and *la Pauline* began to obey the motion of the outgoing tide and the breeze. Slight as the movement was, it was enough to bring on a fresh paroxysm of grief in the case of the bride. I went back to the captain.

"Captain," I said, "I believe you would give very great pleasure to your passengers—to two, at least, among them—if you ordered lunch to be served on deck."

"Why so?"

"Because over there is a young wife who desires to take in every bit of France she can before she leaves it, which she cannot do if she is on the between-decks."

"It would be easy enough," said the captain, "for I only have five passengers at my table."

"Then you agree?"

"I agree."

We were now off Saint-Nazaire, which rises sadly out of sand and heather, with not even a tree to rest the eye. But the young woman's gaze hugged the bare landscape with as much eagerness as though she were looking upon some Swiss meadow or Scotch loch.

"Madame," I said to her, "I have come from the captain to tell you luncheon is ready."

"Oh! I cannot eat anything," she replied.

"Allow me, madame, to tell you that I am certain of the contrary."

She shook her head.

"Seeing," I continued, "that we are not going to have luncheon between-decks but here on deck."

"You asked the captain to do that!" she exclaimed, with as much fervour as though I had realised a desire which she had not even dared to let herself dwell upon.

"Why, yes, I did!" I answered, laughing.

"Oh!" she said, turning to her husband, "how good monsieur is, dear!"

"Upon my word," he said, "you should be most grateful to him; I had not even thought of such a thing."

How is it that even the most devotedly loving husbands, even those just married, never think of things that strangers do? I leave this reflection to the wisdom of any psychologists who may chance to peruse this book.

The table was set on deck; the young woman ate little, but she did not lose sight for an instant of the two banks of the Loire, which were now growing wider and wider apart. As we approached the sea the colour of the water changed from yellow to greenish; then waves began to foam on its surface. When we had doubled Saint-Nazaire, we found ourselves in the angle of a kind of gigantic V, which, at its widest end, displayed to our gaze the limitless horizon of the sea. This was the first time the young woman had seen the sea she was to cross; it was evident that the vision caused her profound terror. The sea was rough without being actually stormy; but it was not its roughness that impressed the melancholy voyager, nor was it the white-crested waves which made her turn pale—it was the idea of its infinity, the feeling of immensity of space that the sight of the ocean always gives. About two o'clock in the afternoon we reached the open sea. Then, on our left lay the isle of Noirmontiers (*nigrum monasteriuni*), which derives its name from a Benedictine monastery, founded there in the seventh century by Saint

Philibert, and destroyed in the ninth century by those Normans whose appearance saddened the last years of Charlemagne; on the right lay Belle-Ile, the isle of Fouquet, which was to give its name later to the heroine of one of my comedies; and, later again, was to become the scene of action of my triple epic *The Musketeers*, and to provide a tomb worthy of my poor friend Porthos. At the time of which I am writing, these various names struck my ears indifferently; but they stayed in my memory none the less, and were to reappear one day decked in all the framework of the dream-fancies of my imagination; floating isles of Delos, which will stop in more or less advanced positions in the realms of the future. In front of us stretched the sea, with its indented crests, merging towards the horizon in a sky dark with clouds, in which the sun was beginning to enshroud itself. We were nearly three leagues from harbour, off the reef called les Pitiers; the bad channels were passed, the wind was south-south-west, and freshening. The pilot announced that his task was done, that he handed over the command to the captain, and that he should return to land. I must say I looked at the means of descent from the ship to the skiff with some disquietude. It was nothing more than a rope-ladder fixed to the round sides of the ship. And, moreover, the ship was making its seven knots an hour. For a moment I wished I need not get off before reaching Guadeloupe. Fortunately, the captain understood what was going on in my mind, and came to the conclusion that a short delay of ten minutes was of no account in a voyage of six weeks.

"Come," he said to me, "go and pay your adieux whilst I lay to the ship."

Then he shouted—

"Down with the helm!"

Instantly the sails quivered: they were doing for me the same as is done when a man falls overboard.

"Clew up the mainsail," continued the captain, "and haul in the sails to the mainmast!"

The ship stopped, or very nearly so. The pilot was already in his boat.

I went up to the poor exile; tears were silently streaming down her cheeks.

"You will be sure and fulfil my commission, will you not, monsieur?" she said in a broken voice.

I bowed my acquiescence.

"You will embrace my mother for me?"

"I promise you I will do so, madame."

"But," said the husband, "if you want monsieur to kiss your mother for you, you ought first to give him the kiss."

"Oh yes, certainly!" exclaimed the young wife effusively; "with all my heart." And she flung her arms round my neck. Here was an unusual situation! That woman and I had never seen one another till the night before, and in the morning we were still strangers to one another; at starting we were merely acquaintances; by luncheon we had developed into friends; parting made us seem like brother and sister. Oh! mysteries of the heart, misunderstood by the crowd at large, but which turn those to whom God has revealed His secrets into beings destined for suffering. I had greater difficulty in leaving these friends of a day than it would have given me pleasure to see friends of twenty years' standing.

"You will not forget my name, will you, monsieur?" the young wife said.

"Try and read the next books that I shall write, madame, and I promise you you shall find that name in one of my very first novels."

There was also, perhaps, underlying the attraction for the ship, my anxiety at the prospect of the more or less perilous descent to which I was about to subject myself. Luckily, I had plenty of spectators to witness my gymnastic manœuvres, and you know how the feeling of being looked at redoubles one's courage. So I went bravely forward towards the ship's side; I caught hold of the main shrouds as well as the ladder, which the pilot, afraid, perhaps, of my falling into the sea before I had paid him his crown, had, to make my descent easier, held taut with one hand, while with his other, by help of a rope fastened through a port-hole, he kept the skiff within reach of the ship. I had not descended two rungs of the ladder before the wind blew my hat off. I did not even try to catch it, for I more than needed both hands to clutch fast hold of the ladder. At last, to my great satisfaction, and without displaying too much clumsiness, I reached the bottom of the skiff. That was one of the happiest moments of my life. I was scarcely seated on one of the seats in the boat before the pilot let go both ladder and rope, and we were thirty feet away from *la Pauline*. I could soon hear the captain's voice shouting—

"Let go the main-sails!"

And instantly the sails stopped quivering and the ship resumed her course. Our two young people stood astern, he waving his hat and she her handkerchief. Meanwhile, the pilot was trimming a little sail; I noticed that it was set by the skiff suddenly heeling over, so if I had not held on to the opposite side of the boat I should have been spilled right into the sea. The joke soon began to appear rather less funny to me—all the more so since the pilot, who could hardly speak any French, and who was chary of using what words he did know of our language, kept staring at the horizon with a fixedness that troubled me. The fact was that the nearer we approached the coast the rougher grew the sea. Night, too, was rapidly coming on. I could still see the three-master, because its pyramids of sails stood out against the purple horizon of the setting sun; but it was evident that they could no longer see us, or that, if they did see us, we must have looked like a gull hidden among the waves. Those who have ever found themselves in a frail boat over a watery abyss, with a moving wall to right and left, immensity of sea before and behind and a stormy sky over their heads, alone know what the wind has told them, as it drives through their hair soaked with foam. In half an hour's time the pilot was compelled to lower his sail. He took to the oars, but they did not grip the waves properly. Here and there we saw high white waves fling their broken crests up into the air, which the wind carried to us in fine, ice-cold rain. These were the places where the waves broke against the rocks. Luckily the flow was carrying us landwards; but at the same time that the flowing tide served us, the wind blew us past the mouth of the Loire and drove us along the coast of Croisic. I myself had no notion where we were. Night came on faster and faster, and the circle of darkness contracted more and more, until we only had about twenty paces of horizon.

I made up my mind to hold on tight to the bottom of the boat, and to trouble about nothing else except preventing myself being pitched into the sea; but, seated at the bottom as I was, I was half soaked in the water we had shipped when we were sailing. Two hours went by in this fashion, and I must say they seemed the longest hours I ever lived. Once, when I rose to look about me, I saw the pilot make a quick movement, and next instant the barque bounded up as though it were gone crazy; we passed under a sort of cataract which came from the dark crest of a rock. I thought all was over that time; the water ran down the collar of my shirt and streamed right through to my gaiters. I shut my eyes and waited; at the end of five minutes, as I still felt I was in the boat, I opened them again. We were neither better nor worse off than before, and nothing had changed except that we could now hear the noise of the surf against the shore; we were evidently not farther off than the length of a couple of cables. The pilot held on to the helm and, driven by the flowing tide, left all the work to the sea; his sole task (and no easy one it seemed to me) being to steer us through the rocks. Suddenly he got up and shouted to me—

"Hold on tight!"

The advice was more than useless; I was holding on to the seat tightly enough to have left my finger-prints on it. I felt a violent shock, as if the bottom of the boat had raked a bed of shingle. The pilot passed rapidly across me and jumped into the sea. I did not in the least understand this evolution, but, on getting up, I caught sight of him standing up to his chest in the water, dragging the boat towards him by a rope. Fifteen paces from us was the cliff. I had a great mind to jump down beside my man, but he realised my intention and sang out—

"No, no; stay still!... We are just in."

Indeed, the first wave pushed the boat so near to the strand that it ran aground.

"Now," said the pilot, coming towards me, "get on to my back."

"What for?"

"To prevent your getting wet."

The precaution was good, but came a little too late in the day seeing I was already soaked through like a sponge.

"Thanks for your thoughtfulness," I said, "but you need not take the trouble." And I leapt into the sea.

At that moment came a wave which went right over my head.

"Capital!" I said, "now my bath is complete!... Oh! what a confounded idiot I am to take such trips as this when there is no occasion to do so at all! Oh!..."

The last exclamation was wrung from me by the satisfaction I felt at being once more on *terra firma*.

We had landed in the little creek that lies between Saint-Nazaire and le Croisic, a league and a half nearly from either of these two towns. So I had my choice. But le Croisic was a league and a half out of my way, while Saint-Nazaire, on the other hand, was just so much nearer. There was no need for hesitation, and I decided immediately upon Saint-Nazaire. As to the pilot, he remained with his skiff. The wind was whistling as harshly as upon the Elsinore stage just when the ghost of the King of Denmark is to appear. I had only one way of warming myself, which was to keep moving as hard as I could. I held out five francs to the pilot, instead of three as I had promised him, and with bare head, my hands tucked into my pockets, with not a rag on me dry, soaked with that delightful sea-water which never does dry, I set off at a quick trot to follow the coast-line. I reached Saint-Nazaire an hour later, and knocked at the door of the only inn of the place, which made all kinds of difficulties in the way of opening its doors and receiving, at eleven o'clock at night, a man without a hat. The dialogue that took place with a view to my gaining an entrance being prolonged endlessly, and not promising to end to my satisfaction, I conceived the idea of throwing a five-franc piece through the window on the first storey, out of which the landlord was leaning to talk to me. The host would then be certain of payment for my bed. The coin rang on the wooden floor of the room, and the innkeeper picked it up, lit a lamp, and, making sure that my money was good metal, decided to let me in. Ten minutes later I stood quite naked in front of an immense fire of heather, which roasted me without warming me thoroughly; but I was so delighted to feel the earth under my feet that I forgot all about the extreme cold I had suffered, and paid no attention to the other extreme of heat. The host had now grown as amiable as at first he had been crusty. He offered me a shirt of his own, which I accepted; warmed my bed himself, and carried my clothes away to be baked in the oven. He had been baking bread and flat cakes that day, and the oven was still warm. My cast-off garments were put in it on an iron oven-plate, and, thanks to this idea, I found my clothes were as dry next day as tinder. At eleven o'clock I was back at Paimbœuf, by night I was at Nantes, and the next day I reached Tours, where I duly delivered to Madame M——— her daughter's messages.

The same day, I found a disengaged place in the mail coach and engaged it. I was sick of the Carlist language that I had heard for six weeks and wanted to see my July sunshine once more and my revolutionary Paris and my buildings all riddled with shot. When I arrived, it was pouring in torrents; M. Guizot had become Prime Minister and they were scraping the front of the Institut!

———————————

BOOK V

CHAPTER I

Confidential letter from Louis-Philippe to the Emperor Nicholas—The Czar's reply—What France could do after the Revolution of July—Louis-Philippe and Ferdinand VII.—The Spanish refugees—Reaction in the Home department—Scraping of the public monuments—Protest

The last sentence in my previous chapter virtually shows how far the reaction in Paris had progressed at the moment I returned there after my absence of six weeks or two months.

The conversation between the lieutenant-general and the Republicans on the night of 3 July will be recollected, and how Louis-Philippe had then revealed his system of *juste milieu*, a system which had been so repugnant to our young men that Cavaignac had exclaimed—

"Oh! if that is how things are going to be, Monsieur, we need have no anxiety, for you will not hold out for four years!"

Cavaignac was not mistaken in his prophecy, although he was wrong as to the date—merely a chronological error, after all. Moreover, a letter, made public by the very man to whom it had been addressed, a prince, whose aristocratic and hereditary pride took pleasure in humbling a king sprung from a Revolution, had published, far more clearly than the light words of a conversation, the programme of the new reign. Copies of this letter actually sent from St. Petersburg were in circulation: it was from the King of France to *Monsieur, his brother*, the Emperor of All the Russias. M. Athalin had brought it by special courier; but it was to be delivered separately from the official letter which announced the lieutenant-general's accession to the throne: this was the letter intended only to be read by the Emperor of Russia, but was naturally the only one of the two that was read by the whole world.

It seemed inexplicable to men who for the last fifteen years had followed the policy adopted by the Duc d'Orléans towards the Elder Branch; to those who were acquainted with his conduct towards Charles X. and the young Duke of Bordeaux, during the days which preceded his nomination to the lieutenant-generalship, and those which followed; also to those who knew the part the Palais-Royal had played in that great *mise-en-scène* of the expedition to Rambouillet, which had ended not exactly in the flight (Charles X. maintained his dignity safe and sound as far as Cherbourg), but in the departure, of the Royal Family. The staunchest of King Louis-Philippe's friends denied that the letter was written by him; they said it was apocryphal altogether.

As I ought to explain the charges I have brought against the Government of King Louis-Philippe, in my capacity both as an ordinary citizen and also as a man of letters, for the benefit of friends past and present, who were surprised at it, I may perhaps be permitted to continue to enumerate my reasons for my political repugnance, which led to my sending in my resignation to the king at a time when my interest—if self-interest had been allowed to triumph over my conscientious scruples—should have rather incited me to make up to the princely fortunes when they advanced to the estate of kingship.

I have mentioned the impression made on me by the letter from the Duc d'Orléans to King Charles X., that had been carried by M. de Mortemart; I have told how the handshaking, the singings of the *Marseillaise* and the forehead bathed in perspiration, had driven me out of the Palais-Royal at the very moment when the young Duc de Chartres was making his entry into it; I have also described the shame that had glued me motionless before the placard wherein the Duc d'Orléans laid claim to being a Valois, ignoring the most elementary historical facts, and, renouncing Saint-Louis for an ancestor, claimed François I. as head of his House—of all our kings the most debauched, impolitic and faithless to his word. Furthermore, the three sons of the king, the Duc d'Orléans, the Duc d'Aumale and the Duc de Montpensier, well knew that my defection was honourable and disinterested, that I never boasted, by calling them my friends, although they more than once did me the honour to call themselves mine. It will be seen when I shall have occasion to speak of them (and it will happen frequently in the course of these Memoirs) how faithful I am to them in their misfortunes, and that the memories which flow from my heart and pen, as we follow the exiles in their retirement, are reverently given.

But to return to the king's letter to the Emperor Nicholas. It may sound absurd to say it, but it was a real grief to me, just as the czar's reply caused me feelings of shame. I think that if a country is to be truly great and generous and strong, each individual citizen belonging to it ought to be in a measure a nerve in the general organisation, and feel individually any impulses given to it as a nation, or to its glory or honour.

Here is the letter. Long though it be, we will follow it with the reply, our only commentary being to italicise certain passages.

> "MONSIEUR MON FRÈRE,—I have to announce to your Majesty my accession to the throne, by a letter that General Athalin will present you, in my name; but I wish to speak to you with complete confidence in regard to the sequel to the *catastrophe that I would so gladly have averted.*
>
> "For some long time past I have had to deplore that King Charles X. and his Government did not follow a policy

better calculated to fulfil the expectations and the wishes of the nation; I could not in the least foresee the momentous issues that have come to pass, and I even thought that, but for want of being able to obtain a frank and loyal spirit in the tone of the Charter and of our institutions, it would only have needed a little more prudence and moderation to enable the Government to have gone on as it was for a long time to come; but, since 8 August 1829, the composition of the new Ministry had alarmed me greatly. I could see how far its attitude was disliked and suspected by the nation, and I shared in the general feelings of disquiet as to what measures we might expect from it. Nevertheless, fidelity to law and love of order have made such progress in France, that resistance to the Government would certainly not have expressed itself in such extreme forms, had not the Government itself, in its madness, given the fatal signal by its audacious violation of the Charter, and *by its abolition of all the guarantees of our national liberty*, in defence of which there is scarcely one single Frenchman who would not be willing to shed his blood. No excesses have followed that terrible struggle.

"But it was difficult to prevent some shaking in our social condition, and that very exaltation of spirit which deterred the people from excessive disorder carried them at the same time towards experiments in political theories which might have precipitated France and, perhaps, even Europe into terrible calamities; it was under this state of things, sire, that all eyes turned on me: *the very vanquished party itself felt me to be necessary to its salvation*; I was the more necessary, probably, in order to prevent the conquerors from taking immoderate advantage of their victory; I have, therefore, accepted this noble and painful task, and I have waived aside all personal considerations which arose, urging me to refuse the crown, because I felt that the least hesitation on my part might compromise the future of France and the peace of all our neighbours. The title of Lieutenant-General, which left everything unsettled, excited dangerous mistrust, and it was imperative to hasten to get rid of the provisional state, as much to inspire necessary confidence as to save the Charter. It was essential to preserve this, the importance of which our august brother the late Emperor realised thoroughly; and it would have been sorely compromised if people's minds had not been promptly satisfied and reassured.

"It will not escape your Majesty's perspicacity and great wisdom, that, in order to attain this salutary end, it is most desirable that affairs in Paris should be seen in their true light, and that Europe, doing justice to the motives that have guided my actions, should uphold my Government with that confidence to which it has the right to look forward. May your Majesty not lose sight of the fact that, so long as King Charles X. reigned over France, *I was one of the most submissive* and faithful of his subjects, and that it was only when I saw the action of the laws paralysed, and the exercise of royal authority totally annihilated, that I felt it my duty to defer to the national vote by accepting the crown which was offered me. It is to you, sire, that France is looking: she loves to think of Russia as her most natural and powerful ally; the guarantee of such an alliance lies in the noble character and the many qualifications for which your Imperial Majesty is noted.

"I beg you to accept the assurance of my great esteem and of the unalterable friendship with which I remain your Imperial Majesty's affectionate brother, LOUIS-PHILIPPE"

A letter so full of tender protestations, so humble and obsequious as this, deserved, indeed, a polite reply.

Here is that sent by His Majesty of All the Russias:—

"I have received from the hands of General Athalin the letter of which he was the bearer. Events, ever to be deplored, have placed your Majesty in a position of cruel alternative; and you have adopted a determination which seemed to you the only means left of saving France from the greatest calamities. I will not pronounce judgment upon the considerations that have directed your Majesty; but I will pray to Providence to bless your intentions and the efforts you are about to make for the welfare of the French people. In concert with my Allies I accept with pleasure your Majesty's expressed desire that peace and friendship should be maintained between you and all the European states; *so long as these relations are based upon existing treaties, and with a firm resolution to respect the rights and obligations and the conditions of territorial possession which those treaties have ratified,* Europe will find in them a guarantee of peace very necessary to the tranquillity of France herself. Called upon in conjunction with my Allies to cultivate these conservative relations with France under her present Government, I, on my part, will give them all the careful consideration they demand, *and am pleased to offer your Majesty the assurance of my good disposition, in return for the sentiments you have expressed towards me.*

"I beg you at the same time to accept the expression of my kind feelings towards you.

NICHOLAS"

That was all Louis-Philippe got in return for his fraternal outpourings! Nicholas might just tolerate his position if he respected the treaties of 1815, and he offered him his *dispositions* in exchange for the sentiments he had put forth in his letter. Now here was exactly where his new situation proved embarrassing. We have spoken of the July Revolution as being the last flash of Waterloo; and, indeed, as soon as the Revolution was an accomplished fact, every generous-hearted mind in France turned its thoughts towards Belgium and Italy and Poland. Belgium, in those days, was still, it will be remembered, a part of Holland, as annexed territory. Italy was then, as it is still, groaning under the tyranny of Austria. Poland was divided up between Prussia, Russia and Austria, and had not even the consolation left it of gathering its scattered members together in the same shroud.

Now, kind-hearted people were asking for a remodelling of Europe: they wanted to give to the flocks which are called nations pastors chosen by themselves; they refused to recognise those butchers, with whom the heartless diplomatists, who sat at the green-covered table at the Vienna Congress, had divided a hundred million bodies and souls, almost at haphazard. But this was just what Louis-Philippe did not want. He represented the bourgeoisie, which was made up of lawyers, men of business, bankers, money-brokers and financiers; and the bourgeoisie has its own god all to itself, which has no sympathies in common with the god worshipped by great minds and noble hearts.

The situation was so lofty that the blinking eyes of that bourgeoisie lowered, utterly dazzled, before they could raise themselves to such a height. For, indeed, after the Revolution of 1830 France could fling at kings the defiance of an unbounded ambition; it could not only act on its own individual strength, but also, by allying other peoples with it, it could increase its power and neutralise that of kings. What was necessary for this? It is enough to look at the general condition of the European monarchies; at Russia, with its vulture of the Caucasus and its gangrene in Constantinople; to Austria, with its twofold cancer of Italy and Hungary; to Holland, with its hostile Belgium; to England, with its unsubdued Scotland and its starving Ireland, to see that if we did but raise our voices a little louder we should not merely be masters at home, but could extend our supremacy over the whole of Europe. At one time, it seemed as though France was going to adopt this wide and splendid policy towards Spain. It is true, though, that the motive which moved Louis-Philippe in his action with regard to Spain was an entirely personal feeling. As stupid, almost as despicable as his grandfather, Ferdinand of Naples, who would not recognise the French Republic in his day, Ferdinand of Spain did not wish to recognise the Revolution of July, or, at any rate, he wished to ignore the prince who had just inherited the throne after that Revolution, in almost as mysterious a fashion as he himself had succeeded the last of the Condés. So, on the first impulse of anger, King Louis-Philippe received a deputation of three of the members of the Spanish Committee, MM. Loëve-Weimars, Marchais and Dupont, introduced by M. Odilon Barrot; he treated his brother Ferdinand in scurvy fashion and all but offered a rope with which he hoped to see him hanged.[1] He went even farther, and placed a hundred thousand francs at the disposal of La Fayette to support the enterprises of the Spanish Revolutionists. From this side, at all events, they believed themselves safe from political reaction. M. Girod (of l'Ain), Prefect of Police, openly distributed passports to the Spanish refugees who were on their way to the Pyrenees; the *impériales* of every public conveyance were reserved for these exiles, who returned to their homes in the face of all the world; and, all along the road, besides these specially privileged travellers, bands of fifty, a hundred and a hundred and fifty men were to be met with, with beating drums and flying banners, marching towards Bidassoa. Finally, M. Guizot (a native of Ghent), in other words a Reactionary, declared quite openly that "when, in 1823, France won back Spain to its Absolutist ideas, she committed a political crime; she therefore owes Spain reparation. Such reparation should be given, signal and complete!" M. Guizot said these words to M. Louis Viardot and asked him to publish them broadcast.

It will be seen that we do not grope in the dark—that we are not making accusations recklessly: we quote not only the words that were said, not only the men who said them, but also the men to whom they were said.

Thereupon all those victims of Ferdinand VII., such as Mendizabal, Isturitz, Calatrava, the Duke of Rivas, Martinez de la Rosa, the Count of Toreno, General Mina, Colonel Moreno, Colonel Valdès, General Torrijos, General Chapalangara, General Lopès Baños and General Butron all raised their hands to Heaven and cried *Hosannah!*

Arms were sent so publicly by MM. Guizot and de Montalivet, that the Spanish Ambassador, M. d'Ofalia, took note of the fact diplomatically.

Now, we have remarked that Ferdinand VII. of Spain was as stupid and almost as cowardly as his grandfather Ferdinand IV. of Naples; we should really have said that he was more cowardly, for at the mere sound of arms in France, at the mere cries of liberty which were echoed in the South, at the mere roll of drums approaching the frontier, he made the *amende honorable* and received Louis-Philippe with every expression of regret at having held back so long. And, although the new king had, as we have said, almost offered the rope wherewith to hang him, he really preferred the sinner's repentance to his death. Without saying anything to them, he withdrew the hand he had held out to the Spanish refugees and, left to themselves, or, rather, delivered over to the vengeance of Ferdinand, they were killed, some on the battlefield, and others, sad and painful and shameful as it is to tell, were chased as far as the frontier and taken and shot down on French territory!

Oh! sire, sire, was it not the shades of these martyrs which appeared to you on 24 February, frightening you into the inert and fugitive king who fell down on the place de la Révolution, at the foot of the Obélisque, on the very spot where the head of King Louis XVI. had fallen?

And Italy, stirred up by promises given her by La Fayette, promises which the old general thought he could keep; Italy, who, in order to carry out her revolution, only asked for an Army Corps to be stationed on the Alps, looked in vain towards the West; for the route taken by Hannibal and Charlemagne and Napoleon remained unoccupied.

As for Poland—we know M. Sébastiani's famous saying: "Order reigns at Warsaw!"

In domestic legislation, reaction was just as obvious. First, they had chosen M. Talleyrand as Ambassador to London, that political Mephistopheles, who had watched the Republic, the Directory, the Empire and the Restoration perish in his hands beneath his skeleton smile. The abolition of the penalty of death had miscarried in the Chamber. Lastly, orders had been given to efface the bullet marks of July from the front of all public buildings. Certainly, this latter Ordinance did not pass without raising opposition. Upon my return to Paris the walls were still pasted with a protest, which I may be permitted to quote, as the tone of the times is clearly shown in the few lines of which it is composed; and, further, because the chief merit of these Memoirs should be the preserving intact and reproduction of the character of the times in which I lived, for the benefit of the future, which is always inclined to become hazy. This is it:—

"REVERENCE FOR MONUMENTS

"Each glorious epoch of our history has its own special trophies and monuments: the hero has his bronze statue and his Arcs de Triomphe; but what living witness will there be to teach the races to come the doings of that cycle of the Three Days and its immortal people? What pages of history will tell future ages at what a cost the monarchical system of a thousand years, ancient in despotism, was destroyed? What monument will teach our posterity that there, behind these mutilated columns, their fathers fell in defence of liberty? Is our Charter, patched up in a day, a fitting monument to the sovereignty of the people? We have nothing to show but our tombs and the traces of the bullets on our walls and the marks made by grapeshot which adorn the pediments of our palaces. Those are our bas-reliefs and inscriptions, our celebrations of that great week; in them the People read their triumph and the King sees there the lessons he ought to learn. On those blackened walls, the temples of Science and of Art, the bullets of Charles X. have written, in ineffaceable characters, the love and gratitude and impartiality we might have looked for in a Bourbon! There, if the imprint had been religiously preserved, we might, perhaps, have discovered the traces of the balls of yet another Charles! What Vandal hand, then, has dared to attack these noble reliques? Some sacrilegious order, given by I know not what authority, would efface those sublime breaches! If they disappear, it will soon be forgotten that thousands of victims fell for a principle, and that their blood flowed for an ephemeral liberty which only shone upon us for three days! Are they friends? Can they be brothers who dare thus to insult our deeds? The Austrians, Russians and Prussians paid respect to our Column, our Arcs de Triomphe, and shall the shameful insignias of the conqueror of the Trocadéro still soil the Arc-de-Triomphe of the conqueror of Austerlitz?

"*Courage, men of the morrow! Courage! Continue your heroic work!* Tear down those wooden crosses, those tricolour flags that adorn the tombs of our brothers, and then you will have succeeded in effacing every last trace of our Revolution!

"*(Signed)*

LANNOY, student of the École polytechnique;
PLOCQUE, advocate;
TH. MASSOT, advocate;
GUYOT, medical student;
ÉTIENNE ARAGO;
CH. LOTHON, student of the École polytechnique."

You see these poor July fighters did not make any great demands; they, who had seen the Republic snatched from them, who had been enclosed in the treaties of 1815, to whom a king had been given, the son of a regicide, who had renounced the Convention, only asked that the bullet marks of the Swiss and Royal Guards imprinted on the façades of their public monuments should be allowed to remain intact. Their demand, as in reason bound, was judged exorbitant and refused accordingly. Thus, just as I said before, when I returned to Paris, M. Guizot was Minister, and they were scraping the Institut.

[1] Here are King Louis-Philippe's very own words:— "As for Ferdinand VII., they can hang him if they wish: he is the biggest blackguard that ever lived!"

CHAPTER II

The drama of Saint-Leu—The bravery of the Duc d'Aumale—The arrest of MM. Peyronnet, Chantelauze, Guernon-Ranville and Polignac—Madame de Saint-Fargeau's servant—Thomas and M. de Polignac—The ex-ministers at Vincennes—The abolition of the death penalty in the Chamber—La Fayette—M. de Kératry—Salverte—Death to the ministers—Vive Odilon Barrot and Pétion!

But, before returning to these patchings up of damaged walls (which played an important part, as we shall see, in due season), let us finish with the dark tragedy of Saint-Leu, and with the last of the Condés, who was found one morning hanging, like an old rusty sword, from the catch of a window. I say *let us finish with the dark tragedy of Saint-Leu*, because, in the preceding chapter, I believe I alluded to the *mysterious* death of the Prince of Condé. Now that death was certainly very mysterious; but my reader must not interpret this epithet in any other sense than the one I give to it. One of my most intimate friends (the same who, on the morning of 17 August 1847, on coming out of the sleeping-chamber of Madame la Duchesse de Praslin, had breakfasted with me, after washing his hands a second time from the bloodstains of that unfortunate woman, and who that morning had said to me, "I swear to you that the Duc de Praslin killed his wife!")—this friend, the celebrated Surgeon Pasquier, as skilled as Dupuytren and as honest as Larrey, repeated many times to me the following sentence:—

"I took the body of the Prince of Condé down from the window; well, on my soul and conscience, I declare he hanged himself there!"

I questioned him the more insistently upon this subject, because I had known the poor prince at Villers-Cotterets, I had dined at the same table with him at M. Deviolaine's, and he had been kind to me, when I was quite a boy, and a stranger and totally unknown to him. Well, upon my word of honour, I, too, in my turn, believe implicitly what Pasquier told me many times; which he repeated again exactly in the same terms when, less than a couple of years ago, we both crossed the Channel together to pay our last respects to the dead king at Claremont (a respectful duty, which, from some unknown family susceptibility or other, I regret I was unable to pay personally). I believe that, if the king had not also died before his time, as many of my friends have died, as the one to whom these Memoirs are dedicated has died, I would invoke his testimony, which would be devoid of all affection towards that Royal Family of which he often had reason to complain to others, including myself; his testimony, I say, would not fail me. And I believe it is right to say and write and print this, and to swear to it by the dead man, as I should have done were he alive, when the rumour reached me in the retreat I had voluntarily chosen in a foreign land, that they were going to raise a doubt as to the question of its being suicide. However, it matters little. Had Madame de Feuchères been accused and convicted of the crime of which science and the law have declared her innocent; had Madame de Feuchères confessed this crime; had Madame de Feuchères been condemned to expiate it on the scaffold; had Madame de Feuchères, in a last confession, accused of moral or material complicity those whom vile hatred has tried to stain with this complicity; had Madame de Feuchères uttered this monstrous lie; had she published this dastardly slander; even then, for all noble minds, for all honest hearts, no shadow of suspicion could ever have attached to those whom she tried to reach—cursed be the parties which make use of such weapons for attacking their enemies! As in the case of the dauphin, when he tried to snatch the sword from the Duc de Raguse, they only wound and stain their own hands with blood! The author who writes history is bound to tell the truth, and I believe I have ever done so: it is cowardly for such as wield the pen, and write for the public, not to contradict calumnious statements. I therefore emphatically deny this one. It would certainly have been finer and nobler of the Duc d'Orléans, who was already rich in his own rights as a prince, and also drawing wealth, as king, from the civil list; it would have been a grand act, I repeat, if the duke had renounced the fatal succession, and handed over the vast legacy to a benevolent institution, a foundation in the cause of art, in aid of a national misfortune at that time or in the future. But those who have read these Memoirs know how miserly the king was, and if they may have blamed me for publishing the fact, they will understand what I now wish people to infer. Well, then, the prince's character being realised and his temperament admitted, we declare that it would have been altogether beyond the power of the man who could cover six pages with figures to discover a bonus of sixty-six centimes, to renounce a legacy of sixty-six millions at the moment when that long-wished-for and expected inheritance came, as it were, of its own accord into his hands.

But now let us pass quickly from this subject, as we said at the beginning of this chapter it was our intention to do, and let us be particularly careful not to fix the responsibility for this fortune, which was left him, on the young and noble hero of La Smala.

Alas! so many calumnies, so much indifference and forgetfulness follow exiles that it is, indeed, necessary that some voices should, from time to time, recall to the country that produced them the names of those beloved sons who were worthy of her love!

An officer who had received his first epaulettes from the Duc d'Aumale once replied to me, when I was praising the bravery of the poor exiled duke in his presence—

"Brave? Why, he was no braver than anybody else!"

No braver than anybody else! As to this, I heard Yousouf, whose own courage I hope nobody will dare to dispute, tell what I am sure he will be ready to repeat:—

"When we found ourselves with only our two hundred and fifty men face to face with the forty thousand souls that composed La Smala, I asked the prince, 'Monseigneur, what are we to do?' He replied, 'Go in, by Jove!' When he said it I thought I must have misunderstood him, so I repeated my question, and when he again said, 'Go in, I tell you!' *I began to shudder.* I took up my sword, of course, because I was a soldier, but I said to myself, 'Then that will be the last of us, for we shall all be lost!'"

No braver than anybody else! though Charras (whom nobody ever accused of Orléanist leanings or of knowing fear, being one of those rare natures who love danger for its own sake, *un soldat de nuit*, as connoisseurs term them)— Charras himself said to me, in speaking of that same taking of La Smala—

"To go as the Duc d'Aumale did, with two hundred and fifty men, into the midst of such a population as that, one *must either be but twenty-two years of age with no knowledge of the meaning of danger, or else have the very devil inside one! The women had only to stretch the tent ropes in front of the horses, in order to throw them down, and to throw their slippers at the soldiers' heads, to exterminate them all, from the first to the last!*"

No, indeed! the Due d'Aumale's courage was of a different order from the rest of the world's: he was braver even than the bravest of men.

In due course I will relate what he himself told me about it at this period, the first time I saw him after his return.

Now let us return to the re-plastering of the walls, from which we have been turned aside by this digression on the death of the Prince de Condé and the bravery of the Duc d'Aumale; I write, I repeat, as I feel, and, above all, from conviction; and I proclaim with an equally impartial voice the avarice and scheming of the father and the courage and loyalty of his children. Moreover, the discussion which arose as to whether the walls of Paris should remain in their mutilated condition or not; whether they should bear the immutable impression of the dates of 27, 28 and 29 July; or whether those dates should be effaced from the stones as it was hoped they would be effaced from people's hearts; this discussion, we say, had a far more significant meaning than the scrapers of houses and restorers of buildings were ready to acknowledge. It was really a question of the saving of the heads of the ex-king's ministers, which were violently imperilled by this public prosecution. Four of them had been arrested: these were, in the order of their arrest, MM. de Peyronnet, de Guernon-Ranville, de Chantelauze and de Polignac.

Let us give a few details concerning these different arrests; the papers of their day duly register the facts and they are talked of, discussed at the time and then gradually forgotten; only the cruel, stupid fact remains; then history steps in, which limits itself to stating the mere fact, robbed of all its details and of its picturesque side.

What does it matter to history?—does it not represent the 1 bare bones of events and nothing more?...

Well, we much prefer a living being to a mummy, and a mummy to a skeleton. Consequently, we will always try to write living history, and it shall not be our fault if it appears in the dryasdust form of mummy or skeleton.

M. de Peyronnet was the first to be arrested at Tours. On Monday, 6 August, at two o'clock in the afternoon, a post-chaise, passing through that town, having awakened suspicions, was surrounded by the National Guard. There was but a single person in the chaise, who affected to speak no language but German. He first of all represented himself to be a courier from the House of Rothschild and refused to answer the questions put to him, pretending he did not understand them; but, when his postillions were questioned, they declared that a second traveller had got out of the carriage a kilometre's distance before they reached the first houses probably with the intention of going round outside the town. Two of the National Guardsmen were at once sent off in the direction of the Bordeaux road and they soon caught sight of a man walking with long strides over the rising ground by Grammont. A gamekeeper, who had just passed the man, was signalled to by the Guardsmen and accordingly arrested him. Ordered to say who he was, the stranger showed a passport giving the name of Cambon; but they searched him and the letter P embroidered on his handkerchief and snuff-box awoke doubts on the subject of his identity. Two other persons coming up, one of whom gazed attentively at the stranger, declared that he recognised him to be M. de Peyronnet. The ex-minister was unlucky: the new arrival, who had recognised him, happened to be an ex-magistrate whom he had deprived of his post. The other, without knowing him personally, had had dealings with him connected with a young man of Tours, called Sir jean, who had been sentenced for a political offence; he had asked M. de Peyronnet to pardon the young man, or, at all events, to lessen his punishment, and he only received a brutal refusal in return. So both these people had a particular hatred towards M. de Peyronnet, and, seizing him by his coat collar, they took him into the town. Taken to the prison at Tours, without the insults and ill-treatment he had been subjected to in the least affecting the calm expression of his countenance, M. de Peyronnet had been put into the cells.

Another arrest was made at Tours that same day: that of MM. de Chantelauze and Guernon-Ranville. The day previously, they had presented themselves at the top of the embankment of Barthélemy; but, learning that carriages and travellers were being searched, they withdrew. The following morning, peasants came across two men in the country who seemed to have lost their bearings, and arrested them, taking them to a little village called la Membrole and handing them over to the police, who took both of them bound to Tours. It was not until after some time of hunting that they found the Prince de Polignac; it was believed he must have crossed the frontier, when it was discovered, from a telegraphic despatch on 18 August, that he had just been arrested at Granville. This was how the arrest was made. He was travelling with the Marquise de Saint-Fargeau, passing for her servant, and was clad in livery. When they reached the neighbourhood of Granville, he put himself under the protection of a gentleman named M. Bourblanc d'Apreville, who hid him in a seaport inn. In spite of his disguise, perhaps even because of it, suspicions were aroused and were increased by the fact of his landing in the night. When he was the least expecting to be recognised, two of the National Guards suddenly entered his room. The prince turned away when he saw them and hid his face in his hands.

"Have you your papers?" they asked.

"By what authority do you put such a question to me?" the prince responded.

"Have you your papers?" the men asked a second time and more imperatively.

"No."

"Well, in that case, you must come with us to prison."

At that moment, Madame de Saint-Fargeau, who had been warned of what was happening, entered the room, laid claim to her servant and protested against the rude treatment to which they were subjecting him. But M. de Polignac was arrested in spite of the marquise's protests, bound and taken to prison in the town. Next day, he confessed to the mayor that he was the Prince de Polignac. He was taken under an escort of the National Guard that same day away from Granville. His journey through Coutances and his arrival at Saint-Lo were very nearly fatal to him: the population threatened to tear him in pieces; and, for a brief period, it seemed as though the efforts of his guards, who tried to defend him, would prove useless; arms were stretched over the guard of soldiers and policemen, endeavouring to hook him out from their ranks; one man even managed to get a pistol put to his throat and would probably have fired if, by good fortune, someone had not held up his arm. The prince was very pale, but whether from fatigue or terror could not be told. From Saint-Lô, M. de Polignac had written to the Minister of the Intérieur to protest against his arrest and to plead his rank as a peer of France, which allowed him the privilege of not being arrested except by an order from the Chamber of Peers itself.

By a strange chance, I happened to be able to give details of M. de Polignac's journey that no one else received, and probably I, and the principal actors, are the only persons now who recollect them.

The prince was placed in the care of Thomas. When I say Thomas, my readers will know quite well to whom I refer. He was that brave and loyal friend of Bastide who, like Bastide, risked his life and sacrificed his fortune for the cause of liberty. He had promised to take the prince safe and sound to Paris, at the price of his own life if need be. From that moment, the prince could rest easy, for he knew he would either reach his destination safely with his conductor or neither of them would do so. The carriage which took the ex-minister of France to Paris started in the dark. But, although Thomas had undertaken to conduct M. de Polignac safe and sound to Paris, he had no intention whatever of letting him escape on the way thither. And this was the dialogue that took place between prisoner and conductor. Thomas, with that astonishing *sang-froid* which never deserted him, whether he was threatener or threatened, drew forth a dagger and pistol from his pocket and showed them to the prince.

"You see, monsieur, I have taken my precautions: if you were to try to escape, I should kill you, it's my duty. But, as I do not desire to restrict your liberty at all during our journey, nor to humiliate an unfortunate man like yourself, whom I respect, give me your word of honour that you will make no kind of attempt to escape and you shall be as free as I am."

"I give it you, monsieur," replied the prince, who believed he was safer in Thomas's hands than fleeing alone across country.

From that moment, the prince could get down from the carriage when he liked, walk up the hills on foot, and wander about at his own pleasure. The conversation, of course, was likely to turn upon one topic only, namely, the events that had just transpired, in which these two actors had each played his own part—one in the high quarters of the palace, the other in the streets. Replying to Thomas's conscientious and somewhat severe reflections upon what he looked upon as the *crime* of the Ordinances, which had led to the fall of Charles X. and the arrest of the prince, M. de Polignac replied, with a sigh—

"Oh, my poor Thomas, who would ever have thought things would have come to such a pass and ended in such a wreck as this?"

And once, the prince, who knew his Corneille, followed this melancholy expression with these lines:—

"Chimène, qui l'eût dit?
Rodrigue, qui l'eût cru?"

The prince sighed at the thought of the lot that awaited him, but resignedly: he wore more the expression of a Christian martyr than of a vanquished general. He interrogated Thomas as to the probable issue of the great trial that would ensue.

"Good Heavens!" replied Thomas, "the whole matter depends on the type of jury that is summoned to judge your case. If you are tried by a jury, both you and your colleagues will be condemned to death; if you are tried before the Chamber of Peers, you will be merely sentenced to imprisonment."

"That is exactly my own opinion," M. de Polignac calmly replied.

After this coincidence of ideas, silence fell between the two travellers, during which time daylight began to lighten the darkness that had enshrouded the first portion of their journey.

Thomas was struck with the sight of the ex-minister's long, easily recognisable profile, sharply defined against the increasing light as the horses' feet rattled on the pavement of a town where the shops were being cheerily opened, and the citizens were leisurely standing in little groups in the square, eager for any fresh news that might be going about. Thomas thought their carriage was the object of some attention. He was, however, obliged to change horses at the hôtel de la poste, which was situated in the square, and, short though their halt was, it might prove quite long enough for the prince to be recognised and for the news to create a sensation throughout the town, with what result it was impossible to calculate. Thomas wore a cap with a broad peak; he threw this over the prince's aristocratic face and wrapped his comforter round his neck. Thomas called this proceeding *extinguishing* his prisoner. When the inquisitive townsfolk came and looked in at the door of the carriage and saw, by the side of Thomas's round, open, cool face, a bonneted figure shrouded in a neck-wrapper, no suspicion was aroused in their breasts, and the carriage started off with fresh horses at a tearing pace. This manœuvre was repeated at nearly every place of relay. When Thomas related these incidents, it was with a certain degree of melancholy. He did not forget that prison, and perhaps even death, awaited his travelling-companion at their journey's end, he who on more than one occasion, indeed, was to confront in a court of justice the alternative of death or imprisonment.

On 28 August, the three prisoners from Tours and the one from Saint-Lo reached Paris almost simultaneously. They were all four shut up in that portion of the château of Vincennes that was called the Queen's pavilion (pavillon de la Reine). Three of them were new men. Indeed, they were scarcely known to anybody before the fatal day of misfortune that overtook them. They had gained their notoriety, or, rather, their unpopularity, by the printing of a hundred thousand copies of Barthélemy's and Méry's verses, and by the oral skits recited against M. de Peyronnet in particular, by the celebrated Chodruc-Duclos. We shall have occasion, later, to speak of this modern Diogenes (we allude, of course, to Chodruc-Duclos and not M. de Peyronnet), who, for seven or eight years, troubled the galleries of the Palais-Royal, where, at all hours of the day, he displayed his unbuttoned coat, his hardly decent trousers, his waistcoat fastened together with string, his sandal-shoes, his battered old hat and the thick growth which covered the lower half of his face, which had earned him the nickname of *the man with the long beard*. Then, as we have said, apart from these verses of Barthélemy's and Méry's, and the Bordelaisian legends made up by Chodruc-Duclos, MM. de Chantelauze, Guernon-Ranville and de Peyronnet were almost unknown. It was very different in the case of M. de Polignac: apart from the claim of his family that they had descended from the same stock as Sidoine Apollinaire, the Polignacs are of historic celebrity.

In the first place, they were old conspirators: Cardinal Melchior de Polignac, the author of l'*Anti-Lucrèce*, had plotted against the regent at the beginning of the previous century; Prince Jules de Polignac had conspired against Napoleon in the beginning of the present one; and their women had played their part during the French Revolution: the Comtesse Diane and the Duchesse Jules, those two inseparable friends of the queen, will both be remembered; the Duchesse Jules in particular, to whom Marie-Antoinette gave a *layette* of a hundred thousand crowns and a duchy worth a million and a half.

Comte Jules de Polignac, the promoter of the Ordinances, was her second son: he was made prince in 1817 or 1818, by Pius VII., a prince of Rome, of course.

Having emigrated in 1789, he had returned to France in 1804, together with his eldest brother, Armand, on purpose to take part in the conspiracy of Cadoudal and Pichegru; he was about to be condemned, or was, I believe, even condemned, to death, but the persistent intercession of Josephine saved his life.

All these facts went to magnify the importance of the prisoner, whose trial was soon to take place. After an exile of twenty-six years, including imprisonment, ambassadorship, peer-age and ministry, he returned in 1830, under the incubus of a second fatal accusation, to the same dungeon at Vincennes where he had been incarcerated for the same cause of Monarchism in 1804. The order had been issued for the transference of the prisoners from the pavillon de la Reine to the dungeons. M. de Polignac was the first to leave it.

I have seen him several times at the house of Madame du Cayla: he was an extremely fine-looking man, with his white hair and lordly bearing, his haughty manners and a pre-eminent air of distinction. But it should be admitted that none of these qualities impressed the people very much: they are often a reason for condemning a person: in the first Revolution, a fine skin and beautiful linen were quite sufficient grounds for sending a man to execution.

There were several courts to pass through before you could get from the pavillon de la Reine to the dungeon, and these courts were crowded with soldiers of the Gardes Nationaux and from the garrison. M. de Polignac appeared bare-headed, between two grenadiers: there was some slight disorder in his dress which was not usual; when he reached the staircase, his strength, if not his courage, failed him: he reeled and kept himself from falling by leaning his hand on the end of a grenadier's gun. The bearing of M. de Peyronnet was quite different: extremely brave, he sometimes made the mistake of extending his courage to the point of insolence; he also kept his hat on and looked to left and right disdainfully as he went. A low man out of the crowd took aim at him, crying—

"Down on your knees, you who ordered the people to be fired upon!"

M. de Peyronnet shrugged his shoulders, remained with folded arms and never either hastened or slackened his pace. M. de Chantelauze looked ill and pale and downcast and seemed overcome by the gravity of the situation. M. de Guernon-Ranville showed a nervous courage and ill temper.

The three commissioners appointed to examine the ex-ministers were MM. de Bérenger, Madier de Montjau and Mauguin.

From 17 August, directly the arrest of the ministers was known, the abolition of the death penalty was proposed in the Chamber by M. Victor de Tracy and supported by La Fayette. On the 6th of the following October M. de Bérenger, charged with the report of the examination of the prisoners, asked for the adjournment of the proposition. Then La Fayette rose a second time, and, with that weighty personal bearing which men who have seen, and done, and suffered much acquire, he exclaimed—

"It is proposed to adjourn the question of the abolition of the death penalty, gentlemen; but, doubtless, those who propose to do so have never had the misfortune to see, as I myself have seen, their families, friends and the leading citizens of France dragged off to the scaffold; they have not, I say, had the misfortune of seeing unfortunate persons sacrificed under the pretext that they were *Fayettists*. I am entirely opposed to the death penalty, especially for political offences. I therefore implore the Chamber to take M. de Tracy's proposal into consideration."

M. de Kératry immediately mounted the tribune and, with that eloquence which is more remarkable for heart than head, made the following speech:—

"I attest before you all that, were it possible to assemble the parents and friends of the courageous victims of July in this building and to ask them 'Do you demand blood for blood? Decide!' the silent jury would shake their heads in token of refusal and return to their noble griefs and deserted hearths.... If I am wrong, I will appeal in spirit to the manes of the noble victims themselves; I will call upon them to reform this unworthy sentence; for I know that brave souls, who risk their lives for a sacred cause, do not shed blood except during the conflict."

These two speeches, of which I have only given the most salient points, roused such enthusiasm in the Assembly, that it was decided, there and then, to send an address to the king, to propose the suppression of the death penalty in cases laid down by the Commission. That same evening, a special sitting was held and the address was read and sent.

But it must be mentioned that the enthusiasm which had carried away the Chamber did not lay hold of the people, nor move the Republicans in the very slightest degree. Now, why did the people, usually generous, why did the Republicans, thoroughly interested in the abolition of the scaffold on which the heads of some among their number might easily fall, declare in favour of the death penalty? Because they knew very well that this Augustan clemency was artificial, that it would be proclaimed loudly as long as it might be useful to the political situation of the moment; but that they would soon return to following the old track from the place de Grève and the place de la Révolution. Because, with gloomy looks and pressed lips, they said to themselves what Eusèbe Salverte alone had had the courage to say in the Chamber:—

"A man urged by hunger and misery, by the sight of his wife and children without bread, a man who has not eaten anything for three days, attempts to steal and is taken in the act, kills in order to escape the galleys and is condemned to death and executed. Then Society cries out, 'Bravo, quite right! the man was a thief, an assassin and an infamous wretch; he deserved the scaffold: long live the scaffold!' But a statesman in cold blood orders the massacre of ten thousand of his fellow-citizens, on purpose to climb to his ambitious ends across their heaped up bodies. Such a man inspires you with pity and not with horror. You would say to him, 'You wished to have our heads chopped off, but to keep your own on your shoulders, and go into a foreign country to enjoy the riches you have amassed. Time will look after such a theft, passions will die down, public and private grievances be appeased; the history of our troubles, written on our walls by the print of bullets and grapeshot, will no longer be legible; then, public compassion will rise up against the length of your exile: it will demand your respite, and, for the third or fourth time, you will bring your country to the edge of the abyss, into which you will finally succeed in flinging it.' Why should such a distinction be made? Unless it is, because, not having had the courage to strike down your victim yourself, as the poor starved wretch did, you pay soldiers and make them the instruments of your crime!"

This is what M. Salverte had said; this is what the people and the Republicans were saying.

Now, as they are soon going to begin again to fire upon the people and the Republicans; as they are going to begin July over again with diametrically opposite results; as for eighteen years it is the conquerors of the Three Days who are going to be the conquered, it is good to draw the dividing line very distinctly and not merely to state, as they did—

"The Chamber and Royalty of July desired the abolition of the death penalty, but the people and Republicans would not agree to it."

You are mistaken, they did wish it; but, as a principle which should safeguard humanity at large, and not as a means of delivering a few privileged guilty people from justice. What they did not want was that as exceptional tribunals are created for the purpose of punishing, there should not be established, this time, exceptional tribunals for absolving. They wanted the people to be looked on as a sovereign power, and that those who had caused them to be shot down, should be dealt with in the same way as those who, later, were to fire on the king. Why, therefore, should a greater indulgence be granted to MM. Polignac, de Peyronnet, de Chantelauze and de Guernon-Ranville, who killed or wounded three thousand citizens, than to Alibaud, Meunier and Lecomte, whose plot fell through, when firing on the king, and who neither killed nor wounded a single person? It will probably be argued that the difference in punishment arose from sentence being delivered by different tribunals. But this was not so: the sentence which condemned some to prison, and others to the scaffold, came from the same jury—the Court of Peers.

The people were right, then, after seeing Maréchal Ney condemned to death, to complain loudly when they knew the ministers were going to be let off. They did not wish their heads to fall, guilty though they were; no, the people wished they should do in 1830 what they failed to do in 1793. They wanted their condemnation and that they should appeal against the sentence to the people direct. Then, as M. de Kératry said, they would have received pardon. But they were not even consulted: it was the king, who owed his crown to the Revolution, his civil list of eighteen millions of income and ten or twelve royal castles, who pardoned them, and not the people who had been shot down, assassinated and decimated.

Thus an undertone of discontent spread over the city, whilst the anger that was settling in the base of the social scale began to rise to the surface in hot bubbles.

On 18 October the walls of the Luxembourg were covered in the night with menacing placards. Two or three of those bands of men, only to be found during ill-omened seasons, came out of the catacombs, so to speak, and spread through the town singing *La Parisienne* and crying, "Death to the ministers!" Some even went further and carried a flag on which the above bloodthirsty wish was written in huge letters.

This band started from the Panthéon, crossed the Pont Neuf and went in the direction of the Palais-Royal.

The ministers held counsel together. At these rumours and cries and the uproar which filled the square, as on the day when they carried the head of the Princesse de Lamballe on a pike, the king and M. Odilon Barrot advanced to the edge of the terrace. The people never uttered a single cry of "Vive le roi!" but shouted "Vive Odilon Barrot!" at the top of their voices.

M. Odilon Barrot was greatly embarrassed by this popularity, which was thus contrasted publicly with the unpopularity shown towards the king.

But Louis-Philippe laughed.

"Oh!" said the king, "don't heed their cries, Monsieur Barrot; in 1792, I heard the fathers of these very people shout, 'Vive Pétion!' as now these men are shouting 'Vive Barrot!'"

CHAPTER III

Oudard tells me that Louis-Philippe wishes to see me—Visit to M. Deviolaine—Hutin, supernumerary horse-guardsman—My interview with the king about la Vendée and the policy of *juste milieu*—Bixio an artilleryman—He undertakes to get me enrolled in his battery—I send in my resignation to Louis-Philippe

It was in the midst of all these troubles that I had arrived; and what I have just told in the preceding chapter and the very want of method in my telling it, depict plainly enough the strange state of exasperation which people's minds had reached. I had handed my report to General La Fayette and he, no doubt, had sent it to the king; for, five or six days after my return, I received a letter from Oudard asking me to go and see him. I therefore at once presented myself at the Palais-Royal; in spite of all that the old head of my office had done to me, I had a real affection for him. My conviction was that, like M. Deviolaine, he had thought me stupid, and that, under this delusion, he had set himself to oppose my work.

"How is it," Oudard asked me, "that you have been back in Paris eight or ten days and we have not seen you sooner?"

"But, my dear Oudard," I said, "you know very well I no longer regard myself as a member of these offices."

"Allow me to reply to this, that, so long as you do not send in your resignation, we look upon you as belonging to us."

"Is that all?" I said, picking up a pen and paper. "Then it won't take long to alter it!"

"There!" said Oudard, stopping my hand, "you always find time to commit some foolish act or other.... At all events, I should be much obliged if you would do it somewhere else than in my office."

I laid down the pen and resumed the seat I had been occupying in front of the fireplace. There was a moment's silence.

"Do you not wish to see the king?"

"What for?"

"Why, if only to thank him for the pardon he granted you for your false money-coiner."

"It was not for me that he did that, it was for you."

"You are mistaken: your letter was laid before him and on it he wrote 'Granted.'"

"You shall thank him for me, dear friend: you know much better than I do how to address crowned heads."

"Bah! You were very particular as to how one should address Charles X."

"Ah! that was a different thing! he was a king of the old order with the tradition of his race.... He was a Bourbon and not a Valois."

"Chut! Don't say such things here!"

"Because they will cause shame or, perhaps, feelings of remorse?"

Oudard shrugged his shoulders.

"You are incorrigible!" he said.

Another short silence intervened.

"So," said he, "you have no desire to see the king?"

"None whatever."

"But suppose he wants to see you?"

"The king? Go along, you are joking!"

"Suppose I was commissioned to settle the hour for an audience with him!"

"You know, of course, my dear fellow, I should not have such bad taste as to refuse.... But I do not believe you have received any such commission."

"Then you are wrong again: the king expects you at eight o'clock to-morrow morning."

"Oh! my dear fellow, how disagreeable the king will find me!"

"Why?"

"Because I am a perfect bear when I am made to get up at such early hours as that."

"Will you dine to-day with me?"

"With whom beside?"

"Lamy and Appert.... Will that please you?"

"Excellently well."

"Then at six o'clock to-night."

We shook hands and separated. I took advantage of being at the Palais-Royal to pay a series of calls. I went first to see Lassagne, who was as good-natured and amusing as ever; then I saw Ernest, who had risen a peg higher; then my friend de la Ponce who, from my old habits, thought I had come to ask him to put on his coat and hat; then, lastly, on M. Deviolaine. I entered his room, as usual, unannounced. He was as short-sighted as a mole and was writing with his face close to his paper, effacing the letters that he traced with his pen with the hairs of his nostrils. At the noise I made as I approached his writing-table, he lifted his head and recognised me.

"Ah! there you are," he said, "Monsieur Bully!"

"Here I am, true enough."

"I advise you to return to Soissons!"

"Why?"

"Because you will get a warm reception there."

"Bah! have they become wicked there?"

"I wonder you weren't ashamed to cause such a scandal in your own part of the country."

"By-the-bye, I have something to ask of you."

"For yourself?"

"God forbid!"

"Then for whom?"

"For my fellow-companion on that occasion."

"Which? There were three of you."

"Hutin."

"What do you want for him?"

"I want a place as supernumerary in the Horse Guards!"

"Good! Do you think such posts are given away like that!"

"Of course!"

"What has he done to deserve such a favour?"

"Done? Why, you know he went to Soissons with me."

"A fine recommendation, indeed!"

"What will you bet that you will give me the post for him?"

"What will you bet?"

"Twenty-five louis."

"Did one ever see such a rascal as you are!"

"Let us bet...."

"Why? You may put a pistol to my head, as you did to the commandant of Soissons."

"Oh dear no! I know well enough such a method would not succeed with you."

"That is a fortunate thing for me."

"But I shall get someone to ask you for the favour whom you will not care to refuse."

"Who is that?"

"General La Fayette."

"General La Fayette! He has something better to do than to draw up petitions!"

"You are right; I will ask it direct from the king."

"From the king?"

"Yes; I shall see him to-morrow."

"Have you asked for an audience?"

"I?"

I shook my head.

"If you have not, how can you see him?"

"I shall see him because he wishes to see me."

"The king wishes to see you?"

"At least, so he has sent me word by Oudard."

"What does he want to see you about?"

"I have no idea.... To converse with me, I suppose."

"To converse with him! Good heavens, what an incredible cheek the fellow has! What shall you tell the king if you do talk to him?"

"What he is quite unaccustomed to hearing ... the truth."

"If you think you will make your way with such principles as that, you are greatly mistaken."

"My way is made ... and you know better than anybody else in the world that neither you nor he helped me to make it."

"Oh! by the gods! I feel as though I were talking to his father once more."

"We might be more unlike, you will admit."

"I thought your friend Hutin was well off."

"Ah! we are coming back to him?"

"Why not?"

"He is rich, since he is asking for a place as supernumerary."

"A runner after young ladies!"

"What the devil else should he run after? After boys?"

"A poacher!"

"I have heard you say a score of times that it was good poachers who made good keepers."

"We will see. Send him to me the first time he comes to Paris."

"I will bring him along myself."

"Nothing of the kind! You have such a way of getting round me...."

"Ah! yes, say that to *Henri III.* and *Christine*, and you will see what they will reply!"

"What are you doing now?"

"Nothing."

"Idle fellow."

"But I shall soon be at work again in all probability."

"What will you do?"

"I shall fight."

"Fight against whom?"

"Against the powers that be: there!"

"Be off with you, and the quicker the better! I never heard such a thing—Fancy coming to talk such treason to me!"

"*Au revoir*, cousin!"

"I your cousin? It is a lie; I'd rather be cousin to the devil! Féresse! Féresse!"

Féresse appeared.

"Do you see this gentleman?" M. Deviolaine said, pointing at me with his finger.

"Yes," replied the astonished Féresse.

"Well, when he presents himself at my office, you can tell him I am not at home."

"I don't care a ——— for Féresse! I shall enter without his leave!"

"You would enter without asking him?"

"Most certainly."

"Well, then, I shall fling you out of the door!"

"You?"

"Do you suppose I should hesitate to do so?"

"You?"

"Would you like a sample now?"

"Upon my word I should!"

"Ah! you dare me to it? Then look out."

M. Deviolaine got up and flew furiously at me. I threw my arms round his neck, and kissed him on both cheeks. He stopped short, and something very like a tear glistened on his eyelid.

"You can go, Féresse," he said.

Then laying his hand on my shoulder—

"What troubles me is that with such a character as yours, you will die in a garret like your father before you!... Come, Hutin shall have his post—off with you. I must get to work."

But before I left the building I had posted a letter to Hutin telling him to come to Paris as fast as he could, and telling him the news which he was not expecting. Let us say at once, that three months later Hutin was made a supernumerary, and eighteen months later he was *entered on the lists*, which in bureaucratic parlance means that he received a salary.

Next day I was at the king's palace as eight o'clock was striking. I had donned my riding uniform of the National Guards for this important occasion. Whether by chance or by premeditation, the king received me in the same chamber in which he had given me audience the day before the first representation of my *Henri III.*, when he was Duc d'Orléans. I did not find him changed either in looks or manner; he had the same affectionate smile and good-natured expression that were so difficult to resist; the smile which had won him Laffitte's fortune, Casimir Périer's health and M. Thiers' reputation.

"Good-day, Monsieur Dumas," he said to me.

I bowed.

"So you have returned from la Vendée."

"Yes, sire."

"How long were you there?"

"Six weeks, sire."

"I have been told that you made a very exhaustive study of the country, and one deserving enough to be brought under my notice ..."

"By General La Fayette, doubtless?"

"Precisely."

"I thought he had done more than that, and had himself presented my report to you, sire."

"Quite true.... But I find a lacuna in that report."

I bowed in token that I was waiting to hear more.

"You were sent by General La Fayette," the king continued, "to study the possibility of establishing a National Guard in la Vendée, and you hardly mention either the possibility or impossibility of such a thing."

"True, sire, on the ground that the study of the locality convinced me that the establishment of a National Guard in the departments of la Loire-Inférieure, Maine-et-Loire, la Vendée and Deux-Sèvres would for the time being be ruinous to the middle classes of society, which have their business to attend to as notaries, drapers, cloth-weavers, locksmiths, joiners, barristers,—trading either wholesale or retail, in a word,—but have no time for horse exercise and drilling. It would, moreover, be a dangerous measure for this reason: the citizens who wore the uniform would become *Blues* again, and those who did not wear it would be *Chouans*. That is why I have nearly abandoned the idea and laid stress on the opening out of roads, on the furthering of communication, to act, as they say in medicine, as a species of dissolvent, rather than by revulsives: let the Vendeans get away from the influence of the nobles, and their women from the influence of the priests, and no more Vendean insurrections will be possible."

"Well, Monsieur Dumas, I am of a different opinion from yours. I believe that a Vendée is no longer possible, because there are no Vendeans left. Tell me where are the Elbées, the Bonchamps, the Lescures, the Laroche-Jaquelins and the Charettes?"

"Sire, where they were in 1789.... However, la Vendée need not be feared, now, or in the immediate future; I would go further still, and say that it would never again rise by itself, but somebody might throw himself into la Vendée and cause it to rise."

"Who? Not the dauphin—he has not energy enough for that; nor the Duc de Bordeaux—he is too young; nor Charles X.—a king would be out of place at the head of a handful of rebels."

"The king knows general history too well not to be acquainted with the history of Hungary: *Moriamur pro nostro rege Maria-Theresa!*"

"The Duchesse de Berry?"

"She is much talked about."

"You are right. I have myself thought so often; but, remember carefully what I tell you, Monsieur Dumas: there will be no Vendean rising without England, and I am sure of England."

I did not urge on the king that there might be a terrible, implacable, fierce Vendean outburst, like that of '92 and '93; I did not tell him that there might, perhaps, be twenty, thirty, or forty thousand men in arms as before; nor that there would be disastrous, fatal and deadly battles, such as those of Ponts-de-Cé, Torfou and Antrain; I did not tell him that the rising of the west would be supported by a rising in the south and by a foreign invasion. I said that there was a chance, a probability and almost a certainty of fighting, and that men would be killed, that fresh hatreds would be born out of the renewed bloodshed, and that the king would be too careful of the spilling of French blood not to set himself in opposition to such proceedings as far as he had means in his power.

The king smiled.

"I tell you, Monsieur Dumas, that I have put my finger on the pulse of la Vendée.... I am a bit of a doctor, as you know."

I bowed.

"Well! there is nothing going on there, nor will there be."

"The king will allow me not to attempt to combat his opinion," I replied, laughing, "but to remain of my own way of thinking?"

"Of course! You know that my influence does not extend over people's opinions, unfortunately, or I should have tried to modify yours and those of some other friends of yours."

"Meanwhile, as the conversation has fallen on this subject, your Majesty may wish me to say what I think?"

"On the disposition of la Vendée?"

"And on the policy of the king...."

"Tell me what you think of both."

"Well, I think that a foreign war, upon the Rhine or in Italy, would be a popular one at the present moment; that the king does not care to bring about such a war, and that he is not sorry to have an excuse for not doing so."

"Ah! indeed!"

"La Vendée would offer him such an excuse."

"How so?"

"No doubt, as the king said just now, he is a doctor; when he has to answer those who talk of the Belgian, Italian or Polish nationality, he will say: 'Pardon, messieurs; before busying ourselves with the affairs of other peoples, France has first to cure herself of an internal inflammation.' When they turn their gaze in the direction of la Vendée, and hear the sound of firing and see the smoke of battle, no one will have anything to reply, the king will then only concern himself with people of his own nationality and even the most fiery propagandists will see that we have not taken upon us the responsibility of foreign bloodshed."

The king bit his lips; I had evidently hit home.

"Monsieur Dumas," he said, "politics are a melancholy profession.... Leave it to kings and governors. You are a poet; attend to your poetry."

"Pardon me. I do not follow."

"I merely mean that, being a poet, you see things as a poet." I bowed again.

"Sire," I said to him, "the ancients called their poets *Vates*."

The king signed with his hand, implying, "Monsieur Dumas, your audience is at an end; I know what I wanted to know from you and you can retire."

I understood the sign, and I did not wait to have it repeated. I went out as far as I could backwards, so as not to shock those ideas of etiquette of which the Duc d'Orléans had tried hard to give me a lesson one day when King Charles X. had come to the famous ball at the Palais-Royal.

I met Oudard on the staircase.

"Have you seen the king?" he asked me.

"I am just leaving him," I replied.

"Well?"

"Yesterday we were only half at variance."

"And now?"

"To-day it is otherwise; we are wholly so."

"Blockhead!" he muttered.

I waved him an adieu with my hand, and ran laughing down the stairs.

As I was returning home I met Bixio on the Pont des Tuileries; he was clad in a blue military coat with red epaulettes and forage cap and had a ball of red horsehair on his shako with stripes of red down his trousers.

"Hullo," I said, "what are you in?"

"In the artillery."

"Is there an artillery, then?"

"Certainly."

"Of whom does it consist?..."

"Of all our Republican friends: Grouvelle, Guinard, Cavaignac, Étienne Arago, Bastide, Thomas and myself, etc...."

"I should like to join it too."

"That will be difficult because of your position near the king."

"Mine? I have broken off with him completely!"

"Then you are free?"

"As free as air! Besides, there is another way of making myself freer still...."

"Which is?"

"To send in my resignation this very day."

"If that be the case, I will undertake to get you admitted. ... I believe they are one or two men short in the 4th Battery; you haven't any special preference, have you?"

"No."

"Besides, it is mine."

"In that case, I have a preference; have me received into the 4th Battery."

"I will mention it to-night to Cavaignac and Bastide."

"Is it agreed upon?"

"Rather, yes!"

"*Au revoir.*"

"*Au revoir.*"

I went home; took paper, pen and ink and wrote the following letter of resignation:—

> "SIRE,—My political opinions being entirely out of harmony with those your Majesty has the right to insist upon in persons who compose your Household, I beg your Majesty to accept my resignation of the post of Librarian. I have the honour to remain, yours respectfully, etc.,
>
> "ALEX. DUMAS"

I apologise for the style, which was that of the period. Then I put a short note to Bixio in the post containing this one line:—

"*Alea jacta est!*"

We shall see later how, as my letter never reached the hands of the king, I was obliged to send in my resignation a second time, which was inserted in the papers and repeated in the Preface to *Napoleon.*

CHAPTER IV

First performance of *la Mère et la Fille*—I have supper with Harel after the performance—Harel imprisons me after supper—I am sentenced to eight days' enforced work at *Napoléon*—On the ninth day the piece is read to the actors and I am set at liberty—The rehearsals—The actor Charles—His story about Nodier

On the same table upon which I had just written my letter of resignation lay a letter in a handwriting that I recognised as Harel's. I opened it in fear and trembling that he was going to speak to me again about the wretched *Napoléon* drama, which had become quite a nightmare to me. But nothing of the kind: he sent me a box for the first performance of *la Mère et la Fille* and an invitation to supper with him afterwards. I sent my ticket to Marie Nodier, keeping one place for myself. I had neglected my dear friends of the Arsenal for a long time and was very anxious to see them again. I reached the Odéon by eight o'clock.

I have previously expressed my opinion upon *la Mère et la Fille*: it is one of Mazères' best plays, and quite Empis' best. Frédéric was sublime in his artless, poignant grief, his restrained despair. The other parts were, in theatrical parlance, *bien tenus*—well sustained. Marie and Madame Nodier wept, and so did Madame de Tracy; the authors won a triumphant ovation in tears.

Lockroy, Janin and I reached Harel's house by midnight, when we congratulated him on his success. Harel received our compliments rubbing his hands together and stuffing snuff up his nostrils with never a word about the *Napoléon* play. I could not tell what had come over him, and began to think that he had given the play to another to write. This silence seemed all the stranger to me since M. Crosnier was making fabulous sums with his *Napoléon à Schoenbrünn*.

The supper was in the style of those sumptuous delightful ones that Georges was wont to give us. She made a glorious queen at such feasts, as she dispensed the finest fruits from Chevet with her beautiful, goddess-like hands. When Harel, Janin and Lockroy were present, there was the very finest flow of wit imaginable. At three in the morning we were still at table. Notwithstanding all this, there were signs in the atmosphere which savoured of some conspiracy: glances were exchanged, smiles returned and significant words bandied about. When I asked for explanations, everybody gazed in astonishment; they laughed in my face, and I felt as though I had just come from Carpentras. True enough, I had come from Quimper, which was nearly the same thing. We all rose from the table, and Georges took me into another room with the excuse that she wanted to show me something extremely beautiful. What was it she showed me? I cannot say: but, whatever it was, it was fascinating enough to keep me from returning to the salon for over a quarter of an hour. When I returned, Lockroy and Janin had disappeared and only Harel remained. It struck half-past three, and I thought it about time to retire; I picked up my hat and was preparing to depart the way I came, when Harel said—

"No, no, everybody has gone to bed.... Follow me this way."

I followed him unsuspectingly.

We went through Georges' room again, then through a dressing-room and finally passed into a room with which I was unacquainted. Two candles were burning on a table which was piled up with books and papers of all sizes and dimensions, with pens too of every description. A comfortable bed was resplendent in the gloom with its purple eiderdown in striking contrast with its white sheets and counterpane. On the bearskin rug by the bedside lay slippers all ready to put on. On one side of the fireplace was a velvet sofa, and on the other a great big tapestry-covered arm-chair.

"Well," I said, "what an invitingly comfortable-looking room! Anybody ought to sleep and work well in such a one."

"Ah!" said Harel, "I am indeed enchanted that it pleases you."

"Why?"

"Because it is for you."

"How for me?"

"It is yours; and as you will not leave it until you have written me my *Napoléon*, I had to make things as comfortable as I could for you, to prevent your being in a bad temper during your imprisonment"

A shiver passed over me from head to foot.

"Harel!" I exclaimed, "don't let us have any foolish tricks, my friend!"

"Exactly so. You made a big mistake in not starting the work when I first asked you.... And I made just as stupid a mistake in not giving it to someone else to write ... but I had spoken to you; and I keep my word. I therefore think we have both shown ourselves quite stupid enough for two men of intellectual attainment, and it is high time we came to our senses once more."

"Come now! you cannot be thinking what you are doing! I have not even the very faintest plan drawn up for your *Napoléon*."

"You told me you re-wrote *Christine* in one night."

"I should need all kinds of books: Bourrienne, Norvins, *Victoires et Conquêtes*..."

"There is *Victoires et Conquêtes* in that corner, there is Bourrienne in another and Norvins is on the table."

"I should want the *Mémorial de Sainte-Hélène*."

"There it is on the mantelpiece."

"My son...."

"He shall come and dine with you."

"And my mistress?"

"Ah!" said Georges, who now came into the room, "you have just done without her for six weeks, you can surely do without her for another fortnight."

I began to laugh.

"At least you will tell her what has happened?"

"She has been told."

"By whom?"

"By me," said Harel, "and she has already received her reward."

"What was it?"

"A bracelet."

I seized hold of Georges' lovely hands, and addressing my remarks to Harel, I said—

"Upon my word, my dear friend, you do things in a way it is impossible to get round.... To-morrow I will set to work on your *Napoléon* and in a week you shall have it."

"You are in a great hurry to leave us, my dear boy!" Georges said, curling her queenly lip.

"Good!" I said. "The play will be finished when I say it is finished.... It is Harel who is in a hurry, not I ..."

"Harel will wait," said Georges in her grand Cleopatra and Medea style.

I bowed; I had nothing further to say.

Harel pointed out a toilet table and its fittings, and observed that my room had no other means of access than through that belonging to Georges; then he went away with her and shut me in. They had even gone so far as to send to my rooms for my trousers. That same night, or rather morning, I set to work and thought out the part of the spy, and the way to divide up the drama. When the rôle of the spy was thought out, the rest was clear enough. History itself provided the divisions of the play.

"From Toulon to Sainte-Hélène!" Harel had said to me. "I am willing to lay out a hundred thousand francs, if need be!"

It would have been difficult to provide me with a wider margin.

The next morning I began to write. As fast as the scenes were composed I passed them over to Georges, who in her turn sent them on to Harel, who in his gave them to a charming fellow called Verteuil to copy out. Verteuil is now secretary to the Théâtre-Français.

The drama was done at the end of the week. It consisted of twenty-four scenes and contained nine thousand lines. It was three times bigger than an ordinary play, five times longer than *Iphigénie* and six times longer than *Mérope*.

Frédéric was to play the part of *Napoléon*. I had debated that choice beforehand; physique seemed to me to be most important in such a creation. The success of the *Napoléon* at the Porte-Saint-Martin was due primarily to Gobert's likeness to the emperor; and nobody could have been less like Napoléon and especially Bonaparte, than Frédéric.

"My dear fellow," Georges had said to me, "remember this: a genius like Frédéric can play any part well."

The reason struck me as being so good that I gave in, and the part was given to Frédéric.

By the ninth day the piece was copied out; Verteuil, with the assistance of two copyists, had only taken one day longer to copy it out than I had to write it.

It was not good work, far from it; but the title would assure a popular success, and the part of the spy would be enough to secure literary success.

They assembled on the ninth day to hear it read, and I read as far as Moscow; next day I continued to the end. The part of Frédéric alone contained four thousand lines—that is to say, it was as long as all the parts in *Le Mariage de*

Figaro put together. But to cut nothing out of it during collation seemed impossible, and it was therefore decided that any cutting down should be done at rehearsals. Everybody set to work with an energy I have rarely seen, even learning passages that were likely to be omitted, which is a most difficult thing to get an artist to do. Frédéric, Lockroy and Stockleit were enraptured with their parts. I was set at liberty the night of the reading. There was a supper given me on my release, as there had been before my incarceration.

These suppers at Georges' house were delightful; I reiterate this statement, for they are amongst my happiest memories of the past; no one could possibly have been more beautiful and queenly, more scornful and caustic, more like a Greek courtezan, or a Roman matron, or the niece of a pope, than was Georges (in her varying moods). The contrast between Georges and Mars was incredibly great; Mars was always as affected, reserved, tight-laced and self-contained as the wife of a senator of the Empire. And then there was Harel, who was so alert mentally that he always reminded one of a man sitting on a glass stool in touch with an electric battery, with sparks at all his finger-tips, and at the end of each of his hairs.

When *it came to the actual theatre*, it was found to contain over a hundred different parts. For five or six days there was a perfect chaos to unravel; I believe I would rather have put the world to rights as described in the Book of Genesis than this world of *Napoléon*. All the parts melted down, compressed and put together (not including the supernumeraries), made between eighty and ninety persons with speaking parts. Jouslin de la Salle, stage manager, quite lost his head over it, and Harel emptied three snuff-boxes full at every rehearsal.

As we have said, Harel laid out a hundred thousand francs in the mounting of the play; but not even M. de Rothschild's cashier would have been capable of calculating the number of brilliant, sparkling, comic expressions he also expended.

In the midst of all this hurly-burly I followed up that everlasting study of dramatic situations and of character which I am looking for always and everywhere, sometimes even in places where they don't exist. Here is an example, for instance:—

Amongst my troop-leaders, acting in—I know not now what part—one of those small rôles called *accessoires* (emergency parts), I had noticed a good-looking young man of between twenty-five and twenty-six years of age, holding a gun as though he had never done anything else all his life long, and, what was still more unusual and important, speaking his part fairly well.

I must ask my readers to forgive me for being obliged sometimes to use theatrical slang; it expresses things often much better than ordinary language does.

Well, it also seemed to me that my *accessoire's* face was familiar to me; and he, on his side, without being too forward, seemed to smile at me as much as to say, "It is not only at the theatre I have seen you." Now where had he seen me? Where had I seen him? This I wanted to find out. I had asked his name; it was Charlet, the same name as our famous lithographer. The name awoke no recollection in my mind. One day, however, right in the midst of a movement of the Old Guard, I stopped in front of him.

"Excuse me, Monsieur Charlet," I said to him, "it seems to me I have seen you somewhere.... Where, I cannot tell; but I will bet my hat you are not a stranger to me. Can you assist my memory?"

"Quite true, monsieur," he answered; "we have seen each other three times before, as one does catch sight of people at special times: once in the rue Saint-Honoré, once on the Pont de la Grève and once at the Louvre."

"Oh yes, I remember ... on the Pont de la Grève you commanded the attack when the standard-bearer was killed?"

"That was it," he replied.

"You are an actor?"

"Well, as you see, I am trying to become one."

"Why did you wait until I spoke to you?"

"I am timid."

"Not in the face of bullets, anyhow!"

"Oh! bullets only kill, when all is said."

He began to laugh.

"I am indeed," he went on, "as timid as I say, to a point you would not believe possible.... For instance, I know M. Charles Nodier."

"You know Charles Nodier?"

"Yes, and quite sufficiently well to have asked him for an introduction to you, or to M. Hugo, or anybody else, but I never dared ask him for one."

"You did wrong: Nodier is a capital fellow, and would most certainly have given you such an introduction."

"I am well aware of it ... although I began by wanting to kill him; but, as afterwards I prevented him from being killed, we are quits."

"What the deuce are you telling me?"

"God's truth."

"How did it come about?"

"Oh! bah! it is too long a story; besides, it is not very interesting...."

"Wrong again, my friend," I said to him; "I am not like ordinary people: everything interests me. As for what you say about the tale being long, well, if it bores me, I will ask you to cut it short."

"We are not in a suitable place here. Indeed, Jouslin de la Salle has already twice tried to silence us."

"They will only think I am asking you your part."

Then he burst out laughing, a good open laugh, showing lovely white teeth.

I like people who can laugh, however poor they are, for it shows they are good-hearted and possess a sound digestion.

"Listen," I said to him, "you are not in the next act."

"No, nor in the one after that ... I only come on again at the burning of Moscow."

"Then let us go up to the foyer and then you can tell me this story."

"Ah! nothing would please me better."

We went from the theatre to the foyer, and sat down in that magnificent gallery which, at night especially, looks like a portico of Herculaneum or an atrium of Pompeii, in the fine shadows that cross it.

"Well?" I asked Charlet, putting a hand on his knee.

"Well," he said, "it was last 27 July—at that time I was a journeyman cabinet-maker—I heard it being said in the faubourg Saint-Antoine, where I was engaged in cutting up some wood, that there had been a riot in the place de la Bourse the previous night, and that there were crowds gathered round the Palais-Royal at that very moment. I was furious over the Ordinances, although I did not thoroughly understand where they curtailed our liberty; but I did understand it to be a sort of challenge thrown down to the citizens. I had long been waiting for this moment, and I did not stop to be told twice, but rushed off to see what was going on. When I reached the *Marché des Innocents* I heard platoon-firing in the direction of the *halle aux Draps>* then I caught sight of several wounded men, some dragging themselves along as best they could, others carried upon litters, and all expending their remaining strength in shouting 'To arms!' This spectacle exasperated me, and, without quite knowing, as I said, which was in the wrong, the People or Royalty, I began to shout in my turn, 'To arms!' A wounded man, who had no strength left to hold his rifle, gave it to me, and some man, I know not who he was, stuffed my pockets with cartridges; workmen and armed bourgeois, some with swords and some with carbines, were running towards the rue aux Fers, and I ran with them.... Now, whether I ran faster than everybody else, or whether I was more excited, somehow I found myself at their head, and they, seeing me at their head, took me for their leader. Upon entering the rue aux Fers we found ourselves opposite a regiment of the Guard; the first line fired: we were so close to the soldiers that the smoke from their rifles enshrouded us like a cloud; in the middle of this cloud I distinguished a young man stagger and fall down dead a few steps from me. I ran up to him; he was hit in the chest by a bullet that had gone right through, had come out at his back, and must have penetrated his heart. I took him in my arms and carried him away.... I was scarcely fifty yards from the troop; but it had ceased firing. For there was nobody in the street but myself, the dead man whom I was holding in my arms and a tall man with a pale face, who wore a red ribbon in his blue frockcoat: it was not worth while wasting powder over us three. I did not really quite know what I was doing; I carried my dead man to the rue de la Ferronnerie, and the man in the blue coat with the red ribbon followed me. This persistence in keeping me in sight made me suspicious of him; I stopped, and, seeing that he was coming up to me, I saved him half his distance by going to meet him. At length we met. I judged from his gentle, sad face that he did not wish to do me harm; however, when I had lain the dead man on the ground, I made my gun ready for any emergency; but, without taking any notice of my hostile precaution, he laid a hand on my shoulder, and, leaving it there, whilst I gazed at him in much surprise, he said: 'My friend, I have been following all your actions for the past hour.' 'I noticed that you had,' I said, 'and that was why I came towards you instead of waiting till you came up to me.' 'Are you the leader of these men?' 'Yes.... What does it matter to you, though?' 'It matters much,' he replied, 'for I too am a man.'

"There was so much sweetness in the voice of the unknown that I, who had begun by asking myself whether to put a bullet through him as I saw him following me, felt fascinated and looked on him with a certain respect. 'Well then,' I said to him, 'if you are a man you must see that they are killing our brothers, and you must help us to massacre all these villains of soldiers.' He smiled sadly. 'But those soldiers are also men,' he said, 'they are your brothers too; only, you act of your own free will, whilst they receive orders which they are obliged to obey. Do you know what the world calls what you are doing your best to bring about? It calls it a Revolution; and do you know what that means, eh?' 'I don't know whether I am raising a Revolution or not, nor whether a Revolution is a good or an evil thing; but I do know what I want.'

'What is that?' 'I want the Charter, *Vive la Charte!*' And then, in a word, I added, trying to struggle against the moral influence this unknown person was obtaining over me in spite of myself: 'Who are you? What are you asking of me? Why do you follow me?' 'I follow you because you interest me.' 'Very well, you also interest me to the extent of offering you this advice: believe me, you had better take another route.... 'You will not?' 'Very well, my friend. Then in that case I shall leave you. Good-evening!' A dozen men had collected round me; I picked up the dead man and took my way with my little troop towards the École de médecine, which I meant to reach by crossing the Seine by the Pont au Change; but great was my astonishment to come across my man again at the corner of the rue de la Vannerie; he was not content this time to give me advice, but took hold of my arm and tried to draw me in another direction. 'Ah! what the devil do you want with me? We must attend to this!' I cried, stamping my foot, and giving the dead body to the others to carry. 'I want to prevent you and your companions from going to certain death,' he said. 'There is a whole regiment on the Quai aux Fleurs; what can your fifteen or twenty men do against a regiment?' '*Sacrebleu!*' I cried, 'you exasperate me beyond bearing! What does it matter to you if I am killed?' 'My friend,' he said to me, 'you must have a father or mother, sister or wife.... Well, I wish to save them tears.' I felt touched in spite of myself, but I was in the centre of men who had chosen me for their leader, and I would not draw back.... 'You are mistaken,' I said; 'I possess none of those ties, so be good enough to go your way and leave me to go mine.' Then, unhanding myself violently from him: 'To the École de médecine!' I shouted to my companions. 'To the École de médecine!' they repeated. And we rushed on to the place du Châtelet. Sure enough, there was a regiment drawn up on the other side of the Seine on the Quai aux Fleurs! '*Vive la ligne!*' we shouted, making for the Pont au Change and shaking our guns. But, instead of fraternising with us, the colonel ordered us to withdraw; we took no notice of his injunction, but continued on our way. We were not more than a third of the way across the bridge when the regiment fired upon us. It was indeed a carnage! Two or three men fell round me; the others took to flight and deserted our dead man. I do not know why I was so set on this dead body; I thought it might be useful both as a standard and as a safeguard. I picked it up and beat a retreat to the place du Châtelet. What remained of my recent troop was waiting for me, and in the forefront was that persistent man of the blue coat and red ribbon. 'Well, my poor fellow,' he said, 'what did I tell you? Three or four of your men are killed and as many wounded! It is a miracle that you are alive; they probably fired fifty rounds at you! For Heaven's sake do not do any more such mad things.... Come, follow me!' 'Oh! that is the way the wind blows, is it!' I said, 'you red-ribboned man; do you know that you are beginning to annoy me intensely, and that if you push me much further I shall end by telling you to your face what I am thinking about you?' 'What is that?' 'Why, that you are probably a *spy!*'"

"When some of my men heard the word *spy* they exclaimed, 'What, do you say he is a spy?' And, taking aim at the unknown, they exclaimed: 'If he is a spy, let us shoot him!' I was terrified at this action, for something told me that the man did really mean kindly by me. 'No, no!' I cried, 'what are you thinking of? Down arms, *sacrebleu!* 'But you said he was a spy,' several voices explained. 'I did not say that; on the contrary, monsieur is a neighbour of mine, and knows me; you heard him mention my mother, and remind me that if I got killed she would be left without anyone to support her.... A spy indeed, go along!'

"I went up to my unknown friend and held out my hand; he took it and pressed it cordially. He was as cool as though his life had never been endangered in the slightest. 'Thank you, my friend,' he said to me; 'I will never forget what you have just done for me. You are right, I am no spy; I will tell you more: I am of your political opinions, but I saw the first Revolution, and that more than satisfied my taste for revolutions.... So now, as I do not wish to see you killed, I will bid you adieu!' He left us and knocked at the door of the café of the Pont au Change, which, after some difficulty, admitted him. We others went off in the direction of the Quai de la Mégisserie, in order to reach the Pont Neuf; but we had scarcely gone forty yards along the quay before we received a volley from the rue Bertin-Poireé that killed four of our men; and, at the same moment, a squadron of mounted police issued from the place des Trois-Marie and advanced towards us, filling the whole width of the quay. I looked all round me, and found I was alone. I fired my gun in the middle of the police and saw one man fall. They had their muskets in hand and fired. I could feel the balls whistle past me, but not a single one hit me. The thought of death never entered my head; I was like one possessed! I receded as they advanced and discharged my rifle a second time, then I hid myself behind the fountain of the Châtelet. I decided to be killed there rather than take to flight. I had reloaded my gun and was taking aim the third time, when I felt someone seize me by the collar of my coat and draw me backwards. I turned round quickly, and it was my blue-coated, red-ribboned stranger once more! 'My friend,' he said, 'you are quite mad. Come and have a glass of eau sucrée with me, and that will bring you to your senses.' I felt in my pockets to see if I had enough to pay my reckoning and found I had ten sous, all I should require; so I replied: 'All right, my mouth is very dry; I will gladly drink something.' I had chewed seven or eight cartridges; and powder, you know, makes one very thirsty. I followed my man, and the café door closed behind us. 'Two glasses of eau sucrée!' he called out. 'Oh, not eau sucrée for me, please,' I said; 'it is too insipid!' 'What will you have then?—a small brandy?' 'I would rather have a kirsch.' 'All right, kirsch be it.' They served me with a glass of kirsch and brought him eau sucrée. 'Well,' he said, 'you are alone; all who were with you are either killed, wounded or fled.' 'True,' I replied; 'but others will take their places.'... 'To be killed, or wounded, or flee in their turn. You poor children! If only revolutions really gave you something in return! but, after each revolution, I have noticed that the people are more unhappy than before.' 'Bah!' I said, 'all the more necessary, then, that we should have a downright good revolution!' 'What are you by trade?' the unknown inquired of me. 'Journeyman cabinet-maker in the quartier de l'Arsenal.' 'How is work in the Faubourg Saint-Antoine?' 'There is plenty.' 'Succeed in making your revolution and then see in six weeks' time how it is.'

"'Well, the belly may be pinched, but at least we shall be free!' 'You may be starved and have less liberty even than before!' He rose. 'Listen, my friend,' he said; 'you told me that you lived in the quartier de l'Arsenal, I think?' 'Yes.' 'Well then, if, as I fear, work runs short, remember me,... come to the Arsenal Library and ask for the librarian,—if I can do you a good turn be sure I will.' He went to the counter, paid, and left. I had noticed signs of understanding going on between the proprietor of the café and my unknown friend, and I stayed behind to find out with whom I had been holding intercourse. As I was going up to question the proprietor of the café, he approached me. 'Do you know the person who has just gone out?' 'No, indeed; I should like to know who he is.' 'You say well, for he is one of the best men on earth!' 'The deuce!' I said, 'so much the worse!' 'Why so?' 'If you only knew what name I called him!' 'Called *him!* 'Yes, him;—I called him a spy!' 'You called M. Charles Nodier a spy?' 'What, the man who has just left here, and with whom I have been drinking, is M. Charles Nodier?' 'The very same.' 'Oh! my God!' 'Well, what are you going to do?' 'Run after him—catch him up and beg his pardon.... Spy—M. Charles Nodier!' I shook the door the proprietor had bolted, with all my might. The firing began afresh at this moment, and five or six bullets pierced the shutters and broke the panes of glass. 'My gun!' I shouted,—'where is my gun?' 'Oh!'the proprietor said, 'your gun is upstairs.' 'Upstairs,—why?' 'Because I have no desire you should be seen going out of here with your rifle, and to have everything in my café smashed and broken. When it is dark I will return you your gun, and you can go away.... Upon my word, from what M. Nodier told me, you have done quite enough with it for to-day!' A second discharge was heard, and several more bullets came through the shutters. 'Come, come,' said the master of the café, 'it is not safe down here.... Let us go upstairs to the first floor!' So, taking me by the arm, he drew me towards the staircase. 'M. Charles Nodier!' I repeated as I followed him, half stunned; and I had called him a spy! I could think of nothing else the whole time I spent in the café of the Pont au Change, and I was there until nine o'clock. I returned home, and lay all night thinking of my day's adventure."

At this moment the manager came into the foyer.

"Oh, Monsieur Dumas," he said, "they are hunting for you everywhere....
And you here too, Charlet,... you must pay a fine, my friend!"

"A fine! And why?" said Charlet.

"Because they did the scene over again, and you were not there."

"A pretty mess I have got myself into!" said Charlet.

"Well! I am doing good business!"

"Don't be uneasy, I will settle it all with Jouslin de la Salle.... Have you seen
Nodier again since?"

"Oh! not very likely, indeed! after having called him a spy! While I was still
warm with excitement I could have managed to say something to him, but
to present myself again to him in cold blood? Never!"

We returned to the theatre, and, as I had promised, I got him off the fine he
had incurred through my fault.

He was the same Charlet that Arago had met on 29 July, at the Marché des
Innocents, in command of General Dubourg's escort.

We have met again since then; I will relate the occasion and tell what Nodier
did for him.

CHAPTER V

I am officially received into the Artillery Corps of the National Guard—*Antony* is put under rehearsal at the Théâtre-Français—Ill-will of the actors—Treaty between Hugo and the manager of the Porte-Saint-Martin—Firmin's proposition and confidence—Mademoiselle Mars' dresses and the new gas lights—I withdraw *Antony* from the Théâtre-Français—I offer Dorval the part of Adèle

After my liberty had been restored me by my implacable gaoler and beautiful gaoleress I returned home and found several letters waiting for me, two only being of importance. One was from Bixio; he had knocked three or four times at my door, and, finding it obstinately closed, he had written to tell me that my admission, when proposed to the heads of the Artillery, had been adopted by a large majority; he was requested to ask me in their name if I should like to enter the same battery as M. le Duc d'Orléans. If such was my wish they would manage to gratify it. Now, the king had decreed that the Duc d'Orléans should join the first artillery battery of the National Guard; he reckoned upon the prince's conciliatory and excellent disposition to win over to him a corps which proudly boasted itself to be an active basis of Opposition; and, as the centre of democratic opinions, principles and interests, completely given over to the bourgeoisie. After my rupture with the king it was out of the question that I should wish to come in contact with his son. I therefore replied to Bixio that I thanked the heads of the Artillery Department for admitting me into their corps, and that they could place me anywhere it suited them, except in the first battery.

The second letter came from the Théâtre-Français. As the censorship had for the moment disappeared, and *Antony* was a free agent; it was therefore a question of beginning to rehearse it at once, so I rushed off to the Théâtre-Français, where I found Mademoiselle Mars and Firmin. My readers know that Mademoiselle Mars had accepted the rôle of Adèle, and Firmin that of Antony; the remaining distribution of parts was settled there and then. The play was capitally mounted, specially in the subordinate parts; Rose Dupuis played the Comtesse de Lacy; Menjaud, the young poet; Monrose, the subscriber to the *Constitutionnel*; and Madame Hervey took Madame de Camps. I say the play was capitally mounted as far as the subsidiary rôles were concerned, not that I wish in the very least to attack the genius of Mademoiselle Mars or of Firmin; but great as may be the talent of these artists—except when contrasted with an all-embracing and powerful genius like Talma's—there are parts that depend more or less for success upon the personal character of the individuals who act them. Now, no woman could have been less capable of understanding the entirely modern character of Adèle than was Mademoiselle Mars,—a character full of subtle contrasts, of strength and weakness and of extremes of passion and repentance. On the other hand, no man could have been less capable than Firmin of reproducing the gloomy melancholy, bitter irony, fiery passion and philosophic ramblings of the personality of Antony. Mademoiselle Mars possessed grace, wit, charm and the art of elocution and coquetry in the highest degree; but she was wanting in that poetic gift which gilds all other qualities with the undefined mystery that constitutes the charm of Shakespeare's women. Firmin possessed Mademoiselle Mars' qualities in a lesser degree, but he was lacking in the fatalism which creates an Orestes in all ages.

Tameness is one of the principal requirements of modern drama. Now, Mademoiselle Mars dared not, and Firmin could not, be tame. Let us go further, and state that the Théâtre-Français itself was a bad setting for the picture. There are certain atmospheres in which some creations cannot exist.

The rehearsals of *Antony* were going on concurrently with those of *Napoléon*. But there was this difference between the two pieces and the two theatres: at the Odéon, everybody was satisfied with his or her own part, and from the manager to the prompter everyone did his best to help me, while at the Théâtre-Français everyone was dissatisfied with his part, and from manager to prompter everybody hindered the author and his work. My reader knows Mademoiselle Mars already. I pointed her out at a rehearsal of *Hernani* pulling to pieces the rôle of Doña Sol. I am sorry I was in such a hurry, I could have shown her in *Antony* pulling the part of Adèle to pieces. On his side, Firmin plucked the part of Antony as hard as he could. Every feather of slightly vivid colouring made a blur on the kind of grey tint that they wished to give to a work whose ruling theme had, in the first place, been colour, so that by dint of plucking out gently each feather the part was quietly transformed into that of a lover on the stage of the Gymnase.

By the end of a month of rehearsals the piece, deprived of all its salient features, might have been reduced to three acts or even to a single one. One fine morning the suggestion was made to me to suppress the second and fourth acts, because they made the play too wearisome. I had taken such a disgust for the work that I was quite ready to suppress it entirely; I had even got to the point of believing that *Napoléon* was the real work of art, and *Antony* the common ordinary run of work. They settled the day for the production of it, because *they must get it out of the way as it blocked the theatre*, which was in urgent haste to put on *Don Carlos, ou l'Inquisition*, a drama from which they were expecting great things, but whose author desired to preserve his anonymity at the first performance; and with good reason too.

Meanwhile Hugo had sought me out; he had come to realise that we should never be looked upon at the Théâtre-Français by its actors and frequenters, and even by the public itself, as anything but usurpers; the stupid heresies that they had attributed to us concerning Molière, Corneille and Racine had sprung up in the orchestra; and everyone who was above the age of fifty came nightly to bask voluptuously under the shadow of our audacity! Consequently, Hugo had looked about for and found a theatre which was not an Olympus, where our triumphs would not be regarded as sacrilege, and where those he should cater for would be plain ordinary mortals and not gods. This theatre was the Porte-Saint-Martin. He had entered into negotiations with its manager, M. Crosnier, for the taking of *Marion Delorme*. Thus was realised the prophecy made by Crosnier to Hugo when, on 16 July 1829, the latter had said to him—

"Monsieur, you have come too late; there are two plays of mine accepted, which have priority over yours."

To which Crosnier had replied—

"By Jove! monsieur, who knows? In spite of these two acceptances I may, after all, be the one to play your works!"

When treating with Crosnier, Hugo had negotiated in my name as well as his own, subject to my agreement thereto. I thanked him for his friendly attention; but the only two plays I possessed were in rehearsal, one at the Odéon and the other at the Théâtre-Français. I should therefore have to wait till I had produced another piece. But I did not need to wait for this. The nearer the day of the first representation of *Antony* approached, the more I became conscious of the ill feeling throughout the theatre. On the other hand, those of my friends who had been present at the rehearsals had gone away shaking their heads, and when urged by me to give them opinions they frankly confessed that *they could not see any play in it at all.* I was completely demoralised, for the further I advanced in my dramatic career the more I lost that early confidence in myself which had kept me up through all the tribulations connected with *Henri III.* I began to think I must be deceived, and that there could be absolutely nothing in *Antony*.

Two things happened at the time which ought to have driven me to the extreme of discouragement, but which, on the contrary, restored all my determination. The day of the *première* was fixed for the following Saturday, and it was then Tuesday or Wednesday, when Firmin took me aside.

"My dear friend," he said to me, "I did not want to refuse to act the part of Antony for you, first, because I will play all the parts you assign me; secondly, because having given me the rôle of Saint Mégrin, which is a good one, you acquired the right to give me a bad one after it...."

He waited for me to stop him midway, but I, on the contrary, let him say his say out. So he went on—

"But you see, I represent the principal character, and I do not wish to take the responsibility of the failure of the play upon myself."

"So you believe it will be a failure?"

"It is my firm conviction.... I do not know how it comes to pass that you, who know the theatrical world intimately, have ventured to risk such a monotonous part.... Antony is a heavy twaddler, who from the first to the fifth act does nothing but repeat the same thing over and over again; who gets angry for no reason at all, a species of monomaniac who rages unceasingly, and wages furious warfare against his fellow-men."

"So that is the effect Antony produces on you?"

"Yes."

"It does not surprise me; it is exactly what I wished it to do."

"Well, that does not matter; I have warned you, remember."

"Yes, but it is not enough to warn a man of his fall: you should afford him a means of escaping his fall."

"Oh!" said Firmin, "I, as you know, am an actor and not an author; I act pieces, but I don't create them."

"But have you no suggestion to make?"

"Yes, I have ... but I dare not say it."

"Say it, of course."

"You will jump as high as the ceiling!"

"What matter, if I do not come down on your feet!"

"Well, then!"

"Well, what?"

"If I were in your place I would take the play to Scribe."

"No," I replied, "but I will take it to Crosnier."

And, going up to the prompter, I said—

"Garnier, please give me my manuscript; there's a good fellow."

The prompter handed me the manuscript; and Firmin watched me take it, astonished. Mademoiselle Mars was waiting all this time until I was free.

"Well, my good fellow," she said in the dry tone she always used when she wished to prepare an author for something disagreeable, "have you done talking with Firmin? And have you a word left for anybody else?"

"Oh madame!" said Firmin, "you had but to speak; I am not in the habit of taking your authors away from you."

"As far as parts such as this man gives me are concerned, you can take him away from me as much as you like."

"Good!" I said,—"this sounds promising!"

Then, going up to Mademoiselle Mars—

"Madame," I said to her, "I am at your service."

"Ah! that is fortunate! Do you know what I am going to tell you?"

"No, madame, I do not know; but if you will be so good as to inform me, I shall."

"I do not intend to act my part in your play on Saturday."

"Oh! why not, if you please?"

"Because I have spent fifteen hundred francs on my dresses, and wish them to be seen."

"But why can they not be seen on Saturday as well as on any other day?"

"Because we had been promised a new chandelier for Saturday, and the man has just put us off for another three months. When there is another chandelier I will play in your piece."

"Ah! madame," I said to her, "there is only one thing likely to put a stumbling-block in the way of your kind intention...."

"What is that?"

"In three months my play will have been acted."

"How can it?"

"It will be."

"Where?"

"At the Theatre Porte-Saint-Martin.... Adieu, madame—Au revoir, Firmin!"

And out I went, carrying my manuscript with me. As I went down the stairs that led from the theatre to the orchestra I turned my head round and saw Mademoiselle Mars and Firmin together, each exchanging questioning glances and gestures. I regret I am unable to transmit the conversation that ensued between them to posterity. I ran off at once to Madame Dorval, who was then residing in the boulevard Saint-Martin, in a house with an exit to the rue Meslay. By chance she happened to be quite alone. When I was announced she had my name repeated twice to her.

"All right!" I shouted from the dining-room; "it is I. But perhaps you wish to have me shown outside the door?"

"Oh! you're a pretty fellow!" she said to me, in those drawling accents that were sometimes such a charm in her; "I have not seen you for six months!"

"What would you have me do, my dear!" I said, entering and throwing my arms round her neck,—"during that time I have produced a child and a revolution, without reckoning that I have been nearly shot twice.... Is this how you greet the ghosts?"

"I cannot embrace you, my *good dog*."

This was the pet name of friendship—even, I may say, of love—that Dorval had given me.

Her *good dog* has remained faithful to his poor Dorval to the end!

"Why cannot you greet me more warmly?" I asked.

"Because, like *Marion Delorme*, I am renewing my virginity."

"Impossible!"

"True, on my word of honour! I am becoming respectable."

"Ah! my dear, I mentioned making a revolution, here is another one. Who the devil caused this to come about?"

"Alfred de Vigny."

"Do you love him?"

"I cannot speak of it; I am mad over him!"

"What has he done to keep you to such good resolutions?"

"He composes little *Élévations*[1] for me."

"In that case, my dear, accept my sincere compliments; for, in the first place, de Vigny is a poet of very great talent; next, he is a true nobleman: both these attributes are better worth having than a mulatto like myself."

"Do you think so?" Dorval said, in a tone of voice she alone knew how to use.

"It is my turn now to swear on my word of honour!"

"Then you didn't come to make love to me?"

I burst out laughing, and made some exclamation or other.

"No, I could not have received your attentions ... fancy, he treats me like a duchess."

"He is perfectly right."

"He calls me his angel."

"Bravo!"

"The other day I had a small lump on my shoulder, and he told me wings were beginning to sprout."

"You must be immensely amused, my dear."

"Yes, indeed! Piccini did not accustom me to such treatment as that."

"And Merle?"

"Still less so.... By the way, you know Merle and I have married?"

"Really?"

"Yes; it was a means of getting separated from one another."

"But he ought to be the happiest man on earth?"

"You think so! He has his *café au lait* in the morning, and his slippers by his bedside at night.... Do you wish to say good-day to him?"

"Thanks, no! I have come for you."

"Ah! you are very cunning, my big dog.... But I had forgotten, he is not here, he is away in the country."

"I have some news to tell you."

"What is it?"

"That I have withdrawn *Antony* from the Théâtre-Français."

"Oh! you have done well! It was the same with Hugo, you know; he took *Marion Delorme* from them and brought it to us. I am playing the part of Marion."

"Well, what do you think of the piece?"

"I think it extremely fine.... I do not know how I shall get on, however. Just think-verses. Can you imagine me as a tragedienne"

"But I do not think it is your first attempt."

"Oh! in *Marino Faliero*, you mean?"

"Goodness! how the part of Helena did bore me! You saw me in that, didn't you?"

"Yes."

"I was pretty bad in it, was I not?"

"Honestly, you were not very good; but I hope you will do better in Adèle."

"What is Adèle?"

"Antony's mistress, my dear."

"Are you bringing *Antony* to us, then?"

"Why, of course!"

"And am I to take the part of Adèle, my good dog?"

"Of course!"

"Three cheers, then! Upon my word, no matter what happens I must kiss you.... Oh! how bad it is of you when I told you I mustn't ... Hullo! what is that in your pocket?"

"The manuscript."

"Oh! give it me to look at."

"I am going to read it to you."

"What! do you really mean it?"

"Certainly I do."

"Like this, to me alone?"

"Certainly."

"Oh! Why, then, you must think me a great actress?"

"De Vigny only treats you like a duchess; but I mean to treat you like a queen."

She rose and made me a curtsey.

"The queen shall be your servant for ever, monsieur, in proof whereof I am going to give you a table and offer you ... what shall it be? What do you like best while you are reading? Will you have eau-de-vie, rum or kirsch?"

"I prefer water."

"All right, then; wait a moment."

She went into her bedroom, where I followed her.

"Oh! why do you follow me in here?"

"Why should I not?"

"It is forbidden."

"Even to me?"

"To everybody!... Alexandre! I give you warning I will ring my bell!"

"Ah! indeed!"

"Alexandre!"

"I would like to settle that question. I bet you will not ring."

"Alexandre!"

She hung on to the bell-rope and rang loudly. I flung myself into an arm-chair and began laughing like a madman. The chambermaid came in.

"Louise!" said Dorval, with perfect dignity, "fetch a glass of water for M. Dumas."

"Louise!... in a wash-hand basin," I added.

"Impertinent fellow!" said Dorval.

She threw herself upon me and hit me with all her strength. Just when she was beating me with the greatest avidity, someone rang the outdoor bell. She stopped short.

"Ah!" she said, "do go quickly into the salon before anybody sees you here, there's a good dog!"

"Suppose I take myself off altogether?"

"What?"

"Suppose we put off our reading till this evening?"

"That would be better still."

"Shall I go out by the way you know?"

"Yes, yes.... Till to-night! Would you like me to give Bocage a hint?"

"No. I want to read it over to you first."

"As you like.... But come, off with you!"

"Oh! how tiresome it is of de Vigny to come just at this moment!"

"What can you expect, my poor friend! We are not to have everything our own way in this world.... Good-bye until to-night."

"Until to-night, then."

She shut the door of her bedroom quickly just as the sitting-room door opened.

"Oh! good-day, my dear Comte," she said; "come and sit here by me ... I was expecting you impatiently...."

Meanwhile, Louise lifted the Persian portière curtain and beckoned me to follow her. I put a louis in her hand. She gazed at me in astonishment.

"Well, what is the matter?" I asked.

"Things are to be, then, as though Madame had not rung?"

"Precisely."

"Shall we not see you again?"

"Oh yes, I return to-night."

"Ah! now I understand."

"Well, no, you do not."

"That is possible too: I can't help it. What is to be done? For the past six months the world has been topsy-turvy here. Ah! monsieur, you whom Madame loves so much, you ought indeed to tell her that she is lost!"

She was right, poor Louise!.. But we will explain in another place why she was right.

---

[1] Alfred de Vigny published his delightful poems called *Élévations* at this time.

CHAPTER VI

My agreements with Dorval—I read *Antony*—Her impressions—She makes me alter the last act there and then—Merle's room—Bocage as artist—Bocage as negotiator—Reading to M. Crosnier—He falls into a profound slumber—The play nevertheless is accepted

---

I returned that night and found Dorval alone and expecting me.

"Upon my word!" I exclaimed, "I did not dare hope for a tête-à-tête."

"I said I had a reading."

"Did you say who the reader was?"

"Oh no! but first come here, sit down by me and listen to what I have to say, good dog!"

I let her lead me to an arm-chair and I sat down.

She stood in front of me with both her hands in mine and she looked gently and kindly at me.

"You love me, don't you?" she said.

"With all my heart!"

"You love me really?"

"Don't I say so?"

"For myself?"

"For yourself."

"You do not wish to cause me pain?"

"Good God, no!"

"You wish me to play your part?"

"Of course, since I have brought it to you."

"You do not want to spoil my career?"

"Why! you must be mad to suggest such a thing!"

"Very well, then, do not tease me again as you did this morning. I should not have strength enough to defend myself, and ... and I am happy as I am; I love de Vigny and he worships me. You know there are certain men one cannot deceive, men of genius who, if they are once deceived,—well, so much the worse for the women who deceive them!"

"My dear Marie," I said to her, "you are the noblest and best-hearted woman I know. Here is my hand upon it—I will not exceed the bounds of friendship."

"Oh! let us understand one another: I do not say such a condition shall last for ever."

"It shall last, at all events, until you give me back my promised word."

"Agreed. If, some day, I am tired of our bond, I will write to tell you."

"To me?"

"To you."

"Before all others?"

"Before all others, for you know quite well how I love you, my good dog!... Oh! now we will read—I hear it is splendid. Why would not that stuck-up minx Mademoiselle Mars play the part?"

"Oh! because she had spent fifteen hundred francs on her dresses and the chandelier does not give sufficient light to show them off."

"You know, I cannot afford to spend as much as fifteen hundred francs on my dresses; but you need not be anxious, I will find means to bedeck myself properly! Adèle, then, is a society woman? How I shall enjoy playing such a part! How well you must know how such a type should be acted! I, who have never played anything but the fishwife kind of woman!... Come, quick, sit down there and begin reading."

I began to read, but she had not the patience to sit in her chair: she got up and leant on my back and read over my shoulder with me. After the first act I looked up and she kissed me on my forehead.

"Well?" I asked her.

"Well, it seems to start very oddly! Things will come to a pretty pass if they go on in the same way as they have begun."

"Wait and see."

I began the second act. As I proceeded with my reading I could feel the agitated heaving of the excellent actress's bosom against my shoulder; at the scene between Adèle and Antony, a tear dropped on my manuscript, then a second and a third. I raised my face to kiss hers.

"Oh! how vexatious of you!" she said, "to interrupt in the middle of my enjoyment, do go on!"

I continued, and again she wept.

It will be recollected that Adèle flies at the end of the act.

"Ah!" said Dorval, sobbing, "there's an honest woman! I should never have been able to do that!"

"You," I said, "are a love!"

"No, monsieur, I am 'an angel'! Let us go on with the third act!—ah! my goodness! if only he rejoins her!"

I read the third act and she listened, trembling with excitement. It ends with the broken window and the handkerchief applied to Adèle's mouth, and by Adèle being flung into her room, after which the curtain falls.

"Well, what next?" said Dorval.

"Of course you know what Antony does after that?"

"Why, he ravishes her, I suppose."

"Rather! only she does not ring——"

"Oh!"

"What?"

"Good!... What an ending to a third act! You do not mince matters! This act will be a little bit difficult to play. You just see how I will say, 'This door will not shut!' and 'No accident has ever happened in this inn!' There is only the cry when I catch sight of Antony; I think Adèle would be too delighted to see him again to cry out."

"She must utter a cry, though."

"Yes, I understand; it sounds more moral.... Come! go on, go on, good dog!"

I began the fourth act. At the scene where the insult takes place, she put her hands round my neck and I felt her bosom rising and falling, as well as her heart beating against my shoulder; I could feel it almost bursting through her garments. At the scene between the vicomtesse and Adèle, where Adèle three times repeats, "But I have done nothing to injure this woman!" I stopped.

"Good Lord! man, why do you keep on stopping?" she exclaimed.

"I stop because you are strangling me!" I replied.

"Why, so I am," she said; "but such things have never been done on the stage yet. Oh! it is too real, it is horrible, it stifles one, oh!..."

"But you must listen to the end, nevertheless."

"Willingly enough."

So I finished reading the act.

"Oh!" she said, "you may be quite at rest, I can answer for myself. Oh! how feelingly I will say, 'She is his mistress!' Your plays are not difficult to act, but they break one's heart.... Oh! let me have my cry out!... You great big dog, where have you learnt to know women like this? You know them through and through!"

"Come, pick up your courage. We shall soon have finished it now."

"Go on!"

I began the fifth act. To my intense astonishment, although she wept much, it seemed to produce a less moving effect upon her than the others.

"Well?" I asked.

"Oh! it is splendid, I think, excellent!"

"That is not the truth: you do not like it, really."

"Yes, I do."

"No, you do not!"

"Well, then, do you honestly want my opinion?"

"Yes."

"I think the last act is a little too mild."

"See what differences of taste people have! Mademoiselle Mars thought it too strong."

"I wager it was not like this to begin with?"

"No, I ought to confess it was not."

"She made you change it?"

"From beginning to end!"

"Come now!"

"But, if you like, I will alter it back again."

"Indeed, I do wish it!"

"Oh! it will be easy enough to do."

"But when can you do it?"

"To-morrow, or the day after, or some day."

She looked at me, turned my chair round on one of its legs and fell on her knees in front of me.

"Do you know what you ought to do, good dog?" she said.

"What ought I to do? Tell me."

She took out one of her little combs and began combing her hair while she talked.

"I will tell you: you ought to re-write that act for me this very night."

"I am willing; I will go home and set to work."

"No, without going home."

"Why."

"Listen: Merle is in the country; take his room, they shall bring you some tea there; from time to time I will come in and see how your work goes on. You will have finished by the morning and will then come and read it to me, by my bedside. Ah! that will be most delightful."

"What if Merle should come back?"

"Bah! we would not let him in."

"Very well: you shall have your act to-morrow before your breakfast."

"Oh! good dog, how very charming you are! But, you know?..."

She raised her finger.

"Since it is agreed between us!"

"All right! What are you going to do this evening? Will you have supper first or begin working?"

"I prefer to set to work."

She rang.

"Louise! Louise!"

Louise came in.

"Well, madame, again?" she asked.

"No.... Make a fire in Merle's room."

"But Monsieur said he would not return."

"It is not for him, but for Alexandre."

The maid looked at me.

"Yes," said I, "it is all right; it is for me."

"Oh! how funny!" she said. "But—"

"You see," I said to Dorval, "it is improper."

"You need not be shocked, Louise. He has a bill of exchange and fears arrest at his own house to-morrow morning, so he will sleep here—that is all; only, you must not mention it."

Worthy Dorval! she could only think of two motives for not sleeping in one's own home—a mistress, or a bill of exchange.

"Oh!" said Louise, "all right! I see it ought not to be spoken about!"

"Specially not to M. le Comte, you understand?... The more so that there is no harm in it."

Louise smiled.

"Oh! Madame takes me for an ordinary lady's-maid, I suppose.... Has Madame any other orders for me?"

"No."

Louise went out.

We were left alone. I, as always, filled with admiration for that naïve, impulsive-natured woman who ever obeyed the first instincts of her heart, or the first dictates of her imagination; she, like a gleeful child who takes an unexpected holiday, or tastes some hitherto unknown pleasure. Then she stood up before me, unaffectedly, in attitudes delightfully natural and, in fittingly sorrowful accents, she went through the whole of her part, without forgetting one salient feature in it, saying each word as she felt it, with striking correctness, bringing out effects, even in the most commonplace of my scenes (those which were put in merely as connecting links with the main ones), that I never thought of when I wrote them, and, every now and then, jumping for joy and clapping her hands and exclaiming—

"Oh! you will see, my good dog, you will see what a grand success we shall make of it!"

Oh! splendid personality, which death thought to obliterate when it struck her down in my arms! I swore the memory of her genius should not be destroyed by death. I will make thee live again, as I promised thee, and, as those who had a right to exact a false version from me have authorised me to tell the truth, I will indeed do so: at every flourish of my pen thou shalt rise from the dead, throbbing with life, with the womanly weaknesses that belonged to thee and the qualities which made thee the artist thou wast; exactly, in short, as God created thee, without veil or mask: to treat such a personality like any ordinary being would be to insult thy genius!

Louise re-entered in a quarter of an hour's time: everything was ready in Merle's room. It was fated that I should from henceforth create my plays at the houses of those for whom they were intended.

At half-past eleven I set myself to work upon my fifth act; by three in the morning it was re-written; by nine o'clock Dorval was clapping her hands rejoicingly and crying—

"How I will act it! 'But I am lost!' Wait a bit; now hear: 'My daughter, I must kiss my daughter!' and then: 'Kill me!' and so on to the end!"

"Then you are quite satisfied?"

"I should think so, indeed! Now we must send and fetch Bocage to breakfast with us and hear it all."

I knew very little of Bocage's talents. I had only seen him act the curé in *l'Incendiaire* and the sergeant in *Napoléon à Schoenbrünn*, two rôles which did not at all assist me to imagine him in *Antony*. I was, therefore, prejudiced against him, and spoke of Lockroy and of Frédéric, of the ease with which we could obtain the services of either of them at the reopening of the theatrical year; but Dorval stuck to her point: she maintained that Bocage was the only actor who could give to Antony the necessary appearance suitable to the part of Antony; so she sent to fetch him.

Bocage was then a handsome fellow of about thirty-four or thirty-five, with dark hair and fine white teeth, and beautiful mysterious eyes, which could express three things essential on the stage—roughness, determination and melancholy: among his physical defects were that he was knock-kneed, his feet were too large, he had a dragging gait and he spoke through his nose. As Dorval's letter was urgent, he rushed off to us at once. We breakfasted, and afterwards I read *Antony* through again.

"Well, what do you think of it, Bocage?" Dorval asked, directly I had pronounced the concluding words, "She resisted me, so I killed her!"

"Upon my word," replied Bocage, "I really hardly know what I have been hearing. It is neither a play, nor a drama, nor a tragedy, nor a novel; it is something of them all, and certainly most striking! Only, can you imagine me as Antony?"

"You will be superb!" replied Dorval.

"What do you say, Dumas?"

"I know too little of you to say anything; but Dorval knows you and is ready to answer for you."

"Good! But I should need a special make-up for the part. I could not act it in ordinary everyday clothes."

"Oh! don't trouble yourself about that," I replied; "we will discover a suitable costume between us."

"What is our next move?"

"You must inform Crosnier that you have just been listening to a drama that suits you and Dorval; that it is by me, and that I am willing to sign the same agreement with him that Hugo did."

"Capital!"

"But, understand, Bocage—there must be no official reading before acceptance; the piece is to be taken whatever happens: there can be a semi-official reading to the manager after its acceptance."

"All right, I understand! Dispense with reading before the other members of the company: you bring your plays and they are simply to act them. What are your terms?"

"The same as Hugo's."

"It shall be settled to-night."

I took a cab and went to tell Hugo what had happened. I received a little note from Bocage that very evening; it only contained these few lines:—

> "I have seen Crosnier. It is all settled; you are to read to-morrow at 11 a.m. in his office *semi-officially*—he quite understands.—Yours, BOCAGE"

Next day I presented myself at the appointed hour to M. Crosnier. I scarcely knew him; for I had only seen him once or twice. He had taken a third or fourth share in five or six pieces; amongst others, in a parody of Schiller's *Intrigue et Amour*, played under the title of *La Fille du Musicien*. I do not even know whether this piece, which was very successful, was not acted later than the time I am now talking of. He was an accomplished, clever man, with fair hair and little of it, grey eyes, a mouth but scantily furnished with teeth and his manners were nice and affable: he has since amassed a very large fortune, I believe, to which his relations with Cavé have done no harm. In conclusion, his was exactly the temperament to understand *La Petite Ville*, and the least suited to understand *Antony*.

I began my reading. By the third act, M. Crosnier was politely striving against his drowsiness; by the fourth, he was sleeping as comfortably as possible; by the fifth, he was snoring.

I went out without his hearing me do so, I have no doubt. Bocage was waiting for me in the salon to hear the result of the reading: I showed him his sleeping manager through the half-open door and left him a receipt for a thousand francs. According to our agreement, M. Crosnier owed me a thousand francs for the reading.

"Diable!" exclaimed Bocage, "is the agreement signed, then?"

"No; but I have your letter of yesterday's date, which is as good as a contract, and I will await your reply at Dorval's house."

Bocage alone could divulge what passed between himself and Crosnier. I fancy there was some friction between them. However, half to three-quarters of an hour later, he arrived at Dorval's house with the thousand-franc note. But Crosnier deferred the play for three or four months: he did not wish to risk his winter's successes with a work he considered *so uncertain of pleasing the public*.

"Never mind, *certain or not*, that will not prevent its making money, my good dog, I will answer for that!" said Dorval.

So that is the story of *Antony*, of its withdrawal from the Théâtre-Français and its appearance at the théâtre de la Porte-Saint-Martin, with your humble servant as its father, and Bocage and Dorval as its godfather and godmother.

APPENDIX

NOTE A

Comme nous nous y étions attendu en heurtant aussi carrément que nous le faisons les hommes et les choses, une réclamation s'est produite, respectable par le sentiment qui l'a dictée; elle est du fils de M. de Liniers.

Cette réclamation nous a été communiquée par la rédaction du journal *la Presse*, et nous avons désiré qu'elle fût publiée dans son intégralité.

Nous croyons devoir la reproduire ici, en conservant les réflexions dont l'avait accompagnée *la Presse*.

AU RÉDACTEUR

"ORLÉANS, 4 *mars* 1853

"MONSIEUR,—Les *Mémoires* publiés par M. A. Dumas dans votre journal (nos des 19, 23 et 24 février) sont venus, par hasard, à ma connaissance. Dans le récit fait par l'auteur d'un épisode de sa vie en 1830, la conduite de mon père se trouve présentée sous un jour qui tendrait à jeter sur lui une déconsidération imméritée.

"Permettez au plus jeune de ses fils, témoin oculaire du fait principal, de défendre une mémoire honorable et chère, et veuillez donner place dans votre journal à sa juste réclamation.

"Je me trouvais en 1830 près de mon père; j'étais dans son cabinet au moment où M. Dumas s'y présenta. En rectifiant les faits altérés par lui, je dirai ce que je sais, ce que j'ai vu.

"Au moment où éclata la révolution, il se trouvait, sous les ordres de mon père, non pas huit cents hommes, mais un nombre à peine suffisant pour former un peloton d'instruction. Dès la veille de l'arrivée de M. Dumas, M. de Liniers avait été prévenu que cette faible garnison était dans le même esprit que le régiment, qui se trouvait alors à Paris, il ne pouvait compter sur elle pour défendre la poudre confiée à sa garde. Une certaine agitation se faisait remarquer dans la ville; on savait la lutte engagée à Paris; la garde nationale s'organisait; les communications étaient interceptées: il ne fut pas même possible d'envoyer une ordonnance à Laon pour prendre les ordres de M. le général Sérant. Dans cette, situation critique, mon père se rendit le soir chez M. de Senneville, f sous-préfet à Soissons, et il fut arrêté entre eux que les poudres seraient remises à la garde nationale, si elle les demandait, et même en cas d'attaque.

"Il restait à maintenir la tranquillité dans la ville; elle fut maintenue, et la révolte des prisonniers, qui avait inspiré un moment de graves inquiétudes, fut comprimée par l'énergie de mon père.

"Le vicomte de Liniers savait donc bien ce qu'il avait à faire; son plan avait été arrêté à l'avance, et M. Dumas, qui n'avait pas encore paru, ne lui dicta en aucune façon la conduite qu'il avait à tenir.

"Le lendemain matin, M. Dumas se présenta dans le bureau de mon père, qui s'y trouvait avec son secrétaire, ma mère et moi. Il demanda que les poudres lui fussent livrées, et présenta à cet effet un ordre signé par le général Gérard. Mon père refusa. En ce moment parut un planton porteur d'un rapport de service; M. Dumas, alors, et à l'instant où le soldat se retournait pour se retirer, sortit un pistolet de sa poche, et lui dit; 'Si tu me fais arrêter, voilà pour ton commandant!' Mon père reprend alors avec calme: 'Vous pouvez m'assassiner; car, vous le voyez, je suis sans armes.—Prenez garde, monsieur le vicomte,' reprit M. Dumas, 'vous voyez que je suis armé; il faut me livrer vos poudres.—Non pas à vous,' répondit mon père, 'mais à une députation de la garde nationale seulement, puisque je me trouve dans l'impossibilité absolue de défendre le dépôt que le roi m'a confié.'

"M. Dumas sortit alors pour aller chercher cette députation, qui, quelques instants après, entra en armes dans la cour; il monta dans le bureau, et y trouva M. de Lenferna et un autre officier. Le commandant de place, exécutant alors ce qui avait été convenu la veille entre lui et le sous-préfet, donna l'ordre de remettre les poudres à la garde nationale.

"Tels sont les faits dans leur simple vérité. Le récit fait par M. Dumas, cette scène étrange d'intimidation, ces quatre officiers français menacés par lui, effrayés par lui, attendant patiemment qu'il voulût bien leur brûler la cervelle, s'ils n'aimaient mieux obéir à ses ordres, tout cela rencontrera certes autant d'incrédules que de lecteurs; l'honneur de braves et loyaux officiers n'a rien à redouter de ces exagérations, et toute cette mise en scène se réduirait à avoir effrayé tout au plus une femme, et menacé avec un pistolet un homme sans armes pour se défendre. M. Dumas cite à l'appui de son récit *le Moniteur* du 9 août 1830, dans lequel l'épisode de Soissons est raconté (il en est le narrateur sans aucun doute); il ajoute: 'Ce récit n'a pas été démenti; donc, il est vrai.' M. Dumas est encore dans l'erreur: mon père a protesté; il a démenti à deux reprises différentes; mais, à cette époque où la bonne foi n'était pas de rigueur, on refusa les colonnes du *Moniteur* à la réclamation de l'ex-commandant de place de Soissons. Il n'était pas, il est vrai, partisan du nouveau gouvernement.

"Je n'entends, du reste, engager aucune polémique avec M. Dumas; j'ai rétabli la vérité des faits, et je ne répondrai à aucune attaque de sa part, dans les journaux; il est facile, mais triste, de ternir la vie des hommes les plus honorables quand ils ne sont plus. Si mon père vivait, il n'eût certes pas laissé à ses fils l'honneur de défendre sa conduite, il s'en serait chargé lui-même.

"Un dernier mot, pour terminer cette rectification, si longue bien malgré moi: mon père reçut, en quittant Soissons, les témoignages de sympathie les plus flatteurs. Le général Gaillebois, qui remplaça le général Sérant, lui offrit son influence pour lui faire obtenir un emploi. Les plus honorables habitants de Soissons, ceux mêmes qui ne partageaient pas ses opinions politiques, voulurent lui serrer la main, et lui exprimer leurs regrets de ne plus le voir parmi eux. Ce souvenir d'estime des habitants de cette ville fut toujours précieux à mon père; c'eût été manquer à sa mémoire de ne pas prouver qu'il en fut toujours digne.

"Recevez, monsieur le rédacteur de *la Presse*, l'assurance de ma considération distinguée.

"LE CHEVALIER DE LINIERS"

"M. Alexandre Dumas, à qui nous avons communiqué cette réclamation, mû par un sentiment de convenance qui sera apprécié, a désiré borner sa réponse à la reproduction du rapport qui a paru dans *le Moniteur* du 9 août 1850. Il est vrai que M. de Liniers essaye d'infirmer l'autorité de ce rapport en alléguant que l'hospitalité du *Moniteur* n'a pas été accordée à la réponse itérative de son père. Il est regrettable, si *le Moniteur* a réellement refusé ses colonnes, que l'ancien commandant de la place de Soissons n'ait pas eu l'idée d'adresser ses plaintes à l'un des journaux légitimistes qui paraissaient en 1830, à la *Gazette de France* ou à *la Quotidienne*, qui se seraient évidemment empressées de les accueillir. Dans l'état des choses, nos lecteurs ont à choisir entre cette réclamation, évidemment tardive, et un récit contemporain qui a reçu une publicité officielle, qui se présente avec la garantie de cinq signatures, et qui n'a pas été contredit en temps utile.

"Voici le rapport de M. Alexandre Dumas:

Rapport à M. le général la Fayette sur l'enlèvement des poudres de Soissons

"Conformément à la mission dont vous m'avez fait l'honneur de me charger le 30 juillet dernier, je suis parti à l'instant même pour la remplir, accompagné de l'un des signataires du présent rapport. À trois heures, nous sortions de la barrière.

"Sur toute la route, on nous prévint que nous trouverions à Soissons résistance aux ordres du gouvernement provisoire, qui n'était pas encore reconnu dans cette ville. En arrivant à Villers-Cotterets, un jeune Soissonnais, signataire de ce rapport, nous offrit de nous faire accompagner de trois ou quatre jeunes gens qui seconderaient notre mouvement. À onze heures et demie du soir, nous étions à Soissons.

"À sept heures du matin, ignorant quelles seraient les dispositions de la ville, nous visitions les ruines de Saint-Jean, où nous savions qu'étaient renfermées les poudres, afin d'être prêts à nous en emparer de force, si on ne voulait pas reconnaître notre appel aux citoyens de Soissons. Le jeune homme qui s'était chargé de nous aider nous quitta alors pour aller rassembler les quelques personnes dont il était sûr, et, moi, je me rendis chez M. le docteur Missa, que l'on m'avait désigné comme un des plus chauds patriotes de la ville; son avis fut que nous ne trouverions aucune aide auprès des autorités, et qu'il y aurait probablement résistance de la part du commandant de place, M. le comte de Liniers.

"Comme il était à craindre que les trois officiers logés à la poudrière ne fussent avertis de mon arrivée et de l'ordre dont j'étais porteur, je me rendis d'abord chez eux, accompagné de trois personnes que m'avait amenées M. Hutin (c'est le nom du jeune Soissonnais). En passant devant la poudrière, j'y laissai un factionnaire. Quelques minutes après M. le lieutenant-colonel d'Orcourt, le capitaine Mollart et le sergent. Ragon se rendaient prisonniers à ma première sommation, et promettaient sur parole de ne pas sortir, disant qu'ils étaient prêts à nous livrer les poudres sur un ordre du commandant de place. Les trois braves militaires, comme nous en fûmes convaincus par la suite étaient, du reste, bien plus disposés à nous aider qu'à nous être contraires. Je me rendis aussitôt seul chez le commandant de place, tandis que le jeune homme que j'avais amené avec moi et M. Hutin se faisaient ouvrir les portes de la cathédrale, et substituaient au drapeau blanc les couleurs de la nation. M. le commandant de place était avec un officier dont j'ignore le nom; je lui montrai le pouvoir que j'avais reçu de vous: il me dit qu'il ne pouvait reconnaître les ordres du gouvernement provisoire; que, d'ailleurs, votre signature ne portait aucun caractère d'authenticité, et que le cachet manquait. Il ajouta de plus qu'il n'y avait à la poudrière que deux cents livres de poudre. Cela pouvait être vrai, puisqu'un ancien militaire me l'affirmait sur sa parole d'honneur. Je sortis pour m'en informer, mais en le prévenant que j'allais revenir. Je craignais peu contre moi l'emploi de la force armée; j'avais reconnu dans la garnison le dépôt du 53ᵉ· J'appris que, dès la veille, tous les soldats s'étaient distribué des cocardes tricolores.

"J'acquis la certitude qu'il y avait dans la poudrière deux cents livres de poudre appartenant à l'artillerie, et trois mille livres appartenant à la régie.

"Je revins alors chez M. le commandant de place; je savais le besoin qu'on éprouvait de munitions à Paris; je voulais, comme je vous avais promis sur ma parole de le faire, m'emparer de celles qui se trouvaient à Soissons, sauf, comme vous me l'aviez recommandé, à laisser à la ville la quantité nécessaire à sa défense. M. le commandant de place avait alors auprès de lui trois personnes dont deux m'étaient connues, l'une pour le lieutenant de gendarmerie, marquis de Lenferna, l'autre pour le colonel du génie, M. Bonvilliers. Je soumis de nouveau à l'examen de M. le commandant la dépêche dont j'étais porteur; il refusa positivement de me délivrer aucun ordre, à moins, me dit-il, qu'il n'y fût contraint par la force. Je crus, effectivement, que ce moyen était le plus court: je tirai et j'armai des pistolets à deux coups que j'avais sur moi, et je lui renouvelai ma sommation de me livrer les poudres. J'étais trop engagé pour reculer; je me trouvais à peu près seul dans une ville de huit mille âmes, au milieu d'autorités, en général, très-contraires au gouvernement actuel; il y avait, pour moi, question de vie ou de mort. M. le commandant, voyant que j'étais entièrement résolu à employer contre lui et les trois personnes présentes tous les moyens que mes armes mettaient à ma disposition, me dit qu'il ne devait pas, pour son honneur, céder à un homme seul, lui, commandant d'une place fortifiée et ayant garnison.

"J'offris à M. le commandant de lui signer un certificat constatant que c'était le pistolet au poing que je l'avais forcé de me signer l'ordre, et de tout prendre ainsi sous ma responsabilité. Il préféra que j'envoyasse chercher quelques personnes pour paraître céder à une force plus imposante. J'enfermai M. le commandant de place et la société dans son cabinet; je me plaçai devant la porte, et je fis dire aux personnes qui m'avaient déjà accompagné de venir me rejoindre. Quelques minutes après, MM. Bard, Moreau et Hutin entraient dans la cour et M. le commandant me signait l'ordre de me délivrer toutes le poudres appartenant à l'artillerie. Muni de cet ordre, et voulant opérer le plus légalement possible, j'allai trouver le maire, qui m'accompagna à la poudrière. Le colonel d'Orcourt nous montra la poudre: il n'y en avait effectivement que deux cents livres. Le maire les exigea pour la ville.

"Tout ce que j'avais fait jusque-là était devenu inutile; je réclamai alors les poudres de la régie: elles me furent refusées. J'allai chez l'entreposeur, M. Jousselin; je lui offris d'en acheter pour mille francs; c'était ce que j'avais d'argent sur moi; il refusa. C'est alors que, voyant que ce dernier refus était la suite d'un système bien arrêté par les autorités de n'aider en rien leurs frères de Paris, je sortis avec l'intention de tout prendre par force. J'envoyai M. Moreau, l'un des plus chauds patriotes de Soissons, arrêter, en les payant au prix qu'exigeraient les voituriers, des chariots de transport; il me promit d'être avec eux dans une demi-heure à la porte de la poudrière. Son départ réduisit notre troupe à trois personnes. Je pris une hache, M. Hutin son fusil, et Bard (le jeune homme qui nous avait accompagnés de Paris) ses pistolets. Je laissai ce dernier en faction à la deuxième porte d'entrée; je l'invitai à tirer sur la première personne qui essayerait de s'opposer à l'enlèvement de la poudre, et M. Hutin et moi enfonçâmes la porte à coups de hache. J'envoyai M. Hutin presser M. Moreau, et je l'attendis au milieu de la poudrière. Deux heures après, tout était chargé sans opposition de la part de l'autorité. D'ailleurs, tous les citoyens qui venaient de se soulever nous auraient prêté main-forte.

"Nous quittâmes Soissons à six heures et demie du soir, accompagnés des pompiers, qui s'étaient réunis à nous, de plusieurs jeunes gens à cheval et armés, et d'une trentaine d'hommes qui nous servirent d'escorte jusqu'à Villers-Cotterets. Notre sortie se fit au milieu des acclamations de tout le peuple, qui se découvrait devant le drapeau tricolore flottant sur notre première voiture.

"À dix heures, nous étions à Villers-Cotterets; l'escorte de Soissons ne nous quitta que pour nous remettre entre les mains de la garde nationale de cette ville, qui, à son tour, nous accompagna jusqu'à Nanteuil.

"Voilà le récit exact de ce que j'ai cru devoir faire, général, pensant que, si j'allais trop loin, vous le pardonneriez à mon inexpérience diplomatique, et surtout à mon enthousiasme pour une cause dont, pour la troisième fois, vous êtes un des plus nobles soutiens.

"Respect et admiration.

"*(Signé)*

AL. DUMAS
BARD, rue Saint-Germain-l'Auxerrois, 66, à Paris
HUTIN, rue Richebourg, I, à Soissons
LENOIR-MORAND, capitaine de sapeurs-pompiers, à Veilly

J'atteste la vérité de ce rapport

(Signé) GILLES"

(Extrait du *Moniteur* du 9 août 1830.)

NOTE B

AU RÉDACTEUR DU JOURNAL *LA PRESSE*

"MONSIEUR,—Les *Mémoires* de M. Alexandre Dumas, que vous publiez dans votre journal, sont devenus, depuis quelque temps, des mémoires sur la révolution de 1830. Je ne saurais me dispenser de réclamer contre ce qu'ils contiennent sur le gouvernement provisoire de cette époque.

"Ce gouvernement ne s'était pas créé de lui-même. Il avait été constitué par une réunion de députés qui s'était formée immédiatement après la publication des ordonnances.

"L'autorité militaire supérieure avait été remise à M. le général la Fayette, et la direction des opérations actives à M. le général Gérard. Quant à l'autorité civile, on en avait investi une commission de sept membres à qui l'on avait confié les pouvoirs les plus larges, mais à qui l'on avait imposé en même temps, non sans une intention secrète, le titre fort restreint de *commission municipale*. Les sept membres de cette commission étaient MM. Laffitte, Casimir Périer, Gérard, Lobau, de Schonen, Audry de Puyraveau et moi. MM. Laffitte et Gérard, retenus par d'autres travaux, n'ont pris aucune part à nos délibérations; M. Casimir Périer y a paru seulement quatre ou cinq fois. De ces sept membres, je suis maintenant le seul qui survive, et je n'aurais pas le droit de réclamer pour mon compte, que ce serait, à mes yeux, un devoir de réclamer pour celui de mes anciens collègues.

"La commission municipale de 1830 n'a pas constitué un gouvernement aussi inactif, aussi introuvable que M. Alexandre Dumas se complaît à l'affirmer. Il s'en serait convaincu lui-même à cette époque, s'il eût seulement jeté les yeux sur les murs de Paris, placardés chaque jour de nombreux décrets. Il les retrouvera dans les journaux du temps, si cela lui convient. Nous ne nous réunissions pas chez M. Laffitte, comme il le dit: tous nos actes étaient datés de l'hôtel de ville, où était notre siège, et où chacun pouvait nous parler. M. Dumas reconnaît lui-même que nous y avons reçu, dès le 29 juillet, c'est-à-dire dès le jour même de notre installation, MM. de Sémonville, d'Argout et de Vitrolles, qui venaient conférer avec nous au nom de Charles X; il reconnaît également que, quatre ou cinq jours plus tard, nous avons reçu M. de Sussy, qui voulait déposer entre nos mains le décret royal rapportant les ordonnances; il reconnaît, enfin, que nous avons reçu une députation républicaine présidée par M. Hubert. Il nous eût trouvés comme tout le monde, si toutefois il nous eût cherchés réellement, et il eût été entendu, s'il avait eu des choses importantes à nous faire connaître; autrement, j'avoue qu'il eût été fort peu écouté.

"De notre conférence avec MM. de Sémonville, d'Argout et de Vitrolles, il ne rapporte que le mot de M. de Schonen, si connu de tout le monde: *Il est trop tard!* Mais ce mot ne terminait pas la discussion; au contraire, il la faisait naître, car il s'agissait précisément de savoir s'il était ou n'était pas trop tard. Charles X disposait encore de forces considérables: aux troupes qui l'entouraient allaient se joindre quarante pièces d'artillerie qui venaient de sortir de Vincennes, un régiment suisse qui arrivait d'Orléans, et le camp de Saint-Omer, qui était appelé. Loin de penser à prendre l'offensive, nous craignions une attaque. La nuit du 29 au 30 juillet fut pleine d'alarmes, et nous n'avions avec nous que deux ou trois régiments de ligne dont nous ne pouvions pas nous servir, parce qu'ils avaient stipulé, en acquiesçant à la cause populaire, qu'on ne les exposerait pas à combattre contre leurs frères d'armes. Aussi nous parut-il indispensable d'ordonner la création de vingt régiments de garde mobile. On se trompe, et l'on juge d'après les événements, quand on croit que Charles X était à bout de ressources dès le 29 ou le 30 juillet: la faiblesse de son caractère et l'incapacité de ses conseils ont été pour beaucoup dans le changement de sa fortune.

"Suivant M. Dumas, nous aurions accueilli M. de Sussy avec une bienveillance marquée; M. Dumas se trompe: M. de Sussy fut sans doute écouté avec politesse, mais non avec bienveillance. Ce qui le prouve, c'est que le dépôt qu'il voulait faire entre nos mains fut nettement refusé. La réception du décret et sa publication, que demandait M. de Sussy, n'entraient pas, d'ailleurs, dans nos attributions. La réunion des députés s'était réservé la haute question politique, c'est-à-dire le droit d'organiser le gouvernement définitif. Nous n'avions à nous occuper de cette question que dans le sein de la réunion même, et comme en faisant partie.

"En nous quittant, M. de Sussy se transporta à la Chambre, et fit remettre le décret à M. Laffitte, qui présidait et qui refusa également de le recevoir: il n'en prévint pas l'Assemblée. M. Dumas ignore, sans doute, qu'il existait alors dans le peuple et dans la Chambre deux tendances opposées. La Chambre se repentait de la révolution, qu'elle avait faite sans le vouloir ni le savoir. Elle était disposée à traiter avec Charles X. M. de Mortemart, nommé premier ministre à la place de M. de Polignac, avait fait demander à la réunion des députés, devenue fort nombreuse depuis la victoire, à être admis à lui communiquer les intentions royales. La réunion s'était empressée de lui répondre qu'elle le recevrait le même jour; elle avait décidé en même temps qu'elle s'assemblerait au palais législatif pour l'entendre, et s'était même occupée de la question d'étiquette. Les questeurs devaient d'abord le recevoir dans un salon; des huissiers seraient ensuite allés au-devant de lui, et l'eussent introduit dans la salle. Pour apprécier la déférence que les députés avaient mise à se transporter au palais législatif, il faut se rappeler que, jusqu'alors, ils ne s'étaient réunis que chez l'un d'eux; ils ne devaient s'assembler officiellement, au lieu ordinaire de leurs séances, et avec le caractère de Chambre, que le 3 août, jour fixé par l'ordonnance de convocation, c'est-à-dire deux ou trois jours plus tard.

"La séance eut lieu, mais M. de Mortemart ne parut pas. De là le décret qui, le jour même, après une assez longue attente, conféra la lieutenance générale au duc d'Orléans. Je n'ai jamais douté, quant à moi, que, si M. de Mortemart se fût présenté, les événements n'eussent pris une direction différente.

"Le peuple n'était pas comme la Chambre: il ne voulait plus de Bourbons. Le duc d'Orléans lui-même, après sa proclamation comme roi, ne put se faire accepter qu'en s'abritant sous la popularité du général la Fayette, et en parcourant les rues de Paris pendant plusieurs jours, donnant des poignées de main aux uns, faisant des discours aux autres, et trinquant avec le premier venu: je dis les faits, je ne crée pas.

"Au moment où, suivant M. Dumas, nous étions en conférence avec M. de Sussy, arriva la députation Hubert, qui, voyant la porte fermée, l'ébranla à coups de crosse de fusil. On ouvrit. Alors, parut M. Hubert, suivi de quelques amis, et portant une proclamation au bout d'une baïonnette. Les membres de la commission furent *saisis d'épouvante* et *s'éparpillèrent* un instant au milieu de la salle.

"Je ne sais si M. Dumas a voulu faire du pittoresque; mais je sais qu'il n'y a pas un mot de vrai dans son récit.

"Voici ce qui arriva:

"La députation avait demandé à être introduite, et le fut immédiatement. Elle n'était point armée, et se composait de quinze ou vingt personnes; M. Hubert était à sa tête. Je crois me rappeler qu'en effet M. de Sussy était encore présent; je crois même me rappeler que nous voulûmes saisir l'occasion de le rendre témoin d'une scène populaire; il ne pouvait qu'y puiser des enseignements pour la cour de Charles X. M. Hubert, qui n'avait ni proclamation écrite, ni baïonnette, parla au nom de la députation, et d'abondance. Il insista notamment sur deux points: sur la nécessité de consulter la nation, et sur celle de ne pas constituer le pouvoir avant d'avoir stipulé et arrêté des garanties pour les libertés publiques.

"Ce discours eut un effet que M. Hubert n'avait certainement pas prévu. Il mit en saillie une divergence d'opinion qui existait dans la commission, mais qui était jusque-là restée inaperçue.

"J'avoue franchement que, sur plusieurs points, j'étais de l'avis de l'orateur. On lui fit une réponse qui venait du cabinet du général la Fayette, qui avait été préparée en arrière de moi, qui manquait de franchise, et qui excita plusieurs fois, de ma part, des gestes ou des mots de surprise et de désapprobation. La députation s'en aperçut. Ce léger incident a même été signalé dans plusieurs brochures de l'époque.

"Tout se passa, du reste, poliment, convenablement, et je crois même pouvoir certifier que, lorsque la députation se retira, M. Audry de Puyraveau ne glissa pas en secret un projet de proclamation dans la main de son chef; autrement, il se serait donné un démenti à lui-même, car il avait approuvé la réponse.

"Je dois ajouter ici que les négociations entreprises par M. de Sussy, et dont le bruit s'était répandu au dehors, avaient tellement alarmé la population, que, pour prévenir un soulèvement populaire, nous fûmes obligés de publier la proclamation qui prononçait la déchéance de Charles X.

"Je ne puis me taire sur une scène où M. Dumas me fait figurer personnellement avec M. Charras. Il aurait été question d'une lettre à écrire aux officiers d'un régiment où je ne connaissais personne; je me serais plaint du général Lobau, et M. Charras aurait menacé de le faire fusiller; sur quoi, j'aurais bondi de surprise; M. Charras m'aurait pris par la main, et, me conduisant à l'une des fenêtres de l'hôtel de ville, il m'aurait montré la place en me disant: 'Il y a là cent cinquante hommes qui n'obéissent qu'à moi, et qui fusilleraient le Père éternel, s'il descendait sur la terre, et si je leur disais de le fusiller!'

"M. Charras était, à cette époque, un jeune homme fort peu connu et n'ayant aucune influence. Je ne me rappelle ni l'avoir vu ni lui avoir parlé à l'hôtel de ville. Dans tous les cas, s'il m'eût tenu le langage qu'on lui prête, ou je l'aurais fait arrêter, ou je me serais éloigné sans daigner lui répondre.

"M. Dumas est certainement venu à l'hôtel de ville, puisqu'il l'affirme. Voici ce qu'il a dû y voir:

"Sur la place, sur les quais et dans les rues adjacentes était une population compacte et serrée, attendant les événements, et toujours prête à nous appuyer de son concours. Sur la place, au milieu de la foule, se maintenait un passage de quatre ou cinq pieds de large. C'était une espèce de rue ayant des hommes pour murailles.

"Quand nous avions à donner un ordre exigeant l'appui d'une force quelconque, nous en confions, en général, l'exécution à un élève de l'École polytechnique. L'élève descendait le perron de l'hôtel de ville. Avant d'être parvenu aux derniers degrés, il s'adressait à la foule, devenue attentive, et prononçait simplement ces mots: *Deux cents hommes de bonne volonté!* Puis il achevait de descendre, et s'engageait seul dans le passage. A l'instant même, on voyait se détacher des murailles, et marcher derrière lui, les uns avec des fusils, les autres seulement avec des sabres, un homme, deux hommes, vingt hommes, puis cent, quatre cents, cinq cents. Il y en avait toujours le double de ce qui avait été demandé.

"D'un mot, d'un geste, je ne dirai pas en une heure, mais en une minute, nous eussions disposé de dix, de quinze, de vingt mille hommes.

"Je demande ce que nous pouvions avoir à craindre de M. Hubert, de M. Charras et de ses prétendus cent cinquante prétoriens? Qu'il me soit permis d'ajouter que des hommes qui étaient venus siéger à l'hôtel de ville dès le 29 juillet avaient prouvé par là même qu'ils n'étaient pas d'un caractère facile à effrayer. Pendant les jours de combat, le gouvernement avait décerné des mandats d'arrêt contre sept députés au nombre desquels je me trouvais, ainsi que plusieurs de mes collègues de la commission. Charles X avait même annoncé, le lendemain, que nous étions déjà fusillés. Quand nous n'avions pas reculé devant le pouvoir, aurions-nous reculé devant des jeunes gens, fort honorables sans doute, mais qui, il faut bien le dire, étaient sans puissance?

"Jamais autorité ne fut obéie aussi ponctuellement que la nôtre. Jamais peuple ne se montra aussi docile, aussi courageux, aussi ami de l'ordre que celui de Paris en 1830. Nous n'avions pas seulement pour nous les masses inférieures, nous avions la garde nationale, la population tout entière. Lorsqu'il fut question de l'expédition de Rambouillet, l'autorité militaire nous demanda dix mille hommes. Sa dépêche nous était arrivée à neuf heures du matin; à neuf heures et demie, nos ordres étaient expédiés aux municipalités que nous avions créées; à onze heures, les dix mille hommes étaient rassemblés aux Champs-Élysées, et se mettaient en mouvement, sous le commandement du général Pajol. Il avait suffi d'un coup de tambour pour les réunir. Leur nombre s'élevait à vingt mille et même à trente mille avant qu'ils fussent arrivés à Cognières, près Rambouillet. Au milieu d'eux, à la vérité, régnait un immense désordre. Charles X était entouré d'une garde fidèle, d'une nombreuse artillerie, et la cause nationale aurait pu éprouver une sanglante catastrophe. Elle n'en eût pas été ébranlée: Paris, dans vingt-quatre heures, aurait fourni cent mille hommes qui eussent été promptement organisés et disciplinés. La guerre civile fut prévenue par un mot du maréchal Maison, mot qui n'était pas exact quand il fut prononcé, mais qui le serait devenu le lendemain, et qui a trouvé son excuse dans ses heureux effets.

"Que si l'on me demande ce que nous avons fait de cette confiance sans mesure qui nous était accordée, je répondrai que ce n'est pas à moi qu'il faut adresser la question. La puissance souveraine, alors, était dans la Chambre, dont le public ignorait les dispositions intérieures. La Chambre obéissait tant aux événements qu'à M. Laffitte, et M. Laffitte, en outre, tant par lui que par le général la Fayette, disposait des masses populaires. Le crédit de la commission ne venait qu'en troisième ordre; mais, comme il grandissait, tous les jours, il inspira des inquiétudes, et on chercha le moyen de s'en débarrasser.

"J'ai déjà signalé la dissidence qui existait entre l'opinion publique et la législature; il s'en déclara bientôt une autre dans le sein de la législature même.

"Parmi les députés, les uns voulaient constituer la royauté d'abord, sauf à s'occuper plus tard des garanties; les autres demandaient qu'on s'occupât des garanties et des changements à faire dans l'organisation du pays avant de constituer la royauté. Commencerait-on par faire une constitution, ou commencerait-on parfaire un roi? Telle était donc la question.

"Les partisans de la royauté faisaient valoir les inconvénients d'un gouvernement provisoire, et la crainte de l'anarchie; ceux de la constitution répondaient que, dans l'état du pays, et ils en donnaient Paris pour preuve, l'anarchie n'était pas à redouter; ils ajoutaient qu'il fallait mettre les institutions publiques en accord avec la situation nouvelle, et ne pas s'exposer à une continuation de lutte avec la royauté, ce qui, disaient-ils, aurait pour résultat inévitable une seconde révolution et l'anarchie même qu'on voulait prévenir. Les premiers répliquaient qu'il n'y avait point de situation nouvelle; qu'il pouvait être question, au plus, de changer la personne du prince; les seconds, que le peuple avait fait plus qu'une révolution de palais, et qu'il importait à la royauté même, dans l'intérêt de sa stabilité, d'être reconstituée sur d'autres bases, et de recevoir la sanction du pays.

"Le parti Laffitte et la Fayette passa tout entier du côté de ceux qui voulaient une royauté immédiate, et leur assura une majorité considérable. Il agit même sur la commission municipale. M. de Schonen, un de ses membres, immédiatement après l'acceptation par le duc d'Orléans de la lieutenance générale, avait demandé que la commission se démît de ses pouvoirs. J'avais représenté que l'autorité nouvelle était déjà engagée dans de mauvaises voies, ce que nous savions tous, et qu'en retardant notre démission de quelques jours, nous parviendrions peut-être à l'éclairer. Sur mes représentations, la discussion avait été ajournée; mais, le lendemain, sur les instances secrètes du général la Fayette, et en mon absence, elle avait été reprise et la démission envoyée. On n'y trouvera pas ma signature. Au surplus, c'est moi qui avais tort. On avait voulu simplement débarrasser le nouveau pouvoir d'une coexistence qui pouvait le gêner; mais il nous convenait à tous de lui laisser la responsabilité de ses actes. Quant à la question de primauté entre l'établissement d'une constitution ou celui d'un roi, on sait qu'elle fut résolue par une révision de la Charte en vingt-quatre heures.

"La commission n'a existé comme gouvernement que pendant cinq jours, et, si l'on veut se reporter aux circonstances et à ses actes, on verra qu'elle les a bien remplis. Elle fut priée par le lieutenant général d'organiser la ville de Paris, ce qu'elle fit, et ce qui continua quinze jours de plus son existence devenue fort étroite. Son œuvre finie, elle se retira. Si elle ne s'est pas occupée plus activement de la grande question politique, c'est, comme je l'ai déjà dit, parce que chacun de ses membres appartenait à la réunion des députés, et y portait son opinion et ses votes.

"Dans ces divers événements, il avait été tenu fort peu de compte du parti républicain, et il y en avait une raison fort simple, c'est que ce parti n'existait pas alors, ni à Paris ni en France. Il se réduisait, à Paris, à cent cinquante ou deux cents adeptes, jeunes gens, il est vrai, pleins d'activité et de courage, mais qui n'avaient d'importance que par leur chef, le général la Fayette. Or, le général la Fayette n'était pas de leur parti; aussi en furent-ils abandonnés dès le premier pas.

"Je ne veux point dire par là que le général la Fayette n'était pas entré, sous la Restauration, dans la conspiration de Béfort et dans plusieurs autres; j'ai assez connu les affaires secrètes de ce temps pour ne pas l'ignorer; mais ces conspirations n'étaient pas républicaines. Je ne veux pas même dire que, dans les deux dernières années de sa vie, il ne se soit mêlé sérieusement à quelques combinaisons contre Louis-Philippe, et je reconnais qu'à cette époque le parti républicain avait déjà plus d'action; mais le général la Fayette recherchait surtout le mouvement et la popularité. M. Laffitte disait de lui, avec beaucoup d'esprit, sous la Restauration: 'La Fayette est une statue qui cherche son piédestal; que ce piédestal soit un fauteuil de dictateur ou un échafaud, peu lui importe.'

"Si M. Dumas veut savoir les motifs qui ont déterminé le général la Fayette à abandonner le parti républicain, il peut les demander à M. Odilon Barrot, qui a dû les connaître.

"M. Odilon Barrot s'était présenté à nous à l'hôtel de ville, non pas le 28, mais le 31 juillet; il était porteur d'une lettre de M. Laffitte, qui nous priait de le nommer notre secrétaire. Nous le connaissions tous, et il jouissait dès lors d'une réputation trop honorable pour que la recommandation ne fût pas accueillie. M. Mérilhou et M. Baude nous étaient déjà attachés en la même qualité; M. Barrot leur fut adjoint. Mais la mission qu'il avait reçue de M. Laffitte n'était pas de rester auprès de nous: elle était de s'établir auprès du général la Fayette, avec qui il avait déjà, par sa famille, des rapports d'intimité. C'est lui qui a servi d'intermédiaire entre M. Laffitte et le général la Fayette, ce qui lui a donné une assez grande action sur les événements. On craignait que le général la Fayette ne conservât quelque rancune contre le duc d'Orléans, à raison de certains actes de la première révolution, et qu'il ne se laissât entraîner par les jeunes gens qui l'entouraient à une tentative républicaine.

"Je voudrais finir, et je vous prie, cependant, de me permettre d'ajouter encore un mot.

"On a dit, dans votre journal, et M. A. Dumas a répété, je crois, que M. Casimir Périer nous avait refusé deux millions que nous lui demandions pour une affaire importante. J'ai attaqué assez vive-men M. Casimir Périer pour avoir le droit de lui rendre justice. Il n'a jamais eu à nous refuser, et nous n'avons jamais eu à lui demander n' ni deux millions ni aucune autre somme. Les caisses de l'État étaient à notre disposition, et elles étaient pleines. Nous avions notamment sous nos mains celle de l'hôtel de ville, qui contenait de dix à douze millions. C'est sur cette dernière caisse que nous avons fait nos dépenses. Elles ont été arrêtées à cinquante-trois mille francs, par la cour des comptes, qui a proposé de laisser cette somme à notre charge.

"La révolution de juillet n'a été l'œuvre ni de quelques hommes ni d'un parti; elle est sortie du soulèvement de la France entière, indignée d'un parjure et encore blessée des humiliations de 1815. Comment cette unanimité si noble et si pure a-t-elle été remplacée, peu de temps après, par des haines de parti et par des scènes de troubles et de désordre? Le gouvernement n'a-t-il pas contribué lui-même à cette transformation? Quel a été son but? Quels ont été ses hommes? Quelles ont été les fautes des partis, les erreurs et les faiblesses des hommes? Voilà ce que l'histoire doit rechercher et enseigner. Les mémoires privés peuvent certainement lui être utiles, mais sous une condition, c'est qu'ils apporteront la vérité.

"Dans le mouvement de réaction qui a succédé si promptement aux trois journées, les membres de la commission, rendus entièrement à leurs fonctions législatives, ont presque tous suivi des routes différentes. On peut les juger diversement: la vie d'un homme public appartient au public. Mais ils peuvent aussi se rendre intérieurement ce témoignage que, pendant leur courte existence comme gouvernement, et tandis qu'ils étaient à l'hôtel de ville, ils ont rendu quelques services au pays. Nul ne saurait se représenter l'état de trouble et de confusion où était Paris le 29 juillet. Les rues, les boulevards étaient couverts de barricades dont celles de 1848 n'ont point donné l'idée. La circulation des piétons en était gênée, celle des voitures impossible, et il ne fallait pas penser à les détruire, car aux portes de la ville était une armée, et cette armée pouvait reprendre l'offensive. Toute la population était sur pied. Parmi les combattants, il y avait un grand nombre de blessés qui réclamaient des secours. Il y avait aussi un grand nombre d'hommes qui, sous les armes depuis plus de soixante heures, manquaient de subsistances. Nous leur envoyâmes de l'argent, et ils le refusèrent. 'Nous nous sommes battus pour la patrie,' disaient-ils: 'elle nous doit du pain, non de l'argent.' Or, il n'y avait point de magasins, point de rations préparées. À chaque instant arrivaient des soldats, des compagnies entières qui abandonnaient la cause de Charles X: c'était un tourbillonnement d'hommes et d'événements dont il serait impossible de peindre la rapidité.

"Au milieu de ce mouvement immense, il fut pourvu à tous les besoins; tous les droits ont été respectés. Les communications entre Paris et les provinces, par la poste et le télégraphe, se rouvrirent dès le jour même du 29. Le lendemain, de nouvelles municipalités furent créées et installées. L'on ne fut troublé ni dans ses propriétés ni même dans ses opinions. Le peuple s'était livré vis-à-vis de deux ou trois personnes à des démonstrations alarmantes: sur un seul mot de nous, il s'arrêta.

"Nous avons pu protéger même des adversaires politiques; ceux d'entre eux qui voulurent quitter la capitale reçurent des passe-ports. Paris reprit promptement sa physionomie ordinaire, et, au bout de peu de jours, il aurait pu se demander s'il y avait eu une révolution.

"Ces résultats ont été dus à la sagesse du peuple, je m'empresse de le reconnaître: nous n'eussions rien pu sans lui, puisqu'il était notre unique instrument. Qu'il me soit permis néanmoins d'en réclamer une modeste part pour la direction qui lui fut donnée, et pour la rapidité des mesures prises et de leur exécution. En nous rendant à l'hôtel de ville, nous avions compromis notre fortune, et exposé notre vie. Qu'on ne nous en sache aucun gré, je ne m'en plains pas; mais, du moins, quand on parle de nous, qu'on en parle sérieusement; c'est un égard qui me paraît nous être dû, de même qu'à tous les hommes publics; j'en appelle à M. Dumas lui-même.

"Je m'arrête et vous prie, monsieur, de vouloir bien publier ma lettre; j'ai dû attendre, pour l'écrire, que M. Dumas eût fini ou à peu près avec l'hôtel de ville. Vous la trouverez peut-être trop longue; je n'ai fait, cependant, que toucher, pour ainsi dire du bout de la plume, les hommes et les choses de 1830. Je n'ai pas osé m'étendre davantage; j'aurais craint de trop importuner vos lecteurs.

"Veuillez agréer l'expression de ma considération très-distinguée.

"MAUGUIN, *Ancien député*

"SAUMUR, 8 *mars* 1853"

AU RÉDACTEUR

"MONSIEUR LE RÉDACTEUR,—Votre journal de ce jour (15 mars) renferme une lettre de M. Mauguin infirmant quelques-uns des faits que je rapporte dans mes Mémoires.

"J'ai pris, en écrivant ces Mémoires, une résolution: c'est de ne répondre que par des preuves officielles, des documents authentiques ou des témoignages irrécusables aux dénégations qui pourraient m'être opposées.

"Ainsi ai-je fait, il y a quelques jours, à propos de M. le chevalier de Liniers; ainsi ferai-je aujourd'hui à propos de M. Mauguin.

PREMIÈRE INFIRMATION

"Au moment où, suivant M. Dumas, nous étions en conférence avec M. de Sussy, arriva la députation Hubert, qui, voyant la porte fermée, l'ébranla à coups de crosse de fusil. On ouvrit. Alors, parut M. Hubert, suivi de quelques amis, *et portant une proclamation au bout d'une baïonnette.* Les membres de la commission furent *saisis d'épouvante*, et *s'éparpillèrent* un instant au milieu de la salle.

"Je ne sais si M. Dumas a voulu faire du pittoresque, mais je sais qu'il n'y a pas un mot de vrai dans son récit."

Voici ma réponse:

"M. Hubert fut choisi pour porter cette adresse à l'hôtel de ville; il partit en costume de garde national, et accompagné de plusieurs membres de l'assemblée, parmi lesquels étaient Trélat, Teste, Charles Hingray, Bastide, Poubelle, Guinard, tous hommes pleins d'énergie, de désintéressement et d'ardeur. La députation fendit la foule immense répandue sur la place de Grève. HUBERT PORTAIT L'ADRESSE AU BOUT D'UNE BAÏONNETTE....

"Les uns s'égarent dans l'hôtel de ville, les autres trouvent la porte du cabinet de la commission municipale fermée. Ils demandent à entrer, on ne leur répond pas. INDIGNÉS, ILS ÉBRANLENT LA PORTE À COUPS DE CROSSE. On leur ouvre, enfin, et *ils aperçoivent le comte de Sussy causant amicalement avec les membres de la commission municipale.*"

(Louis BLANC, *Histoire de dix ans.*)

SECONDE INFIRMATION

"M. Hubert, qui n'avait *ni proclamation ni baïonnette*, parla au nom de la députation, *et d'abondance*; il insista notamment sur deux points....

"Tout se passa, du reste, poliment, convenablement, et je crois même pouvoir certifier que, lorsque la députation se retira, M. Audry de Puyraveau ne glissa point en secret un projet de proclamation dans la main de son chef; autrement, il se serait donné un démenti à lui-même, car il avait approuvé la réponse.

"Je ne sais quelle était la réponse approuvée par M. Audry de Puyraveau. Voici la mienne:

"Seul (dans la commission municipale), M. Audry de Puyraveau avait une attitude passionnée! *Remportez vos ordonnances!* s'écria-t-il alors (s'adressant à M. de Sussy); *nous ne connaissons plus Charles X!* ON ENTENDAIT EN MÊME TEMPS LA VOIX RETENTISSANTE D'HUBERT LISANT POUR LA SECONDE FOIS L'ADRESSE DE LA RÉUNION LOINTIER....

"La députation républicaine se disposait à sortir lorsque, s'approchant d'Hubert, et TIRANT UN PAPIER DE SA POCHE, M. Audry de Puyraveau lui dit avec vivacité: TENEZ, VOICI UNE PROCLAMATION QUE LA COMMISSION MUNICIPALE AVAIT D'ABORD APPROUVÉE, ET QU'ELLE NE VEUT PLUS MAINTENANT PUBLIER. IL FAUT LA RÉPANDRE."

(LOUIS BLANC, *Histoire de dix ans*, imprimée et publiée à quinze éditions, du vivant de M. Audry de Puyraveau et de M. Mauguin.)

TROISIÈME INFIRMATION

"Je ne puis me taire sur une scène où M. Dumas me fait figurer personnellement avec M. Charras. Il aurait été question d'une lettre à écrire aux officiers d'un régiment où je ne connaissais personne. *Je me serais plaint du général Lobau*, et M. Charras aurait menacé de le faire fusiller; sur quoi, j'aurais bondi de surprise; M. Charras m'aurait pris par la main, et, me conduisant à l'une des fenêtres de l'hôtel de ville, il m'aurait montré la place en me disant: *Il y a là cent cinquante hommes qui n'obéissent qu'à moi, et qui fusilleraient le Père éternel, s'il descendait sur la terre, et si je leur disais de le fusiller.*"

RECTIFICATION

"D'abord, j'ai mis dans la bouche de Charras, non ces paroles tronquées par M. Mauguin, mais celles-ci, qui, à mon avis, sont bien différentes:

"*Et, si le Père éternel trahissait la cause de la liberté, ce qu'il est incapable de faire, et que je leur disse de fusiller le Père éternel, ils le fusilleraient!*"

"Reprenons la troisième infirmation où je viens de l'interrompre.

"M. Charras," poursuit M. Mauguin, "était, à cette époque, un jeune homme fort peu connu et n'ayant aucune influence. *Je ne me rappelle ni l'avoir vu ni lui avoir parlé à l'hôtel de ville.* Dans tous les cas, s'il m'eût tenu le langage qu'on lui prête, ou je l'aurais fait arrêter, ou je me serais éloigné de lui sans daigner lui répondre."

PREMIÈRE RÉPONSE À LA TROISIÈME INFIRMATION

"La garde nationale de Saint-Quentin demandait deux élèves de l'École polytechnique pour la commander; elle avait envoyé, en conséquence, une députation à la Fayette, et lui avait, en même temps, fait passer l'avis qu'il serait facile d'enlever le régiment caserné à la Fère. La Fayette mande auprès de lui deux élèves de l'École, et les envoie à la commission municipale. Ils arrivent accompagnés de M. Odilon Barrot. Seul, M. Mauguin se promenait dans la salle. Instruit de l'objet de leur visite, *il prit une plume, et commença une proclamation qui s'adressait au régiment de la Fère.* Mais M. Odilon Barrot interrompit son collègue par ces mots: *Laissez-leur faire cela; ils s'y entendent mieux que nous!* M. Mauguin céda la plume à l'un des deux jeunes gens.

"La proclamation faite, le général Lobau se présente: *on la lui donne à signer, il refuse et sort.* IL NE VEUT RIEN SIGNER, dit alors M. Mauguin; *tout à l'heure encore, il refusait sa signature à un ordre concernant l'enlèvement d'un dépôt de poudres.*— IL RECULE DONC? répondit un des élèves de l'École polytechnique; *mais rien n'est plus dangereux, en révolution, que les hommes qui reculent.* ...JE VAIS LE FAIRE FUSILLER!—Y PENSEZ-VOUS! répliqua vivement M. Mauguin, FAIRE FUSILLER LE GÉNÉRAL LOBAU! UN MEMBRE DU GOUVERNEMENT PROVISOIRE!—LUI-MÊME, reprit le jeune homme EN CONDUISANT LE DÉPUTE À LA FENÊTRE *et en lui montrant une centaine d'hommes qui avaient combattu à la caserne de Babylone*, et JE DIRAIS À CES BRAVES GENS DE FUSILLER LE BON DIEU, QU'ILS LE FERAIENT!" M. Mauguin se mit à sourire, et signa la proclamation en silence."

(LOUIS BLANC, *Histoire de dix ans*.)

DEUXIÈME RÉPONSE À LA TROISIÈME INFIRMATION

"MON CHER DUMAS,—Je viens de lire, dans le numéro de *la Presse* que vous m'avez envoyé ce matin, une lettre où M. Mauguin conteste l'exactitude d'un récit que vous avez publié, *et où mon nom figure à côté du sien.*

"Vous me demandez la réponse que j'ai à y faire. Je vous avoue que je tiens assez peu à ce que l'on nie ou affirme telle ou telle des scènes où j'ai pu être acteur plus ou moins obscur dans notre grande lutte de juillet 1830; mais, puisque vous y tenez, JE DÉCLARE QUE LA SCÈNE DE L'HÔTEL DE VILLE EST, sauf quelques détails de peu d'importance, EXACTEMENT RACONTÉE DANS VOS *Mémoires*. Les souvenirs de M. Mauguin *le servent mal*. JE SUIS SUR DE LA FIDÉLITÉ DES MIENS. Ils concordent, d'ailleurs, parfaitement avec *l'Histoire de dix ans*, publiée il y a longtemps déjà, et où vous avez, sans doute, puisé les faits contestés *aujourd'hui* par M. Mauguin.

"Tout à vous.

"CHARRAS

"BRUXELLES, 13 *mars* 1853"

QUATRIÈME INFIRMATION

"On a dit, dans votre journal, et M. Dumas a répété, je crois, que M. Casimir Périer nous avait refusé deux millions que nous lui demandions pour une affaire importante; il n'a jamais eu à nous refuser et nous n'avons jamais eu à lui demander deux millions ni aucune autre somme."

RECTIFICATION

"Je n'ai pas dit qu'on eût demandé à M. Casimir Périer *deux millions*, somme qui, effectivement, vaut la peine qu'on y réfléchisse avant de la donner.

"J'ai dit:

"La moitié des combattants mourait de faim sur les places publiques, et demandait du pain. On se tourna d'un mouvement unanime vers M. Casimir Périer, le même qui proposait, la veille, d'offrir quatre millions au due de Raguse. *Ah! messieurs*, répondit-il, *j'en suis vraiment désespéré pour ces pauvres diables; mais il est plus de quatre heures et ma caisse est fermée.*"

RÉPONSE A LA QUATRIÈME INFIRMATION

"Sur ces entrefaites, on vint annoncer que beaucoup d'ouvriers manquaient de pain; il fallait de l'argent. On s'adressa à M. Casimir Périer, qui répondit: IL EST PLUS DE QUATRE HEURES; MA CAISSE EST FERMÉE."

(Louis BLANC, *Histoire de dix ans.*)

CINQUIÈME ET DERNIÈRE INFIRMATION

"La commission municipale de 1830 n'a pas constitué un gouvernement aussi inactif, aussi introuvable que M. Alexandre Dumas se complaît à l'affirmer. Il s'en serait convaincu lui-même à cette époque, s'il eût seulement jeté les yeux sur les murs de Paris, placardés chaque jour de nos nombreux décrets."

RÉPONSE

M. Mauguin m'accuse à tort de ne pas rendre justice à l'activité de la commission municipale; car, justement, à propos du premier de ses décrets, j'ai écrit ceci dans mes Mémoires:

"Voilà donc la bourgeoisie à l'œuvre, et recommençant, le jour même du triomphe populaire, son travail de réaction!

"Reconnaissez-vous, abordez-vous avec des cris de joie, embrassez-vous, hommes des faubourgs, jeunes gens des écoles, étudiants, poètes, artistes; levez les bras au ciel, remerciez Dieu, criez *Hosannah!* Vos morts ne sont pas sous terre, vos blessures ne sont pas pansées, vos lèvres sont encore noires de poudre, vos cœurs battent encore joyeusement se croyant libres;—et déjà les hommes d'intrigue, les hommes de finance, les hommes à uniforme, tout ce qui se cachait, tremblait, priait pendant que vous combattiez, vous vient impudemment prendre des mains la victoire et la liberté, arrache les palmes de l'une, coupe les ailes de l'autre, et fait deux prostituées de vos deux chastes déesses!

"Tandis que vous fusillez, place du Louvre, un homme qui a pris un vase de vermeil; tandis que vous fusillez, sous le pont d'Arcole, un homme qui a pris un couvert d'argent, on vous calomnie, on vous déshonore là-bas, dans ce grand et bel hôtel que, par une souscription nationale, vous rachèterez un jour, enfants sans mémoire et au cœur d'or! pour en faire don à son propriétaire, qui se trouve ruiné n'ayant plus que quatre cent mille livres de rente!

"Écoutez et instruisez-vous!—*Audite et intelligite!*

"Voici le premier acte de cette commission municipale qui vient de s'instituer:

"*Les députés présents à Paris ont dû se réunir pour remédier aux graves dangers* QUI MENAÇENT LA SÛRETÉ DES PERSONNES ET DES PROPRIÉTÉS.—*Une commission a été nommée pour veiller aux intérêts de tous, en l'absence de toute organisation régulière.*"

"Comment concilier, maintenant, la prise de cet arrêté avec ce que dit M. Mauguin, dans la lettre à laquelle nous répondons, de ce même peuple qui, selon la commission municipale, *menaçait la sûreté des personnes et des propriétés?*

"Voici ce que dit M. Mauguin:

"Jamais autorité ne fut obéie aussi ponctuellement que la nôtre; *jamais peuple ne se montra aussi docile, aussi courageux, aussi ami de l'ordre que celui de Paris en 1830.*

"Convenons que la commission connaissait bien mal ce peuple ou, le connaissant, lui faisait gratuitement une bien grave insulte!

"Mais la commission ne connaissait pas le peuple; elle ne l'avait pas vu.

"Cela tient à ce que la commission ne fut constituée que le 29 juillet au soir, et que le peuple se battait depuis le 27 au matin.

"Nous attendons les nouvelles dénégations qui peuvent se produire, et nous promettons d'y répondre aussi promptement, aussi catégoriquement, aussi victorieusement qu'à celles de M. le chevalier de Liniers et à celles de M. Mauguin.

"ALEX. DUMAS

"BRUXELLES, *ce* 13 *mars* 1853"

NOTE TO P. 357

In the Brussels edition of 1853, Dumas adds: "Happily, these lines of Barbier supply all I could wish to have said:—

Oh! lorsqu'un lourd soleil chauffait les grandes dalles
Des ponts et de nos quais déserts,
Que les cloches hurlaient, que la grêle des balles
Sifflait et pleuvait par les airs;
Que, dans Paris entier, comme la mer qui monte,
Le peuple soulevé grondait,
Et qu'au lugubre accent des vieux canons de fonte
La *Marseillaise* répondait;
Certe, on ne voyait pas, comme au jour où nous sommes,
Tant d'uniformes à la fois;

C'était sous des haillons que battaient les cœurs d'hommes;
C'étaient, alors, de sales doigts
Qui chargeaient les mousquets et renvoyaient la foudre;
C'était la bouche aux vils jurons
Qui mâchait la cartouche, et qui, noire de poudre,
Criait aux citoyens: 'Mourons!'
. . . .

Mais, ô honte! Paris, si beau dans sa colère,
Paris, si plein de majesté,
Dans ce jour de tempête où le vent populaire
Déracina la royauté;
Paris, si magnifique avec ses funérailles,
Ses débris d'hommes, ses tombeaux,
Ses chemins dépavés et ses pans de murailles
Troués comme de vieux drapeaux;
Paris, cette cité de lauriers toute ceinte,
Dont le monde entier est jaloux,
Que les peuples émus appellent tous la sainte,
Et qu'ils ne nomment qu'à genoux;
Paris n'est maintenant qu'une sentine impure,
Un égout sordide et boueux,
Où mille noirs courants de limon et d'ordure
Viennent traîner leurs flots honteux;
Un taudis regorgeant de faquins sans courage,
D'effrontés coureurs de salons
Qui vont, de porte en porte et d'étage en étage,
Gueusant quelque bout de galons;
Une halle cynique aux clameurs indolentes,
Où chacun cherche à déchirer
Un misérable coin des guenilles sanglantes
Du pouvoir qui vient d'expirer!

Ainsi, quand dans sa bauge aride et solitaire,
Le sanglier, frappé de mort,
Est là tout palpitant, étendu sur la terre,
Et sous le soleil qui le mord;
Lorsque, blanchi de bave et la langue tirée,
Ne bougeant plus en ses liens,
Il meurt, et que la trompe a sonné la curée
À toute la meute des chiens,
Toute la meute, alors, comme une vague immense,
Bondit; alors, chaque matin

Hurle en signe de joie, et prépare d'avance
Ses larges crocs pour le festin;
Et puis vient la cohue, et les abois féroces
Roulent de vallons en vallons;
Chiens courants et limiers, et dogues, et molosses,
Tout se lance, et tout crie: 'Allons!
Quand le sanglier tombe et roule sur l'arène,
Allons! allons! les chiens sont rois!
Le cadavre est à nous; payons-nous notre peine,
Nos coups de dents et nos abois.
Allons! nous n'avons plus de valet qui nous fouaille
Et qui se pende à notre cou.
Du sang chaud! de la chair! allons, faisons ripaille,
Et gorgons-nous tout notre soûl!'
Et tous, comme ouvriers que l'on met à la tâche,
Fouillent ces flancs à plein museau,
Et de l'ongle et des dents travaillent sans relâche,
Car chacun en veut un morceau;
Car il faut au chenil que chacun d'eux revienne
Avec un os demi-rongé,
Et que, trouvant au seuil son orgueilleuse chienne,
Jalouse et le poil allongé,
Il lui montre sa gueule encor rouge et qui grogne,
Son os dans les dents arrêté,
Et lui crie, en jetant son quartier de charogne:
'Voici ma part de royauté!'"

END OF VOL. IV

Milton Keynes UK
Ingram Content Group UK Ltd.
UKHW020755200524
442968UK00006B/823